Deems Taylor: *A Biography*

Deems Taylor: *A Biography*

James A. Pegolotti

With a Foreword by Gerard Schwarz

Northeastern University Press
Boston

Northeastern University Press

Library of Congress Cataloging-in-Publication Data

Pegolotti, James A.
    Deems Taylor : a biography / James A. Pegolotti ; with a foreword by Gerard Schwarz.
        p. cm.
Includes bibliographical references (p.   ) and index.
    ISBN 1-55553-587-9 (cloth : alk. paper)
    1. Taylor, Deems, 1885–1966. 1. Composers—United States—Biography. I. Title.
    ML410.T19P4 2003
    780′.92—dc21   2003005448

Designed by Judy Arisman

Composed in Perpetua by Wellington Graphics, Hanover, Massachusetts. Printed and bound by Thomson-Shore, Inc., Dexter, Michigan. The paper is Dexter Offset, an acid-free stock.

MANUFACTURED IN THE UNITED STATES OF AMERICA

07   06   05   04   03   5   4   3   2   1

Frontispiece: Deems Taylor at his Hollow Hill home in Stamford, Connecticut, in 1930. *(Courtesy of Michael W. Davis)*

To the memory of my parents,
Giacomo and Ida Pegolotti,
who, on their wedding day in 1921, left Cogolo,
their small Italian mountain village in Trentino,
to find a better world in the United States.

Contents

Illustrations

Foreword

Like so many of us in the latter part of the twentieth century and the early twenty-first century, my first acquaintance with Deems Taylor was seeing him as the host in *Fantasia,* a movie that has had a tremendous impact on all of us in the world of classical music. He was the appropriate spokesperson, being well known for the remarkable work that he did on the radio, especially as the intermission commentator for the New York Philharmonic broadcasts.

My next encounter with Deems Taylor was when I was working on my American Music series with the Seattle Symphony for Delos records. I had the score to Taylor's *Through the Looking Glass,* a piece that I thought was simply a retelling of the marvelous story by Lewis Carroll. Upon studying the work I realized that it was fantastic; it had beautiful melodies, exquisite harmonies, and marvelous orchestration. I vividly remember recording it with a sense of delight at this remarkable composer. Then I read his books *Of Men and Music* and *The Well-Tempered Listener,* which were so informative. I decided to delve into other music that he had composed and studied his operas *The King's Henchman* and *Peter Ibbetson.* Once again I found him a remarkable composer, and in 1999 I conducted a concert version of *Peter Ibbetson* with the Seattle Symphony and many wonderful soloists, to great acclaim.

Through Jim Pegolotti's informative, fascinating, and beautifully written biography, I have finally come to know the man as well as the music. And what a fascinating man Deems Taylor was, in both his personal life and his professional life, and through his innovative ways of looking at the world. Single-handedly, he probably did more for classical music in the first half of the twentieth century than anyone else in the United States. I'm thrilled with what Jim Pegolotti has achieved, through his extensive research and readable style, to commemorate this remarkable composer, writer, and personality.

Gerard Schwarz

Acknowledgments

In a wonderful way, this book has come about through the help of two Connecticut institutions of higher learning: Western Connecticut State University (WCSU) and Yale University. WCSU provided me with a faculty leave of six months in 1996 to work in the Yale University Music Library, and Kendall Crilly, the director, kindly gave me complete access to the then uncatalogued Deems Taylor Papers. During those months, he and Suzanne Eggleston, the assistant director, gave me as much assistance as could ever be desired. Similarly, the staff of the Beinecke Library, where the Mary Kennedy Papers are housed, provided full attention and help. As my research continued over the following years, Richard Boursy joined the Yale Music Library staff and catalogued the Taylor collection in excellent fashion. Richard became my private "think tank" on so many matters. The help and encouragement of Ken, Suzanne, and Richard made this book a joy to research. My thanks to them is deep and complete.

To my equally good fortune, Joan Kennedy Taylor, Deems Taylor's daughter, from our first meeting put faith in a neophyte author whose only previous book-length work was a chemistry Ph.D. thesis on trifluoromethylallyl alcohols. She immediately gave generously of her time, as well as of materials from her personal collection. In no way could this book have been written without her help, advice, and encouragement.

Others of the Taylor family have also helped, especially Michael W. Davis, a grandnephew of Taylor's who has taken on the role of family genealogist. He gave me access to all his family materials, including the annual journals kept by Deems's father, Joseph Schimmel Taylor, an invaluable source of history, and provided many of the photographs for this book. Michael Cook, Deems's only grandchild, shared memories of his grandfather and grandmother. Elizabeth MacDonald, a cousin, and Robert Stranathan Jr., a nephew, also supplied information. Four years of correspondence across the Atlantic with Lucille Térouanne, Taylor's third wife, presented a treasure trove of information about the last third of his life. Her generous sharing of recollections has made the biography much richer with details and insights.

A wide variety of other people have helped shape this book, either in conversation or in correspondence. Each has brought a building block toward the larger construction, and I am thankful to each and every one: Elizabeth Barnett, Heywood Hale Broun, Emily Coleman, Norman Corwin, Jeff Davis, Roger Dettmer, Boyd Dolan, Hugh Downs, Frank Egan, Linda Rodgers Emory, Rita Falbel, David Falvay, Yolande Betbeze Fox, Margaret Friesner, Richard Frohlich, Barbara Gillis, John Steele Gordon, Paulette Greene, Carolyn Guszki, Byron Hanson, Marion (Mrs. Ross) Hastings, Richard Hecht, Harry Herforth, Eleanor Holm, Michael Keith, Edward Jablonski, Minelda Jiras, Richard Lamparski, Leila Hadley Luce, Fraser Macdonald, James McKenzie, Sidney Mear, Donald Ott, John Joseph Patton, Alfred Pessalano, Joseph Poprzeczny, A. Clyde Roller, Elis Ronbeck, Dorothy Sarnoff, Eugene Schwarz, Anna Sosenko, Jim Steinblatt, Henry Z. Steinway, Judith Anne Still, Ann and George Stone, Nathan Stutch, Sister M. Helen Jean Sullivan, Sidney Svedrofsky, Herbert Bayard Swope Jr., Nancy Howe Webster, Jane Paige Weld, Toni Winters.

As a former librarian, I fully appreciate the time and effort it takes to respond to requests from an author. Therefore, I am doubly grateful to the archivists of the following institutions for their help. Some responded beyond the call of duty, and in those cases I have noted their names: Academy of Motion Picture Arts and Sciences, Chicago Symphony Rosenthal Archives (Andrea Cawelti), Circus World Museum and Parkinson Library (Erin Foley), Columbia University, Curtis Institute of Music (Elizabeth Walker), Dartmouth College (Sarah Hartwell), Ethical Culture Feldston School, Georgetown University, Hampden-Booth Theatre Library (Raymond Wemmlinger), Library of Congress (Alice L. Birney), Mercyhurst College (Earleen Glaser), Metropolitan Opera Archives (John Pennino), National Institute of Arts and Letters (Kathryn Talalay), New York Philharmonic Archives, New York Public Library, New York University Fales Library (Marvin Taylor), Paterson (N.J.) Free Public Library, Pennsylvania State University (Sandra Stelts), Princeton University (Margaret Sherry Rich), Radcliffe College, State Historical Society of Wisconsin, Syracuse University, University of Arkansas, University of California at Berkeley, University of Delaware,

University of Georgia, University of Maryland (Beth Alvarez), University of Michigan Bentley Historical Library, University of New Hampshire, University of Pennsylvania (Nancy Shawcross), University of Rochester, University of Texas at Austin, University of Virginia, *Vineyard Gazette* (Eulalie Regan), Walt Disney Archives (David Smith), Paul Whiteman Archives of Williams College (Sylvia Kennick Brown), Yale University Beinecke Library (Patricia Willis).

I give special thanks to Richard Davis for providing me the use of his summer home in Maine on two separate occasions for weeks of isolation and writing at critical times in the development of the manuscript. I thank Linda Gerber and Joan Haines for a similar use of their vacation home. Louis Lotorto saved me a trip to Los Angeles by going to the Disney Archives and transcribing *Fantasia* story conferences: *grazie,* Luigi. Thanks likewise to Michael Keith for giving me a recording of Taylor's *Jurgen,* which he produced via his synthesizer.

The sabbatical research time made available to me by Western Connecticut State University set the book into motion. My gratitude is to both WCSU and the citizens of the state of Connecticut, whose taxes provided the sabbatical pay. Also special thanks to Katherine Sholtz, library director of Ruth Haas Library, to her successor, Ralph Holibaugh, and to librarians Annette Curtis, Jane Fowler, Lorraine Furtick, Mary Kay Loomis, Vijay Nair, Joan Reitz, Xiao Hua Yang—all of whom had to cover some of my duties in my absence. Thanks also to the ever-helpful Neera Dean in the circulation department. Research today relies greatly on an effective interlibrary loan department, and WCSU's has been extremely helpful, from the early assistance of Rosemary Hughes to the ever-friendly and cooperative Joanne Elpern and her staff. They are the jewels in any researcher's crown.

I am indebted to Gerard Schwarz for taking the time to write the foreword to this book, and for his positive support throughout the endeavor. Our communication began when I wrote to thank him for recording the *Through the Looking Glass* suite with the Seattle Symphony. It was a thrill to attend the concert version of *Peter Ibbetson* that he conducted in spring 1999 in Seattle, and to hear a live example of Taylor's music for the first time. More than any one event, that spurred me on to the completion of this book. Once into the writing, it was through the special, patient help of William Frohlich of Northeastern University Press that the book improved draft after draft. I am grateful to him, his assistant, Sarah Rowley, and copy editor Anne Rehill, who did a terrific job.

Lastly, how can a book go into print without the help of friends who happened to be in the right place at the wrong time and had to read various draft versions: Herbert Janick, Western Connecticut history professor emeritus, who as head of the "Holiday Diner Salon" gave me weekly boosts of encouragement; Carl Myhill, Western Connecticut mathematics professor emeritus, who kept saying, "It can be done"; Betty Neville, a longtime friend, who gave of her expertise from previous editorial experience; Howard Tuvelle, Western Connecticut music professor emeritus, who, cigar in hand, patiently listened to me read chapter after chapter; Richard Boursy of Yale Music Library, whose knowledge of the Taylor papers saved me from making many an error; Elise Knapp, Western Connecticut English literature professor emeritus, whose enthusiasm was unrelenting and her insights unerring; Paul McCarthy, S.J., a chemist friend and expert on umlauts, who e-mailed his comments all the way from Sandy, Utah; Joan Reitz, Western Connecticut librarian, whose perceptive comments, after reading the second draft, helped shape many chapters; Harriet and Edward Rosenberg, who read the final manuscript—she an astute judge of appropriate content from her years of teaching literature and writing, and he a Western Connecticut mathematics professor emeritus who (luckily for me) had honed the virtue of nitpicking to its highest possible level; and finally Stephen Sosin, my longtime companion, who read all the drafts of the book and caught many errors. He listened to endless stories about Deems Taylor and dreamed only of the day when the book would be completed and I could return to more mundane matters.

The author gratefully acknowledges the following permissions:

Material from the unpublished letters and writings of Deems Taylor and the unpublished letters of Mary Kennedy are used by permission of Joan Kennedy Taylor, literary executor of the estates of Deems Taylor and Mary Kennedy.

Material from the unpublished letters of Lucille Térouanne to the author is used by permission of Lucille Térouanne.

Portions of the letter from Gladys Brown Ficke to Arthur Ficke dated February 18, 1927, from the Yale Collection of American Literature, are used by permission of Yale University.

The letter from Jane Anderson to Theodore Dreiser dated March 24, 1910, is used by permission of Van Pelt–Dietrich Library, University of Pennsylvania.

Material from the writings of Newman Levy is used by permission of Margaret Friesner, literary executor of the estate of Newman Levy.

The line illustration depicting Deems Taylor as a centaur is reproduced by permission of Disney Enterprises, Inc.

All the quotations from the letters and other writings of Edna St. Vincent Millay are used by permission of Elizabeth Barnett, literary executor, the Edna St. Vincent Millay Society.

Material from the published and unpublished letters of John O'Hara is used with the permission of United States Trust Company of New York, as trustee under the will of John O'Hara.

Material from the unpublished writings of Robert Benchley is used by permission of Nathaniel R. Benchley, literary executor of the estate of Robert Benchley.

All the quotations from the letters of Otto Kahn are used with permission of the Princeton University Library.

The monograms used to decorate the first page of each chapter were created by Deems Taylor for the following personalities (see page 163 to view a selection of these at a larger size):

Deems Taylor (chaps. 1 and 20); Edna Ferber (chaps. 2 and 13); Alfred Lunt (chaps. 3 and 14); William LeBaron (chaps. 4 and 15); Ethel Kelly (chaps. 5 and 16); Guthrie McLintic (chaps. 6 and 17); Edna St. Vincent Millay (chaps. 7 and 18); Donald Ogden Stewart (chap. 8); Winthrop Ames (chap. 9); Peggy Wood (chap. 10); Alexander Woollcott (chaps. 11 and 19); Roland Young (chap. 12).

Introduction

When New York University bestowed its Gallatin Medal upon an aging Deems Taylor in 1962, his fellow composer William Schuman read to the assembled guests a long list of the honoree's talents—"composer, speaker, popularizer, writer, author, critic, translator, editor, and judge of Miss America"—then summed up Taylor's life in seven words: "He is a man for all reasons." A similar tribute to Taylor at the time of the award came from the highly respected New York music critic Louis Biancolli: "Nobody has quite equaled—or is ever likely to equal—Deems Taylor's diverse contribution to American music and the allied arts."

Indeed, even today it would be difficult to find anyone who could match Taylor's varied talents. A New York City native, he thrived in his hometown from pre–World War I to post–World War II, years when the United States, building confidence in both its own music and literature, reduced its reliance on European cultural values. These were years when radio became the common thread of entertainment for the whole country, elevating music of all types to a new level of appreciation. Taylor's natural abilities as a composer, writer, and golden-voiced radio commentator fit the era like a cultural glove.

From his father's Mennonite upbringing he gained an intense work ethic as well as self-sufficiency. He considered himself first and foremost a composer, spurred to that decision by music he wrote for varsity shows while a student at New York University. When Taylor returned from a World War I journalistic assignment in France, he turned what was to have been a musical suite of his impressions of war into his most popular work, *Through the*

Looking Glass, based on Lewis Carroll's adventures of Alice. In so doing, not only did he present a beautifully crafted orchestral work that quickly entered the repertoire of most major American orchestras, but he also leaped in fame over many of his American contemporaries, notably John Alden Carpenter, Charles Wakefield Cadman, and Charles Tomlinson Griffes. Although such composers usually studied extensively in Europe, New England, or both, Taylor had only several months of instruction in music theory, and he then learned orchestration on his own.

No sooner did he bring his musical talents to the attention of the cultural elite of New York than he also impressed them with his writing ability by becoming the music critic for the Pulitzer family's *New York World.* Newspapers before the age of radio had full rein as dispensers of news and opinions, and their music critics were held in high regard. Readers loved Taylor's reviews, for he brought to his writings wit as well as the musical knowledge gained from being an active composer.

He did have a goal: to write an opera and have it produced at the Metropolitan Opera House. From the musical pulpit of the *World* he banged the drum for American music and American operas so loudly that in 1925 he received not one but three commissions for musical works, among them the first opera commission ever offered by the Metropolitan. For his librettist he reached out to Edna St. Vincent Millay, then at the peak of her fame as a poet; together they created *The King's Henchman,* which premiered to glowing reviews in 1927. The Metropolitan quickly commissioned Taylor for a second opera, *Peter Ibbetson.* This time the composer chose to be his own librettist. It premiered in 1931 and became immensely popular, with sold-out performances over five seasons.

But it was radio that brought Taylor the greatest fame and recognition, mainly because of his popular intermission talks from 1936 to 1943 for the New York Philharmonic broadcasts. "If one judges a critic's influence by the sheer numbers of people he reached," writes the music historian Mark Grant in *Maestros of the Pen,* "the greatest figure among American composer-critics—vastly more influential than Virgil Thomson, more comparable to Leonard Bernstein—was the native New Yorker Deems Taylor." Taylor's voice was distinctive and pleasant, and his manner often clever and informative. He never talked down to an audience, for he knew, as do all good teachers, that you must gain the confidence and attention of your students if you want to educate them. He transformed the best of his broadcast essays into three books, one of which, *Of Men and Music,* became the best-selling book on music of the 1930s. Even the *New Yorker* agreed on Taylor's radio fame. In one of its cartoons, a man returns from work to find his wife listening to the conclusion of a music program on the radio. "I don't know who did the playing," she tells him, "[but] Deems Taylor did the talking."

Taylor's championing of American music and musicians through his radio work and his books and articles had few equals in his time. He inspired others by twice proving that an American composer could write successful operas. When Walt Disney began planning *Fantasia,* his masterful meshing of animation and classical music, and found that he needed an on-screen host, Taylor was the natural choice.

He seemed to know everyone of importance in the arts, from George Gershwin to Jerome Kern, from F. Scott Fitzgerald to John O'Hara, from Dorothy Parker to Ayn Rand. In conversations he had no qualms about speaking his opinions; often he won arguments with his wit, something that David Sarnoff, the head of NBC, discovered one day in 1937. Sarnoff had called an important meeting of people in the music community. He wanted their opinion on public relations for the arrival of Arturo Toscanini, drawn back to America to conduct the NBC Symphony, an orchestra assembled specifically for him. Taylor was among those invited. As Sarnoff droned on in praise of Toscanini, Taylor calmly volunteered that there were other conductors equal in ability to him. Flustered, Sarnoff turned directly to Taylor and inquired, "Are you saying that Toscanini isn't the greatest conductor in the world?"

Taylor's answer produced a roar of laughter: "Well, I didn't say he wasn't at the Last Supper. I just said he didn't sit at the head of the table."*

Although relatively quiet in his political leanings, Taylor believed passionately in free speech. When the Daughters of the American Revolution denied Marian Anderson access to Constitution Hall in Washington for her 1939 concert, Taylor wired the DAR that he believed their action subverted the clear meaning of the U.S. Constitution. (This is elaborated further on in the text.) In 1947, when the House Un-American Activities Committee summoned some of Hollywood's best writers and directors to testify, a group later known as the Hollywood Ten, Taylor lent his name to those who spoke out against the committee's vicious personal attacks. He knew the power of words.

Taylor loved women; of that there is no doubt. He had three wives, each lovely and each fascinating. His second wife, Mary Kennedy, provided him with his only child and his longest marriage—thirteen years. Mary believed firmly in his abilities as a composer and rued the day when her husband de-

* I heard this story from Frank Egan, at that time a page boy at NBC, who was present to hear the interchange.

cided that he had to rely on radio for financial support. During his marital intersessions, the charming Taylor, though quite bald, always found a beautiful woman for companionship. He was amusing, charming, and often loyal to a fault.

I came to know of Deems Taylor and his life because of my interest in the cultural history of the twentieth century and my love for classical music, much of which developed from concerts that I heard on the radio as I was growing up in the early 1940s. As a youngster on my parents' dairy farm near Eureka, California, I turned on the family radio after cow-milking chores in the evening. I looked forward to nightfall, because then I could tune in the CBS and NBC stations 250 miles to the south in San Francisco. Eureka had neither NBC nor CBS network stations, and in those days of AM radio, one had to wait for the sun to go down to bring in distant stations. Because they were broadcast in the daytime over CBS, I didn't hear Deems Taylor's famed intermission talks during the Sunday broadcasts of the New York Philharmonic, but I found special pleasure in evening "good music" programs, especially *Voice of Firestone* and its back-to-back Monday partner, *Bell Telephone Hour.*

Decades later, during my studies to become a librarian in 1988, I worked in the Bethel (Connecticut) Public Library and stumbled on material about Howard Barlow, the conductor on *Voice of Firestone,* who had lived his last years in that town. I found out that Barlow and Taylor were good friends, and in my research I came to better understand the importance of Taylor as a composer, critic, and radio personality in the 1930s and 1940s, an importance that seems to have slipped through history's fingers. I began to read Taylor's books of insightful essays on music, then listened to many of his compositions, from off-the-air recordings as well as the few available commercial recordings. Having always admired both composers and humorists, I found in Taylor a man worth writing about.

A reader cannot hear music by turning these pages but will experience, I hope, something of the life of this extraordinary man. Here was a man so well known in his time that he readily received a letter sent to him from Paris in 1928, addressed simply:

> Deems Taylor, Esq.
> Somewhere in New York City
> Try Vanity Fair or Metropolitan Opera House
> or just stand at 42nd Street and yell his name . . .
> someone will tell you where he lives.

Deems Taylor: *A Biography*

1. *The Early Years of (Joseph) Deems Taylor, 1885–1906*

How Taylor Was Given the Name Deems

On December 22, 1885, the cries of a baby boy born that day filled the crowded flat at 152 West Seventeenth Street in Manhattan. For Katherine Johnson Taylor the birth had been a difficult ordeal because of the size of the infant, who weighed ten pounds and measured twenty-one inches. Fortunately, Joseph Schimmel Taylor, her highly organized husband, had anticipated possible difficulties and brought his mother, Mary, from Pennsylvania to be with them to help when their first child was born. Ten days later, Taylor wrote to his foster family to tell about his new son: "His name is Joseph Deems Taylor. . . . He has black hair, blue eyes, and is as fat as his Papa used to be. He is a very 'good' baby, and does nothing but eat and sleep. . . . Kathy is just ready to get out of bed. She had a pretty severe time, but came through it all very bravely."[1]

There was also a certain bravery in the Taylors' providing their son with the middle name of Deems, for in doing so they abandoned a long-standing family tradition in which the mother's family name always became the child's middle name. Instead, Joseph senior wished to impart to his son the strength of a pastor he much admired, the Reverend Charles Force Deems. And he would very likely never have met the Reverend Deems if it hadn't been for his mother's family, the Schimmels, and their ventures with apple butter.

George Schimmel, the family's American patriarch, arrived in Philadelphia from Rotterdam, Holland, in 1753. He settled on a farm in Bucks County, eastern Pennsylvania, and married a Miss Eschbach. One son, Christian Schimmel, was the sole product of that union. When Christian grew up and married a Miss Yoder, they too had only one child, John Johann Schimmel. But John Johann married Hannah Oberholtzer in 1824, and the one-child tradition exploded with the production of nine Schimmels: seven brothers and two sisters.

All of the brothers worked on the family farm, but one of the youngest, Jose, saw other possibilities for his life and spent his spare time in the kitchen preparing fruit butters and other preserves. Since apple orchards dotted the area, he concentrated his efforts on producing an exceptional apple butter, an endeavor that eventually proved successful.

While Jose experimented, in 1850 his sister Mary married Thomas B. Taylor, another farmer from Bucks County. Taylor died a decade later, leaving Mary to raise their three children. Relatives and friends helped her as best they could for the next two years. By this time the Civil War was raging. Mary wed a neighbor, John Ritter, who was a widower with six children of his own. But life took another terrible turn for her when Ritter died two years later. Now she was a widow with nine children.

Under the circumstances, Mary had no choice but to place all nine children into the care of nearby relatives. So it was that her son Joseph Schimmel Taylor, who would become the father of Deems Taylor, found his home with the Jacob Moyer family in Passer, Pennsylvania, only a half-mile from his mother's house. The Moyers welcomed eight-year-old Joseph and called him JoJo, a nickname that stayed with him throughout his life.

The hundred-acre Moyer farm was situated about a dozen miles southeast of Allentown. The mildly undulating terrain featured woods, meadowland, and acres of apple trees, all of which demanded a great deal of work and attention. For six years JoJo worked on the farm, gathering apples and making cider in season, feeding chickens, collecting eggs, and helping with the milking. Amusements were limited, but when JoJo wasn't shaping toys with the many tools available in the woodshed, Grandfather Moyer taught him to read German. Years later he recalled how happy those times were:

> The Moyer household was of the kind which constitutes the moral backbone of this country. They lived in the fear of God and made the Bible the rule of life. They were members of the New Mennonite church and belonged to the Springfield congregation [a few miles from the farm]. . . . After the service hosts of friends and relatives were invited to go home with us . . . and this Sunday dinner was an institution forever to be remembered. Meat, potatoes, pre-

serves, three or four kinds of pie, and Oh, such conversation. Unfortunately when the company was large I had to wait for the second table. . . . Frequently the guests remained for supper; but at four o'clock I had to change my clothes and go for the cows. . . . That is the one objection I have to farming. It isn't nice to have to milk on a Sunday night. If you wish to appear in company in the evening you have to change a second time; for it would never do to come to the parlor with the odor of cows upon the person.[2]

JoJo also exhibited an amazing memory that may well have been photographic. To impress visitors, he would announce that he could memorize advertisements and—for a penny—recite them in reverse. Though JoJo's mother and the Moyers recognized his unusual memory and intellect, they knew he needed to learn a trade to assure he would be able to earn a living. Thus in 1870, at fourteen years of age, he was apprenticed to tradesmen in the nearby towns of Milford Square and Hagersville to learn to be a carriage painter.

At this time young JoJo also decided to become a member of the Springfield Mennonite Church, so every Sunday he walked six miles for instructions in the faith, an interest that wasn't surprising, for Mennonite traditions ran strong in his family. Not only were the Moyers Mennonites, but JoJo's grandmother Hannah bore the family name Oberholtzer, a key German family in Mennonite history. This Swiss Anabaptist sect, named for its leader, Menno Simon, had come to Pennsylvania in the 1680s to escape religious persecution. Like the Quakers, they resisted warlike actions. The values of frugality, hard work, piety, and helpfulness permeated the Mennonite world and found a place in JoJo's heart. He was received into the congregation in 1872. Time would prove that nothing Deems Taylor received from his father had greater impact than the work ethic of the Mennonites.

After JoJo completed his apprenticeship, he spent several years painting carriages, but his active mind ultimately found this work unappealing. He determined instead to become a teacher and entered the Pennsylvania State Normal School in Millersville to complete the necessary program to gain a certificate. The Millersville school, the first of Pennsylvania's state-sponsored colleges for training teachers, had only about a hundred students. The educational regimen was hard, but JoJo derived particular enjoyment from singing, either in the choir or in small groups. During choir practice he noticed the beautiful voice of Katherine Moore Johnson, a member of the class a year behind him. JoJo became entranced with Katherine. In 1878 he graduated at the head of his class of thirty-two neophyte teachers (eight women and twenty-four men). For his first teaching opportunity JoJo selected Mount Joy township, just ten miles north of Millersville, where Katherine remained to complete her final year.

JoJo's first year of teaching, he admitted years later, was "afflicted with the intellectual malady of nearly all fresh graduates, an overestimate of his own importance."[3] Perhaps that attitude did not sit well with the Mount Joy school board, because after one year he left to teach at Ebervale, in the coal-mining region of northeastern Pennsylvania. The choice again may not have been accidental, since Katherine had begun her career only five miles away, in Hazleton. At the end of his second year of teaching, in 1880, JoJo proposed marriage to Katherine and she accepted. However, they hardly rushed to the altar: Katherine remained to teach in eastern Pennsylvania for another year, at Wilkes-Barre, while JoJo chose a one-year appointment in Huntington at the Brethren Normal School, now Juniata College.

By the time JoJo had completed his third year of teaching, in 1881, he realized that he could never get married and start a family on his meager income. Fortunately, his uncles Jose and Owen Schimmel came to his rescue. Jose had by now developed a superior apple butter, and when he took jars of the preserve to Philadelphia, they sold so well that he established a canning factory there, J. O. Schimmel and Company. Continued success convinced Jose to open factories in Chicago and New York. He chose his brother Owen to take apple butter to New York City, then virgin territory for the sweet spread. By the late 1870s Owen had begun tempting New Yorkers with Schimmel apple butter, and by 1881 he needed a reliable assistant as a bookkeeper. Remembering that JoJo had an incredible memory and agility with numbers, Owen made him an offer to come to New York City. JoJo quickly accepted, leaving his rural roots to join in his uncles' business.

When JoJo arrived in New York he found no Mennonite churches, so he joined Uncle Owen in worshiping at the Church of the Strangers, where he met and became friends with the pastor, Reverend Charles Force Deems. The minister had come to New York from North Carolina, where he was well known as a preacher, writer, and educator with the Southern Methodist Episcopal Church.[4] Deplorable conditions in North Carolina after the Civil War, as well as debts to some Northern creditors, spurred his move northward. With a wife and four children, Reverend Deems settled in New York City and initiated the *Watchman,* a weekly newspaper that urged national reconciliation and a forgive-and-forget philosophy regarding the Civil War. The newspaper survived only a year, after which he returned to his ministerial vocation.

What Reverend Deems heard from preachers in New York's pulpits were denunciations of "rebels" and the "rebellion." Such attitudes convinced him that his true mission was to provide a church of worship and comfort for Southerners who had found their way to New York. To accomplish this, he founded the Church of the Strangers, initially using the chapel of New York University at Washington Square for services. During his quest for a permanent home for the church, Reverend Deems fortuitously met Frankie Crawford Vanderbilt, the second wife of the shipping and railroad magnate Commodore Cornelius Vanderbilt. She became a member of his church, and a friendship between Deems and the Commodore resulted. Though the richest man in the country had never been one to give to charity, the charms of his Southern wife and the enthusiasm of Reverend Deems persuaded him in 1870 to provide the necessary fifty thousand dollars to establish a home for the Church of the Strangers on Mercer Street.[5]

By the time JoJo arrived in New York, his uncle Owen had become an important member of the church's advisory council. JoJo also plunged into the life of the religious group, soon becoming one of its officers. He dedicated himself to helping Reverend Deems, even to writing the Church of the Strangers' official history, *A Romance of Providence.*[6]

Occasionally JoJo managed to get to Pennsylvania to visit Katherine, who had contracted a throat infection that ended her teaching career. She knew that her fiancé needed to build his savings before they could marry, so she waited patiently and passed the time doing needlework at the family home in Oxford, some forty miles west of Philadelphia. Three years later, in 1884, the couple married and moved into a lower Manhattan flat, a term that at the time suggested stark rooms with few amenities. JoJo worked for his uncle until he discovered that teachers' salaries in New York were double those of Pennsylvania. He promptly lost his taste for the apple butter business and took a position at a starting salary of $1,080, augmented with evening instruction and work with private pupils, and a promise of pay as high as $3,000 per year.

All this was explained in the previously mentioned letter of December 31, 1885, which JoJo wrote to his foster parents. But the main purpose of the letter was to relay the good news of his first child, Joseph Deems Taylor.

In what became a lifetime role as a traditional supportive wife, Katherine agreed with her husband's wishes to name the child not only for his father, but also for the forceful Reverend Deems. It was not until graduation from college that Joseph Deems Taylor simplified his name and became Deems Taylor.

Six-year-old Deems with his mother, Katherine, in their Manhattan flat in 1891.
(Courtesy of Yale University Music Library)

Childhood Recollections

If environment predisposes a child's future direction, then young Taylor was certain to find a love for music. Katherine and JoJo, who had gained some formal training in the Millersville college choir, undoubtedly sang "Rock-a-bye Baby," "Oh Promise Me," and other popular tunes of the day, as well as hymns such as "I Will Sing the Wond'rous Story." But it was Taylor's parents' interpretations of the latest Gilbert and Sullivan operettas, particularly *H.M.S. Pinafore* and *The Mikado,* that found prominence in the home. Years later Taylor remembered that when he was six years old, his parents' warblings were distinctly Savoyard:

> [W]e were not wealthy. The piano, for instance, the traditional re-
> sult and symbol of affluence, was missing. We did, however, possess

a parlor organ: a Mason & Hamlin, and a good one; and what time he was not teaching day or night school, my father used to play and sing a good deal . . . about some kind of little bird that died, and whose name was Tit Willow. . . . Also every once in a while, to some statement of my mother's my father would retort, "What, never?" Without even waiting for her to speak he would instantly answer himself, "Well hardly ever!" and burst into laughter. My mother would laugh, too. It seemed to me almost unbearably silly for two such aged people to go on like that over a simple question and its perfectly satisfactory answer.[7]

Apparently young Taylor was not aware of the repeated question of H.M.S. *Pinafore*'s sailors to their braggart captain, but he was intrigued by the black dots on the printed sheets of music that provided the impetus for his parents' vocalizings. Fascinated, he began his life as a composer, drawing his own musical staves that varied from four to six lines, "all generously filled in with large fat notes placed at random."[8] In this manner, he composed a seven-movement work in youthful Sturm und Drang mode: *Love, Hatred, Sorroe, Gladness, Anger, Joy and Fetig.* The artistic embellishments on the staves provided early evidence of a budding talent for drawing.

Along with music, books and writing held an honored place in the Taylor family. JoJo read prolifically and chronicled family events in annual journals. He was a proud man, especially of his own self-discipline. His description of a trip in July 1890 to an educational meeting in St. Paul, Minnesota, speaks volumes about the man: "I have been absent 23 days, traveled 4059 miles; spent $120 which is an average of 3 cents a mile. . . . Never made a single mistake of any sort. Was not sick a minute. In short, I have more than realized my highest expectations." This dedication to detail helps explain why, twenty-five years later, Joseph Taylor became superintendent of all the schools in the Bronx and the author of numerous books and papers about education.

One can imagine how proud the parents were to find that their son quickly gained a love for reading. "I do remember," Taylor wrote years later, "that at the age of seven I read a biography of Mozart and decided to become a composer. This idea was not encouraged, and was later abandoned by me in favor of becoming a member of the fire department."[9] At the same time that the youngster was contemplating career changes, the Taylors welcomed their second and last child, Katherine Ralston Taylor, born in October 1892. For six-year-old Deems, the arrival of a sister was not anticipated. According to family lore, he wanted his parents to get him a pet goat, but instead he got a sister. Perhaps it was for this reason that in later years, the J. M. Barrie novel

Sentimental Tommy became one of young Taylor's favorites: little Tommy Sandys, the book's hero, suffered a similar unexpected fate of sharing parental affection.[10]

The Taylors' new child was given the same first name as her mother, thereby necessitating nicknames. Katherine the mother became Mummie, and Katherine the daughter, Katy. As pleased as they were to have a second child, the parents did not let an infant deter them from planning a trip the following summer to what would be the nineteenth century's final great world's fair, the 1893 Columbian Exhibition in Chicago. Little Katy was left with Mummie's parents in Oxford, Pennsylvania, while JoJo, Mummie, and Deems took their ten-day trip to investigate the display of growing U.S. industrial power and strength.

It was the second great U.S. world's fair. The first had been the 1876 Centennial Exposition in Philadelphia, commemorating the Declaration of Independence. At that fair, the machinery powering the industrial revolution had held center stage. As 1892 drew near, and with it the four-hundredth anniversary of the voyage of Columbus to the Americas, Congress saw another opportunity for a grand show. However, the inevitable congressional political maneuverings about where the fair should be located consumed so much time that the World's Columbian Exhibition opened to the public in 1893, a year late. The Chicago fair attracted huge crowds, drawing 27 million visitors in its one summer of existence from a U.S. population of some 65 million.[11]

Approaching the site, visitors saw a gleaming White City built on 685 acres fronting Lake Michigan. The buildings, designed in a Beaux Arts style officially labeled "Neo-classical Florentine," were set beautifully upon canals and lagoons, an attempt to construct the ideal city in scale and elegance. More exciting than the architecture to some of the visitors was the extensive use of electricity—for an electric railway, the first Ferris wheel (250 feet in diameter, its thirty-six cars could carry up to 1,440 passengers), and brilliant night illumination of the gargantuan white buildings.

Taylor's father detailed the trip in his journal. Ever the educator, he made sure that the family saw all the major exhibition halls and visited the Midway, the lengthy entertainment strip that bestowed its name on all such succeeding sites. Seven-year-old Taylor rode the Ferris wheel with his mother—"Price is 50 cents; children full fare." He loved Hagenbeck's Animal Act. There is no record of what music he heard on the Midway, but John Philip Sousa was there with his band, and farther along were Africans from a Dahomey village, drumming and chanting their native harmonies. Undoubtedly he also heard ragtime, a new phenomenon that, with its driving, striding piano style, became popular in the United States by the end of the century but was a novelty when the Columbian Exhibition opened. Fair goers heard it played by "pianists from all over the central United States [who] converged on the amusement thoroughfare called the Midway, as well as the huge Chicago red-light district that extended from Eighteenth Street to Twenty-second and from Dearborn all the way to the Illinois Central tracks. Few were the players who went unemployed."[12] Among these musicians was Scott Joplin, who six years later published "The Maple Leaf Rag" and ascended to the throne of "King of Ragtime." Young Taylor must have found this American music exciting, very different from the tunes of Gilbert and Sullivan. All in all, the six days spent at the fairgrounds filled him with visions of architecture and music. When the family returned to New York, JoJo made his customary financial assessment of the trip: ten days from beginning to end, at a cost of ninety-five dollars.

After the visit to the Columbian Exhibition, Joseph Deems's main preoccupation remained reading. A Pennsylvania cousin recalled the nine-year-old arriving from New York, stepping off the train "all aglow. He had just read Kipling's 'The Brushwood Boy,' a story with a dream-like, fantastic background. . . . The story had inspired him . . . and he was shocked to find that his cousin and his other Philadelphia playmates had never heard of it. . . . He was an indefatigable reader. Once when he had exhausted my library, I suggested in a joke that he might try my new dictionary. And sure enough, I found him a little later poring over it."[13]

In the world of the 1890s, the piano ruled supreme as the instrument of choice for family music. Taylor's musical talents took a big step when his parents bought him one and provided a piano teacher for a few months of lessons. "The necessary routine was most irksome to him," his teacher recalled years later, "and his interest had to be awakened by giving him the beginning of harmony, which I did. . . . [It was] as an incentive for him to do some creative work which he did in the little pieces he made up for me. . . . He hated the work necessary to read new music but he did it. It was a task he labored through for the joy afterward in making his own music."[14] These lessons and some later months of music theory became Taylor's only formal excursions into music study.

During his elementary school years, the young man brought home testimonials of merit "for punctual attendance, correct deportment and diligent attention to study," but it was later revealed that his "school life was largely Hell because his father was a teacher," and "to make matters worse, [he] spent one year in a school of which his father was the principal."[15] What appears to emerge from all this is that Joseph Deems had to continually face a father who demanded perfection similar to his own. JoJo realized that his son was not being challenged in school, so he moved him from one elementary

The Taylor family home on Loring Place in the Bronx. *(Courtesy of Elizabeth MacDonald)*

school to another. For an artistically inclined youngster, the public schools of the 1890s did not provide an outlet; there were neither music specialists nor opportunities to draw or paint. About all the school systems offered for artistic expression was rigorous penmanship. The long-suffering father finally came up with a solution, as his son remembered years later:

> Most of [my father's] theories of education were about 25 years ahead of those of his contemporaries. The basis of his thinking was that the school belongs to the child, and that its curriculum should be flexible enough to pay some attention to the particular abilities and needs of the individual. Naturally, the New York public school system at that time could not do that [since its province] was too broad and the number of its pupils too vast. My father did his loyal best to adjust me to the system, sending me to a succession of four different public schools; but our relationship, theirs and mine, was not a completely happy one. Then he heard of the Ethical Culture School, discovered that its theories, likewise, were about 25 years ahead of its time—and had me enrolled.[16]

It was a fortunate choice for J. Deems Taylor, as he then signed his name. When he entered the Ethical Culture School in 1896, it had been in operation in midtown Manhattan for eighteen years, far from the Bronx that was now his home. The Taylor house on Loring Place sat high above the Harlem

River, with surroundings that still could be called rural. Only a few hundred yards away, the new campus of New York University on University Heights was evolving. Every weekday Taylor boarded the streetcars that took him to West Fifty-fourth Street. With fifteen cents for lunch money, he always bought the best food bargain—a massive bag of Pfeffernuss, German ginger cakes, "hard as stone and garnished with white icing."

The Ethical Culture School proved to be the opportunity he needed. Every one of his embryonic talents developed through the school's offerings: music, writing, carpentry, elocution, and drawing. All had their place here:

> I was taught musical notation. . . . Once a week we had a visitor at assembly, a professional, who would play the violin or the piano, or would sing to us. . . . Those Friday recitals were about all the serious music that we youngsters ever heard. . . . We received art instruction as a matter of course. . . . [W]e worked in a real studio, and again I was taught by professionals. . . . I enjoyed the astounding luxury of being supplied with paper and pencil for working out my spelling and arithmetic problems . . . [for] in those days, in public school, we used slates. . . . We studied elocution. . . . We acted plays in the assembly room for the edification of our fellows.[17]

Fourteen-year-old Taylor, the inveterate reader.
(Courtesy of Yale University Music Library)

One place he loved was a wonderful workshop in the basement, "a small boy's dream." Here he developed his woodworking talents using saws, hammers, planes, chisels, and lathes.

After three years in the lower division, Taylor entered the Ethical Culture High School in the fall of 1899. It was located in a converted brownstone on Fifty-eighth Street between Park and Madison, with smallish rooms that belied their previous use as bedrooms. The following years introduced him to classical Greek and Latin, as well as French and German, and he became the first editor of the school's literary magazine, *The Inkling*. He also discovered that despite all his talents he did have an Achilles heel— mathematics. As he later remembered: "Mathematics were in the care of Miss Mathilde Auerbach. How she labored, with the patience of a pediatrician dealing with a mongoloid idiot, to pound the elements of algebra and geometry into my unresponsive skull! It was no use. Mathematics and I were simply allergic to each other. I had planned to enter college after my third year, provided I could pass the entrance examinations; and my other teachers were willing to recommend me—all but Miss Auerbach, who held out till the end, despairingly maintaining that I was not yet fit to enter the halls of learning."[18]

During summers he visited cousins in Philadelphia. They went by trolley north to Willow Grove Park, where memorable experiences of live music awaited them:

Every summer, in my early years, I used to spend about a month in Philadelphia, visiting my aunt and my two girl cousins. And also, every summer, Victor Herbert took his orchestra to Willow Grove Park in Philadelphia for a season of five weeks, during which he conducted four concerts a day, seven days a week. My cousin Hattie and myself had long been devoted Herbert fans and the prospect of seeing him in action, conducting his own music was so entrancing that we would gladly have spent the entire five weeks at Willow Grove. But we had a problem. To go on one of those Herbert binges we were each given fifty cents. Naturally, we wanted to stay for both the afternoon and evening concerts. But the trolley fee to Willow Grove was fifteen cents each way, a total of thirty cents. Then admission to the park was another fifteen cents leaving us exactly five cents apiece for dinner. Believe it or not we licked that problem. Each of us bought five cents' worth of the cheapest candy we could find. We finally settled on something called licorice shoestrings, which tasted as revolting as it looked. And when we ate it, it made

Taylor family photo, Milford, Pa., in 1901: Katherine Moore (Mummie), Joseph (JoJo) Schimmel, Katherine Ralston (Katy), Joseph Deems.

(Courtesy of Michael W. Davis)

us so sick that we didn't want any dinner, and so sat happily through the two evening concerts.[19]

Herbert's concerts made a strong impression. For the first time Taylor heard the music of Richard Wagner—marches from *Lohengrin* and *Tannhäuser,* overtures to the *Flying Dutchman* and *Rienzi*—all of which began a lifelong admiration for the works of Wagner. In the summer of his sixteenth year, Taylor spent several weeks at Camp Dudley on Lake Champlain. It was in that bucolic setting that his fingers first touched a Wagner opera score: "My first opera was *Tannhäuser.* . . . I did not see a performance of it, but I was personally conducted through the piano-vocal score by a gentleman named James Fuller Berry, who, besides being a rabid Wagnerite, was a professor of mathematics in the New York public high schools. I never went to public high school, and my mathematics was—or is it were?—always terrible; but I am indebted to a mathematics professor for opening before me a world that I had not known existed."[20]

Years later, after the premiere of Taylor's own first opera, Berry sent a letter of congratulations to the composer. His response must surely have pleased the teacher: "Dear Pa Berry, Thanks so much for your note. I wonder if you remember introducing me to the score of 'Tannhäuser' at Camp

Dudley in 1901? That summer turned a page in my life and I have always been grateful to you."[21]

In the summer of 1902, Taylor turned another significant page; he entered college.

College Years at New York University

One of the city's fine institutions of higher education was only a ten-minute walk from the Taylor home. In 1894 NYU had moved its School of Arts and Pure Science (University College) from the Washington Square area of Manhattan to the Bronx, onto a knoll looking west over the Harlem River to the brownish cliffs of upper Manhattan.[22] To build the needed new classrooms on what became known as University Heights, Henry Mitchell MacCracken, the chancellor of NYU, convinced Helen Gould, the daughter of the "robber baron" Jay Gould, to donate construction funds. He promised to name the library for her father, thus helping to rehabilitate his somewhat blighted name. Helen Gould agreed to this plan and gave the financial support. MacCracken then convinced the city's premier architect, Stanford White, to design buildings of strength and beauty for the new campus.

When White saw the site he realized that erosion could ultimately undermine the buildings, so he designed a semicircular retaining wall, a six-hundred-foot colonnaded covered walkway to be constructed of granite. The chancellor soon envisioned another purpose for the classic structure: a Hall of Fame for Great Americans. He sold the idea to his board, which then appointed a committee of prominent men to select which deceased American greats would be honored. Busts of the chosen would fill the spaces between the colonnades. This Hall of Fame gave uniqueness to the campus when it opened in 1900.[23]

For most, travel to the new campus meant taking elevated railways, trolley cars, or horse-drawn carriages, since subway lines were still under construction. The emerging automobile remained suspicious to most and irritating to the horses that pulled the carriages on the cobblestone streets. But the closeness of NYU made Taylor's choice of a college simple. He had watched the construction and had gone to the dedication ceremony in 1900, snapping photos of the event with his first camera. Now he wanted to be an architect, which built on another of his talents, drawing. Since NYU did not have a school of architecture, he decided on four years of liberal arts there, followed by a school of architecture elsewhere. In mid-June 1902 he took the college entrance exams, did well enough to be accepted, and that September began his daily walks down Loring Place to the campus.

Some three hundred men constituted the total student body of NYU when Taylor enrolled; one hundred of these were in his freshman class, with most in the engineering school that shared the Heights campus. His liberal arts course of study provided little choice within the well-defined areas: sciences, literature, languages (classical and modern), philosophy, and church history. Away from the classroom his social life centered on the Phi Upsilon fraternity, which he joined. Though he continued to live at home, he soon became a favored entertainer at fraternity weekend events.

Taylor also participated in athletics. He weighed 128 pounds and had grown to his full height of 5 feet, 6½ inches. For his first excursions into college athletics, he chose football and track. Having been the quarterback on his Ethical Culture football team, he put his meager body into the fray as part of the scrub team. Unfortunately, the coach assigned him to play tackle, and after he faced an opposing varsity tackle of 185 pounds, his future in football proved neither promising nor long. In the spring he pursued his aspiration to be a runner: "I made the track team, but I don't remember ever winning a race," he later wrote. "I existed for the sole reason that we simply had to have at least two entries for every event; so I was the second entry. . . . The finish of every race was for me a nightmare of numbers; the numbers on the backs of the other contestants. None of which in the least prevented my spending considerable portions of three dogged, panting years trying to beat somebody."[24]

Joseph Deems also joined the glee club in his freshman year, an event that helped push music above architecture as a future calling.[25] NYU in the early 1900s, like most other colleges and universities of its time, had no music department. This was strictly an extracurricular activity and consisted of clubs—glee, mandolin, banjo. Taylor later explained their popularity:

> Membership in these organizations was eagerly sought by everybody who was not actually tone-deaf. Everybody wanted to belong to the musical clubs because twice during the term, at Christmas and at Easter, these organizations were allowed to go on a week's concert tour. . . . [The program] began, invariably, with Bullard's Winter Song, sung with awful earnestness by the glee club. . . . Following that, the banjo club would assemble and play a march, which was always on the "patrol" order—that is, it began very softly, grew very loud in the middle, and ended very softly. This always created a terrific sensation. After loud applause the club would play it all over again. . . . Next, a specialty by myself, consisting of a melodrama, with myself playing all the parts. I stole it from a vaudeville act that I had seen on 14th Street. . . . Then, something else by the glee club generally comic—a young man sitting on a sofa with a young

woman, and stealing a kiss—something sidesplitting like that. Last
of all, "Here's to the land I love," from The Prince of Pilsen, rendered with magnificent élan by the combined glee, banjo, and mandolin clubs. Then a dash for the train, and so back to the humdrum
of academic life. Our principal patrons were Y.M.C.A.'s desperate
for entertainment [and] girls' boarding schools desperate for the
sight of a boy. . . . I might add that we seldom played return engagements.[26]

Taylor developed a special friendship with Reinald Werrenrath and William LeBaron, two of his fellow glee clubbers. He admired Werrenrath's vocal talents and LeBaron's writing skills. In fact, Werrenrath and Taylor shared
a unique ability in the glee club: they were the only members who could read
music. Werrenrath's parents both were professional singers, and he hoped to
follow in their footsteps. LeBaron, who had transferred to NYU from the
University of Chicago, had aspirations to write plays for Broadway. In the
years ahead Taylor, Werrenrath, and LeBaron played significant roles in helping each other develop successful careers in the arts, but at that time Taylor
still saw architecture as his future. Whether he knew it or not, music's siren
call became more seductive with every passing day.

In the summer between his junior and senior years, he and two other
friends developed their musical talents as a three-piece dance band playing at
a vacation hotel on Shippan Point, a portion of Stamford, Connecticut, on
the Long Island Sound. The Atlantic Coast abounded with massive wooden
summer hotels that attracted wealthy vacationers. For the smartly dressed
crowd, small ensembles provided music at teas and evening socials. At
Shippan Point Taylor's trio consisted of a piano, a cornet, and a violin. Each
earned a free meal and $8.33 per week. Taylor discovered he had a talent for
arranging music, at least for those three instruments. "We played afternoon
tea concerts, and evening hops," he recalled years later. "The latter were simple: no nonsense about rumbas and tangos and sambas—just waltz, two-
step, waltz, two-step. The waltzes were mostly [Victor] Herbert. For the tea
concerts, the 'Gypsy Love Song' from The Fortune Teller was our pièce de
résistance. In fact, we played it so much that we began to be worried for fear
that the rocking-chair brigade might notice its almost daily appearance on
the printed program."[27] Taylor may have tired of some Herbert music, but as
fate would have it, Victor Herbert himself gave the final fatal jolt to his idea
of becoming an architect.

After the musical frolics on the Connecticut shore, Taylor was contacted
by Reinald Werrenrath, who had graduated the previous year. The baritone
had planned to write the music for the NYU varsity show of 1906 with an-

other graduate, but his concert career had already begun and he had no time. Werrenrath urged Taylor, for the good of NYU, the "Violet and White," to compose the music; William LeBaron would write the libretto.

The opportunity for Taylor was too good to let pass. All the important universities of their day had such varsity shows, always with original music and the story by students or alumni. The shows played for several days in legitimate theaters, usually with a professional orchestra, and were covered by newspaper reviewers who knew that exceptional talent often existed in these shows, if in raw form. Some students, such as Richard Rodgers, who went to Columbia University, chose their college because they wanted to compose or write the varsity show.[28]

Actually, Taylor had been predisposed to the joys of stage presentations by his parents, who had taken him to Broadway plays and musicals. He had a vague recollection (having been only four years old at the time) of seeing the great Edwin Booth in *Hamlet,* and the spectacle of *Ben Hur.* In addition, he had seen two classic musicals: Charles Hoyt's 1891 *Trip to Chinatown,* which ran 657 performances and turned farce-comedy into musical comedy, and *Florodora* in 1899, with its sensational sextet of glamorous chorus girls to give young Taylor a new kind of thrill. By his NYU years he was, in his own estimation, "a hardened theatergoer."[29]

Taylor and LeBaron had seen many varsity shows and knew that audiences loved the sophomoric humor tossed out to them by the ebullient all-male student entertainers. What audience members especially loved was the traditional "pony ballet," nothing more than a chorus line of men in drag. One observer of the 1906 Columbia University varsity shows put it this way: "Taken at a distance (and in this case distance always lends a decided enchantment), they appear passably feminine, and elicit generous applause."[30]

To provide for all these expectations, Taylor and LeBaron first had to find a story. They remembered the Broadway hit of some four years previous, the *Sultan of Sulu,* a comic opera with a plot that became a Broadway staple: the interaction of Americans with the ways of natives on tropical islands. The new songwriting team dipped into this story line and created the 1906 NYU varsity show, *The Isle of Skidoo,* in which they sent two Americans to a South Sea island populated by cannibals. Everything seemed to go well for the composer and lyricist until Taylor turned to orchestrating the music. Then he quickly learned that arranging for a full orchestra was far more difficult than for piano, violin, and cornet. He had no choice but to plead with the faculty committee overseeing the show to underwrite the cost of professional orchestration, which it did.

The NYU varsity show played for a full week at the Carnegie Lyceum, a

Taylor, seated on left, with NYU classmates in 1905. Standing on far right is the baritone Reinald Werrenrath. Juniors have light-colored college caps; seniors have dark caps. *(Courtesy of Michael W. Davis)*

thousand-seat theater in the basement of Carnegie Hall. If *The Isle of Skidoo* had little impact on the musical world, it hardly mattered, for though the style was that of Gilbert and Sullivan, the energy and humor were strictly collegiate. The two shipwrecked Americans welcomed by the cannibals to their shores were named Mr. Wright and Mr. Wronng, and the cannibal chief's name was Hooami. In the exchange between the cannibal chief and Mr. Wright, LeBaron managed to predate the classic Abbott and Costello routine of "Who's on First?"

> *Chief:* Hooami.
> *Wright:* That's right. Who are you?
> *Chief (pointing to Wronng):* He's Wright. Me, Hooami.
> *Wright:* That's Wronng. I mean, who are you?[31]

The audiences loved it. So did the varsity show committee, which quickly signed up the new team to prepare the 1907 presentation.

Taylor's college days now approached their end. He finished the requisite senior thesis for graduation, choosing as his topic the plays of the then still relatively unknown George Bernard Shaw.

And what of women in the life of the young collegian? His subsequent recollections of the senior ball—"I took Adele Martin, a queen. She married Bill Wildman almost immediately afterward"[32]—suggest that the charm and wit of future years still hadn't blossomed completely. In the years ahead Taylor would not be able to live without the companionship of women, but for now the fair sex had to wait. The working world beckoned, and he had to find a job. He also decided that henceforth he would not be Joseph Deems Taylor, or even J. Deems Taylor, but just plain Deems Taylor.

2. The Emergence of Taylor as Composer and Writer, 1906–1916

Victor Herbert Changes Taylor's Life

Deems Taylor's musical talents couldn't yet buy him clothes, so he turned to the printed word to make money. It was now 1906, and New York seethed with publishing energy in newspapers, magazines, and books. In Washington, the vigorous president Theodore Roosevelt, himself a New Yorker, had helped spawn a reading public, with books he had written on subjects from biographies to his beloved outdoors.[1] Among the dozen daily newspapers in New York, one could choose the sensationalistic approach of William Randolph Hearst's *Journal* or Joseph Pulitzer's *World,* or select instead the more moderate style of the *Tribune, Sun, Evening Post,* or *Times.* For readers with a literary bent, favorite periodicals included *Century Magazine* and *Life,* the humor publication. In the not-too-distant future Taylor would gain a few extra dollars from poems published in both of these, but for the present he chose to join the staff of *Nelson's Encyclopedia,* a major reference work of its day. Here he wrote articles, proofed the work of others, and found photos to use as illustrations. Though the salary hardly made him a millionaire, he was able to save a little money because he still lived at his parents' home.

On evenings and weekends Deems met Bill LeBaron to develop *The Oracle,* their 1907 NYU varsity show. This time they sent two adventurous Americans not to fight cannibals, but to climb Mount Olympus in search of the Delphic Oracle. As in the past, the Varsity Dramatic Club, producers of the show, announced to NYU students the time and places for tryouts. Of course, the men played both male and female parts. The announcement caught the attention of Newman Levy, a freshman who after graduation would become a well-respected lawyer and writer of light verse. But at this time he was a stagestruck young man, in love with Victor Herbert's operettas as well as those of Gilbert and Sullivan. In his autobiography, *My Double Life,* Levy tells how he went to the audition and "never quite recovered from the impact of that afternoon . . . listening in rapturous delight to sparkling lyrics and gay tunes written by the two young men at the piano."[2] As a neophyte actor, Levy settled for the part of "a beautiful Greek nymph, slim and graceful, with long flowing golden curls . . . part of what was called in those days the Pony ballet . . . [which] could dance and kick in a manner that would do credit to a Rockette."[3]

The Carnegie Lyceum Theater again was the site for the show. This time Taylor, the versatile composer, also became a carpenter. As Levy recalled: "The scene of Act Two was before the Temple of Apollo at Delphi, and the theatre . . . although well equipped with exteriors and interiors was rather shy on Greek temples. So Deems, one morning, went down to the theatre with a lot of lumber, canvas and carpenters' tools and built the temple himself."[4]

The show's title, *The Oracle,* proved prophetic, for the production brought Taylor a wise counselor in the hefty body of Victor Herbert, then the most famous composer of light opera in America. He had produced fourteen operettas in twelve years, including the great successes of *The Fortune Teller* and *Babes in Toyland.* Just a year earlier, a touring company of the latter had been playing in San Francisco at the time of the earthquake on April 18, 1906. Herbert, who Taylor later referred to as "one of the greatest human beings I have ever known,"[5] organized a concert at the immense New York Hippodrome to benefit the people of San Francisco. In September 1906 his *Red Mill* opened on Broadway for a run of 274 performances, far and away the hit of the year.

After *The Red Mill* closed, Herbert, always seeking new musical talent, accepted the invitation of Jack Scannell, the comic lead of *The Oracle,* to come to the Carnegie Lyceum and see the latest NYU varsity show. Scannell knew the Herbert family, but didn't tell anyone that Herbert himself would be in the audience. Taylor, conducting the orchestra, received a surprise message at the end of the first act to come and meet the famed composer in his box. After introductions, Herbert quizzed the young man about his musical training: "My boy, you have talent, but you don't know anything about music, do you? I mean musical theory." The pleasantly startled Taylor admitted to having had no formal musical education but for his few months of piano lessons.

"Well," advised Herbert, "you must study harmony and counterpoint. As it is now, you're like a man trying to write plays who doesn't know how to read and write. You can go just so far. If you want to go farther, you must study."[6]

As a youngster Taylor had idolized Herbert and his orchestra at Willow Grove. Now he could only thank him and promise to follow his advice. With the success of *The Oracle,* the Varsity Dramatic Club again asked the two men to create their next show. LeBaron, now an advertising manager for the coal industry publication *Coal Age,* had savored something of the business world, and for their next plot he suggested that they raise their sights to satire. The resulting *Cap'n Kidd and Co.* in 1908 targeted the barons of business, as is suggested by the lyrics of one of the songs, "The World Isn't Running as It Was":

> *In days of old (you've all been told the tales about nobility),*
> *'Twas quite the thing for ev'ry king to rule with imbecility.*
> *A king there was in ev'ry land; his subjects were a loyal band,*
> *Nobles all, at his command, salaamed with great agility.*
> *But now a king cannot coerce, the way he used to then.*
> *The rulers of the universe are now the bus'ness men!*[7]

William LeBaron, lyricist of the four NYU varsity shows for which Taylor wrote the music. He became head of production for Paramount Pictures in the 1930s.

(Courtesy of Yale University Music Library)

Newman Levy once again was in the chorus line: "I had grown taller and heavier, and I became a show girl, a slender, sinuous glamour girl in a tight-fitting princess dress, a black wig, and long eardrops. I was called by my admiring colleagues of the chorus the Queen of the Ghetto."[8]

Admiration for the show also came from reviewers sent by both the *World* and the *Times*. For the *World* critic it was "a genuine surprise. . . . LeBaron furnished two acts of crisp lines and swinging lyrics, and Deems Taylor . . . turned out tinkling melodies." The *Times* called it "a hit, excelling anything ever done by the club."[9] Not surprisingly, the LeBaron-Taylor team was signed again. Their 1909 show, *The Echo,* hit Broadway pay dirt, thanks to the theatrical impresario Charles B. Dillingham.

The Echo Lights Up Broadway

In 1909 vaudeville still held much of the public's attention in New York theaters, but change was in the air. Though Victor Herbert operettas remained popular, Franz Lehár's *Merry Widow* had come to Broadway from Europe in 1907 and caused a sensation, as had the title waltz that swept the country. Lehár's music opened Broadway to what became a succession of Viennese operettas. That same year, an enterprising Florenz Ziegfeld initiated a revue modeled on the *Folies Bergères* of Paris. Held in the rooftop auditorium of the New York Theatre at Broadway and Forty-fifth Street, soon to be renamed the Jardin de Paris, the show evolved into the glamorous *Ziegfeld Follies,* featuring stars such as Nora Bayes, Sophie Tucker, and Fanny Brice in its early years. Meanwhile, at the four-year-old Hippodrome on Sixth Avenue between Forty-third and Forty-fourth Streets, audiences filled the 5,200 seats to watch spectacles from galloping stallions to galumphing elephants. Ten years later on that very stage, Harry Houdini would make one of those elephants disappear.

Ziegfeld ultimately gained greater fame as a producer of Broadway extravaganzas, but in 1909 Charles Dillingham was the prominent producer of musicals, known for his gentlemanly ways and variety of productions. Dillingham recognized that musical revues—with topical songs, lots of dancing, and a minimal plot—had begun to compete successfully with operettas in attracting audiences. But revues needed songwriting talent, and Dillingham knew that varsity shows often provided a source for that new blood. Having heard of the NYU team's earlier successes, he attended one of the three performances of *The Echo* and liked what he heard. He went backstage to tell the words-and-music team that he wanted to produce *The Echo* on Broadway.

The flabbergasted pair signed a contract on May 1, 1909, the final night of the show, but Dillingham advised them to be patient because the production needed a lot of work. He planned a tryout in Chicago early the following spring, and then would open *The Echo* on Broadway in his own Globe Theater. The delighted twosome had visions of fame and fortune—especially Taylor, who reflected on what Victor Herbert had told him and decided that the time to learn musical theory was right now.

In the spring of 1909, he succeeded in "obtaining a small subsidy from a reluctant father" to begin his music studies.[10] It is likely that Taylor's father did not appreciate his son's seeking fame on Broadway, a street that still had connotations of a world of loose living. Though JoJo kept detailed annual journals, in none of them did he mention any of the NYU varsity shows.

Deems Taylor chose Oscar Coon, an elderly man with a patriarchal white beard, to teach him music theory. Coon earned his living by teaching, writing books on music subjects, and providing orchestrations for publishers. Years later Taylor fondly remembered his teacher and Coon's spartan quarters near Washington Square, a "room whose principal articles of furniture were a cot and bookkeeper's desk, at which he stood to write music. . . . He subsisted, so far as I was ever able to discover, on Scotch whiskey and bananas exclusively. . . . Don't get the impression that he was a drunken eccentric. On the contrary, he was a tough-fibered, intellectually honest, fiercely independent upstate Yankee . . . a profound and devoted musical scholar. . . . The hours that I spent with Oscar Coon were among the happiest and most profitable of my life."[11]

Taylor's 1909 appointment book indicates that he began his studies in April, and during the summer and fall he completed two manuals of music— Richter's *Harmony* and Jadassohn's *Canon and Fugue*—in months versus the normal two years.

While Taylor studied, Dillingham began to shape *The Echo* into a hoped-for Broadway success. Unfortunately for Taylor, Dillingham soon recognized that the score did not have the requisite Broadway-type tunes, so he substituted songs from a variety of songwriters, then a common practice for musical revues. By the time the production went to Chicago for tryouts, though LeBaron's writing remained mainly intact, all that was left of Taylor's music was the opening chorus and an encore dance number.[12] However, "Deems Taylor" remained on the program as the show's composer, a bit of solace for a bruised ego, since the composers of interpolated songs were not officially identified.

Among the songs Dillingham added to *The Echo* was "Whistle When You're Lonely" by Jerome Kern (born in 1885, like Taylor), then an up-and-coming songwriter. Kern was making his money by selling music to Dillingham and other Broadway producers, as many other songwriters did.

During the first intermission of *The Echo*'s Broadway premiere, so the story goes, Bruce Edwards, the director, encountered Jerome Kern in the lobby. "Your music is swell, old man," he said. Whereupon several other men standing nearby turned, smiled, and said, "Thank you!" *The Echo* was Kern's first association with Dillingham, later to become the producer of most of his musicals.[13]

The Echo opened at the Globe Theater on August 18, 1910, to positive reviews that thrilled Taylor. Unfortunately, the thrill of the evening could not be shared by Taylor's parents and his seventeen-year-old sister, Katy, who were in the midst of a European trip. It is likely that when they left in July, the opening of *The Echo* had not yet been set. According to the *Times,* the production provided "a singing and dancing frolic . . . one of the brightest, neatest, cleanest, and most entertaining musical shows that Broadway has seen in many a day. . . . 'The Echo' promises to make itself heard for a good many weeks to come."[14] The plot, as usual in Broadway revues, was tenuous at best, all about the goings-on at a hotel set in the mountains, where echoes provided the basis for the musical's name. A young life-of-the-party society man woos a pretty waitress, to the intense disapproval of his mother. Singing and dancing characters of various types wander in and out, until the final curtain provides the happy-ever-after finale. For the waitress, Dillingham selected Bessie McCoy, then a leading singer-dancer on Broadway. Also featured were new entertainers on their way to stardom: the Dolly Sisters and the dance team of Ben Ryan and George White, the latter dancer to light up future Broadway skies with *George White's Scandals.*

Ticket sales flourished, and Taylor dreamed of becoming a major player on the Broadway scene. He sent Dillingham a letter of thanks: "It is not easy to thank you in words for all that you have done, and still I must try. You have given us a start—the most wonderful sort of a start—in a profession where the start means everything. A newspaper friend of mine said yesterday, 'This production, with Dillingham's name on it, has given you two youngsters a professional standing, in this one week, that other men have spent years trying to attain.' And he was right. Whatever the future may hold for me, I shall not soon forget that it was you who made that future a possibility instead of a dream."[15]

The First Mrs. Taylor: Jane Anderson

In September 1910, with his name on a Broadway marquee, the world seemed bright for twenty-five-year-old Deems Taylor. In addition to *The Echo*'s success, Jane Anderson had entered his life, a beautiful and intelligent woman born in Atlanta some twenty years earlier. For a time she had lived with her father in Yuma, Arizona, then attended Kidd-Key, a women's college in Sherman, Texas. Highly ambitious, she left college before graduating to pursue a writing career in New York City. Her letter of introduction to George Harvey, editor of *Harper's Weekly,* was from none other than Harvey's friend Buffalo Bill Cody.

Taylor met Anderson in November 1909, eight months before *The Echo* opened, and within a few weeks they found occasions to be together almost every day.[16] He had fallen quite madly for the Southern girl, who had the looks and talent he appreciated in women. Though he never described Anderson's attractiveness in any of his known writings, others did. Kitty Crawford, her close friend at Kidd-Key, thought her one of the most beautiful girls she had ever seen, having a face that was "rather broad, with widely-spaced violet-blue eyes, [and] a pert upturned nose."[17] The English novelist Rebecca West later added these details: "She was very beautiful with orange hair that I am sure was of nature, a slender figure, a ravishing complexion, and great charm of manner."[18]

In addition to her physical beauty, Anderson very likely showed Taylor the same tantalizing mixture of coyness and sensuality that is evident in her letter to the author Theodore Dreiser: "Dear Mr. Dreiser: You will believe me strangely unappreciative; the truth of the matter is: since I saw you I have read Sister Carrie. Before, when I had no standard by which to judge my work, I was, anyway, not ashamed of it. You will remember though, please, that after all is said and done I cannot be expected to accomplish very much—at twenty. It *is* a wonderful book; it is truth, life; and shows a marvelous mastery of detail. You have the intuition of the feminine added to your masculine directness and logicality. Very Sincerely, Jane Anderson."[19]

With *The Echo* still playing on Broadway and no sign of closing, Taylor believed he had a secure income from royalties and asked Jane to marry him. Jane, believing she was marrying a rising star, accepted his offer. They exchanged wedding vows on September 27, 1910, with Taylor's parents as witnesses to a ceremony performed by a minister of the Fordham Reformed Church, which his parents had joined upon moving to the Bronx.[20]

Financial success on Broadway seemed assured, so the young couple moved into an apartment at 440 Riverside Drive, a fashionable address that overlooked the Hudson River. But bad news followed, for as good as *The Echo* seemed to reviewers, most theatergoers still preferred operettas, of which they couldn't seem to get enough ever since *The Merry Widow* had appeared on Broadway. Dillingham was forced to tell a downcast Taylor that *The Girl in the Train,* a new operetta from Vienna, would replace *The Echo* at the Globe in October. There was some good news, though: Bessie McCoy would take *The Echo* on the road throughout the Northeast.

Taylor and Jane Anderson, his first wife. They were married from 1910 to 1918.

(Courtesy of Yale University Music Library)

The show played in theaters along the East Coast from Washington, D.C., to Boston for nearly six months, closing the following March.[21] That September, since Taylor had not yet received royalties from *The Echo's* final weeks on the road, he wrote to Dillingham asking when he might expect the money. Taylor's dreams of fame vanished with the producer's response: "Dear Mr. Taylor: In reply to your letter, I suppose the delay was caused in not being able to find out here in the office what you did for 'The Echo' last season. As soon as we can locate your connection with that piece I have no doubt Mr. Rigby will send you a check. Yours very truly, C. B. Dillingham."[22] The staff finally did locate Taylor's connection, and a check arrived to the financially beleaguered composer two months later. In his letter to Dillingham confirming receipt of the money, he spoke to the plight of a poor, starving artist: "Thank you for the check that arrived this evening. I know now how I shall feel at my hanging, when the messenger dashes in with a reprieve."[23]

Since the newly married couple had taken a chattel mortgage and no longer could meet the payments, their new furniture was repossessed. Tail between legs, Taylor took his wife back to the family home in the Bronx until financial times improved. Anderson wrote stories for *Harper's* and made other literary contacts, while Taylor found work for a piano-roll manufacturer in Newark, New Jersey, leaving the Bronx at 5:30 in the morning to get to his job at 8:00 A.M., all for twenty-five dollars per week. The player piano era was at its peak, and piano rolls were big business, with competitors trying to outdo each other.

With this in mind, Taylor proposed to his employer to make a roll of selections from Giacomo Puccini's latest opera, *La Fanciulla del West,* premiered in New York a year earlier. His boss liked the idea and approved the venture, though it would be a six-week endeavor. Taylor loved the project, and when he took the master piano roll to his boss, he expected more than a little praise. Quite the opposite occurred, for when he was asked if copyrights had been cleared, he embarrassedly admitted that they had not. The whole project was wasted, and an enraged manager sent him back to New York permanently. Deems Taylor, the future president of the American Society of Composers, Authors, and Publishers (ASCAP), an organization for which copyright is everything, did not soon forget the experience.[24]

Again without a job, Taylor learned that the word was out that he was the composer "in name only" of a Broadway show. Still, he believed in his talent, and since musical themes stirred in his brain, they needed an outlet. But it wasn't only music that stirred his imagination; he also found himself attracted to writing humor. While at NYU he had submitted some short pieces to the preeminent literary columnist Franklin Pierce Adams, who did publish one of them in his column "Always in Good Humor," in the *New York Evening Mail.* Taylor, never afraid to look for new ways to develop his skills, decided to seek a meeting with Adams. It was a life-changing event.

FPA Meets "Smeed"

Franklin Pierce Adams arrived in New York from Chicago in 1904 to establish the first daily literary column in a New York paper. The column's success intensified ten years later, when he moved from the *Evening Mail* to the *Tribune* and changed the column's name to "The Conning Tower." Anyone interested in Broadway openings, newly published books, or just chatty information about the goings-on in the New York cultural world turned immediately to Adams's column. So well-liked were it and its writer that he became known solely as FPA.

He cleverly avoided writing most of the columns himself, relying instead on his reading public to send him original material, usually brief poems or short pieces that he printed if they were up to his standards. Of course, he did not pay for submissions, believing that the thrill of being published was enough. Many aspiring writers, some of whom later became members of the Algonquin Round Table, had their work published for the first time through FPA's column, and in so doing became known as contributors. Newman Levy, one who later bloomed into a fine humorist, candidly described FPA in an unpublished biography:

> A fascinating, ill-mannered, charming, ugly and brilliant man . . . one of the most cantankerous, irritating persons I ever knew, and one of the most congenial. He was often inexpressibly rude, yet multitudes of men and women sought his companionship and he had a host of loyal friends. He wrote continuously for more than half a century, prose, verse, epigrams, comments on people and contemporary events. . . . He was a mythical person to most of his devoted readers who would rather have gone without breakfast than have missed his daily column and the engrossing reports of his flirtations, his gambling, the books he read, the plays he saw, and the candid revelation of his frailties.[25]

While at NYU Taylor read Adams's column religiously, and in his senior year sent FPA a poem, which was published under the nom de plume "Smeed." All FPA's contributors had literary disguises for their names; some chose to use only their initials ("G.F.K." turned out to be the soon-to-be famous playwright George F. Kaufman), while others selected a mysterious name or phrase ("Daffydowndilly" was the famed editor and poet Louis Untermeyer). Adams never disclosed the identities of his contributors, for he enjoyed providing this sense of mystery, but literary grapevines helped determine who hid behind the veils. In his post-college years Taylor continued submitting works as Smeed, and FPA continued to publish them. As more and more items appeared under the name Smeed, the literati deciphered the coded entry: it was Deems spelled backward.

When Adams received Taylor's request to meet with him, he obliged graciously, for he knew that he had to be kind to his contributors. Taylor outlined his aspirations and financial troubles. FPA gave this advice: "Light verse will keep you in food. It's very simple. Here's what you do. Starting tomorrow, you write one piece of light verse each day. Then you get a lot of stamped envelopes and—keep 'em in the mail. The poems, I mean. As fast as one editor turns 'em down, send 'em to another. The law of averages will take care of you."[26] Literary magazines of the time, such as *Century* and *Life,* welcomed light verse at fifty cents a line, and even the New York newspapers featured such poems. Taylor acted on FPA's advice with encouraging results. He sold several dozen poems and cleverly made eight dollars for one about writing poetry for money.

Nevertheless, neither his light verse nor Jane's stories provided enough for them to enjoy New York's world of music and theater. Once again FPA came to the rescue, as Taylor remembered years later in a poem, "To Tommy":

> *'Twas one-and-thirty years ago, and I was very broke;*
> *My pants were on the shiny side, my checkbook was a joke.*
> *I took my woes to F.P.A., who sent me down to see*
> *A guy who worked on West Street, by the name of P.L.T.*

P.L.T. was P. L. "Tommy" Thomson, assigned by Western Electric Corporation, the country's leading manufacturer of telephones, to initiate a monthly publication for its twenty thousand employees. Thomson needed an assistant editor for the *Western Electric News*. When he interviewed Taylor for the position and asked him how much he wanted in salary, Taylor indicated he'd "be glad to work for ten bucks a week just so long as [he] knew it was coming in every week."[27] He got the job, and in 1912 started a four-year daily trek from the Bronx to downtown Manhattan, as also described in "To Tommy":

> *So I went to work for Tommy, doing K.P. for the NEWS.*
> *I interviewed executives, and jotted down their views.*
> *I collected text and pictures, read the proofs, and ordered cuts,*
> *And I smoothed the troubled waters when the printer drove him nuts.*[28]

No sooner had he settled into his new job than FPA alerted him to the opportunity of becoming a poor man's FPA; the *New York Press* was looking for someone to do a humor column. With a big push from FPA, Deems Taylor landed the job. Continuing with Western Electric during the day, at night he worked on the column.

Taylor was elated. Not only could he choose the materials for the column, but he would also provide the illustrations. On December 10, 1912, the *Press* introduced the Taylor column "Between All of Us." There was no by-line, but the initials "D. T." appeared at the end and with every illustration. Though most of the writing featured Taylor's original humor, some of the items he used came from other newspapers, often with his added witty commentary. Many *Press* readers were not the sophisticates who read the *Tribune* or *Sun,* so they would often have been puzzled by his choice of subjects, such as an extensive commentary on the large size of some female opera singers: "Isolde generally seems to call for an obesity cure, rather than a love-potion," he mused, and summed it up in a quatrain:

> *I've never been an opera star;*
> *I never hope to be one.*

But, take them as they mostly are,
I'd rather hear than see one.[29]

The column lasted four days.

The Siren Song and Cantatas

At the same time that his short life as a columnist for the *New York Press* came to an end, the Boston music publisher Oliver Ditson published Taylor's first art song, "Witch Woman." The need to exercise his compositional urges now resulted in such pieces. He also gained a few extra dollars by doing arrangements for others, but songs did not satisfy Taylor completely. He wanted the opportunity to put into action all the musical knowledge he had acquired from Oscar Coon.

Such a chance came, as he described later, when he read an announcement in the weekly magazine *Musical Courier* "that the National Federation of Music Clubs was offering a substantial prize [five hundred dollars] for the best symphony or symphonic poem by an American composer. That paragraph called for thought, but not for long. 'If Broadway doesn't want me,' I

Oscar Coon, Taylor's only music theory teacher, an "eccentric Yankee."

(Courtesy of Yale University Music Library)

said to myself, 'I'll try Carnegie Hall.' So I went out and bought a quire of music paper, found a poem with a mood that I liked, and set to work. The piece, which I christened 'Siren Song,' was finished and shipped off to Chicago."[30]

Months passed with no announcement, and then came the telegram: "JUDGES HAVE SENT DECISION FOR CLASS ONE—YOUR 'SIREN SONG' AWARDED SECOND PRIZE THREE HUNDRED DOLLARS—CHICAGO ORCHESTRA WILL CONSIDER RENDERING AT BIENNIAL IF YOU SEND PARTS BY WEDNESDAY NINETEENTH—ABSOLUTELY NECESSARY TO SEND AT ONCE DIRECT TO MR. STOCK—WIRE HIM—ACCEPT CONGRATULATIONS—AM WRITING YOU—MRS. JASON WALKER."[31] Second prize! Taylor read the telegram with joy and surprise: his first major composition, and the famed Chicago Symphony was going to perform it under the eminent Frederick Stock. Then his heart sank; he realized he had not extracted the separate instrument parts for the orchestra. Even a professional couldn't do that in five days. He regretfully informed Mrs. Walker that he could not have the parts in time.

On reflection, Taylor decided that if the judges had seen value in the composition—and they included the famed conductor Leopold Stokowski—then he must be a composer. He was even more elated when he learned that the judges had not presented a first prize in the competition. But why hadn't *he* received the first prize? The answer came from a kindly, knowledgeable friend: "My boy, there's only one thing wrong with it—parts of it aren't playable. Look at this harp part—in order to play that, the harpist would need four hands and two assistants to work the pedals."[32]

Taylor learned his lesson and began to study orchestration intensely, recognizing it as a major gap in his musical knowledge. He read the treatise by Hector Berlioz, and he examined minutely the scores of master composers—Mozart, Wagner, Debussy. Tchaikovsky's treatment of the orchestra particularly impressed him. Years later, in speaking with young musicians at the National Music Camp in Interlochen, Michigan, Taylor told them that he learned orchestration so well because "I had the best teachers in the world."[33]

Composing *The Siren Song* and winning the prize convinced Taylor that he needed to push deeper into composition. He published a few more art songs, but these brought little recognition and even less income. What he needed was to compose a big piece to call attention to his talents, and the man that provided the opportunity was his NYU friend Reinald Werrenrath, now a highly popular baritone whose concerts drew large crowds.

Werrenrath also had organized a choral society in the Bronx, and he needed a new choral work, so he called Taylor and offered him a modest payment to compose a short cantata. Taylor accepted and chose Oliver Wendell Holmes's poem *The Chambered Nautilus* as his musical subject.[34] The resulting short work premiered in the Bronx in May 1914. *Musical America,* the influential weekly, sent a reviewer who declared that Taylor "has written music which is modern to the core and free in its harmonic grain, but his modernity is natural and not forced."[35]

The success of *The Chambered Nautilus* spurred Werrenrath to call on Taylor again. The baritone had been invited to participate in the summer MacDowell Festival of 1914, on the grounds of the MacDowell Colony in Peterborough, New Hampshire. One of the most famous festivals in its time, its purpose was to further the memory of Edward MacDowell, whom many considered the first important American composer of concert music. When the director asked Werrenrath if he knew of any cantatas for baritone and female chorus that had not been sung to death, the singer indicated that he knew someone who was composing just such a cantata.

Of course this wasn't true, but Werrenrath quickly contacted Taylor, told him of his predicament, and begged him to accept the challenge and have the vocal parts in three months.[36] Taylor was aware that one of his virtues was the ability to work at top speed with limited time, so he agreed to compose the second cantata for Werrenrath. This time a longer work was needed as a text; Taylor finally chose "The Highwayman" by Alfred Noyes, a poem with poetic hoof beats that had been memorized by countless schoolchildren over the years:

> *The road was a ribbon of moonlight over the purple moor,*
> *And the highwayman came riding, riding, riding,*
> *The highwayman came riding, up to the old inn-door.*

It proved to be a perfect choice, since the cantata was for a baritone (the highwayman) and female chorus (the landlord's black-eyed daughter).

The resulting cantata, nearly thirty minutes in performance, provides memorable melodies for the dramatic words of the poet. Taylor begins with the chorus introducing the highwayman and telling of his attraction for Bess, the landlord's daughter. To musically establish time and place, he uses the English folksong "The British Grenadier" as the march that brings King George's men to the inn to capture the outlaw. (The use of folksongs became a Taylor signature in his operas.) Following the highwayman's death at the hands of pursuing soldiers, Taylor's chorus sings of the time "When the moon is a ghostly galleon tossed upon cloudy sea." Counterpointing the chorus, the ghostly voice of the highwayman makes an eternal promise to his "bonny sweetheart": "I'll come to thee by moonlight, though hell should bar the way."[37] Taylor dedicated the cantata to Oscar Coon.

Major critics were present at the festival and wrote of their pleasure at hearing the new work. They agreed that Taylor could seize a dramatic moment and build on it musically. "With this cantata," wrote A. Walter Kramer of *Musical America,* "Mr. Taylor has produced a work which cannot fail to take a place of distinction in modern literature." Leonard Liebling of the *Musical Courier* lauded the melodic base: "The dramatic moments have point and yet are not brusque, and the lyrical episodes please with the smoothness and grace of the writing."[38] Taylor had produced his first major work, to critical acclaim.

But he knew that fame for choral works came at Carnegie Hall, not in the Bronx or New Hampshire. Two years later he devised a plan by which Kurt Schindler, the director of the Schola Cantorum, New York City's most venerable choral group, would actually ask him for a cantata. He possessed the three talents he knew would get him an audition with Schindler: a fine voice, note-reading ability, and a great German accent, which he had developed from listening attentively to the parents of a college friend who had tutored him in German while at NYU. Taylor got the audition, and among the music that Schindler gave him to sing was the first tenor part of a Bach cantata with lyrics in German. "You have a nice German accent," the conductor told Taylor. "You read music well," he added. "Maybe you have composed a little, yes? Something for chorus maybe?" Taylor heartily confirmed this. "Maybe I could see it, yes?" asked Schindler. The ruse had worked![39]

The Schola Cantorum sang *The Chambered Nautilus* in Carnegie Hall as part of a program that included other new choral works. Taylor's cantata, some ten minutes in length, begins with an instrumental introduction establishing the mood of a calm ocean. Choral voices enter in staggered sequence, giving the effect of the movement of water and the ever-developing layers of the chambered nautilus. Short though it was, the cantata received high praise from the *Times* reviewer: "[Taylor] attacks a difficult problem without hesitation, with the use of the most elaborate means . . . and uses a very full orchestral apparatus not unskillfully. His work is, on the whole, impressive. He has erected an imposing climax upon the last stanza, 'Build thee more stately mansions, O my soul,' for which he has wisely sought greater simplicity and breadth."[40]

The next day the composer received a laudatory note from Schindler: "I was so glad your composition met with such approval and success with last night's audience. I congratulate you once more heartily on this auspicious beginning in Carnegie Hall. I also want to express to you my thanks for the great help you have given me throughout the winter in connection with the work of the chorus, which is proud to have had you as a member."[41] Schindler, a collector of European folksongs for adaptation and publication in the United States, subsequently enlisted Taylor and his wife to help him provide singable English lyrics for these tunes.

After the publication of both *The Chambered Nautilus* and *The Highwayman* by the Boston publisher Oliver Ditson, Taylor's name began to spread in modest fashion as a composer of merit, with *The Highwayman* bringing him his first wide acceptance. Twenty-five years later it would still be referred to by John Tasker Howard as "among the most popular works in this form in our current music literature."[42]

"The Coveted Time-piece"

All the while Taylor continued to send FPA materials for his column; he met socially with the columnist as well. FPA revealed some of their interactions to his readers in the segment of the column where he described his weekly activities (at least those that were publishable). He wrote in the style of Samuel Pepys (1633–1703), whose diary chronicled years of Restoration England. Snippets from the FPA "Diary" indicate how much Adams enjoyed Taylor's company ("To the tennis matches again with Deems Taylor the composer"),[43] while also admiring his musical abilities ("I saw Deems Taylor who hath won a great prize of £60 for the writing of a symphonick poem *[Siren Song]* which I am glad of").[44]

FPA also appreciated Taylor's literary abilities. The proof came in 1916, when FPA awarded "Smeed" a watch as the author of the best annual contribution to his column. For many years the giving of the FPA watch—identified as "the coveted time-piece" in the language of "The Conning Tower"—became an anticipated annual event for the column's contributors, their equivalent to the Nobel Prize for literature. This was not a committee decision: Adams was the sole judge of who would receive the timepiece. In the first years, no formal event was held for the presentation of the award; Adams simply gave it to the winner.

However, by 1916 the contributors, now calling themselves "contribs," were so well known to each other that Newman Levy, co-winner of the first "coveted time-piece," headed a group to form a contribs club dubbed the Contribunion. The now united contribs tried to convince FPA to hold a formal dinner for the presentation, and, though FPA liked the idea, he declined to be present. "I find," he told Levy, "that often when my 'contribs' get to know me they stop sending in stuff."[45] He did promise to send a representative to present the watch, should the contribs pursue the idea of a dinner, which they did.

On January 6, 1916, some fifty of them gathered in a private room at Scheffel's Hall, an old saloon at Third Avenue and Seventeenth Street, for the big event. There would be no surprise as to the recipient of the annual award, since FPA himself had, not so subtly, announced the winner in his column on New Year's Day: "To a jeweller's, and bought a fine watch for D. Taylor, but I begrudged the money not at all." Though most previous awards had been for humorous pieces, this year the subject was death itself: Taylor's description of the aftermath of a tragedy that had occurred in Chicago on July 24, 1915, a day of horror for the Western Electric Company.

On that morning, five chartered steamships stood waiting at the docks in the Chicago River to receive employees of Western Electric for the annual company cruise on Lake Michigan. Without sufficient supervision, one of the ships, the *Eastland,* took on passengers severely beyond its capacity. When a minor stampede to one side of the ship occurred, the ship capsized into the river and eight hundred people drowned.

As soon as the New York office heard of the tragedy, they immediately sent Taylor to prepare the story for *Western Electric News.* After completing the dreadful assignment, he sent FPA a series of vignettes describing Chicago a week after the disaster. He won the watch for one of these: "The Eastland is still lying in the Chicago River, with a hundred people under her. After you've seen her once, you can't forget her. . . . And you stare down at the Eastland, with her long, graceful curves and beautiful knife-like bow, lying on her side in that shallow, filthy river, with black scars on her side where the acetylene torches burnt her. . . . Probably ship owners, and captains and inspectors aren't really devils. Probably they're just Americans. Americans, who never prevent anything until it has happened, once."[46]

True to his word, FPA did not attend the Contribunion dinner, but in his place sent Robert Benchley, a young man newly arrived from Boston to write for the *Tribune.* When Benchley, a complete cipher to his audience, rose to make the presentation, he was observed to be, as Newman Levy later described him,

> [a] solemn, round-faced young man who adjusted a large, bone-rimmed pair of spectacles in an embarrassed fashion, and then beamed out at the audience with the most engaging fatuous grin I had ever seen. "Ladies and gentlemen," he said, "we are gathered here tonight for the purpose of presenting a watch." Mr. Benchley's face and voice suddenly became serious. "It seems appropriate,

The *Eastland* overturned in the Chicago River. Taylor received his first "coveted time-piece" award from Franklin P. Adams for his reflections on this 1915 disaster that killed eight hundred people. *(Courtesy of Yale University Music Library)*

therefore, to give you a brief history of the development of the watch industry in the United States." He reached into his pocket and drew out an enormous sheaf of typescript. A heavy pall descended upon the audience.[47]

As Benchley droned on with detailed statistics of the year-by-year importation of Swiss watches, the contribs sensed the joke and initiated the laughter that was continued by millions across the United States, watching Benchley's "short subject" movies or reading his books of humorous essays. The off-the-cuff monologue on watches evolved into "The Treasurer's Report," Benchley's signature act in Broadway revues and on film.

Five years later Taylor won a second watch, and in so doing became the sole winner of two during the twenty years of the award.[48] His second winning contribution could not have been more different from his piece on the *Eastland* tragedy. This time Taylor thought back on his NYU years and created a lengthy poem. Adams loved Latin, so Taylor chose as his title "Haec Olim Meminisse Iuvabit," a phrase from Virgil's *Aeneid:* "Perhaps one day it will be useful to remember even these things." The poem, in which he reflected on each of his NYU years, took up almost the complete "Conning Tower" column for the day. Seven years later, "overwhelmed by insistent demands," FPA reprinted the entire poem and labeled it "the best history of the higher education in America ever written."[49] (The complete poem is included in Appendix 3.)

Early in 1916, with his musical and writing talents now apparent, and wearing the first of his coveted timepieces, Taylor felt optimistic about himself and the development of his talents. He continued at the *Western Electric News*, while Jane worked with the eminent naturalist William Beebe of the Bronx Zoo, helping him write articles.[50] She and her husband did find one opportunity to combine their literary talents, when Kurt Schindler asked them to provide singable English lyrics to some Finnish and Russian songs he had collected for publication.

Were Taylor and Anderson happy? There is no clear evidence, but he may have indirectly indicated how he felt in the poems chosen for the song cycle *The City of Joy,* composed at that time and dedicated to Reinald Werrenrath. The five songs, based on poems about New York by Charles Hanson Towne, spoke of two lovers, "poor as little church-mice," enjoying the world of Gotham: the joys of spring, of riding on an omnibus, of gazing at the moon together from a roof garden. Romantic as their life appears to have been, the rumbles of war filtering across the Atlantic slowly grew into life-changing episodes for them both.

3. The War Years, 1916–1919

A Modern Marriage

Jane Anderson, in the final analysis, was a free spirit who desired fame and adventure. When the Great War broke out in Europe, she saw an opportunity for the attention and success that so far had evaded her: she would become that rare creature, a female war correspondent. Her goal was to get to England, and for this she needed money. She couldn't rely on her husband; he was too poor. Instead she refined her capacity to insinuate herself into the lives of other men. Why she chose John H. Hobbs, part owner of a small movie theater on Forty-second Street, for this purpose is not known, but she introduced herself to him after sitting through an Amazon travelogue at his theater and asked for an appointment to meet with him.

When they did meet, Jane warned Hobbs that the film was a fake. Though she didn't indicate where this information came from, Hobbs probably assumed it was from her connections to the naturalist William Beebe. Hobbs, grateful for being alerted, agreed to help Jane get her travel money and, together with friends, raised a sum of about one hundred dollars. Jane said good-bye to her husband, still the assistant editor of *Western Electric News,* and sailed for London on September 24, 1915. Her plan was to present a letter of introduction to one of the most powerful men in England, Lord Northcliffe, the owner of the *London Daily Mail* and *London Times.* Theodore Roosevelt, for whom she had done some manuscripts, reportedly had provided her the letter.[1]

Once in England, the beautiful American journalist had few problems making the necessary military connections to provide her with exciting experiences to write about, including doing loops over London in a warplane and being escorted down into a submarine to observe its workings. Lord Northcliffe agreed to publish her articles on war-related experiences. An accomplished opportunist, Jane parlayed the Northcliffe connection into an introduction to the family of the famed Polish-born novelist Joseph Conrad, an episode she described in great detail to her husband in a letter. The April 1916 missive made it quite clear that she had made a very favorable impression on both Conrad and his wife, Jessie.[2]

Her exhausting wartime adventures finally caught up with her physically. In the summer of 1916 she suffered a nervous breakdown, and for many weeks received the hospitality of the Conrads for her convalescence; Mrs. Conrad herself helped nurse Jane back to health.[3] During this time Joseph Conrad took more than a passing interest in Jane. His feelings toward the recuperating beauty, expressed in a letter to his intimate friend Richard Curle, suggest more than benevolent paternalism: "She is seeking to get herself adopted as our big daughter and is succeeding fairly. To put it shortly she's quite yum-yum."[4] A similar indication of Conrad's interest in the redheaded American is found in the 1916 journal of Taylor's father, who writes of receiving a letter from his son with the news that an article by Jane Anderson "will appear in the *Tribune* of August 20. It was revised by Joseph Conrad, who has adopted Jane as a literary protégé—the only one he ever had. He changed only three sentences."[5] Conrad's biographers are unsure whether Jane's relationship with him was sexual, but undoubtedly he found her most attractive, for after she returned to good health and to London, Conrad visited her.[6] In late September, a year after arriving in England, Jane learned that she would be receiving another visitor: her husband.

The *New York Tribune Magazine*

Taylor realized he was going nowhere with the *Western Electric News*. As luck would have it, a call from his career mentor, FPA, offered him a position with the *Tribune*'s new Sunday magazine section. By 1915 the *Tribune* had risen to the top rung of New York newspapers, with highly readable prose from writers of high standards: Grantland Rice, sportswriter; Henry Krehbiel, music critic; George Kaufman and Heywood Broun, drama critics and social commentators; and, of course, FPA and his "Conning Tower." Ogden Reid, the paper's owner, was satisfied with the weekday editions but believed Sunday needed a top-quality magazine. He appointed FPA to develop it, strongly urging him to maintain the progressive attitudes of the daily editions.

To achieve Reid's objective, FPA knew he had to hire additional writers to address current social issues and bring some humor to the magazine. The first one hired was Robert Benchley, whom he would later ask to represent him at the Contribunion dinner. Earlier that year Earl Derr Biggers had introduced him to Benchley, who was a Harvard graduate of the class of 1912 and had been editor of the *Lampoon,* the university's humor magazine. FPA was impressed and contacted him with an offer of forty dollars a week to help develop the *New York Tribune Magazine.* Benchley responded with interest but vacillated on a decision, because his wife, Gertrude, was expecting their first child that November.

Adams grew impatient and told Benchley he was coming to Boston to talk to him face to face.[7] A few days before the meeting, the Benchleys welcomed their son Nathaniel. With a new mouth to feed, Benchley agreed to FPA's offer. By January 1916, he had moved his family to New York and begun work on the *Tribune.* Because the Sunday supplement would not begin publication until April, Benchley was first put to work as a reporter.[8]

With Benchley on board, FPA needed another writer to complement him, someone who knew the New York scene and could match Benchley in wit and imagination. In FPA's mind, Taylor, a native New Yorker with a real talent for writing, fit this bill perfectly. He invited him to the *Tribune* office for a chat and offered him the job.[9] Taylor had had enough of the world of telephones, so he resigned from the *Western Electric News* to join Benchley as one of the chief architects of the magazine.

Benchley and Taylor had already met several times: first at the Contribunion dinner, then a month later at the Dutch Treat Club. The Dutch Treaters, as they called themselves, had been founded eleven years earlier in 1905 by a rambunctious group of male editors, writers, and artists. The members gathered weekly for lunch, with a minimum of structure and a maximum of folderol.[10]

Every year, members of the club devised a show of original verve and ribaldry so notable that reporters were sent to cover it. The *Tribune* assigned Benchley to review the Dutch Treat show of 1916, and there he again ran into Taylor, who had joined the club the year before and immediately been convinced to compose the music for the 1916 show. Joining him in the endeavor was James Montgomery Flagg, who provided the lyrics and the program's cover. Flagg's talent as an illustrator and portrait artist was better known than his literary abilities, and five months later he created one of the most famous posters in American history—a somber Uncle Sam point-ing his finger at the viewer with the words "I WANT YOU for [the] U.S. Army."[11]

On February 28 at Delmonico's restaurant, *The Breath of Scandal* had its sole performance. The show spoofed the daily newspapers that claimed to be lofty purveyors of information about politics, high society, sports, and the arts, but actually thrived on gorgeous "Scandal." On the show's program cover, Flagg depicted Scandal as a voluptuous female nude with a come-hither look, sitting cross-legged on a sofa chair with cigarette held high. Tay-lor's music to the thirteen songs sounded like warmed-over Gilbert and Sullivan, but who needed anything more? Benchley's *Tribune* review of the performance incorporated "such lyrics as were printable."[12]

By the time Taylor began work at the *Tribune* on May 1, 1916, Benchley had been on the staff for five months. After their first week as coworkers, Benchley noted in his diary that he found Taylor "a highly congenial desk-mate."[13] Their friendship deepened as the magazine evolved, with both pro-viding articles—some humorous, some serious, but all on social and political issues. "Brothers All" (June 11, 1916), an early Taylor story, reflected on man's inhumanity to man by his description of a scene from his Western Electric days on Nassau Street, where he had seen a little mouse scurry for its life among the sidewalk habitués. When a shopkeeper stepped on its tail, "a stout, cheery looking individual" sent the mouse into the street with a quick drop kick. From under the wheels of a passing pushcart "came a thin, high squeal." The cheery man stopped to buy an afternoon paper.

> "Hello, Joe," he called affably to the news dealer, "what's new?"
> He hastily glanced over the headlines.
> "Well, I'll be ————! Another neutral steamer sunk by the Ger-mans. Fifty drowned."
> He clenched his fist and scowled. "The damned brutes!"

Taylor's writings on serious topics indicated a deeply sensitive streak, as if the Mennonite beliefs of his father—"No freedom in giving, or doing, or assisting, by which men's lives are destroyed or hurt"[14]—had also permeated his life. In another feature (August 13, 1916), Taylor described a brusque naturalization ceremony in a "large, ugly room with a high ceiling," welcom-ing "hyphenated Americans" into citizenship: "As I came in they were admin-istering the oath of allegiance to one Samuel Kessler, a young Russian Jew. 'Hold up your right hand,' said the man in horn-rimmed glasses. 'Do you hereby declare on oath that you absolutely and entirely renounce and abjure allegiance, mumble, mumble, for'n power or principality, mumble mumble,

mumble—Patrick Gallagher!' Samuel Kessler looked a bit bewildered. He probably wondered what Patrick Gallagher had to do with his becoming a citizen of the United States." Patrick Gallagher, of course, was not part of the oath of allegiance. He was simply the next candidate.

Taylor then asked the reader: "For what is naturalization but a voluntary rebirth, the renunciation of an old life and the choosing of a new? In that moment a man says: 'Though I was born in another country I am not of that country. The things for which it stands are not the things that I desire most. And so I choose this as my native land; here is freedom; here are my ideals!' It is as though a man should choose for himself a new mother."

In other articles, Taylor's capacity as an insightful and humorous social critic emerged. For example, "Do You Wear a Tennis Racket with Your Collar?" (May 14, 1916) provided timeless commentary on how consumers are depicted in print advertisements: "Any little thing pleases them. They go into spasms of joy over their morning cereal. . . . [T]he arrival of a fresh cake of laundry soap brightens their whole day. They smile as they munch their favorite chewing gum . . . except of course when they have been stung by accepting some Cheap and Inferior Substitute. Then the sky darkens. But they soon rally and Demand the Genuine; and lo! Once more the sun comes forth and the little birds burst into song." In his summer essay "Camerabies" (July 23, 1916), Taylor questioned "what the summer vacationist of fifty years ago did with himself. How did one make the time pass in those dark, dark ages when the kodak was unheard of and the amateur photographer as yet unborn?"

Jane Anderson, learning of his new appointment, sent her husband some of her articles from British newspapers, and FPA agreed to publish several on the magazine's front page. The first story, "Looping the Loop over London" (May 28, 1916), carried the byline "Jane Anderson (Mrs. Deems Taylor)." Three months later, in "Over the North Sea in a Messroom Chair" (August 27, 1916), she boasted: "I am the first woman who has been permitted to see the hangars which house his majesty's great fleet of the air; I am the first woman to make a flight in one of Britain's seaplanes, designed for war, created by war." Now her byline was simply Jane Anderson.

Taylor had been disturbed by his wife's April letter, which told him how warmly the Conrads had received her. He knew how she thrived on being among the rich and famous, and wondered whether she might be drifting away from him. He decided he had to go to Europe, and he would use her approach by taking a leave of absence for six months and going to France as a war correspondent for the *Tribune*. FPA granted his request, but there would be no salary and no expense account; the only pay would be for the articles

Taylor sent that the *Tribune* published. Taylor believed that would be enough to keep him going, since he had saved a little money while living with his parents. The plan was now complete: he'd report on the war, and then meet Jane to discuss their future.

However, it wasn't only his concern for his marriage that prompted his decision to go to the site of the European war; another deeply personal issue would be resolved by the trip. Though he considered himself a pacifist, a position consistent with the Mennonite dictums of his father, he wondered whether he might actually be a coward.[15] There seemed to be no better way to find the answer to his question than to go the front.

He still had several months to prepare, however. During August he returned home after work to an empty house; his parents were on vacation in Nova Scotia and his sister, Katy, no longer lived there. In April she had married David Rowland "Rowlie" Davis, an NYU graduate. Rowlie would join the army for a year, and after that take his wife to Buffalo, where he would begin work for the new public relations firm of Barton, Durstine, and Osborn, while she awaited the birth of their baby.

Having neither wife nor family around him, Taylor concentrated on his needs for the European trip. To make his life as a traveling journalist easier, Taylor craved one of the recently developed portable typewriters. He didn't have enough money, so by letter he turned his wiles upon his vacationing parents. He detailed his coming trip and then got to the real point of the letter: "I was also going to get a Corona folding typewriter but . . . it costs $50 and I haven't got no $50 to spend. . . . I was thinking that if any of my friends should ask me what I wanted them to give me for a present when I go away I would say give me a Corona folding typewriter the price is only $50." After one final pitch for the typewriter, Taylor ended with "your loving son. Deems." Then came the postscript: "Please excuse this bum typewriting. I know it isn't good but this typewriter is so old. Not that it isn't a good typewriter, but it's so heavy I couldn't take it along, although goodness knows I will need one."[16] His father read the "very clever" missive and its "long rigmarole about a folding typewriter—the Corona—that weighs only six pounds and costs fifty dollars." He concluded that "the letter is worth fifty dollars as literature, so I'll send him the fifty."[17] Deems's father at least appreciated his literary style.

Taylor bought his typewriter, packed, said good-bye to Benchley and FPA, and sailed on September 30, 1916. The following day, FPA informed "The Conning Tower" readers that "J. Deems Taylor of here left for Europe yesterday to be gone until December." He also printed a poem entitled "Lines on Entering the War Zone":

As I board the boat for Europe, for to visit my Jeannette,
Who has been away a twelvemonth, more or less,
I am wondering whether she's the kind that ever can forget
That I used to run a column in The Press.
Smeed

Taylor's short-lived column in the *Evening Press* had created a running gag in "The Conning Tower." Yet between the lines, Taylor was really asking whether Jane remembered him.

Taylor Goes to War (Sort Of)

During his first weeks in Paris, Deems Taylor breathed the air and essence of the city he would grow to love as much as he did New York. His first letter to Benchley addressed the question of whether he was a pacifist or a coward: "You'll be interested to know that after one month of a twelfth-hand view of this here war I'm a rabid pacifist. The funny part is that everybody else is, too. And the closer view folks have had of it, the more rabid they've become."[18]

The manager of the *Tribune*'s Paris bureau appreciated Taylor's appointment, overjoyed to have someone to send to the front. On December 8, 1916, in the predawn darkness and before getting into the foreign correspondent's car, Taylor sent Benchley a postcard with the simple message: "6:45 A.M. We're starting for the trenches, and gosh——"[19]

He never actually got to the front, but close enough for six unforgettable hours, an experience that he captured in the *Tribune Magazine*'s cover story a month later, "Informative Moment Near No-Man's Land" (January 7, 1917): "[These are] not the views of a soldier . . . merely an uninformed American . . . up against war for the first time." Taylor then described images of war, such as "Lunar landscapes" spotted with "the relics of human beings—or what had been human beings." He told of an episode deeply burned into his memory. A command car just ahead of his car of foreign correspondents took a hit by a German shell and careened off the road: "All at once I began to be frightened."

Returning to Paris, he wandered the streets with camera and notebook in hand, witnessing the scars of war:

> After [the wounded soldier] gets out of the hospital, he comes to
> Paris on leave. And so you see him—no index finger on the right
> hand, no second finger, no thumb. Sometimes the whole hand is
> gone. So often on the streets here you see men who have no noses at

all. You don't mind quite so much after a while. But you never really get used to seeing them; for a man without a nose looks exactly like a death's head. It's rather horrible. You find yourself wondering what his wife thinks, or the girl he used to know. The English call it "shrapnel face." What makes it worse is the fact that most of them are blind.[20]

Taylor was apparently in touch with his wife in England, and arranged for them to meet in Paris in December. What they discussed is unknown, as is the length of their stay together. The only evidence of their meeting is a note that Taylor made in his journal for the week of December 8—"Jane's dress $13.10"[21]—and a note in "The Conning Tower" of December 31: "Deems Taylor and wife are in Paris, Fr., at this writing." It is highly unlikely that Taylor knew of the other reasons for his wife's presence in Paris, specifically her liaison with Joseph Conrad's close friend, the mysterious Polish statesman Jozef Retinger. At that time Retinger had begun what one biographer called "a lengthy affair with the singularly bizarre American adventuress."[22]

While involved with lengthy affairs, Jane also pursued shorter ones, including one with Conrad's son Borys, who was with the British forces on the Continent at the time. When Borys found out that Jane and Retinger were in Paris, having heard so much of the "glamorous lady" from his father, he sought a few days' leave to meet her. It took only one evening at the Crillon Hotel for him to fall for her charms. Borys even overstayed his leave to remain an extra day with Jane. Thanks to friends in the right places, Jane freed young Conrad from possible arrest for being AWOL. After five days with her, Borys admitted that "the only piece of concrete information she had disclosed about herself was that she had once been married to a man called Taylor in the U.S."[23] Of course she was still married, but that did not seem to be a major concern to her. The volatile nature of her affairs would be smartly described by Gilbert Seldes, another of her lovers: "I met Retinger right after the end of World War I, through Jane Anderson (later the divorced wife of Deems Taylor), who was then engaged to be married to at least one of us."[24]

In February Taylor returned to the United States short of money, leaving France with the good wishes of the journalist Paul Scott Mowrer, a war correspondent for the *Chicago Daily News* and a poet as well. The two had rapidly developed a friendship. Taylor had revealed to Mowrer his hope to compose an orchestral suite based on impressions from the war. A few days before Taylor sailed for the United States, Mowrer, knowing that German submarines remained active in the Atlantic, wrote from Rome to wish him a safe trip and urged him to work on his music: "Get busy now . . . and do us that war suite which is germinating. Tomorrow we are going to the sacred lake of Nemi, in the Alban hills. I don't know if it will do any good, but I will offer a prayer for you to Diana, whose shrine this has been for nearly 3000 years. She is said to be a whiz at enabling barren women to conceive; she may surely be able to help a fertile composer to deliver his music."[25] If the goddess Diana did help, she got something confused, because the suite that eventually materialized from Taylor's imagination was about the adventures of Lewis Carroll's Alice.

Taylor's return to New York could not have been pleasant, for not only did his wife remain in Europe, but also the *Tribune Magazine* was on its last legs and FPA could not reemploy him. With no work, he once again had to seek shelter at the home of his parents. Fortunately, he recalled that William LeBaron had ascended the literary ranks to become advertising manager at *Collier's* magazine, a weekly with national circulation. When he contacted LeBaron, his friend offered him the position of supervisor of the editorial page. Taylor accepted gratefully, but rapidly found the work uninspiring. One day during lunch with Lucien Cary, who had been put in charge of the picture page, he learned that Cary was similarly unhappy. Switching jobs was the solution, since Cary knew most about editorials and Taylor knew all about pictures. Cary suggested, "Let's put it up to the boss," the American humorist Peter Finley Dunne. He quickly approved the sensible change, and Taylor became one of the few editors in New York who had been to the war front. He could recognize and identify much of the paraphernalia in battlefield photographs that were a major component of the magazine's illustrations.[26]

The *Collier's* position gave him a stable income, so he happily moved into an apartment at 125 East Thirty-fourth Street. In the evening he worked to transform Kurt Schindler's rough translations of sixty Russian folksongs into melodic English, thereby assisting Schindler in publishing the first "complete English edition of the standard Russian folk-songs."[27] At the same time, Percy Rector Stephens, another major choral conductor in New York, approached Taylor for new arrangements of European folksongs and art songs for his Schumann Club, a women's chorus. (The name refers to Clara Schumann, not her husband, Robert.) When Taylor accepted Stephens's offer, he didn't suspect it would become a four-year project.

Since he was unsure about his marital future, Taylor decided not to wait for his wife's return to have female companionship. He found a special friend in eighteen-year-old Phyllis Duganne, who had also come to New York for a writing career. Whether he told his teenage sweetheart he was married is not known, but Phyllis let her friends believe that she and Taylor were engaged. When he learned that his wife was returning from Europe, he had to tell a tearful Phyllis the relationship was over. Unfortunately, Jane Anderson arrived earlier than expected and went to his apartment to surprise him. There the superintendent informed her, "Mr. Taylor was out—and Mrs. Taylor wasn't there either."[28] Knowing that she was definitely not the Mrs. Taylor of the superintendent's statement, Jane left and began suit for divorce based on adultery, then the only allowable basis in New York State. Anderson's romances, however, were not an issue.

Perhaps Taylor and Anderson understood each other far better than they realized, for the divorce did not end their friendship. After filing the papers, Anderson left New York in an unsettled state of mind and spent time with her friend Kitty Crawford in the Denver area before returning to Manhattan, where she and Taylor connected off and on for the next few years.[29] One researcher determined that in the early 1920s, she "took an apartment in New York City and that she continued to toy with the emotions of her many suitors."[30] In 1922 Jane left for Europe, where she would ultimately become a political tool of the Fascists. Her notoriety would haunt Taylor in later years.

His actions in seeing Anderson extensively after their agreement to divorce is the first indication of a side of Taylor's persona that would trouble him throughout his life: a relationship would end, but he could not simply walk away; he remained loyal. Yet, for psychological reasons that are unclear, throughout his life he would not develop a mature, ongoing relationship with a woman. Perhaps his father had overly shaped his life. Years later, Taylor gave a clue to his feelings about his father's influence on him in a preface he wrote to the book *Plays and Poems of W. S. Gilbert*. Taylor extolled Gilbert's wit and wondered how such talent could come from a man whose father was "utterly humorless" and "serious." He drew the following conclusion: "The almost inevitable reaction against the father's solemnity and morbidity would be the son's pursuit of humor and make-believe."[31]

Indeed, both of these were already central to Taylor's professional life, in both his music and his literary attempts. But humor and make-believe are not the basis for long-term relationships. Nor is the superficial attribute of appearance. For any of his lengthy relationships, in marriage or otherwise, Taylor sought women who were beautiful, intelligent, and youthful. With his glamorous mates he showed his friends that he, a rather ordinary looking man, could attract a woman of outstanding allure. Further, it would be rare that, as with Jane Anderson, he did not stray into a brief affair. As Taylor's relationships ended, perhaps he felt a sense of guilt. After all, he knew he had found physical and intellectual enjoyment in the company of the woman, so why was he letting her go so easily? It seems reasonable to suggest that Taylor's guilt may have transformed itself into extended loyalty. Yet at the same time he may have been incapable, ultimately, of feeling deeply enough about a female to make her his life's companion—like Barrie's *Sentimental Tommy,* whose emotions were skin-deep.

Composing *Through the Looking Glass*

After returning from France and his war experience, the idea of composing a "war suite" remained in Taylor's mind for months. After the Armistice, he received a letter from the Oliver Ditson Company, publisher of both his cantatas, requesting not a war cantata but a peace cantata. He turned them down. "I can't write a Peace cantata; there's no reason why I shouldn't, except that I just can't. . . . It's only about now, for instance that I'm beginning to get a sufficiently perspectived realization of what I saw and felt in France two years ago to be able to make timid motions toward a 'Verdun—Christmas, 1916' that I planned a long time back. Nobody wants that, now, of course, and I don't think I'll ever write it . . . but I haven't got around to peace yet, inside, and so I can't write about it. I wish I could, for I like royalties."[32]

War memories did not inspire musical ideas for Taylor; his world of inspiration lay in fantasy. As did most composers, he carried a notebook to jot down themes as they occurred. This shows that as early as 1914, he considered motifs for specific characters of Lewis Carroll's books. What finally supplanted the war memories were those of the Alice of his youth, as he explained years later:

> I always did like fairy tales, and have liked both the Alice books since I first read them at the age of ten. I and my friends used to have a game in which we would say some of the things that Alice said, or that the creatures she met said to her. For instance, when one of us came into a room, the others would shout, "No room, no room!" or, as in the garden of live flowers, one of us would explain why he was quiet by saying, "We can talk if there's anybody worth talking to." By playing this game, I got to know the books even better, so it was quite natural that when I started to write my first serious symphonic piece of music, it should turn out to be the "Looking Glass Suite."[33]

Taylor worked hard on his composing during the fall of 1918, for it relieved him from the tedium of work at *Collier's* and justified his belief that musical composition truly was his forte. He chose four segments of Carroll's book and transformed them into musical pictures: "Dedication" (Carroll's foreword), "Jabberwocky," "Looking-Glass Insects," and "The White Knight." Still unsure of his self-taught orchestrating abilities, he scored the work for a chamber orchestra of eleven players and then approached Carolyn Beebe and her New York Chamber Music Society to perform it. Beebe's orchestra was highly regarded in music circles for its premieres, and its concerts attracted some of the city's top critics. Beebe found the suite charming and agreed to premiere it at Aeolian Hall, a 1,300-seat venue located on Forty-third Street between Fifth and Sixth Avenues. Aeolian Hall was second only to Carnegie Hall as a concert site in New York City.

On the evening of February 18, 1919, an apprehensive Deems Taylor entered to hear his suite performed. He was certainly in good company, for the program also included a Mozart quintet and a Schubert octet. Before the concert began, Taylor saw the music critic H. E. Krehbiel walk in and seat himself in his typical slumping fashion, a "huge patriarchal figure of a man, with a beautiful head that would have enchanted a sculptor, and a mop of excited, yellowish hair that no comb could ever hope to master."[34] Of the many talented critics on the scene at the time, no one gave a greater sense of infallible judgment than Krehbiel, who had worked for the *Tribune* for nearly three decades. Taylor had met him while there and had come to admire his encyclopedic knowledge of music.

He also knew that a bad review from Krehbiel could hurt his future, but he needn't have worried; Krehbiel's comments the next day were laudatory, comparing the humor and freshness of the suite to the joyous finale of Verdi's *Falstaff*.[35] Krehbiel craftily noted that "Dedication," the first of the four movements, had the requisite seriousness most composers believed was necessary as an introduction to a series of musical impressions. He extolled Taylor's choice of the bassoon, "the conventional clown of the orchestra," as the voice of the Jabberwock, the mysterious creature ultimately slain by the hero. Krehbiel wrote that the bassoon, "in a long unaccompanied monologue," describes the Jabberwock's death throes and then initiates "a fugued section which has a capital subject that is capitally worked out."

In an unsigned review, another critic compounded Taylor's happiness by writing of the "Looking-Glass Insects" movement: "Mr. Taylor knows the instruments; the flute twittered and scintillated. There were the gnats flittering around you and some people unconsciously waved their hands in the direction of their ears." As the suite's finest passage this critic referred to the final part, "The White Knight," with its musical depiction of an unfortunate Don Quixote–type character, prone to many accidental dismounts from his steed. In the orchestra, downward glissandos culminated in musical thuds of wonderful originality. Summing up, the critic wrote: "There was real depth in this and one wondered whether Mr. Taylor would not sometime

write the score of a real grand opera."[36] The reviewer's suggestion was belated; the idea of composing an opera had already entered Taylor's head.

Musical Success in Denver

The positive views of *Through the Looking Glass* buoyed Taylor's spirits enormously. His two cantatas and now the suite reinforced his belief that he'd
been born to compose, but how could he break away from *Collier's* and turn
completely to music? He found the answer through Percy Rector Stephens.
The reason Stephens had originally contacted him in 1917 to do new arrangements for his Schumann Club was simple: he had heard Taylor's cantatas in live performance and recognized an unusual talent. By having him prepare new arrangements, Stephens expanded the repertoire of his choral
group, as well as those of the hundreds of women's groups then existing nationally, many in the "normal schools" that trained teachers.

Taylor's four-year project produced an impressive eighty songs, from
Bach to contemporary composers, with a special emphasis on folksongs: Ar-
menian, Belgian, Breton, Czechoslovak, English, and Scottish. He also provided some arrangements for mixed chorus, several of which, particularly
the Czech "Waters Ripple and Flow" and the English "Mayday Carol," became
standards in the choral repertoire. Not surprisingly, Taylor became enamored of European folksongs, an affection that would later lead him to introduce them into his operas. As a bonus for Taylor's excellent work, Stephens
taught him the essentials of voice production, invaluable knowledge for a future composer of opera.

Stephens had a national reputation for developing fine singers, including
Reinald Werrenrath. Part of this reputation came from summer master
classes that he offered in major cities. Denver was to be the site for his 1919
class, and once Stephens found out how bored Taylor had become with
his work at *Collier's,* he offered to take him to Denver on a two-month working vacation. Knowing that Taylor had to make some money while there,
Stephens arranged for him to present a fee-based series of lectures on music
history to interested Denver music lovers. That clinched the deal. Taylor resigned from the magazine, packed his bags, and left to learn whether life did
indeed exist west of New York City.

On June 22, the *Rocky Mountain News* announced "Percy Rector Stephens, eminent voice teacher, and Deems Taylor, prominent American composer and writer, both of New York City, will arrive in Denver this week for
a two month's sojourn. . . . Men and women will forgather here from numerous states in order to have the advantage of their professional guid-
ance. . . . Mr. Taylor comes here primarily for vacational rest and to com-

plete an orchestral score upon which he is engaged . . . and to deliver a series of seven Thursday evening lectures on 'Music History and Appreciation.'"[37]

Denver was a city of 250,000 in 1919, the heyday of agricultural and oil well development. "The Queen City of the Plains," with its cool summer air from the Rocky Mountains, also attracted many with its reputation of helping people recover from pulmonary ailments. While the mountains bestowed tranquillity, in downtown Denver entertainment was plentiful. The Rivoli Theater provided first-run silent movies and a symphony orchestra to accompany them. The Broadway Theater offered touring drama or musical companies, and the Empress, Denver's vaudeville theater, presented the Shimmie Dancers ("It's alluring, fascinating, tantalizing—but not naughty").[38] On July 1, only three days after Taylor arrived in Denver, the country went "dry," a state of affairs he did not particularly welcome. But he may have appreciated the humor of the *Denver Post*'s Prohibition announcement that "a funeral is now the only place where they pass the bier."[39]

Two newspapers, the *Post* and the *Rocky Mountain News,* served the area. The *News* catered to a more sophisticated readership and provided special coverage of cultural events. A year earlier it had hired Katherine Anne Porter, a young reporter from Texas, to help with this coverage. Porter, who later became one of the country's most admired writers of fiction, read of Taylor's arrival with more than passing interest; she knew him through Jane Anderson, whose acquaintance Porter had made owing to an unusual chain of events.

Three years earlier in Texas, Porter had contracted tuberculosis, then a contagious and feared disease. While being treated in a sanitarium, she met another patient, Kitty Crawford Jenkins, Jane's close college friend, now a journalist and married. A strong friendship developed between Kitty and Porter, so when Kitty received Jane's letters from Europe, she shared them with her new friend, who came to know a great deal about Anderson and her marriage to Taylor. Porter's illness was less severe than Kitty's, which allowed her to leave the sanitarium and return to reportorial work in Texas in 1917. Kitty's recovery lagged; in spring 1918 her husband and family determined that the climate in Colorado would be better for her, so she moved to Denver and rented temporary quarters in a boardinghouse.

Meanwhile, Anderson had returned from Europe and initiated divorce proceedings. Learning that Kitty was in Denver, Jane decided to visit her friend. Once there, she chose to spend the summer in Colorado to complete a variety of writing assignments. Finding a secluded mountain cabin near Colorado Springs, Jane convinced Kitty to move in with her and share the cost. No sooner had the two women settled there than Jane sent for Gilbert Seldes, her most recent amour. Jane was still high-strung from her war adventures and, according to Joan Givner, Porter's biographer, the ménage became uncomfortable. "[Jane] solved the problem by writing to Porter, about whom she had heard a great deal from Kitty. She told Porter that Kitty was lonely and very devoted to and dependent on Porter, and begged her to join them."[40]

Porter accepted, intrigued by the chance to meet Anderson and gain inside knowledge about Joseph Conrad. But Porter's experience soon turned sour, for Jane continually criticized American ways as crude in comparison to those of Europe. Jane also turned the summer into a major drinking session, finally leaving with Seldes. Neither Kitty nor Porter ever saw her again. When the summer ended, Porter took the reporting job with the *News* and moved to a Denver rooming house.[41]

On July 5, 1919, Katherine Anne Porter attended the first of Taylor's lectures, "Music History and Appreciation," in the Recital Hall of Knight-Campbell's, Denver's premiere music company. She was impressed. "We found Deems Taylor's first talk on the history and appreciation of music very out of the ordinary and entertaining," she wrote in next day's *Rocky Mountain News*. "The little group of serious thinkers who braved the rain to hear him were jolly glad they went. . . . There are to be a half-dozen more of these lectures if so dull a name may be applied to talks as informal and charming as these."[42] One reason there may have been so few in attendance was that the series ticket was ten dollars per person, somewhat expensive for the time.[43]

A week later, Porter reported on a more personal musical event: "Deems Taylor played a number of his new Russian songs for us the other day, and our old enthusiasm for all things Russian (save their politics, at a pinch) came back with a swoop. . . . Mr. Taylor probably is the only translator who did 250 songs from the Russian into English without knowing so much as the alphabet of that language. However, Kurt Schindler translated the poems into rough—oh, very rough—English prose, and from this mass of material Mr. Taylor created delicate, stylistic verses for the native music."[44]

Meanwhile the lectures continued successfully. "[Deems] says his lectures are doing well," his father wrote in his journal. "Between sessions he looks up books, makes elaborate notes, and then lectures without any reference to said notes!"[45] Having found a successful method of presentation, Taylor chose as the subject of his final lecture Edvard Grieg, Norway's greatest composer. For his material he relied on his own copy of *Grieg and His Music*, written by the respected New York critic Henry Finck. The lecture went swimmingly: "Because the end was in sight, [Taylor] let himself go. His wit sparkled, he was jocose, he even ad-libbed a little. The session over . . . one man remained until all the others had left. Then grasping the lecturer firmly by the hand, he said: 'I want you to know Mr. Taylor, that Grieg and I were room-mates at Leipzig Conservatory.' Taylor gulped. 'You—er—liked my discussion of him?' The other nodded vigorously, 'I agree with your opinions exactly.'"[46]

Percy Stephens's summer workshop ended with a concert featuring a chorus of sixty voices. Taylor's own songs, and some he arranged, took up much of the program, together with his cantata *The Chambered Nautilus,* which he conducted himself. The reviewers for the two Denver papers varied in their assessment of the concert. The *Post* concluded that Taylor's presence added "much to the success of the affair," while his unusual arrangement of two songs resulted in "a regular debauch in humming." The critic also thought highly of a group of Negro spirituals, noting that of all of them, "particularly the last song, 'Oh, Didn't It Rain?' excited approval."[47] Porter's review in the *News* emphasized Taylor's works; she found his songs and cantata to be the highlights of "certainly the most charming affair heard here in many a day."[48] Taylor was elated: the positive reception by Denver of both himself and his music confirmed that he had a future in music. In addition, he learned that he had inherited a bit of his father's talent for teaching.

Before departing for New York, he met once more with Porter, who sought his advice because she was anxious to go there to develop her writing career. Taylor recommended that she see Heywood Broun, his journalist friend from the *Tribune*. Porter gratefully recalled the suggestion years later: "I went to see Heywood Broun, who advised me not to waste time on a newspaper, but to go and get a well-paid job in the publicity department of a moving picture company. . . . [A] very nice job in the Selznick studio in East Orange, New Jersey . . . paid me well and wasn't much work and I spent most of my time writing a novel."[49]

When Taylor arrived back in New York after the two-day train trip, he found that not much had changed: his marriage was in the divorce courts, more Schumann Club arrangements awaited his attention, and he had no permanent job. However, there was one bright spot for the family. In November Katy gave birth to William Osborn Davis. (Here the middle name honored one of the founders of Rowlie's company.) In the years ahead, young Bill would be the pride of JoJo and Mummie and a special nephew for Deems.

To occupy his time, Taylor decided to complete *Portrait of a Lady,* the rhapsody for piano and orchestra begun in Denver, because at least this was his own music instead of just another arrangement of a folksong. He remained firm in his desire to compose music for the concert stage. If necessary, he planned to return to some sort of editorial job to make a living, but unexpectedly an offer arrived to compose music for a Broadway revue. The Great White Way beckoned again, this time thanks to Mercedes de Acosta.

4. The Theater Beckons Again, 1920–1921

Back to Broadway

Mercedes de Acosta, the daughter of rich Cuban parents, had two passions: theater and women. In later years her relationships with Marlene Dietrich and Greta Garbo set many tongues wagging, but in 1919 she mingled conspicuously with wealthy members of New York society. During a party given by Mrs. John Jacob Astor at her Fifth Avenue mansion, de Acosta met Hope Williams, an amateur actress: "We . . . 'clicked' at once," de Acosta recalled.[1] Williams wanted to be a Broadway star, and de Acosta promised to help by writing a musical with a featured role for her. Gaining support for such an enterprise was not easy, but de Acosta had a friend in Elisabeth Marbury.

Marbury was a power on Broadway—rich, cultured, and charming— and always on the lookout for new talent. Among her finds was Cole Porter, whom she helped to Broadway fame by producing his first musical, *See America First*. Though it ran only fifteen performances, the show established a firm friendship between Marbury and Porter, so when de Acosta asked Marbury's advice on a songwriter for her musical, Marbury suggested Porter. As it turned out he was unavailable, but he recommended Taylor. Now wiser to the world of Broadway, Taylor told de Acosta that before he accepted, he would need proof that there was sufficient money to produce the musical.[2]

De Acosta initially didn't have financial backing, but she did have a plan. During her volunteer war work for the Red Cross she had met and made friends with Mrs. Frank Frueauff, the former actress Antoinette Perry. She knew that Perry's financier husband was wealthy and that Mrs. Frueauff wanted to be a Broadway producer, so de Acosta contacted her and inquired whether Mr. Frueauff might provide some financial support for her new musical, *What Next!* He did agree to help, but only if the production used amateur performers and the proceeds went to a charity. The agreement was quickly worked out and with money in hand, de Acosta contacted Taylor, who now signed a contract to furnish the music for the songs. The lyrics would be by Charles Shaw. To spur the creative process, de Acosta arranged for Taylor to have space in the elegant Frueauff apartment on Park Avenue while he was composing. This not only produced the music for the show but developed a strong friendship between Taylor and the former Antoinette Perry, who would become a silent benefactress in the years ahead. (Perry did become a successful Broadway producer. Her guiding spirit for the American Theater Wing brought her the posthumous honor of having Broadway's highest award named the Tony.)

What Next! was actually a high-class amateur production, an example of the Broadway revue presented by and with wealthy amateurs, often women from New York society who put together musicals for modest Broadway runs. These shows emphasized dance because of the influence of icon Isadora Duncan. Her free-form style and spirited living brought a new sense of art to the moneyed class. De Acosta wanted dance episodes with a special flair, so she contacted Bessie McCoy, who had starred in *The Echo*. Now married to Richard Harding Davis, the most famous journalist of his time, McCoy agreed to help develop the choreography, but would not dance.

On January 26, 1920, an advertisement in the *New York Times* announced a two-week engagement for "What Next! A Musical Comedy by Deems Taylor," at the elegant, though small (299-seat), Princess Theater. All proceeds went to the "N.Y. Protective Ass'n and Girls' Protective League." *What Next!* melded a feeble situation (jewel thieves disguised as a maid and butler in a country mansion) with songs on topical subjects: Prohibition ("I've ruined my condition on account of prohibition") and strikes ("If you want to know what's-whatsky, simply ask Lenin or Trotsky, and they'll tell you that it's strikes, strikes, strikes").[3] The *Times* critic was laudatory: "There have been many amateur shows which have been handled in their entirety by New York society, but never before have these energetic men and maids undertaken anything so ambitious as last night's production. . . . The music, while at times reminiscent, was tuneful. . . . The cast was made up of names well known in society . . . until the last act, when a few professionals were included to lend atmosphere. . . . Miss Hope Williams really carried away the honors of the evening. . . . [S]he was very amusing and displayed surprising talent."⁴ De Acosta's goal for her protégée had been achieved, and Taylor had seen his name on a Broadway theater program as he had with *The Echo,* but this time all the music was his own. He wondered whether his musical life wasn't meant to be on Broadway after all. As if to confirm this possibility, at one of the first performances of *What Next!* Eugene Lockhart was in the audience and contacted Taylor to be part of another musical revue.

Eugene Lockhart, who later became one of the great character actors in movies, arrived on Broadway from his native Canada. Like Taylor, he was blessed with multiple talents. Actor, writer, and composer, Lockhart was the lyricist for one of the big hit tunes of 1919, "The World Is Waiting for the Sunrise." His production plans now focused on *Heigh-Ho,* a musical revue backed by Washington, D.C., society and designed to showcase some of its local talent. The Canadian needed someone to write a few more songs, do orchestrations, and conduct the orchestra during the pre-Broadway run.⁵ Taylor, still eking out an existence, happily accepted Lockhart's guaranteed minimum of one thousand dollars.

At the time Taylor lived in a rented apartment above a garage on East Eighty-third Street. Since Lockhart would not pay him until the fall, he invited Marc Connelly, a contrib friend of his, to move in and share the rent. Connelly had grown up near Pittsburgh, where he worked as a reporter on local newspapers. The lure of New York was to satisfy his ambition to be a playwright, a goal that ultimately gained him a Pulitzer Prize for his play *The Green Pastures.* "Even before I knew Deems Taylor," Connelly wrote in his autobiography, "there were scores of mornings when breakfast had an extra zest because of something in the 'Tower' signed 'Smeed.'"⁶

That Connelly and Taylor should meet because of FPA's column was not surprising, because wit was essential for them both. They had something else in common: both were on the road to baldness. The two would have another roommate who did not share this characteristic; when Connelly accepted Taylor's offer, he learned that "Mrs. Higgins," a cat, also lived there. Taylor throughout his wifeless days needed feline company, and for some unknown reason his cats, one after the other, were all named Mrs. Higgins.

Connelly was surviving at the time by selling a few short stories and reporting for the *Morning Telegraph.* While prowling the theater district for stories, he met George S. Kaufman, another Pittsburgher, who was then a drama reporter for the *Times.* They found common ground in their playwriting aspiration and as fellow contributors to FPA's "Conning Tower." Kaufman and his wife, Beatrice, lived on West Eightieth Street and often invited Taylor and Connelly to dinner; the offers were gratefully accepted by the duo, who trekked across town for the free meals.⁷ These evenings not only helped keep them fed, but also provided opportunities for discussions of plots and plays. Kaufman was brilliant and found in Connelly the first of several coauthors who brought out the best in him. The Kaufman-Connelly team gave Broadway some of the freshest comedies of the early 1920s: *Dulcy, Beggar on Horseback,* and *Merton of the Movies.*

Mary Kennedy Arrives

By this time Taylor had become part of the Broadway social scene, thriving on late-night parties, liquor, and cigarettes. He loved parties; there he smoked his Lucky Strikes (a lifelong obsession) and sipped his favorite Jack Rose cocktails, at least when decent Prohibition applejack was available.[8] It was at such a party of theater people in late August that he spotted Mary Kennedy, a twenty-four-year-old actress with childlike features clearly identifying her Irish heritage. She was in a celebratory mood, because after several years of secondary roles in Broadway plays she finally had gained a featured part in the successful comedy *Not So Long Ago,* starring one of Broadway's great actresses, Eva Le Gallienne.

That night Taylor fell very hard for Mary Kennedy. Months later in a letter to her, he described his initial impressions: "Who is that? . . . She can't be an actress, for she looks like somebody's kid sister. So I decided to go and see. I didn't know your name. Someone must have told it to me. . . . I had a book about stage decoration, in French, and we looked at the pictures. And you said something about reading it and I said, 'It's only French.' And you thought that was funny; so I instantly began to like you, for I meant it to be funny. . . . I remember feeling tremendously—what's the word? Comfortable isn't quite it. Comforted—yes, comforted, somehow."[9]

For his second wife-to-be, he had picked another Southerner. Born in 1896, Mary Kennedy had spent her early years in Jacksonville, Florida, the oldest of three children in an Irish Catholic family. As an eight-year-old, she was taken into her father's room just in time to watch him die, a prayer book in his hands.[10] Her mother sent Mary away to a Catholic boarding school, but once her schooling was completed, she returned to Jacksonville and discovered the city had become the center of a small motion picture industry. The Kalem Company's Civil War stories and three-reel comedies were at the forefront. Mary got a few parts in these movies as an extra, followed by roles in local theater productions. Knowing that New York was the center of both theatrical productions and moviemaking, and with references from friends she had made in her film work, she headed North.

She tried Broadway first and won small roles in plays between 1917 and 1919, one of which, *Lombardi, Ltd.,* provided her with the then rather grandiose sum of $2,900 for the engagement. During this period she also married

James Blaine Hawley. Nothing is known of the marriage except that Mary's final decree of divorce from Hawley was granted only a month before she met Taylor at the party.[11] Mary told him about the divorce but maintained, early in their relationship, that she couldn't marry him because the Catholic Church did not allow remarriage. In the years ahead, though Kennedy would judge her husband's behavior from her strict point of view, he would persuade her that their love, not the dictums of her church, provided the basis for marriage.

Her religious concerns did not bother Taylor, who pursued a totally secular life centered on hard work and acceptance by others. His parents, firm churchgoers, realized their son had wandered far from their religious path in his mature years, something his mother revealed when she wrote to her then famous son and described a dream she had had: "I dreamed last night that we had a reunion of my mother's people at some sort of a banquet. I was so proud. . . . You were there of course and after we were seated you stood up. I thought to myself, 'I believe Deems is going to ask the blessing.' I immediately woke up. The shock one way or the other was the cause I guess!"[12] Mary Kennedy, like Taylor, had exceptional and multiple talents. A fine actress, she was also a writer and had nascent talents as a sculptress. Taylor felt fortunate to have found both an intellectual and emotional soulmate, someone to share his human and theatrical passions, to join him in dreaming about the future. They began an intense correspondence, initially writing from their separate apartments across town, then across states while Mary toured in *Not So Long Ago*. He called her Mashinka, Russian for "Little Mary Darling"; she called him Deems.

In their letters, both displayed emotions bordering on the immature. Deems wrote: "Mashinka, and you *are* my child and you *are* a sweet thing. Don't forget your Shortest Catechism while you're away: Who are you? Whose child are you? . . . Oh, my dear, my dear. Come back to me soon. I didn't know I needed you like this. Don't ever let me go, Mashinka."[13] From the road, Mary wrote: "Deems, I must talk to you. My trunks are all packed, I am bathed and expensively scented. I am warmly tucked in bed and I have to get up at eight-thirty. Being utterly weary, I should go to sleep like a very nice well-trained child, but I must ask you a lot of questions first. . . . Deems are you as nice as I think you are? Do you really like me, or in your secret heart do I just amuse you? . . . Will I ever see you again? Do you like me more or less than you did?"[14]

Emotionally bound to Mary, Taylor turned his full creative attentions to *Heigh-Ho*. He and Lockhart had worked out the show in anticipation of November tryouts in Annapolis, Baltimore, and Richmond. They expected that with this amount of preparation the show would be in good shape for Washington, make a big splash for the society matrons who had invested their money, and then make its leap to Broadway. Unfortunately, as Taylor chronicled in letters to Mary Kennedy throughout the *Heigh-Ho* tour, one difficulty followed another from the very beginning in New York: "I'm slowly going mad. . . . We leave a week from today, I haven't any orchestra, the orchestrations aren't ready, my leading lady can't sing and I've got to try and make her sing. . . . I've got a finale and two interludes still to write, I owe two months' rent, and they're hinting at taking away my piano."[15]

Misfortune on the Road

The worst was still to come. Originally only Washington amateurs were to be used for the chorus and dancers, but theatrical regulations forced the producers to hire New York professional chorines as half the performers. The New Yorkers rehearsed in their own city, then joined the Washington group in Annapolis for dress rehearsal. Lockhart and Taylor arrived the day before the scheduled opening and made a disconcerting discovery: the Washington rehearsal director's ideas did not coincide with those of the New York director's because each had gone blithely ahead and rehearsed his group independently.

As a result, the Washington girls did not look with favor upon their professional coworkers, while the New Yorkers made no effort to conceal their amusement at the amateurs' efforts. Dress rehearsal in Annapolis, the day before the opening, was held without the scenery, which arrived the next morning by train at 4:00 A.M. The stagehands, after lugging the scenery into the theater, discovered that the stage was too narrow for the set. The show opened that night with only one faded backdrop serving for the entire production.[16]

Heigh-Ho survived two nights in Annapolis, then left for Baltimore, where the scenery did fit the stage. Here the mistake was that instead of the usual three-day run, the producers had scheduled *Heigh-Ho* for a week. The future looked stormy to the composer, as he wrote to Mary:

These damn fool[s]. . . . [T]hey had actually counted on getting about six thousand dollars out of Baltimore. They HAD to get it. What we did get, of course, was an awful panning and about twenty-two hundred on the week. . . . Sunday morning Miss Brown arrived with enough to pay the chorus and give the principals something on account. . . . Sunday night at seven they called us again and told us to be at the station at 9:30 Monday morning. . . . We missed the first train . . . and very lucky for me that we missed it, too; for I was in hock at my hotel with an unpaid bill of forty dollars and six dollars in the world; and they forgot me, and had to send someone up from the station to bail me out.[17]

The company limped into Richmond Sunday afternoon, and by 8:45 P.M., when the orchestra seated itself in the pit with Taylor at the podium, the scenery still hadn't been set. He assured the audience there would be a performance and fictionally ascribed the delay to a train wreck, then for two hours he conducted the orchestra, repeating the score four times. Not surprisingly, when *Heigh-Ho* finally opened at 10:45 P.M., what was left of the audience happily whistled and sang along with the singers. A week later a moody, unhappy company left Richmond; no salaries had yet been paid.[18]

Washington papers alerted the public to the arrival of "'Heigh-Ho,' The Gorgeous New Musical Fantasy by Eugene Lockhart and Deems Taylor." The opening actually went smoothly, and the next morning the *Washington Post* critic wrote mildly pleasant things (November 30, 1920): "[The first night audience] responded with a cordial hospitality [to] the matter of song, dance, scenic novelty which only falls short of the definition of a revue by lacking any outstanding specialties. Yet in respect to pulchritude, Mr. Ziegfeld probably would be happy to acknowledge it for a quality that made his annual institution famous. [It was] a graceful evening's entertainment, attractively staged, pleasingly costumed, with music above the musical comedy average."

But by this time the financing of *Heigh-Ho* had crumbled, and Taylor wrote to Kennedy of his desperation: "The marshals and lawyers and things descended in a body tonight and attached everything there was to attach. . . . Maybe God doesn't want me to go into the show business . . . but see here, God, be reasonable. I didn't want to go into the show business. I just wanted to get some money so that I could support Mrs. Higgins [the cat] and write some music. . . . I've got to write an opera, and very soon. I want to write music for the stage and that's what I can do best. And if I don't get to do it pretty soon I'm going to bust wide open."[19]

Two weeks later in another letter to Kennedy, he indicated the clear vision he had of the difficulties that lay ahead. Composing art music rarely provided enough money to put food on the table. "If [a composer] writes Dardanella, he'll make fifty thousand dollars at it. If he writes a better symphony than Beethoven ever did, it will cost him two hundred dollars to have the orchestra parts copied, and his income from it will amount to a hundred dollars, perhaps in five years."[20] Though Taylor exaggerated, the fact remained that he knew writing a major symphonic work would take months of work, and he expected little monetary reward.

Gone were the days when a composer had either the church or some nobleman as patron, times when, as Taylor himself later expressed, the patron "boarded him and paid him a salary, asking in return only that he compose music. On the other hand, the composer ate with the hired hands. His status was that of a servant. Today we have abolished that servitude. We regard the composer with respect and admiration—and let him starve."[21] Taylor's assessment of the composer's problems was rather severe, but nonetheless anyone who had the internal incessant itch to compose large-scale works such as an opera either had to find employment or marry into money. For Taylor, the latter possibility did not appear to be on the horizon.

He returned to New York disheartened, but nevertheless confirmed in his devotion to music: "Music's going to be my life hereafter. If I starve for it, well and good. If I can't make enough money to run this apartment and support Mrs. Higgins and buy a grand piano and lunch at the Algonquin and take an occasional taxi I ought to give it all up and stop complaining, I guess, or else give up my dream of being a good composer. It's not very simple . . . And it's very hard to live in New York without living on the scale of the people I know."[22] Taylor didn't mince words with Kennedy. He liked the good life, the life of parties and socializing, and, when possible, lunching at the Algonquin Hotel as a member of a salon of wits that gathered there regularly.

The Algonquin Round Table and Taylor

To link the name of Deems Taylor with the Algonquin Round Table, the most famous of New York literary salons, may seem out of the ordinary until one realizes that his friends FPA and Robert Benchley were two of the key players in that group. In fact, even before the beginning of the Vicious Circle (a nickname for the group), many of the members had formed an invisible bond as FPA contribs. Taylor had been one of those but had not been present at the creation of the Algonquin Round Table.

That occurred in 1919, when several press agents threw a party for Alexander Woollcott at the Algonquin.[23] Woollcott, dubbed "Old Vitriol and Violets" by James Thurber, was then the drama critic of the *New York Times* and an increasingly powerful molder of theatrical public opinion. Though the party originally was meant as a "roast" of Woollcott, he was so pleased to have so many friends around him that he urged them to continue in the jollity and join him for daily lunch at the hotel.

A love of the theater bound the "Algonks," and as the lunches continued, two groups developed: a primary one that lunched most often, and the secondary group of infrequent attendees. The primary group of the Round Table had a major impact on the New York literary scene: Robert Benchley, Dorothy Parker, Alexander Woollcott, and Donald Ogden Stewart were

drama critics and writers for the magazines *Vanity Fair* and *Life;* George
Kaufman, Marc Connelly, and Robert Sherwood were playwrights; Harold
Ross would found the *New Yorker;* FPA and Heywood Broun were influential
newspaper columnists; Murdoch Pemberton, John Toohey, and Ruth Hale
(wife of Heywood Broun) were press agents; Margalo Gillmore and Peggy
Wood were actresses.

Called a "collection of first-rate, second-raters,"[24] the Vicious Circle
practiced their daggerish wit or devilish puns on each other before releasing
witticisms to the newspaper columnists who awaited their daily dribblings,
many of which have come down to the present. FPA, Alexander Woollcott,
Robert Benchley, and Dorothy Parker proved the most quotable. FPA
thrived on puns, such as his comparison of the attention required of peonies
and dahlias by a gardener: "If you take care of your peonies, the dahlias will
look after themselves." Woollcott's humor could scorch; an example is the
exchange between him and a fellow Hamilton College alumnus at an alumni
reunion: "You remember me, don't you?" asked the man. "I can't remember
your name," said Woollcott, "but don't tell me." Benchley's humor, as he
showed later in numerous movie short subjects, leaned toward the dry. Concerning his literary talent, he stated simply: "It took me fifteen years to discover that I had no talent for writing, but I couldn't give it up because by that
time I was too famous." Parker, described by Woollcott as a "combination of
Little Nell and Lady MacBeth," provided piercing humor, yet with common
sense. Commenting on the very essence of the Algonks, Parker wrote: "Wit
has truth in it; wisecracking is simply calisthenics with words."[25]

Taylor, in his quiet way, could match any of them in witticisms, but often
couldn't match them in finding the money for lunch. He became a member
of the secondary group, those who appeared less often for lunch, people such
as the novelist Edna Ferber, the violinist Jascha Heifetz, and silent Harpo
Marx. Of all those who broke bread around the Round Table, only Taylor
wrote music for the concert hall.

As fascinating as he found the Algonks to be, Taylor astutely put his
finger on their essence in a letter to Mary Kennedy after returning from the
Heigh-Ho debacle. He told of an experience after a lecture on music he had
attended. Someone he'd never met before came up to him and began a
lengthy discourse: "I hadn't talked to him three minutes before I knew that
here was a man to whom music meant something. Something real; something
important not just a nerve stimulant. If he liked my stuff, it meant something.
But all those clever, glib Americans that I know—that Algonquin crowd.
They're representative enough, except that they're more intelligent than the
average. . . . The thing I live for, the thing I *must* do isn't even unimportant to
them. It simply doesn't exist." Feeling sorry for himself because they didn't

appreciate his music, he identified the one thing the Algonquin crowd did respond to: achieving some kind of success.

> Of course, if I wrote the greatest music in the world they'd admire
> me because I was said to write the greatest music in the world; if
> you became the greatest sculptor in the world they'll admire you,
> because everybody says you're as good as Rodin—of whom they
> have heard. . . . Ruth Hale has never heard a note that I've written;
> but she's suddenly become respectful—because Jerome Kern told
> her I had it all over the other serious American composers. Good
> God! And the worst of it is, I do hear these people, and wait to hear
> what they'll say—because I'm an American, God help me, and
> they're my people. And I'll never be anything but an American. . . .
> But whom am I writing for?[26]

The answer to his question was that he was writing for himself, to satisfy that inner urge of a composer, though the plaudits of others were gratefully received. Taylor could easily appreciate the literary abilities of his friends, but few of them had sufficient interest in serious music to appreciate his. Walking the composing road was lonely, even with Mary's firm encouragement. Perhaps he decried the achievement orientation of friends, but deep inside his soul he also sought one of the "brass rings" of music: the composition of the first successful American opera.

Taylor Dreams of Composing an Opera

Taylor's first thoughts about a subject centered on James Branch Cabell's 1919 novel *Jurgen,* one of the Virginia author's sixteen works set in the mythical land of Poictesme. Cabell spent his entire life in Richmond, and in his books he provided cynical commentary on everything from the caprices of love to the tenets of religion. His heroes sought wisdom, truth, and beauty in magical kingdoms, but usually ended up with ordinary lives back home. Cabell intrigued many among the intelligentsia in the 1920s, though he fell quickly from literary grace in the 1930s.

Jurgen became the most famous of Cabell's books, but not only for literary reasons. Parts of it were considered highly sexual in content and caused the New York Society for the Suppression of Vice to sue the publisher and ban its sale. After two years, a judge and jury acquitted the publishers of any alleged indecencies in the book. Inevitably, such notoriety produced underground copies at a price greater than bootlegged liquor during Prohibition. "At current boot liquor quotations," wrote one commentator, "Haig and Haig costs twelve dollars a quart, while any dependable booklegger can unearth a copy of 'Jurgen' for about fifteen dollars."[27]

Symbolism abounded in the medieval setting of *Jurgen,* with puns and anagrams challenging the mind of the reader. Since Taylor was such a pushover for fantasy and literary cleverness, he became preoccupied with the book and its meaning for him. The plot is Faustian. Jurgen is a pawnbroker anxious to find his youth once again, and he makes a pact with the devil that brings him into the sanctuaries of such beautiful women as Helen of Troy.

Taylor at this time was thirty-five years old and approaching middle age. Apparently to him Jurgen was a kindred spirit, seeking continuing youth and beautiful women while decrying "the opportunities of a youth that had been lost."[28] On December 27, 1920, Taylor wrote Mary, still on tour in *Not So Long Ago,* and shared his feelings about *Jurgen:*

> [It's the] saddest book I ever read. I don't know why, exactly. The book hurts me—tears me to small pieces—but somehow it sets me free. It says the word that I've been trying to pronounce for so long. It tells me everything I am, and have been, and may be, unsparingly. . . . I've been sitting here tonight, reading it aloud . . . with the tears streaming down my face and wetting the bewildered Mrs. Higgins, who has been trying to get a little much-needed sleep in my lap. . . . So you have a rather small and subdued Deems tonight, who would very much like to put his head in your lap, and be kissed and put to sleep.[29]

What he didn't tell Mary was that two nights before, on Christmas Eve, he had summoned the courage to write Cabell and thank him for writing *Jurgen.* Within a few days, Cabell responded cordially and with gratitude.[30] This gentle and appreciative answer was all that Taylor needed to write once again, this time to advance the possibility of a collaboration: transforming *Jurgen* into an opera, with Cabell doing the libretto. In this letter Cabell learned for the first time that Taylor was a composer determined to write an opera: "For ten years I have been planning and getting ready to write—grand opera, music drama, lyric drama—whatever you want to call it. Now I'm ready." Taylor went on to explain that he considered the text of a music drama more important than the music; for him, *Jurgen* was a perfect story, "Till Eulenspiegel with a soul." He warned Cabell that there wouldn't be any money in writing a libretto, or even in a production of the opera. Then the gently conniving alter ego of Taylor emerged: "As far as a production is concerned, if I wrote an opera that showed any gleam of promise, I believe I could cajole or blackmail either the Metropolitan or Chicago companies into putting it on."[31] Cabell must have wondered at such a brash statement from a man relatively unknown in the music world.

Though they exchanged several letters about the possibility of a *Jurgen* libretto, two months later Taylor abruptly closed the discussion, albeit in a laudatory manner: "I think you are a great man—saving perhaps Conrad, the greatest writer of English now living." Below his signature in the typed letter, Taylor scribbled the following: "I think I'll do a Jurgen suite."[32] For some reason, he had closed the book on an opera. Perhaps what he had told Cabell had finally sunk in in his own mind: there was no money in writing operas, and he clearly needed money.

With the beginning of 1921, Taylor once again had reached bottom financially, and he shared his misery with the faraway Kennedy: "I've been in a state of complete mental paralysis for over a month now. I'm unable, apparently, to start anything at all. I've pretended to look for jobs, but I haven't really. . . . It's the debts that paralyze me so. When you owe three months' rent (counting January) and four months' piano installments, and for the clothes you're wearing, and the gas company wants to cut you off, and everything has to be paid immediately—why the sheer impossibility of it keeps you from even trying."[33] But two days later he revealed that the sun had started to shine again: "I have honest work. Orchestrating the score of an operetta. It's vile music, and a tedious job, but it's worth about four hundred dollars, and that's something. It'll take about three weeks or so. I've almost got me [*sic*] strength back."[34]

Meanwhile, help with the rent vanished when Connelly moved out, the result of the coinhabitors' getting on each other's nerves. Connelly and Kaufman's play *Dulcy* was in preparation for a Chicago opening, and Taylor may well have allowed envy to invade his brain: "I'm sick of clever people. I know at last why Marc gets on my nerves. It's because I know—or feel that I know, which amounts to the same thing—all there is to know about him. I can anticipate his reactions to anything . . . so he can go now, please. . . . Mrs. Higgins is such a relief. She has no brains at all. I much prefer that to merely clever ones. That's the trouble with cleverness. It's only knack, after all."[35] In the years ahead, it would be a knack that Taylor himself used extensively.

It was during these difficult financial times that James Gibbons Huneker, the music critic of the *New York World,* died peacefully in his Brooklyn home on February 9, 1921. When Taylor read of Huneker's death, an idea germinated.

5. *Taylor Becomes the Music Critic of the* New York World, *1921–1922*

Replacing Huneker

According to the historian Mark Grant, Huneker's death removed from the New York music scene "the most influential and most widely read by other writers and intellectuals of all the music critics in [U.S.] history."[1] Unlike the four other "old guard" members—W. J. Henderson of the *Sun,* Henry Krehbiel of the *Tribune,* Henry Finck of the *Evening Post,* and Richard Aldrich of the *Times*—Huneker had not spent the major part of his career as a newspaper music critic. He lived mainly on freelance writing. Also unlike them, he saw all the arts as his domain. He was equally at home writing about drama, art, and music; he had gained an international reputation from countless articles and some twenty books, including autobiographical fiction. His life began in Philadelphia, where he studied to become a lawyer, but a love for the piano and travel took him to Paris to study piano and harmony. His particular love for the music of Chopin ultimately resulted in a biography of the composer, as well as an edition of Chopin's piano works for Oliver Ditson.

After he had settled in New York, the flamboyant, rotund Huneker habitually chose Luchows, the famed German restaurant on Fourteenth Street, for dining. Beer-assisted repasts often provided episodes that quickly entered the realm of legend in the music community. Particularly notable was an encounter brought about by Huneker's relentless criticism of Vladimir de Pachmann. The Ukrainian pianist parlayed eccentric stage mannerisms and broad interpretations of Chopin's works into a major career, but his pianistic gesturings and delicate manner especially annoyed Huneker. Once, in a particularly nasty mood, Huneker dubbed Pachmann "The Chopinzee," a pun that included a flowery reference to the pianist's masculinity. Such remarks ultimately led to a confrontation at Luchows: "The long-suffering Pachmann stepped up to Huneker, started calling him vile names, and became so insufferable that Huneker picked up a stein of beer and calmly dumped its contents on Pachmann's shirt front."[2] The feud ended years later, but Pachmann's mannerisms would become the subject of a classic review by Taylor, as will be noted.

It might seem that Taylor had overdosed on hubris when, with no music criticism experience, he considered becoming Huneker's replacement. Yet he understood that whoever replaced the great man would immediately become a major player in the New York musical scene. Taylor's goal was to write an opera. He had achieved success in two cantatas and *Through the Looking Glass,* but his name was hardly a household word. It would not have escaped his attention that the more people knew of him, the more they would like to hear some of his music. Might there not also be a desire to hear something such as an opera from him?

But there was a more pragmatic reason for Taylor to seek Huneker's position: he'd then have enough money to convince Mary Kennedy to be his bride. Within a week he had made an appointment with the *World*'s executive editor, Herbert Bayard Swope, to put forward his candidacy.

Joseph Pulitzer's *World* had been a crusading paper with progressive ideas, though often on the sensationalistic side. After Pulitzer died in 1911, the paper slumped in quality. But when one of his sons, Ralph, advanced Swope from star reporter to executive editor in 1920, the paper began a return to greatness. It soon became "a newspaperman's newspaper, brilliantly written, tautly edited, politically and commercially independent, effervescent, irreverent, combative, liberal."[3] Much of the paper's newfound energy came from Swope's dynamism. Mary Kennedy, who along with Taylor would enjoy his summer hospitality in Great Neck in the years ahead, described Swope as "one of the most forceful men I have ever met, . . . a loud talkative man with a mop of red hair, and a big, active body. He was inexhaustible and . . . stored in his big frame the loudest vocal sounds ever exploded by any human being."[4]

Swope's method of improving the *World* was simple: get the best journalists, and, if they are at another newspaper, reel them in one by one. From the *Tribune* he brought both FPA and Heywood Broun, noted for his sports and literary commentary; from the *Times* he lured Alexander Woollcott to smite the mediocre on Broadway. He assembled their columns on the page facing the editorial page and initiated what became a journalistic tradition: the "op ed" page.

Huneker's death created for Swope the obvious problem of finding a replacement. When Taylor arrived for his appointment, the new editor recognized an ambitious man and asked him to explain why he believed he could fill Huneker's shoes. The tactful applicant asked if he might reply after further deliberation and preparation. Swope agreed, and Taylor went home to type a letter that he brought back the next day. Part of it read:

> I haven't written very much about music for two reasons: first, because I've been too busy writing music itself, and second because nobody but newspapers want musical criticism, and the few periodicals that will stand for a serious discussion of music pay so villainously that I haven't been able to afford to write for them, much as I would have liked to. . . . I do know something about music. I have been writing it for ten or twelve years, and have succeeded in winning a certain amount of respect for my intentions, at least, as a serious composer. . . . [I] know a good many people, painters, musicians, and writers, both here and abroad, including most of the concert, opera, and newspaper people in New York. I speak French pretty well, German rather badly, and can read Italian. I know most of the Russian alphabet.

Finally Taylor came to the crux of the matter: "The only thing that I haven't mentioned, so far as I can see, is my fitness to step into James Huneker's shoes. I haven't any. Nobody has; unless, of course, you could get Mencken."[5] Swope hardly believed he could reel in H. L. Mencken, then one of the country's most distinguished journalists and sometime music critic. But he did recognize Taylor's potential, so he extended him the challenge of attending concerts and operas in the next two weeks as if he were the *World* music critic. He was to write reviews and submit them every day by the regular midnight deadline. Taylor happily accepted the role of apprentice critic. At the end of two trying weeks, the neophyte music critic wrote to Mary Kennedy:

> I'm weary, Mashinka. I got up at some unearthly hour—nine o'clock, I think—went to a morning dress rehearsal of a new opera at the Metropolitan, stayed there till two, ate hastily at the Algonquin, went to the National Symphony in the afternoon, wrote a review of it, dined, went to the Philharmonic concert in the evening, and went down to the World office and a wrote a review of that. . . . The only man who's being considered besides me is Philip Hale of

the [Boston] Herald and he's nearly seventy. The two things I write
tomorrow will be the last of the tryout stuff, thank God. I'm to
meet Pulitzer tomorrow afternoon."[6]

An optimistic Taylor emerged from that meeting: "He's quite young . . .
and rather pleasant. He asked me how I learned to write so well, and I told
him, by having something to say and absolutely no fluency in saying it, so that
I *had* to learn to write well in order to write at all. . . . Mencken, I hear,
talked to Pulitzer about me, and said I was the only person in town who
could do the job."[7] This was, obviously, a major recommendation. But even
with such an important encomium to his credit, Taylor had to wait until the
end of summer before he learned that he had been chosen to replace
Huneker. And it was still midwinter.

February's bitter weather matched the level of Taylor's finances. Mary's
play had completed its tour, and she returned to find that her admirer wanted
to see her as often as he could, while he prepared to go onstage himself. In
his college days, Taylor had been "The Great Fango," a one-man show for his
fraternity brothers in which he dexterously manipulated a variety of hats off
and onto his head for various impersonations. Learning that the Amateur
Comedy Club, one of New York's oldest theatrical groups, planned *A Man
about Town,* a vaudeville-type presentation on Broadway to accompany *Mary
Stuart,* a short drama, he dusted off his hats and auditioned. The club added
him to their presentation, and when Woollcott reviewed the opening, he
thought the play worthy of an audience's attention and lauded "the delightful
pantomime which precedes it."[8] The forty performances, Taylor's only
Broadway appearance, helped pay the rent and the restaurant bills.

By this time he had become friendly with a vast number of people in
journalism and on the Broadway stage who knew of his abilities as a composer. Therefore, it was not completely unexpected that he received a call
from the Theatre Guild. This time Broadway wanted him as a composer of
serious music, because the two-year-old organization needed incidental music for their upcoming production of Ferenc Molnár's *Liliom,* a play that had
been a great success in Europe. It was the Theatre Guild's lofty intention to
produce plays by exceptional European playwrights, thereby bringing a
deeper dimension to Broadway than its predominant fare of comedies, revues, and melodramas. (Years later, in 1946, the Guild would also produce a
musical version of *Liliom,* Rodgers and Hammerstein's *Carousel.*)

Most likely Taylor was recommended for the incidental music by FPA,
who planted the idea in the ear of his friend Lawrence Langner, one of the
Guild's founders and the director of *Liliom.* Taylor, ever ready to seize an un-

usual opportunity, agreed to provide the music even though time was short, with only a month until the opening performance.

To choose his music he had the help of Joseph Schildkraut, who would be playing Liliom, the carnival man of mixed virtues. Schildkraut had seen a production of the play in Vienna as a young actor and remembered melodies used there, such as themes from works by Engelbert Humperdinck (the composer of the opera *Hänsel und Gretel*), as well as a Viennese street song. He shared his recollections with Taylor, who built on the suggestions in choosing the themes for Liliom's funeral and a scene in heaven. The music must have made a strong impression, because a few years later a *Time* magazine writer commented, "Liliom audiences may still recall and whistle 'Look Out, Here Come the Damn Police' as vividly as they remember the acting of Schildkraut."[9] The success of *Liliom* propelled Taylor to the top as a leading composer of incidental music for Broadway productions.

The Second Mrs. Taylor: Mary Kennedy

While Taylor was busy with his Broadway tasks, Mary Kennedy went to Jacksonville, Florida, to see her mother. She returned in April and sublet an apartment on Madison Avenue, since all signs pointed to an imminent marriage with Taylor. Every day they met for lunch or dinner, sometimes both. Yet, throughout this time Taylor slipped in a few dates with Jane Anderson, his former wife, who still lived in the area. Very likely Kennedy found out about this and raised the roof, because early in June he sent her an apologetic note: "Forgive me, my dearest. . . . There is no particular excuse for me. I never behaved like this in my life before and I'll try never to again. I'm not very worthy of you, Mashinka, am I? I love you."[10]

Whether theirs was genuine love or emotional dependence, they agreed to marry as soon as his divorce became final at the end of June. Since his New York divorce prohibited further marriages in the state, they decided to be wed in Newark, New Jersey, just a brief train ride from the city. Taylor explained to his wife-to-be that a honeymoon was out of the question since he was nearly broke. But, as if in a theatrical plot, Taylor's friend "Mac, the Singing Policeman," came to the rescue.

Edward "Mac" McNamara could have been a character out of a Damon Runyon story.[11] Burly and with all the facial characteristics of his Irish parentage, McNamara as a young man strode the streets of his hometown, Paterson, New Jersey, as a policeman. His robust but untrained baritone voice made him a favorite in the city of silk mills and immigrants. To Patersonians he was the Singing Policeman, often used by Irish politicians at political ral-

Taylor and Mary Kennedy, his second wife. They were married from 1921 to 1934.
(Courtesy of Joan Kennedy Taylor)

lies to warm up the voters. Like thousands of others, McNamara always attended Paterson's annual spring music festival, which featured soloists from the Metropolitan Opera accompanied by an orchestra and a massive chorus—hundreds of local residents. His voice had such fervor and popularity that in 1913, the festival committee chose him as the featured singer for the final evening, a first for a local boy. Not only would McNamara conclude the festival, but he would follow by just one day a concert by John McCormack, then the world's greatest Irish tenor.

In those preamplification days, the hometown boy triumphed. The eight thousand people in the audience gave him ovation after ovation for his Irish songs and an aria from Gounod's *Faust*. "McNamara is Great Sensation of Festival's Final Concert," headlined the *Paterson Press* the next day.[12] Seated in the applauding audience was one of the most famous sopranos of her time, Madame Ernestine Schumann-Heink; she was also impressed. "A great voice," she told a reporter. "He has a great future."[13] The presence of the Austrian soprano was not accidental, for when she had moved to the United States in 1905, she'd bought a home some ten miles from Paterson. She could have been a model for the saying "It's not over until the fat lady sings," and she was loved by audiences for both her great voice and *gemütlich* charm. For many she also was the "Great Hausfrau," with her many children and her allegiance to her new homeland. She even named one of her children George Washington!

Although taken by McNamara's voice, the diva knew that he needed training and was willing to pay for it. If that went well, she would consider taking him along on her transcontinental concerts as a featured artist, a protégé. She approached him with the possibility and he agreed to the plan, quit the police force, and enrolled at the University of Michigan for nine months of voice training. Schumann-Heink considered the results positive enough, and in October 1914 McNamara joined the soprano as she began her annual tour. For their concert in Sioux City, Iowa, McNamara sang the "Prologue" from *Pagliacci*. "Let us hope," wrote one reviewer, "that it will always be sung as well as Mr. McNamara sang it."[14]

He toured for several years with Schumann-Heink, sharing the stage on one tour with Edith Evans, a talented pianist from Philadelphia. She came to know him for the charming and effervescent human being that he was. After the tour, Edith married John F. Braun, a wealthy Philadelphia businessman and art collector, and they settled in Merion, Pennsylvania, where the baritone visited them occasionally.

With connections provided by Schumann-Heink, the affable McNamara began associating with many important music and newspaper people in New York. Quite incredibly, he gained the unique claim to fame of being given lessons by Enrico Caruso, a fact noted by the *New York Times* under the headline "Caruso Takes First Pupil."[15] But even Caruso could not convince McNamara to try for a concert career. People so adored the Singing Policeman that he became a sought-after guest, staying for especially lengthy visits at the home of Heywood Broun. Marc Connelly later called McNamara "the greatest container of love and affection that I ever met."[16]

In the interconnected world of New York theater, Taylor and McNamara met sometime before the summer of 1920. McNamara took Taylor to meet his friends Edith and John Braun at their Merion home. Edith quickly warmed up to the charming Taylor and applauded his irrepressible desire to compose music.[17] To get to know Taylor better, the Brauns invited him to spend ten days with them at their Camden, Maine, seaside cottage in early August 1920; he happily accepted.[18] As a result, Taylor was well known to the Brauns when McNamara informed them of the upcoming marriage of Taylor and Kennedy. And when he mentioned that Taylor was practically broke, the Brauns graciously invited the couple to celebrate at their home.

On July 11, 1921, after a civil ceremony in Newark, the new Mr. and Mrs. Deems Taylor boarded a train for Philadelphia and a wedding banquet at the Brauns'. McNamara brought the champagne.[19] Knowing his parents would have trouble with a remarriage, Taylor spared them the formalities. Two days later he sent them a telegram: "You have a little daughter-in-law. Arrived Monday noon. Weight 115 lb. Name is Mary. Son doing well. Address in care of J. F. Braun, Merion, Pa. Much love, Deems."[20] Since Mary Kennedy was a member of the Lucy Stone League (an early women's rights organization), she would never allow herself to be called Mrs. Deems Taylor.

The newly married couple began life together knowing that the combined income of a composer and an actress would be unpredictable and sporadic. They agreed to a strict share-and-share-alike approach in pooling their resources. Both loved the theater, a bond that held them close early in their marriage. Many of their friends were actors, playwrights, or producers at a time when more than sixty first-class Broadway theaters welcomed plays into New York every season. Though Mary probably recognized that she did not have the stage quality of her friends Katherine Cornell, Lynn Fontanne, and Margalo Gillmore, three ascending stars on Broadway, she nonetheless wanted to remain an actress. She also aspired to be a mother someday, but soon found out that her husband held no interest in becoming a father. He said of his friends who had children: "Damn bad luck for them."[21] In the years ahead, she came to think of Taylor as a man whose relationships with women were based more on admiration than on love; he likewise had no intention of giving time to a son or daughter.

After their honeymoon, the Taylors rented an apartment on Fifty-seventh Street. For Mary Kennedy, the role of housewife didn't exactly fit; she believed that anything that took more than five minutes to cook wasn't worth the effort. She quickly grew bored with apartment life and within a month contracted to begin a pre-Broadway tour with the play *Other Lives*. Since Taylor still had not heard that he would be the *World*'s music critic, he decided to accompany his wife as the play took a long route from Trenton to Washington, then into Pennsylvania, where it folded. With this unhappy experience the couple returned to New York, where Mary resumed plying another of her talents, playwriting.

For Taylor, the waiting ended in mid-September. Swope summoned him to the *World*'s office and offered him the position of music editor and critic, from October 1 to May 1, at a salary of $150 a week. Taylor accepted enthusiastically.[22] Not only did he now have a major platform from which to attract attention to himself and express his views on music, but he also had a wife who believed deeply in his abilities as a composer. He couldn't wait to get started.

The New York Music Scene in 1921

As the *World*'s music critic, Taylor knew he was in friendly competition with four others, the prestigious old guard of New York's dozen daily newspapers.[23] Every one of these music elders had been a critic for some thirty years; their hearts beat to the strains of Wagner, not the modernists, and they certainly could not suffer politely the insinuation that jazz was serious music. Taylor was the new kid on the block. Recognizing this, Henry Finck of the *Evening Post* sent him a copy of his book *Musical Progress* with this inscription: "Henry T. Finck, a setting star, herewith sends greetings to Deems Taylor, the rising star who, he expects, will shed much needed light on darkest music land."[24] Taylor knew that the process of shedding much needed light would be both time consuming and mentally demanding, so he decided to give up composing temporarily. After all, with only a seven-month contract, he needed to establish a positive reputation if he wanted to be more than a short-term critic.

Taylor was entering his field at a time when the call for new traditions in American concert music was growing ever louder, seeking to break away from the European traditions of romanticism and impressionism. This call sounded particularly from music critics not in newspapers but in monthly periodicals who sought the attention of intellectuals in the arts. The leader of this charge was Paul Rosenfeld, columnist for the prestigious literary magazine *Dial*. He championed such European modernists now in this country as Edgard Varèse and Ernest Bloch, while continually looking over the horizon for the great American composer.

But which orchestra could be expected to play the music of emerging young composers who had points of view that were new to the mainstream scene? When the American composer Henry Gilbert wrote in 1918 that "Musical America is in the grip of Europe,"[25] he referred to the fact that all major conductors and musicians were from Europe and preferred the world of Beethoven and Brahms; such tastes ruled the concert roost. Aaron Copland, Roy Harris, and Roger Sessions, all still in their twenties, needed money to sponsor concerts in which their music could be heard.

Farsighted moneyed women now opened their purses: Gertrude Vanderbilt Whitney helped Varèse and Carlos Salzedo initiate the International Composers Guild in 1921; Alma Morgenthau Wertheim gave funds that helped bring about the League of Composers in 1923. These were two of the most prominent groups to sponsor modernist concerts. Also from the League of Composers sprang the influential monthly *Modern Music,* which gave heart to artists seeking to break away from European traditions.[26]

Whether it was a concert of the usual non-American music or one that brought new composers a chance to be heard, much was happening in 1921 to make the life of a newspaper music critic especially hectic. In those days a review of a concert, or the first performance of an opera, was published the next day. Since most concerts were in the evening, the critic had to race back to the office and dash off a review in time for the morning edition. Opera reviews posed special problems due to the length of the presentations. To make a deadline, the critic usually had to exit the opera house before the conclusion, so if in the final scene of *Aida,* the tomb collapsed on Aida and Radames from the weight of a hefty Amneris standing above them, the event would probably make the front page of the paper—but not the review.

Before the instruments started their tune-ups in late September, Taylor looked over what he might expect for the 1921–22 concert season. The Metropolitan Opera was figuratively draped in black: Enrico Caruso had died that August. Yet even without Caruso, Italians singers—Beniamino Gigli, Giuseppe DeLuca, Giovanni Martinelli—still dominated the male roster of the queen of American opera companies. There was nary an American star in sight. However, in the female ranks, Rosa Ponselle and Geraldine Farrar, both stars of the first magnitude born in the United States, matched the abilities of the Italian Claudia Muzio and the Spanish Lucrezia Bori.

As for the symphonic season ahead, a significant merger had occurred during the summer with the amalgamation of the New York Philharmonic and the National Symphony. The Philharmonic, with principal conductor Josef Stransky and associate Henry Hadley, had thus taken on the two National conductors, Willem Mengelberg from Amsterdam and Artur Bodansky of the Metropolitan Opera. "The National Symphony died and went to heaven," Taylor later wrote, "or at least was absorbed by the Philharmonic, together with its two conductors. . . . This gave the Philharmonic almost as many leaders as a South American army."[27]

Gotham's second major orchestra, the New York Symphony, remained intact, guided by its longtime conductor Walter Damrosch. However, many believed that neither orchestra could match the virtuosity of the visiting Philadelphia Orchestra, conducted by Leopold Stokowski, whose beautiful hands and striking profile captivated audiences. As for the recital season, Taylor saw that once again the great European instrumentalists would dominate and could be expected to fill Aeolian and Carnegie Halls with the likes of the violinists Fritz Kreisler and Jascha Heifetz, and the pianists Sergei Rachmaninoff, Ignacy Jan Paderewski, and Josef Hofmann.

Taylor's First Year as Music Critic

Taylor's first assignment as a *World* reviewer was not at the Metropolitan or Carnegie Hall. Instead, he had an aisle seat for an opera at the magnificent Manhattan Opera House, only several blocks from the Metropolitan. For years, Fortune Gallo's excellent San Carlo Opera Company had kicked off the New York music season, ahead of the Metropolitan and the orchestral season, with productions in this location. Taylor's first review was of a performance of Giuseppe Verdi's Egyptian spectacle, *Aida* (September 29, 1921):

> The San Carlo company's performance of "Aida" last night was not, perhaps, perfection, but it was a spirited one and on the whole extremely creditable. . . . The scenery was pretty bad, but it was so well lighted that it passed muster. It was a shock, though, to find that all the temples in the middle distance at Memphis were in ruins, even in those days. An added attraction of the evening was the Manhattan Opera House cat, who strolled across the stage with his hands in his pockets during the Nile scene to the delight of everybody [in the audience]. . . . It is said that he had been told by one of the stagehands that the cat was a sacred animal in Egypt, and immediately went out to see if there was any truth in the rumor. He is not expected to appear in "La Boheme" tonight.

It didn't take long for readers to sense that a talented and witty critic was now in their midst.

Once the orchestral season began, Taylor's reviews often concentrated on the international celebrities who appeared regularly in New York, such as Richard Strauss conducting the Philadelphia Orchestra in three of his own tone poems. Though Strauss was considered among the greatest living composers, what especially fascinated Taylor about him was his conducting style (November 1, 1921): "It is disconcerting to hear the orchestra mount through thunderous waves of sound and to see Strauss's right arm indicating a mild 'one-two, one-two' that is almost comically disproportionate to the gigantic results it evokes." Taylor later learned that what appeared to be an economy of gestures on Strauss's part was due to the orchestra's having been honed in the Strauss tone poems by Stokowski prior to the great composer's arrival.

In mid-November the Metropolitan Opera season opened for the first time in eighteen years without Enrico Caruso, and five days later Taylor described the impact of "a blond thunderbolt [that] swept out upon the stage of the Metropolitan like a flash of sunlight and caroled her way stormily into the hearts of the audience" (November 20, 1921). With these words, Taylor, ever the connoisseur of female beauty, introduced his readers to the Czech soprano Maria Jeritza in her Metropolitan debut opera, *Die Tote Stadt,* an opera written with her in mind by twenty-two-year-old Erich Wolfgang Korngold, who like the singer had been born in Brno, the capital of Moravia. "She is an actress of extraordinary grace, fire and emotional variety," continued Taylor. "She created the part of Marietta and she draws a portrait of this seductive and tempestuous wanton so detailed and authentic that it is difficult to imagine what 'Die Tote Stadt' would be without her. . . . Her voice is one of tremendous power and range and of considerable beauty, and she colors it wonderfully to express the mood of the moment."

Taylor also commented on Korngold's music, "a mixture of excellence and defects. . . . He is not yet an individual. His score is crammed with reminiscences not only of other men's themes but of other men's minds and reaction. He not only sounds like Puccini and Mendelssohn and Wagner and Bizet . . . he *is* each of these in turn." Here the neophyte did what all music critics love to do: seek out a composer's musical lineage and demonstrate to his audience that he could identify it. Taylor also commented on the composer's knowledge of the human voice: "[Korngold's] writing for the voice is generally bad . . . the soprano part is too high and the tenor part is too low."

As did all the major critics, Taylor supplemented his daily reviews with lengthy Sunday pieces in which he came to grips with major issues in the music world or expanded on an earlier review. In the first Sunday piece after Jeritza's sensational debut, he elaborated further on what he found wanting in Korngold's writing for the human voice. He spoke knowledgeably from his own experiences in writing cantatas and arranging folksongs. Here is Taylor the music teacher writing, a role he would continually embellish in his years as a critic (November 27, 1921): "Every singer has two registers . . . 'chest' and 'head.' Between the chest and head registers there is a break in the voice, which the singer works to conceal—two or three notes which may be sung either as head or chest tones and which are very hard to handle." He gave examples from the Korngold score that forced the singer into repeated notes in the voice break area. He explained that the voice of any singer, unlike other musical instruments, is subject to fatigue: "The result after four or five years of this sort of singing is a worn-out voice."

Two weeks later Taylor saw and heard Jeritza give her first American performance in the title role of Puccini's *Tosca,* an event that caused every future soprano in that role to seek out the cold floor of an opera house as a bosom companion while singing "Vissi d'Arte." Taylor's review of December 2, 1921, explains:

No one who saw Tosca last night is likely soon to forget her. Marie [*sic*] Jeritza made her first appearance in the title role . . . and gave a performance that left a packed house alternately breathless and cheering. . . . It was a performance that took small account of tradition. . . . Just before the "Vissi d'Arte" she crouched on the sofa, from which Scarpia roughly pushed her so that she half slid, half fell, to the floor. It was from this prone position that she sang the whole aria—a vocal feat as difficult as it was effective. Her voice was as beautiful as her acting. Only once or twice did she fall into her fault of "scooping" her high notes. But even then she scooped to conquer.

Taylor's strong sense of theater and music made his opera reviews glow; an example is his description of the acting of Feodor Chaliapin, the great Russian basso, who returned after a fourteen-year absence. The extremely tall Chaliapin provided New Yorkers with their first view of his monumental performance as Boris in Mussorgsky's *Boris Godunov*. As Taylor told it in his review of December 10, 1921:

> Feodor Chaliapin brings something to the opera that is greater than singing, greater than acting. He brings drama. . . . [He] must be the most stupendous stage personality in the world. There is no question of his creating an illusion. . . . When he gazed terrified across the palace chamber at the ghost of the murdered Dimitri, the audience turned startled eyes toward the spot at which he was gazing. And when they saw nothing there they turned again to the Czar, groveling on his knees by his chair, a tortured Rodin figure come to life, so huge, so pitiful—and wrung their hands and suffered his torment with him.

People working in the *World*'s city room late in the evening now became familiar with Taylor and looked forward to his sartorial splendor when he appeared, rushing back from the opera to write his review. Alfred Pessolano, then a copy boy, recalled the scene: "At the far end of this long room, doing his review and critique of an opera, sat Mr. Taylor, at a typewriter, in full dress and wearing a high top hat. . . . [He] made a very impressive sight, in the long unadorned City Room with reporters and editors plainly dressed in their shirt sleeves, but Mr. Taylor in full dress."[28]

It was soon clear to the *World*'s 400,000 readers that Taylor had a special gift with words. In many of his reviews, one or two sentences of unusual insight stood out, as can be seen in the following examples. On Beethoven's Third Symphony, "Eroica," performed by Pierre Monteux and the Boston Symphony, he wrote (November 4, 1921): "The funeral march was tragic, but it was not solemn: a dead hero, perhaps, but still a hero." Of Sibelius's Fifth Symphony, the New York premiere by Josef Stransky and the New York Philharmonic, he observed (November 11, 1921): "Whenever a new Sibelius work is played there is much talk of bleakness, and icy winds, and lonely pine trees, and grim crags, and similar 'furthest north' stage properties. There was little in last night's music to justify such arctic metaphors. Sibelius is not austere; he is plain—which is far from the same thing." And of Mozart's *Così fan tutte*, in its first U.S. performance at the Metropolitan, he declared

(March 25, 1922) "a musical comedy libretto with a score by Mozart that fits it like a glove."

On the whole, readers came to see that Taylor's judgments were reasonable and balanced. Taylor himself had experienced the thrust of the critic's pen and knew the importance of balance in a review. His philosophy was clear: "'Criticism' is not synonymous with faultfinding. A good critic is on the alert, not only for faults, but for merits. He must be capable, not only of disapproval, but of enthusiasm."[29] But as does every critic, Taylor had a composer whose music he was unable to discuss in a balanced way: Gustav Mahler.

Taylor reviewed the first U.S. performance of Mahler's symphonic song cycle *Das Lied von der Erde* (February 2, 1922): "The text is taken from a series of Chinese poems. . . . A great composer could begin where the words left off and create a work of overwhelming beauty and almost religious impressiveness. But Mahler was not a great composer." A year later, when the Philharmonic gave the first New York performance of Mahler's Seventh Symphony, Taylor lauded the playing as "beyond praise" (March 9, 1923), but not so the symphony. He spent the first half of the review piling fact upon fact—that the composer had conducted the first performance in Prague, that the symphony lasted one hour and a half, and that the scoring included a "tenor saxhorn in b flat [which] sounds rather like a trombone with adenoids." When he finally came to a musical evaluation of the work, he called it "the most stupid piece of music that we ever heard. . . . We found most of the themes not only incredibly banal, but vulgar; we found their development long-winded and inept, and we found the scoring scrappy, muddy and ineffective." He ended his review with this reminder: "There are six more Mahler symphonies that have not yet been heard in New York."

A possible reason for Taylor's annoyance with Mahler is that he disliked lengthy symphonies. As his own composing life evolved, he never attempted a symphony himself; his purely orchestral works all had brevity as a quality. In an unpublished poem, he bared his annoyance at composers who overstayed their welcome with symphonies that he considered overlong and often bombastic. In this case, he complained about Anton Bruckner (1824–96), Mahler's Austrian precursor:

> *Permit me, my friend, to explain*
> *Why Bruckner, to me, is a pain:*
> *He says his dull say*
> *In a rather dull way . . .*
> *Then he says it all over again.*[30]

Taylor ended his first season as music critic by providing Henry Finck's "much needed light": he wrote his overall opinion of the year's operatic performances, orchestral works, and recitals. To increase reader interest, he chose best of the year in several categories. His review of the orchestra season (April 16, 1922) named the Philadelphia Orchestra best ("It possesses a beauty and homogeneity of tone, a perfection of discipline"), Damrosch's New York Symphony second, and the Boston Symphony third. For orchestral works performed for the first time in New York, he gave Karol Szymanowski's Symphony No. 2 first place, and for second he chose Charles Martin Loeffler's setting for voice and orchestra of three Irish poems. But time has shown that performances of his third choice, Ravel's *La Valse,* and those of two also-rans—Vaughan Williams's *Fantasy on a Theme by Thomas Tallis* and dances from Manuel de Falla's *Three-Cornered Hat*—have far exceeded those of his favorites.

A week later (April 23, 1922), Taylor's five-thousand-word digest of the Metropolitan Opera season appeared and precipitated a rare congratulatory letter from his father: "That summary of the Metropolitan's season is a masterpiece. No music critic in this town ever took the trouble to do anything like it . . . covering the operas, the books, the singers, the staging, lighting, acting, conductors, manager."[31]

Indeed, Deems did a lively digest of facts: 37 operas received 177 performances; Verdi was the most popular composer, with 7 different operas performed; none was by an American composer. Of the 4 operas new to the Metropolitan stage, Taylor predicted long life for Mozart's *Così fan tutte* and Korngold's *Die Tote Stadt,* but he found little hope for Rimsky-Korsakov's *Snow Maiden* or Lalo's *Le Roi d'Ys.* Of the latter, he correctly wrote: "The best part of the score is the overture, but the Metropolitan Company insisted upon going further." Among new singers he praised Jeritza ("She is undoubtedly Caruso's successor as a popular favorite"), but found the first season of the famed soprano Amelita Galli-Curci "distinctly disappointing . . . for her voice sounded generally weak and she displayed her wonted tendency to flat."[32] He lauded Giulio Gatti-Casazza, the Met's general manager, for establishing an excellent company and attaining a financially successful season, with many sold-out performances.

However, Taylor balanced praise for the Metropolitan with criticism: "The company is not nearly so good dramatically as it is vocally," and the repertoire "not as interesting as it should be. . . . Who wanted 'Ernani' and 'Le Roi d'Ys' and 'Loreley'? Where were 'Le Coq d'Or,' 'The Girl of the Golden West,' 'Otello,' 'La Gioconda,' 'The Jewels of the Madonna,' 'Pelleas,' 'Falstaff'?" As a final criticism, he cited the Metropolitan's staging as its "weakest link," with "frequent inexcusable blunders in the handling of properties and lights and scenery," and "scenery [that] has been allowed to get unnecessarily shabby."

In the last of his Sunday pieces, he addressed the lack of American opera composers by noting that in this field it was necessary "to begin at the top," the Metropolitan Opera. There were no other companies where operas could be tried out, companies that took chances on composers. He argued, "What we need in New York is . . . an operatic company organized for the sole purpose of producing works that need neither a symphony orchestra nor a multitudinous cast to do them justice."[33] Through 1920 Gatti-Casazza's management had introduced just nine operas by American composers at the Metropolitan, and none of them had any lasting quality. From his pulpit as music critic for the *World,* Taylor continually recognized the potential to advance his own candidacy to become the Metropolitan's next opera composer.

Socializing, a Controversial Essay, and Paris

Exciting as the musical year had been for Taylor, his social life had the stamp of bachelor days. Mary did not have any particular interest in attending concerts, nor did she drink. She stayed in their apartment and occasionally offered friends the opportunity to try her modest culinary talents. FPA reported on one such event in his newspaper column: "So to the office and with D. Taylor . . . home, and he had me to stay to supper, which his wife cooked, and not bad neither, albeit there was more ham than was needed and not enough salad."[34] For Taylor, most mingling came with the Algonquin crowd, who even during Prohibition found liquor to be a significant cohesive force. As Donald Ogden Stewart saw it, "Prohibition also added immensely to the joie de vivre . . . [by drinking] you were defying that damned Puritanical law."[35] Now that Taylor worked at the *World* with Algonquin regulars Heywood Broun and FPA, socializing with them was natural.

Since Mary didn't imbibe, she stayed away from occasions that her husband sought out for enjoyment. On some afternoons, Taylor found himself and others of the Round Table in the art studio of Neysa McMein, a preeminent magazine illustrator of her day. The studio, on the same floor as Dorothy Parker's apartment at Sixth Avenue and Fifty-seventh Street, became a type of "Algonquin North" for afternoon gatherings—a large, communal space for the Algonks to carry on their daily exercises in New York badinage while McMein continued to paint, oblivious to the chatter.[36]

Some evenings, after his review had been written, Taylor headed for the home of Heywood Broun, with whom he shared a cubicle at work. Broun wrote his column "It Seems to Me" during the day, whereas Taylor more often worked at night. "Sharing an office with Heywood was like living with a glacier," he would observe years later. "His own desk was literally invisible, buried under a mountain of books, manuscripts, clippings, old newspapers, articles of apparel, and all the other nameless and shapeless objects that accumulate on the desk of a man who never throws away anything. Naturally, there was no question of his using his own typewriter. That was buried far too deep to be practicable. So he used mine. I wasn't in the office as much as he was, so the system worked better than it sounds."[37]

Taylor's friendship with Broun was one of the strongest he ever shared with a man, a friendship that blossomed in the after-hour sessions at Broun's Eighty-fifth Street brownstone. This had become the Broun home in 1921, thanks to the gambling offshoot of the Algonquin group, the Thanatopsis Literary and Inside Straight Poker Club, which for years met regularly on Saturdays. Broun, FPA, Woollcott, and Harold Ross were mainstays, as were Herbert Swope and Harpo Marx.

The purchase of the brownstone, according to Broun's son Heywood Hale "Woodie" Broun, "was made possible because Heywood had won a thousand dollars in a poker game."[38] Each of the three floors had one occupant. Ruth Hale, Broun's wife and a founding member of the Lucy Stone League, lived on the second floor, and Woodie was tucked away on the third. Heywood roamed around the first floor, welcoming such guests as Taylor and McNamara, the Singing Policeman. Alcohol flowed upward from the basement, served by a housekeeper. As liquor loosened inhibitions, arguments raged on many subjects. Years later, McNamara recalled a Broun put-down at the end of one argument. "Mac, it's a shame that with a voice like yours, you don't ever know what the hell you're talking about!"[39]

Discussions of every possible type took place at both the McMein apartment and the Broun home. A month before the concert season ended, Taylor himself became the subject of debate over a chapter he had written for a book grandiosely titled *Civilization in the United States: An Inquiry by Thirty Americans.* Harold Stearns, a brilliant Harvard-educated intellectual, was the editor. He had come to New York first as a newspaper writer, then become an editor of *Dial.* According to Stearns, the concept of the book began in a conversation he had with Van Wyck Brooks, a major literary critic of the time. Stearns then convinced some of the country's best writers and intellectuals to "illuminate by careful criticism the special aspect of that [American] civilization with which the individual is most familiar."[40] Stearns gathered his coworkers together in his Greenwich Village quarters. Among the others participating were H. L. Mencken ("Politics"), Lewis Mumford ("The City"), and George Jean Nathan ("The Theatre"). Van Wyck Brooks recalled that there were few group meetings "of these rebel intellectuals, so called, who were at the same time both bitter and hopeful."[41] Brooks himself supplied the chapter "The Literary Life." How Stearns came to choose Taylor for the "Music" essay is not known. Probably Mencken suggested him, since the influential Baltimorean had also suggested Taylor to Pulitzer for his music critic job.

After Stearns had edited all the chapters, he left for Paris in July 1921 to begin a stay of many years. *Civilization in the United States* appeared in 1922 and initiated a flood of critiques, especially in the magazines read by New York intellectuals. Most considered it significant and thought-provoking in its criticism of U.S. materialism and Puritanism, but far too negative in its assessment "that the America of 1922 is not safe for genius."[42] Nevertheless, it was "the book that inspired many dissatisfied young Americans to go abroad."[43]

Taylor's chapter revealed more bitterness than hope: "We spend more money upon music than does any other nation on earth. . . . There has never been a successful opera by an American offered at [the Metropolitan], and the number of viable American orchestral works is small enough to be counted almost upon one's fingers. We squander millions every year upon an art that we cannot produce."[44] He focused his attention on the American composer of "serious" music, a person he believed "not good enough" to write compositions of lasting importance, who "lacks taste," and who "doesn't know his business." He also believed the American composer to be inferior to "even the second-rate Continental composers."

The essay certainly indicated a Eurocentric thinking, a belief that there would never be American music up to the standards of Europe's, with its composers who expressed individual musical cultures with a nationalistic flair. The United States, apparently, was too heterogeneous to produce such creativity. He did not see this very heterogeneity as the eventual strength of American art; rather, Taylor saw the composer left with only one option: "The American must accept his lot. There is but one audience he can write for, and that is himself."[45]

Taylor was, of course, wrong. As Barbara Tischler pointed out in *An American Music,* many of the younger composers of Taylor's time "were among those who said that the Romanticism of the nineteenth century had played itself out and that new means of musical expression were needed. The emergence of new techniques and approaches to composition, all under the rubric of modernism, provided new opportunities for the American composer."[46] Taylor simply didn't seem to realize that such composers as Aaron Copland, George Antheil, and Roger Sessions would succeed in their new opportunities. His blinders came from his being highly introspective and largely self-taught. He did not seek friends among American composers, old or young; this was part of a self-sufficiency that he would exhibit throughout his life. Certainly he did not gain any friends with those harsh statements.

Nor did his essay gain friends among women. Taylor saw a danger in what he called the "feminization of music." He stated that "women constitute ninety per cent of those who support music in this country."[47] They were the majority in concertgoing, in choral singing, and in forcing "reluctant husbands and fathers to subscribe for opera seats and symphony concerts."[48] With women being the driving force in music as well as "the moral guardians of the race," Taylor argued that a musical Puritanism had resulted. The example he gave was an opera contest conducted by the National Federation of Music Clubs in 1914, a group composed almost entirely of women. The rules made clear that no libretto would be considered if it contained "immoral or suggestive" aspects. As Taylor pointed out, under those regulations the librettos for such operas as *Carmen* and *Tristan* would have been barred from the competition. He probably didn't win any friends in the National Federation either, since it happened to be the same group that had given him the award for *The Siren Song* seven years earlier.

Though some Puritanism did exist, Taylor underestimated the role of women in providing financial support for composers, as was occurring with the development of groups such as the International Composers Guild and League of Composers mentioned before. Certainly he was aware of the part played by Marian MacDowell, the widow of Edward MacDowell, in establishing the MacDowell Colony in New Hampshire. He had written *The Highwayman* for their summer program. Walter Damrosch, reflecting on both the past and the modernist present of the mid-1920s, had a more accurate and fair opinion: "I do not think there has ever been a country whose musical development has been fostered so almost exclusively by women as America."[49]

Taylor's well-written essay undoubtedly stimulated discussion in musical circles. It also marked him as a man with his musical feet in the past, negative about the modernist music. Nevertheless, by selecting him to write the chapter, Stearns added to Taylor's reputation as the country's leading writer-composer.[50]

Once Taylor learned that Swope had extended his contract for another year, he and Mary planned a lengthy summer vacation in Paris. They sailed on June 1. He couldn't wait to introduce her to the City of Light, and to see Paris without its wartime cloud. He also looked forward to sharpening his abilities in the French language he so loved, and to savoring postwar Paris's exceptional artistic energy, which had erupted with the century's greatest explosion of all the arts. Maurice Ravel, Erik Satie, Darius Milhaud, and Francis Poulenc provided French musical momentum, while the resident Russian expatriate Igor Stravinsky stimulated audiences with rhythmically bold and melodically daring compositions. Memories still remained of the tumultuous premiere of *Le Sacre du printemps* nine years earlier, danced by the still pioneering Ballets Russes of Sergey Diaghilev in a portrayal of barbaric pagan rites.

Paris also provided opportunities for the Taylors to satisfy their literary side and meet a great variety of writers. The city offered a comfortable and inexpensive habitat for writers who, for political or intellectual reasons, had determined to leave their homeland. James Joyce, Ernest Hemingway, F. Scott Fitzgerald, and Ezra Pound found acceptance there, and, for these and other writers, Sylvia Beach's bookstore, Shakespeare and Co., provided a place to congregate and ruminate over literary directions. Beach became a heroine to the literary crowd by publishing Joyce's then scandalous *Ulysses*. Since many of New York's literati thrived in Paris in the summer, chance meetings abounded at the bookstore or at the popular cafés.

At some point in their Paris stay, the Taylors met Edna St. Vincent Millay. She had been there for more than a year writing articles for *Vanity Fair*. The petite red-haired poet had already caught the attention of many Americans with her second book, *A Few Figs from Thistles,* and its quatrain "First Fig," which became an anthem for the rebellious youths of the twenties:

> My candle burns at both ends;
> It will not last the night;
> But ah, my foes, and oh, my friends—
> It gives a lovely light!

To what extent Taylor spoke with Millay at the time remains unknown. He did join in some escapades with Algonquin members who were visiting Paris. Edna Ferber recalled some of these doings years later: "In Paris that June I found Aleck Woollcott and Neysa McMein and Donald Ogden Stewart and Deems Taylor and Jane Grant. We whirled around together, we ate ices or drank aperitifs outside the Café Nationale, we saw the Russian Ballet at the Opera in that first tour which gave Scheherazade and Petrouschka to a bedazzled world."[51]

Understandably, shadows of the world war ended less than four years earlier could not be avoided. Woollcott, who had experienced France during the war's final year as a writer for *Stars and Stripes,* arranged a tour of battlefields for his friends, a visit that remained in Stewart's memory for years: "The important emotional product of this battlefield tour was an overwhelming rejection of any remaining romanticism on the subject of war."[52] In the fields they saw tips of bayonets visible above ground, their dead French owners having been buried alive when exploding German shells covered them with earth. In the graveyard of soldiers, Ferber recognized a curious democratic process: "Hundreds and thousands of little white crosses, the neatest imaginable, row on row, marked the new cemeteries of the French countryside. You had only to read the names to realize that really nothing could be more democratic. Karl Bauers. Tony Mazzetti. Leo Cohn. Joyce Kilmer. Ignace Prybzbyzski. . . . No arrangement could have been fairer."[53]

Besides the lengthy visit to Paris, Taylor had another reason for going to Europe: he had an appointment in July to visit Richard Strauss. The meeting would be at Strauss's summer home in the Bavarian town of Garmisch, and Taylor looked forward to seeing with his own eyes the domestic environment of the man who had written *Sinfonia Domestica,* the musical depiction of a day in the life of a husband, wife, and child.

When Taylor arrived in the village accompanied by Harry Osgood of the *Musical Courier,* he asked for directions to the famous composer's house, but few seemed to know anything at all about a composer in town. As it turned out, Strauss's "local fame seemed to rest chiefly upon the fact that he is the best skat [German card game] and pinochle player for miles around."[54] When they finally arrived at the walled residence, they found Strauss cordial and well tanned, pruning fruit trees. They conversed in the garden about the composer's recent tour of the United States, his first in seventeen years, and he indicated that he had found the orchestras he had conducted "excellent." As for the staging of the operas at the Metropolitan, he believed they lacked "dramatic instinct," but agreed with Taylor that some—"where the words are so important"—should be given in English. Frau Strauss interrupted their conversation to summon them in for tea. As the great composer entered the house, he carefully wiped his feet three times on succeeding doormats. This simple incident remained etched in Taylor's memory: "For in that moment I saw, for a flash, the truth. Here was no Titan or demigod; before me stood only a married man."[55]

By late July the Taylors were back in New York, two months before the music season opened. This gave Deems an opportunity to add another segment to the *Looking Glass* suite. While in Paris he had asked his wife's advice about orchestrating it for full orchestra. She urged him to do so, but also suggested he add a short piece depicting Alice in "The Garden of Live Flowers." He liked the idea, because a segment of musical chatter would nicely separate the reflective mood of the opening "Dedication" from the drama of "Jabberwocky." By September the newly orchestrated and augmented score was completed.

To have the fully orchestrated suite performed, Taylor approached Walter Damrosch, a dominating force in music for decades. Damrosch had conducted at the Metropolitan, convinced Andrew Carnegie to build his hall, and for thirty years had led the New York Symphony, an orchestra created by his father, Leopold, as the Damrosch Symphony. He was also a composer of operas, with his *Cyrano* performed six times at the Metropolitan in 1913. Damrosch loved New York, and he enjoyed playing works by American composers. After examining the score of *Looking Glass,* he guaranteed Taylor a performance the following spring. Until then, for Taylor it was back to work as a critic.

One of the first things he looked for on his desk when returning to the *World* was the Metropolitan's announcement of its season. There were to be forty operas for 1922–23, and Taylor wrote his appraisal of the company's choices, with specific mention of the lack of any American work (October 22, 1922):

> The Metropolitan Opera Company's announcement is out, with the grand, five-star final list of novelties and revivals for the coming season. And a pretty unexciting list it is. . . . Here in New York we have the largest and richest opera company in the world. Its activities are underwritten by a group of wealthy men whose combined fortunes reach a staggering sum . . . and what fresh fare does this richest opera company offer us in this year of our Lord 1922? It offers us two novelties, one by a German, one by an Italian . . . Nothing from France, nothing from Russia. . . . There are no operas announced to be sung in English, and no American revivals. Why not? Simply, adored reader, because the English-speaking portion of the Met audience (and that means the majority) takes no interest in hearing operas sung in English or in hearing operas by Americans.

It was a strange blend of chastising both the Metropolitan and its audience, but as time would tell, the powers behind the Gold Curtain were reading the *World* and trying to decide what to do about this very matter.

6. *The* World *Years, 1922–1923*

Modernist Music

"It is rather thrilling to hear a symphony orchestra after months of silence," Taylor wrote toward the beginning of his second season as the *World*'s critic (October 18, 1922). "There is nothing quite like those first waves of smooth, powerful, superhuman sound, so mysterious and so moving in their wordless eloquence." Of course, the waves were usually the very agreeable sounds of a Beethoven symphony or a Strauss tone poem, but the deeper Taylor entered the world of music criticism, the more he faced the surge of modernists, whose dissonance and atonality were increasingly influential. It had to be a problem for him, because as a composer he merged the romantic with the impressionist. Melody was essential to Taylor's way of thinking: "We all want tunes. Of course we don't admit it, or call them tunes. We talk of 'flowing melodic line,' or 'pregnant melos' or 'thematic material of deep significance,' but tunes we mean. Every viable musical composition ever written has survived only because it contains one or more musical phrases . . . that can be remembered" (December 11, 1921). Taylor never retreated from this belief, but he did temper his criticism of the modernists by acknowledging that they were composers who believed as deeply in their work as he did in his own.

In a Sunday piece before the concert season began in fall 1922, Taylor noted that the Hungarian conductor Fritz Reiner, newly arrived in the United States, had told an interviewer that he believed the future of music "rests in the hands of the youngest and most radical composers including

[Arnold] Schoenberg . . . [whose] later works, such as the 'Five Orchestral Pieces,' are so difficult to play and to hear that most of the great music centers prefer to talk about them. Schoenberg must be played well in order to be at all comprehensible. Hearing him played badly is worse than not hearing him at all" (October 1, 1922).

Reiner's thoughts puzzled Taylor, because the previous season he had heard the Philadelphia Orchestra under Stokowski perform the *Five Orchestral Pieces* in a "brilliant" manner. "Yet the better the orchestra played," Taylor wrote in concluding the piece, "the worse Schoenberg seemed to sound. However, we must confess to a sneaking and slightly morbid curiosity to hear them again—merely, we add hastily, to see whether they could possibly sound as bad as we thought they did." Taylor apparently was joined by the majority of the audience in a similar criticism. Even Paul Rosenfeld, the *Dial* critic who usually boosted modernist composers, wrote that "[t]he assemblage sat like patients in dentist chairs, submitting resignedly to a disagreeable operation."[1] (It should be noted that New York often lagged behind in bringing modernist music to the concert stage; the Schoenberg work had been heard in Boston six years earlier.)

But there was another Schoenberg that Taylor did admire, as he explained in his December 13, 1922, review of *Verklärte Nacht,* composed by Schoenberg before he had moved dramatically toward atonality:

> One wonders what Mozart would have thought of "Verklärte Nacht." The masterly writing for the six instruments he would most certainly admire. Nor would he mind the occasionally drastic harmonies. For the work is early Schoenberg, a Schoenberg who was writing with his heart instead of with his mind, as he came, unhappily, to do later; and Mozart, who was a bit of an innovator himself in his day, would be quick to sense the superb form and musical logic of the work. . . . What a pity that Schoenberg should have ceased being the George Moore of music to become its James Joyce.

Taylor's literary tussles with modernist music persisted throughout his *World* years, then resurfaced when he became the intermission commentator of the New York Philharmonic Sunday afternoon broadcasts.

Broadway Summons Taylor

The success of the *Liliom* incidental music brought more offers for incidental music to dramas. Now feeling more assured of his *World* work, Taylor agreed to compose for three Broadway productions planned for spring 1923. He was especially pleased when the theatrical producer Winthrop Ames asked him to compose songs for *Will Shakespeare,* a three-and-a-half-hour epic on the life of the Bard of Avon. Ames had the highest respect of theater people because of his elegant taste in productions and his low-key manner. Ames needed songs to be sung in a tavern by a group of wandering singers, who included Katherine Cornell on her way to becoming a Broadway luminary. Robert Benchley, then the drama critic for *Life,* reviewed the opening of the play and found the music appealing: "Deems Taylor has written some very catchy songs for [the strolling singers] . . . but in common with all Elizabethan 'hey-nonny' singers on the stage, they give the impression of having had glee-club rehearsals every Tuesday and Thursday night since August to prepare for this one burst of spontaneous song."[2] For *Humoresque,* the Fannie Hurst tearjerker about a young, talented violinist who is killed in the Great War, Taylor set to music Alan Seeger's poem "I Have a Rendezvous with Death."

The third production presented a greater challenge: the Theatre Guild was to present Elmer Rice's *Adding Machine,* one of the greatest satires of business ever shown on the American stage. Rice modeled his play on German expressionism, then currently in vogue as a means of distorting events for emotional effect. To echo the dullness of the office work routines of the characters, he gave them names such as Mr. and Mrs. Zero, Mr. One, Mrs. Two, and Boss. The central character, Mr. Zero, a bookkeeper who crunches numbers with a pencil, is thrown out of his job when Boss purchases adding machines. Lashing out against the perceived inhumanity of the change, Zero kills Boss. He is executed after a trial, then experiences Purgatory followed by Heaven ("Elysian Fields"), and finally a reincarnation. Audiences left the theater more than a bit puzzled.

Taylor composed music to be played by a string quartet during three scenes: the murder, the graveyard, and Zero in the Elysian Fields. But after he had written the requested music for the Elysian Fields scene, the director changed his mind. "A few days before the opening," Rice recalled in his autobiography, "Moeller [the director] decided he wanted music throughout the scene, which ran for half an hour, putting upon Taylor the task of producing quickly a great amount of music. I supplied him with a bottle of whiskey and left him alone in my hotel room to work against time. He did the job, but Moeller changed his mind again and most of the new music was never used. Taylor had reason to be resentful, but he took it all in good part."[3] If nothing else, Taylor prided himself on being a fast worker!

Siren Song Finally Performed

As a composer and music critic, it was only a matter of time until Taylor faced a dilemma: whether to review a performance of one of his own works.

Early in 1923 the predicament arose when Henry Hadley, the first U.S.-born conductor of importance, programmed *Siren Song*. Hadley had helped found both the Seattle Symphony and the San Francisco Symphony, but despite his qualifications, major American orchestras still looked to Europe for their musical leaders. He did take a significant upward step in 1921, when the New York Philharmonic board agreed to appoint him its associate conductor. A composer himself, Hadley recognized an unusual opportunity to help others gain acknowledgment of their works by including at least one composition by a contemporary American on every program he conducted.

Hadley's missionary work for American composers began the following year, when the New York Philharmonic became the resident orchestra for New York's first outdoor summer concerts. While Andrew Carnegie had given the city its finest concert hall, the philanthropist Adolph Lewisohn built a stadium on the City College of New York campus in northern Manhattan. He then funded summer concerts at the site that later became known as Lewisohn Stadium. Every evening for six weeks, a different stadium concert drew large audiences, often close to ten thousand people. Though other conductors shared the podium with Hadley, he had to conduct more than a dozen concerts himself. Since he wanted new American works to play throughout the summer, he asked many composers for new works. When the request came to Taylor, he provided Hadley with a revised *Siren Song,* the score that a decade earlier had won him the top award of the National Federation of Music Clubs.

Hadley conducted the premiere on July 18, 1922, while the Taylors were still in Europe. He liked the score so much that he programmed it again six months later, during the Philharmonic's regular season. It was for this Carnegie Hall concert that Taylor had to answer the question: Should I review my own work? Of course, the obvious answer would be no. But he remembered something from his NYU days: his senior thesis had been on George Bernard Shaw, who now unknowingly showed him the way to write the review (January 12, 1923):

> The novelty of the evening was another of the American works that Henry Hadley is introducing this month, a symphonic poem, "The Siren Song," by Deems Taylor. The work was written in 1912. . . . As George Bernard Shaw points out in the preface to "The Irrational Knot," human beings are entirely renewed every seven years, so that an author may properly treat a twenty-year-old novel of his own as the work of a stranger. Such being the case, perhaps a reviewer may be similarly distant toward his own eleven-year-old symphonic

poem. So far as we are concerned, "The Siren Song" is virtually a posthumous work, written by a young man. . . . We thought it a promising work with a certain freshness of feeling and a disarming simplicity of utterance that partly atoned for its lack of well-defined individuality. . . . On the whole, "The Siren Song" interested us. We should like to hear more works by the same composer.

Richard Aldrich of the *Times*, a more objective reviewer, was quite enthusiastic: "Mr. Taylor's music is itself poetical, highly imaginative at points, pictorially suggestive. . . . The composition as a whole is of striking beauty and effectiveness, the product of a melodic invention none too common in an arid time."[4] Still, so far as is known, *The Siren Song* was never heard again.

Ten days later, Taylor's Sunday piece evaluated the first half of the concert season (January 21, 1923): "The musical year is about half over and it has not been a particularly exciting one. What we have missed more than anything else has been new orchestra music of outstanding importance." Perhaps this paucity of inspiration was the reason Taylor decided to leave his native city in midwinter and go to the even colder Midwest for several weeks, seeking musical warmth among their symphony orchestras. It was an inspired trip, because he would be the first of New York's music critics to acknowledge that bountiful bouquets of music awaited west of the Hudson River.

A Unique Journey: Orchestras of the Midwest

On January 31, 1923, Taylor initiated his two-week train journey to hear and report on concerts of six major orchestras of the Midwest: Cleveland, Cincinnati, Chicago, Detroit, Minneapolis, and St. Louis. Of these, only the Cleveland Orchestra had given concerts in New York City, and those very rarely. For the average New York concertgoer, the quality of Midwest orchestras was unknown. Throughout the trip, he sent back daily detailed accounts of the people he met and what he heard, stories that gave *World* readers a new view of music in the rest of the country.

The orchestra conductors he met were pleased to have a New York critic report on their performances. Fritz Reiner, the new conductor of the Cincinnati Symphony, who had previously appeared to be at odds with Taylor's view of modern music, took special pleasure in welcoming the writer. After the Cincinnati concert, the Reiners hosted him at their home. Taylor knew, of course, that close ties with conductors also benefited him in the long run, for when they sought new works to perform, they might think to ask the composer Deems Taylor. That is exactly what happened in Chicago, where the symphony's longtime conductor Frederick Stock invited Taylor to return another year and conduct one of his compositions himself.

Of the daily assessments that Taylor sent home, it was his five-thousand-word summary article, "The Orchestra Next Door" (February 18, 1923), that raised the eyebrows of East Coast orchestral sophisticates. He shared with them examples of fresh programming ideas he had encountered, such as a Reiner concert that "contained no symphony, nothing by the three Bs [Bach, Beethoven, Brahms], nothing . . . [earlier] than the end of the nineteenth century; and it was one of the most fascinating programs I ever heard." He also cited dozens of compositions that had rarely, if ever, been heard in New York, another indication that his hometown didn't have a lock on music. Finally, he gave his assessment of how the orchestras of the Midwest compared with those of the East:

> For, after painstakingly making all possible allowance for the fact that first impressions are not necessarily trustworthy and that the unfamiliar is often more impressive than the accustomed—even so, I cannot help feeling that the East can teach the Middle West very little about symphonic music. . . . I did hear the Chicago Orchestra, which seemed to me easily equal as regards purity of tone and perfection of ensemble to anything we have in the East. . . . The players themselves seem imbued with a spirit totally different from the air of conscious competence that emanates from the average Eastern orchestral musician.
>
> . . . Incidentally, our Eastern orchestras have not always made the most favorable impression in the world when their travels have taken them into the Middle West. I heard a good deal of adverse comment. . . . Some people still remember a concert given [in Cleveland] by a New York Orchestra two or three seasons ago, when, during a symphony slow movement . . . one of the trombone players sat at his desk for ten minutes in full sight of the audience reading a newspaper.

Taylor's concluding words spoke wisely of the future: "The Middle West is extravagant and young, and thirsty, and eager. The East is 'cultured' and middle-aged and self-satisfied. They still come to us for the final stamp of approval; but the hope for the future lies with them unless we bestir ourselves. We guard the flame. They fan it."

Through the Looking Glass **for Full Orchestra**

On March 11, 1923, only a month after his return from the Midwest, Taylor went to Aeolian Hall, as he had done four years earlier almost to the day, to hear his *Through the Looking Glass* suite. But this time it was the full orchestra version in its premiere performance, as promised by Walter Damrosch and the New York Symphony. Taylor had provided his own program notes, identifying "Lewis Carroll's immortal nonsense fairy tale" as the basis of his music, "and the five pictures it presents will, if all goes well, be readily recognizable to lovers of the book." The suite still began with "Dedication," the melodically gentle depiction of Carroll's "child of the pure unclouded brow and dreaming eyes of wonder!" But then, with no interruption the new segment was introduced, the skittery conversation in the "Garden of Live Flowers," followed by the bassoon-driven "Jabberwocky," frenetically buzzing "Looking-Glass Insects," and sadly heroic "White Knight."

Much to the composer's satisfaction, reviewers were even more positive than those for the original chamber orchestra version. Typical was the opinion of Richard Aldrich, the veteran *Times* critic, who told his readers that they needn't fear modernism in Taylor's music: "He is not in the new movement. He not only can write melodies, but does. . . . He has skill in orchestration; and altogether he fills his music with a feeling for beauty as well as with humorous descriptive touches."[5] The suite's reception spurred interest throughout the orchestra world.

A year later, in 1924, the two-year-old Hollywood Bowl summer concerts premiered it on the West Coast. Both Leopold Stokowski and Willem Mengelberg, major driving forces in music, programmed the suite with the Philadelphia Orchestra (1924) and New York Philharmonic (1925), respectively. Henry Woods introduced it to Great Britain at an August Promenade concert in Queen's Hall in 1925. British reviewers, particularly in the *London Times,* seemed annoyed that an American would attempt to translate Lewis Carroll's masterpiece into music: "In the movement called 'Jabberwocky' . . . at the monster's appearance, [the composer] starts off a ridiculous fugue, which sounds like something by Bach gone wrong and orchestrated in modern style by one who shall be nameless. For the rest, the music succeeded only in being turgid—which Lewis Carroll never was, even in his mathematical treatises."[6] But Americans enjoyed the suite, making it one of the most performed works by an American composer in its time. As one indication of this, Frederick Stock and the Chicago Symphony programmed *Through the Looking Glass* every year for ten years straight.

Taylor, though bolstered by the reception to his suite, at the end of the

1922–23 music season was apathetic about what he had heard over the preceding months. Concerning important new orchestral music, he did find Delius's *On Hearing the First Cuckoo of Spring* "a lovely bit of tone painting" (April 29, 1923). But the Metropolitan Opera disappointed him, having produced neither an outstanding production nor an American opera. "If one rates an opera company," he told his readers, "according to the language that predominates at its performances (and this seems fair), it is evident that the Met, despite the large number of American singers on its roster, is an Italian opera company" (April 22, 1923). He would not let the Metropolitan forget his belief that they should do more for American composers—and the English language.

With the completion of his second season as music critic, Deems Taylor found continued editorial acceptance of his approach to criticism. Herbert Bayard Swope, still the executive editor, in a touch of unusual largesse, gave him a five-hundred-dollar bonus and a contract for two more years. However, he didn't raise his salary.

The Swopes of Great Neck

Taylor's ego had been nicely stroked in the spring of 1923 with performances of *Siren Song* and *Looking Glass,* but Mary's also needed uplifting. She returned to the stage as a French maid in *The Love Habit,* an Americanized French farce that ran for two months. Toward the end Florence Eldridge left the play, and for the first time Mary Kennedy gained a lead role. Thanks to all these enriching experiences, the Taylors entered the summer of 1923 in high spirits, enhanced further by weekends at the Swopes' Great Neck estate, a gargantuan three-story structure with twenty-seven rooms and eleven and a half baths. There the *World's* editor and his wife, Margaret, lavished food, drink, and entertainment on their guests, principally the Algonquin crowd and friends from Tin Pan Alley and the Broadway stage. Literary friendships also blossomed at the Swopes', for it was there in October 1923 that Taylor first met F. Scott Fitzgerald. At the time, Scott and Zelda rented a home adjoining the Swopes' to the south, and what Fitzgerald saw and enjoyed was the embryo that grew into *The Great Gatsby.*

The rich and famous saturated the Great Neck area. Ring Lardner owned the property bordering the Swopes' on the north, while to the northwest were the homes of George M. Cohan and Sam Harris, the Broadway producer and Cohan's partner. Farther to the west lived Groucho Marx and Ed Wynn, while across the inlet on another of the fingers of land jutting into the Long Island Sound were the homes of Eddie Cantor and the longtime ASCAP president Gene Buck. Dotted about were mansions of prominent families: Astor, Harkness, Guggenheim, Loew, Frick, Kahn. If a summer tidal wave had swamped the Sound inlets, it would have wiped out most of the financial United States as well as Broadway's best.[7]

But it was the Swope estate where writers and Broadway people gathered as preferred guests. The songwriter Howard Dietz remembered Margaret Swope as the hostess who set up housekeeping "on a grand scale. She engaged two shifts of servants. If you happened to be hungry at 4 in the morning, you could get a steak. Everybody drifted Swopeward."[8] It was a style and ambiance that Taylor, in a letter to Woollcott, referred to as "living like Swopes."[9]

Besides food, croquet kept many of the guests occupied from Friday to Monday. Swope, a competitor from toes to head, loved the game. The normally nonathletic Woollcott also found it to his liking, initiating a vicious competition with the editor both in daytime and after dark. One evening the neighboring Lardners sat on their porch, chatting with Dorothy Parker and Marc Connelly, when they noticed something unusual: cars seemed to be lining up to leave even though it wasn't even ten o'clock at night, a time when the Swopes usually started to serve dinner. Ring Lardner Jr. later described what his parents observed: "The cars were being arranged so all the headlights converged on the croquet court, and full realization dawned when they heard the familiar daytime sound of mallet striking ball."[10] Woollcott, in typical fashion, wrote an article about his croquet experiences, calling it "With Mallets toward None."

Swope's son, Herbert Jr., was in his preteen years then, and recalls meeting visitors such as Jascha Heifetz, Helen Hayes, and Boris Karloff, all gathered in the large living area where everyone gossiped, ate, and drank, while at the piano would be George Gershwin, Irving Berlin, Oscar Levant, or Taylor, "a delightful man, with a bright little face with glasses."[11] Mary Kennedy accompanied her husband to many weekends at Great Neck and wrote in her journal that "[Swope] filled his house at this time with everybody who was talked about or working on important jobs. To be left out of Swope's list was to argue yourself unknown. He was fond of us. Deems was his direct antithesis—quiet, shy, small voiced, but always standing up to him, and giving him what he adored, a chance for intelligent conversation."[12]

The Taylors Buy an Old Connecticut Home

Taylor the bon vivant thrived at the Swopes', but summer was not all play for him. He had committed himself to compose a ballet pantomime for the new Katherine Cornell play, *Casanova,* which was slated for a late September opening. Peggy Wood, one of the original Round Table members and friend to both Mary and Deems, invited the composer to come to the rolling hills of Stamford, Connecticut, where she and her husband, the poet John V. A. Weaver, had purchased a run-down farm. She promised him the peace and quiet he needed to finish the *Casanova* score. Deems accepted the offer, worked hard during the week, then welcomed his wife to join him on the weekends.

Peggy Wood lost no time in trying to persuade Deems and Mary of the glories of owning a Connecticut farm, particularly the joys of taking a run-down old home and remodeling it. As the carpenter side of Taylor clicked in, the pep talk worked. With the help and advice of a realtor, the Taylors soon found themselves gazing at a home Deems later described as

> a typical Connecticut farmhouse of the late 18th or early 19th cen-
> tury, built on the side of a hill, two stories and a half high at one end
> and three and half at the other, and there was a large chimney stick-
> ing out of the exact center of the ridgepole. We went inside, and
> found ourselves in a long, narrow room devoted to the storing of
> chicken feed. For no particular reason we went down the cellar
> steps into a large, evil-looking room filled with broken harness,
> cobwebs, and more chicken feed. . . . I opened a hinged board par-
> tition at one side of the room, and caught a glimpse of an immense,
> disused stone fireplace. The lath and plaster hung loose from a cor-
> ner of the ceiling. . . . We turned and left; and, as we reached the
> yard, I heard, to my bewilderment and horror, a voice saying, "Let's
> take it." It was my voice.[13]

The property was on Haviland Road, a country way wandering over the mild undulations of tree-covered earth in an area of northern Stamford some five miles north of the train station. From the house, perched on the highest point of the property, one looked north to Hunting Ridge, where Heywood Broun and Ruth Hale would soon plant their rural feet. Down from the house was a marshy area that provided plenty of room for croaking frogs and hatching mosquitoes. The Taylors named their nineteen-acre Connecticut retreat Hollow Hill.

Before Taylor could transform some of the rooms with his carpentry skills, the first summer's work required "scraping off several generations of wall paper and gray paint, uncovering the fireplaces, and abolishing board partitions."[14] Most of the time Taylor did the work without Mary, who had little interest in restructuring a home. One thing he desperately needed was an automobile, because after a train and taxi had brought him to the house from New York, how else was he go to stores for needed materials or take away all the trash? Somehow his plight found its way to the ears of Antoinette

Perry Frueauff, who answered his country prayers. Continuing her friend-ship from the days of *What Next!* she presented Deems with an old Ford sta-tion wagon.[15] By summer's end the house had running water pumped from the well, but much remained to be done before it could be termed livable.

When the warm days had passed, making money again became the cen-tral issue for the Taylors. In addition to their New York apartment, they now had the added joys of mortgage payments, repair costs, and property taxes. Taylor sequestered himself in the city after Labor Day to finish the *Casanova* music. The results were more than satisfactory, for when the play opened in late September, an apparently stimulated John Corbin of the *Times* hailed the ballet pantomime, choreographed by Michel Fokine, as "a thing of exquisite fancy, redolent of sensual love in carnival, rhythmic with aphrodisiac pain and longing."[16] (The music was published years later as Ballet Music from *Casanova*.)

Meanwhile, in spite of enjoyable times together at the Swopes' and the excitement of buying their own home, something was going awry between Mary and Deems. Perhaps it was the emotions of becoming landed gentry with the added expenses, or simply the fact that they seldom had private time together. Whatever it was, Donald Ogden Stewart, who socialized reg-ularly with them, recognized a problem during a September visit. When he wrote to thank Mary for her hospitality, he told her of his concern: "My, my—how full your life is of many, many things—but don't you sometimes think, little girl, that after all your true function is to make a cozy little 'nest' for Mr. Taylor? . . . I am a very poor judge of such things because I suppose that really at bottom you and Deems care for each other and will work your problems out . . . and I hope that some day our paths may cross under per-haps happier circumstances. My kindest regards to your husband. I hope he goes on with his music for I believe that he has a real 'gift.'"[17]

Stewart's last comment suggests the issue may have centered on Mary's belief that her husband was not pursuing his composing talent sufficiently. Nothing gave her more pride in him than his music, something she expressed in a letter sent to him in Baltimore while he was with the pre-Broadway *Casa-nova:* "I am sure your 'Casanova' will be a brilliant success, and I will have more brilliantine to add to my plumage."[18] Clearly she saw his success as also enhancing her standing. In fact, they both were seeking accomplishments in their own rights, and competition can be at the heart of many a lovers' spat. Whatever set them apart, it was not the last of their difficulties.

7. *The* World *Years, 1923–1924*

A Murderous Review

While her husband returned to his role as music critic, Mary tried to keep busy with playwriting. But with evenings mainly spent alone, she became frustrated and decided to return to the stage. Through her excellent Broadway connections she gained a major part in a new mystery thriller, *In The Next Room*. (One of the coauthors, Eleanor Robson, later married August Belmont and became the first woman member of the Metropolitan Opera board.) The play opened in late November to stellar reviews. A five-month Broadway run was followed by a lengthy tour. Mary had her wish and was busy until the following summer.

Taylor began his season as always, by surveying the offerings of the Metropolitan. Its announcement of the 1923–24 season showed him that his efforts to prod the Metropolitan Opera into producing American works had not borne fruit. He told his readers that he saw a dreadful sameness in every aspect of the company, nothing to create excitement (October 14, 1923): "The list of singers is much the same. . . . The new scenery will be in the same hands. . . . There are no new conductors or stage managers. . . . The trouble is that our opera house is too good and too successful. It enjoys a social monopoly, and it makes money, and its achievements are not seriously challenged."

The excitement began in early October, when the eccentric Russian pianist Vladimir de Pachmann, once the butt of Huneker's critical jibes, arrived for his first New York recital in twelve years. The overflow audience cheered when the seventy-five-year-old artist walked onto the Carnegie Hall stage. Taylor's review described him as "a chunky little old man with a head something like Franz Liszt's portraits [with] the same high forehead, eagle nose and long gray hair" (October 12, 1923). Though generally admired for his interpretations of Chopin's music, Pachmann still continued the peculiar habit of chatting with his audience while he performed. This charmed many that night but irritated others, especially Taylor.

He started his review with jolting words: "Three thousand people saw murder done last night in Carnegie Hall. No, that won't do for a beginning. It is the truth, but it sounds too sensational, blurted out like that." He decried the pianist's well-known ploy of beginning to play, then stopping to make asides, most of which were audible solely to the occupants of the first few rows, people who then laughed nervously like children listening to a rather juicy little story. Taylor couldn't restrain his critical anger:

> And so de Pachmann played the adagio from Beethoven's pathetic [*sic*] sonata. It is short, and very simple—just a tune, really; and only a great man could have written it. For it has the miraculous power of suggestion that all great art possesses. It pleases the imagination. It links you for the moment with eternal things; you glimpse something of the vast beauty and sadness of life. And in the middle of it the little man raised his hands and beat time and grinned at the audience and said something. And the man in the row behind one laughed aloud, and then everybody giggled. . . . And Beethoven died and went to hell, and everybody was frightfully amused at Mr. de Pachmann.

Even the *World*'s Ralph Pulitzer wrote to congratulate Taylor on the "admirable de Pachmann criticism,"[1] but Alexander Woollcott, another critic of the arts and Taylor's Algonquin friend, couldn't let the comments go unanswered. He also had attended the concert and sat "so close that it was possible to hear every groan and every chuckle, possible to see every gesture of hand and shoulder." Woollcott found the concert "a dramatic performance," and thus within his domain, as a theater critic, for commentary. What he saw and heard engrossed him completely, and he did not appreciate the critical "bricks" hurled by Taylor and others. He trumpeted that Pachmann's actions emanated from the pianist's very nature. "After all," Woollcott wrote, "it is a part of de Pachmann, and one did not come away from [Sarah] Bernhardt's last 'Camille' denouncing her for being a grandmother with a wooden leg." Woollcott even suggested that the mutterings of the pianist were truly prayers to God.[2] Knowing how Woollcott loved to goad his fellow Round Tablers, Taylor refused to take up the challenge and do battle.

A month later, Pachmann returned to New York for another recital. Since Taylor had to review *Madame Butterfly* at the Metropolitan the same evening, he did not go to hear the pianist this time, but next morning he read the *Tribune*'s review by Francis Perkins: "Mr. de Pachmann's silence was the feature of his second recital last night at Carnegie Hall, such silence as, it was said, had not reigned for many a year. Whatever the cause of this silence, the veteran pianist addressed his audience only through his piano in a program devoted entirely to Chopin, which was pleasing for those who had come for purely musical reasons. . . . His performance of some of the numbers on last night's program would have been hard to rival." When the concert concluded, "not a word had been spoken—the recital had actually been a piano recital."[3] A satisfied grin must have crossed Taylor's face.

Four days later, Wanda Landowska walked onto the Carnegie Hall stage for a concert that brought the harpsichord into the modern era. Accompanied by Stokowski and the Philadelphia Orchestra, the petite Polish woman played concertos by Bach, Handel, and Mozart. It was the first two concertos that she played on a harpsichord, an instrument that most in the audience, including Taylor, had never before heard. "She is a greatly gifted player," he wrote, "equipped with a finger technique whose velocity and surety are remarkable even in this day of technical prodigies. . . . The instrument that Mme. Landowska plays is not the transmogrified piano that passes muster for a 'harpsichord' as at most modern concerts of ancient music, but a genuine reconstruction of the sort of instrument upon which Bach and Haendel played" (November 21, 1923). In putting the harpsichord at center stage, this concert may well have helped develop the current fascination with baroque music.

Despite his predictions, by mid-season Taylor observed that the Metropolitan's productions had gained both physical luster and unusually fine singing. Though he had recently called the Metropolitan an "Italian opera company" for its heavily Italian repertoire, Taylor now expressed his unending gratitude for an exceptional production of *Die Meistersinger von Nürnburg,* populated mainly by American and Italian singers. The critic loved Wagner's lyric masterpiece: "If we were told that every opera on earth were to be destroyed save one, and that we were delegated to pick that one, we should pick 'Die Meistersinger' without a moment's hesitation. . . . It breathes a spirit of tolerant humor and mellow humanity that is almost unequaled in dramatic literature" (November 11, 1923). Thinking back to his early season concerns about the Metropolitan's quality, he admitted that he had "never dreamed that it could be so much fun to be wrong." There was a basic fairness in Taylor's bones.

While deep into another season of reviews, Taylor remained committed to honing his talents as a composer as well as performing his critical responsibilities. However, on one occasion his writing and composing talents collided in what could have proven fatal to his *World* career. It happened because Jane Cowl, a major Broadway actress, decided to produce an English version of Maeterlinck's *Pelléas et Mélisande* drama. With fourteen scene changes, Cowl needed music to cover the stage resettings and, knowing Taylor's abilities, asked him to provide it. He accepted the challenge and chose segments from the Debussy opera based on the Maeterlink play, arranging his choices as string quartet interludes.

Eager to hear the results of his partnership with Debussy, Taylor looked forward to the opening night of December 4, only to learn that on the same evening he was scheduled to review a piano recital by the popular Russian-born pianist Mischa Levitzki. He looked over a copy of the pianist's Carnegie Hall program and realized he had previously heard Levitzki play every one of the programmed pieces. A perfect solution to his problem came to mind: he would write a review beforehand and have a friend attend the concert in his place. Then after the *Pelléas* performance, they would meet and Taylor would show his prewritten review to his friend. If the friend found the review adequate, Taylor would wire it to the *World*.

The plan worked perfectly. After attending the Cowl play he met his friend, who approved the review, and off it went. Two days later he received a summons from the editor, and when he reached the office he noticed a small pile of letters scattered about Swope's desk. Taylor later recalled that the next portion of the interview was a "rather spirited monologue, delivered, with gestures, by my revered employer."[4] Swope indicated that all the letters asked the same question: Why had Taylor written a glowing review of Levitzki's "lucent and imaginative reading of the Chopin [B minor] sonata,"[5] when in fact Levitzki had played the Schumann G-minor sonata? A red-faced Taylor had been caught faking information, the mortal sin of reporting. All he could do was level with the editor. He confessed that his musical ego had overwhelmed his journalistic one, then gave an explanation: Levitzki had changed his program at the last minute, and his friend, somehow missing the announcement, had probably slept through the sonata.

No doubt it was only Taylor's overall reputation in Swope's eyes that saved him that day. However, such a juicy story quickly made its way around the music community. Years later when the story reached Andre Kostelanetz, then a star conductor of radio orchestras, it had become totally transformed into falsehood. In this version Taylor was actually fired from the

World for having skipped a performance of *Aida* at the Metropolitan but sent in a review of same, only to discover the next day that *Faust* had been substituted at the last moment![6]

Stravinsky's *Rite of Spring* Arrives

With modern music and its dissonances making more frequent appearances on programs, Taylor found opportunities to expand on the possible musical virtues in such pieces. It must be remembered that many of the creations of European composers found their way slowly, and not necessarily chronologically, across the Atlantic. For example, Stravinsky's four-year-old *Song of the Nightingale* preceded his eleven-year-old *Rite of Spring* to the New York stage by several months. When Taylor heard the former in its U.S. premiere, he praised it as "a masterpiece . . . [of] 'modern' music in the most extreme sense of the word." Though he considered it "ugly enough at times," he also found that "its most excruciating dissonances convey a sense of logic and inevitability." He compared it to "other modern music whose chief characteristic seemed to be a willful and deliberate ugliness" (November 3, 1923).

Taylor was willing to give the modernist composers their due, but within limits. As he heard more and more of the live performances of modernist works, he attempted to explain how these works differed from the European musical past. In a lengthy Sunday piece of December 9, 1923, he emphasized his belief that music affects principally the listener's emotions, not the intellect:

> Music is a language, but not for ideas. It reaches the emotions, or the spirit, if you like, through a series of sounds that are essentially meaningless, so far as concerns the intellect. . . . Consequently when the rebellious modern composer dares us to give him any good reason why he should not write in four keys simultaneously, and three kinds of rhythm, he is fighting a windmill. There are, of course, no logical limitations upon what he can and cannot write. The question is how does his music sound. . . . If his music is vital and communicative and important, it will live, though all the critics in Christendom shut their ears and scream. If it is propaganda music written chiefly to exhibit the composer's contempt for rules that any one is free to break, it will die. . . . Truth and time will determine the verdict.

Taylor again emphasized emotion over the intellect when, two months later, he reviewed the first New York performance of Igor Stravinsky's *Rite of Spring* (February 1, 1924):

It is foolish, of course, to attempt anything like detailed criticism of as monumental a work like "The Rite of Spring" after one hearing. One can but record reactions. Briefly, then—and much too briefly —this listener can find no word short of "masterpiece" to describe the score. It is music of almost unbelievable complexity of orchestral texture, yet essentially as stark and primitive in outline as the wall pictures of a cave-man. It is not beautiful, in any external sense of the word, but it has a power and truth that strike deep, that awaken age-old emotions and desires, almost terrifying in their unfamiliarity. This is great music.

As a composer, Taylor held that rhythm had to be the servant of musical themes, a belief he indicated a year later after hearing *Rite of Spring* on four different occasions: "I must confess that it no longer impresses me as being an immortal masterpiece. The shock of its rhythms is no longer potent. . . . The slow movement of Brahms' second symphony, on the other hand, a piece of music whose rhythm serves merely to make its themes articulate, moves me now just as profoundly as when I heard it for the first time" (March 15, 1925). Fifteen years later, a tuxedoed Taylor on the silver screen introduced *Rite of Spring* to millions in Walt Disney's *Fantasia*.

Jazz and George Gershwin

Two weeks after Stravinsky's *Rite of Spring* made its emphatic New York debut, another twentieth-century milestone was heard for the first time anywhere: George Gershwin's *Rhapsody in Blue.* It happened on Lincoln's birthday in 1924, a snowy New York day, but an especially memorable one for Taylor. He had looked forward to reviewing the widely advertised Paul Whiteman concert, "An Experiment in Modern Music," in which Gershwin would premiere a work for jazz orchestra and piano. The composer himself would be at the piano for the afternoon concert in Aeolian Hall.

Taylor had met the gifted Gershwin three years earlier in Tin Pan Alley at the office of Harms, Inc., a major music publisher. Charlie Mill, head of the orchestra department, had invited Taylor into his office and said, "'[T]here's a kid I want you to meet. He wrote that hit of Al Jolson's, "Swanee," and I think he's a comer.' Upon which he went to the door of his office and yelled, 'Hey, George!' and a very young man, with polished black hair, came in and was duly presented. Our host suggested that he play his new hit, which, with no hesitation at all, he did; and sang it too."[7]

The February 12 performance was not Gershwin's first appearance on a concert stage. Taylor had seen him three months before that at Aeolian Hall, when he reviewed the annual New York recital of the Canadian-born mezzo-soprano Eva Gauthier. The four-foot, ten-inch singer, elegantly gowned in black velvet, opened her program with Italian and English airs, then songs by Bartók and Schoenberg.[8] After these presentations of modernist composers, her accompanist, Max Jaffe, left the stage. In his review of November 2, 1923, Taylor described what happened next:

> [After] a pause, the singer reappeared, followed by a tall, black-haired young man who was far from possessing the icy aplomb of those to whom playing on the platform of Aeolian is an old story. He bore under his arm a small bundle of sheet music with lurid red and black and yellow covers . . . and then Eva Gauthier sang "Alexander's Ragtime Band" . . . while young Mr. Gershwin began to do mysterious and fascinating rhythmic and contrapuntal stunts with the accompaniment. . . . The audience was as much fun to watch as the songs were to hear for it began by being just a trifle patronizing and ended by surrendering completely to the alluring rhythms of our own folk music.

Two days later in his Sunday piece (November 4, 1923), Taylor expanded his point of view on the recital's inclusion of "six examples of genuine, homebrewed American jazz" in a formal recital of art songs. He told his readers that the "six jazz numbers stood up amazingly well, not only as entertainment but as music. Some of them had their vulgar moments—but it is not for a reviewer who hears the 'Marche Slav' . . . a dozen times a season to open the subject of vulgarity. . . . They conveyed no profound message—but neither does a good deal of [Richard Strauss's tone poem] 'Also Sprach Zarathustra.'" Taylor was impressed by their "melodic interest and continuity, harmonic appropriateness, well-balanced, almost classically severe form, and subtle and fascinating rhythms—in short, the qualities that any sincere and interesting piece of music possesses."

In the 1920s, the word *jazz* was the equivalent of "popular music." Taylor continued, describing his own feelings about the genre:

> Jazz is fundamentally and irreducibly two things. It is, first, syncopation. . . . The other feature of American jazz is its constant use of cross-rhythms. . . . Why shouldn't occasional jazz numbers be placed on programs of serious music? It is folk music if ever any music was. . . . Miss Gauthier did a brave thing when she sang jazz the other night, and a thing that was worth doing. . . . Not that there is any need to magnify the importance of jazz. It is not the only music in the world, and it is not the best. I would flee an all-jazz recital as

wholeheartedly as I would flee an all-Mahler recital. But it is something genuine and amusing, and utterly American—the only utterly
American music that I know.

What is particularly interesting in these comments is Taylor's spin on
popular songs being the "folk music" of America. His reflective writing on
the Gauthier concert gained high plaudits years later from Gershwin's first
biographer, Isaac Goldberg, who wrote that "In the critical literature of our
native music this . . . must go down as a seminal, a pioneer document."[9]
The Gauthier concert receded in importance after Paul Whiteman's on
that snowy afternoon in February. Whiteman, then the most famous leader
of a dance orchestra in the United States, had never conducted a formal jazz
concert, but he explained why the time appeared right to do so: "I believed
that jazz was beginning a new movement in the world's art of music. I
wanted it to be recognized as such. I knew it never would be in my lifetime
until the recognized authorities on music gave it their approval."[10] The "Experiment in Modern Music" consisted of seventeen arrangements of popular
tunes in a jazz manner, a "Suite of Serenades" by Victor Herbert, and the premiere of the Gershwin *Rhapsody in Blue.* Taylor's review (February 13, 1924)
told of the afternoon's high point:

> Just before the closing number, a brilliant adaptation of Elgar's
> "Pomp and Circumstance," George Gershwin played a "Rhapsody in
> Blue" of his own composition for piano and jazz orchestra. In a way
> this was the most interesting offering of the afternoon for it was an
> experiment in treating the jazz instrumental and thematic idiom se-
> riously, and it was by no means an unsuccessful one. . . . Mr.
> Gershwin's piece possessed at least two themes of genuine musical
> worth and displayed a latent ability on the part of this young com-
> poser to say something of considerable interest in his chosen idiom.

In his Sunday piece that followed four days later (February 17, 1924),
Taylor elaborated on the Whiteman concert and lauded the arrangers of jazz,
explaining that popular music composers rely on arrangers to give their melodies "harmonic and rhythmic interest of its own [and] the fascinating color
and lilt of jazz music. . . . A few, like Jerome Kern and George Gershwin, really write their music, but the average American popular composer is totally
illiterate, musically speaking. He plays the piano by ear, and sometimes only
with one finger; he cannot write down his own music or read it when it is
written for him." Taylor then correctly predicted that if Gershwin learned
how to orchestrate his own works, he would have an important place in music history as a coalescer of jazz with "serious music." He recognized in

Gershwin "the link between the jazz camp and the intellectuals. . . . His 'Rhapsody in Blue,' for orchestra and piano revealed a genuine melodic gift and harmonic sense. . . . Moreover, it was genuine jazz music, not only in its scoring but in its idea. It was crude but it hinted at something new, something that has not hitherto been said in music. Mr. Gershwin will bear watching; he may yet bring jazz out of the kitchen."

Those who believed that jazz belonged in the concert hall often quoted Taylor's final comment. However, few composers beyond Gershwin ever succeeded in meshing the elements of jazz with the formal structures found in classical music to the pleasure of critics. Even Gershwin's Concerto in F, now considered a masterpiece in combining the concerto form and jazz, received generally negative reviews at its premiere. As Carol Oja notes in *Making Music Modern,* "Critics came down much harder on *Concerto in F* than they had on *Rhapsody in Blue.* But then its pretensions—in both music form and performance venue—raised the stakes."[11] The influential critic Paul Rosenfeld, who had no love for jazz, put his finger on the problem when he stated, "Jazz is an 'entertainment.'"[12] Undoubtedly a prejudice against the increasing importance of the black musician in entertainment played its part, as critics continued to see jazz in terms of its relation to the ragtime legacy. Jazz and concert music were not born to be wed, they felt.

Taylor the "Beggar on Horseback"

On the same day that George Gershwin entered music immortality with his *Rhapsody,* Taylor also received critical acclaim for the music he had composed for Kaufman and Connelly's play *Beggar on Horseback,* which premiered that evening to completely positive reviews. Winthrop Ames produced and directed the work, which was based on Paul Apel's controversial German play *Hans Sonnenstössers Höllenfahrt* (Jack Sunpusher's trip to hell). Ames saw the need for music for a dream pantomime, the centerpiece of the production. When Taylor read the script, he was captivated because *Beggar on Horseback* was a fantasy, so he quickly accepted Ames's offer. The music would be his best as a composer of incidental music for Broadway.

Ames directed the play as a burlesque on German expressionism. In the story, big business collides with artistic creation. Neil McRae, the central character, is a composer without the financial means to write the symphony that stirs within him. As the plot develops, McRae decides to marry a rich businessman's daughter who has a crush on him. By doing so, he can gain the money he needs for composing, but must leave behind the girl next door, whom he truly loves. As he sits contemplating his plan, he falls asleep and dreams that his ogre father-in-law demands that he give up all artistic creativity and help manufacture "widgets," the family's product. (The word *widget,* coined for the show, later took on a life of its own.) Deeper into the dream, Neil staggers to the family's "palatial, but over-decorated mansion" and murders his in-laws, his wife, and her brother—all with a letter opener.

Ames's production crossed the theater of the absurd with audience participation, for no sooner has the dream murder been committed than newsboys race down the aisles tossing out editions of *The Morning-Evening* with a front-page photo of the murderer and the headline: "Four Killed in Music Plot—Slays Kin over Symphony." The trial for the murderer-composer proceeds with a judge who is the father-in-law reincarnated. After a guilty verdict, McRae is sent to work for the rest of his life as a popular songwriter, a job he completely abhors! Once awakened from the nightmare, he determines to seek a life as a serious composer—and with the girl next door.

It must have been Connelly who suggested the title *Beggar on Horseback,* coming as it did from an Irish proverb: "Set a beggar on horseback and he'll ride to the devil." For the pantomime, Ames and the playwrights found the right moment, as recalled by Connelly: "It came when Roland Young, [who portrayed] the musician, was on trial for murdering a grotesque set of in-laws. . . . To prove that the killings were justified because of the in-laws' crassness, our hero presented a dance pantomime that his in-laws had sneered at. It was called 'A Kiss in Xanadu,' and Deems Taylor wrote an enchanting score for it. Mr. Ames created the wordless action in which a king and queen, bored with each other, seek romantic diversions in a moonlit park and fail to recognize each other behind masks."[13]

Reviewers at opening night loved the play. "A sly and caustic satire. . . . with novel and richly colored theatric inventions," wrote John Corbin, the *Times* reviewer.[14] Reflecting on the play four days later, Corbin called the pantomime "quite the most richly colored and airily graceful thing of its kind in modern memory," with "novel and sparkling" music.[15] "A Kiss in Xanadu" received such universal praise that Taylor later published the music.

It seems quite likely that the model for "beggar" Neil McRae was none other than Deems Taylor, Connelly and Kaufman's old composer friend.[16] Connelly, having lived with Taylor for more than a year, could hardly have been unaffected by the composer's concerns over the difficulties of having enough money to pursue his art. Several snippets from the play support this likelihood: At one point McRae is told, "But there's no reason why you shouldn't subsidize yourself." Taylor had often told friends he would "subsidize" his composing through writing. At another moment McRae's girlfriend asks, "You do see his genius, don't you?" The question parallels completely Mary Kennedy's belief in her husband's abilities as a composer. And finally, no comment strikes more deeply into Taylor's persona, with his love of fantasy and wit, than "Who ever accused you of being a grown man?" It was as if the playwrights had found the psychological key to Taylor's adventures with women.[17]

In an odd twist of fate, *Beggar on Horseback* became a launching platform for Stephen Sondheim, one of the great songwriting talents of the twentieth century. While an undergraduate at Williams College, Sondheim also dreamed of a future as a composer, and when *Beggar on Horseback* came to his attention, he converted the play into his first musical, the college show *All That Glitters.*[18]

The Accidental Demolition of an Orchestra

The excitement of the Whiteman concert and the Broadway opening of *Beggar on Horseback* quickly diminished as Taylor returned to his regular chores. Whenever possible he attempted to meld humor with insight: "One wonders sometimes whether Prof. Einstein hit upon his theory of relativity while attending an operatic performance," he wrote at the beginning of the review of one Metropolitan production (February 28, 1924), "for at the opera, as nowhere else—except possibly at the dentist's—one realizes that time is only relative, that the actual duration of an event has little to do with its apparent length. The second act of 'Lohengrin,' for instance, seems hours longer to the consciousness than it actually is, and one totters forth from [Verdi's] 'Ernani' surprised to find that New York has altered so little with the passage of the years."

In March, Stokowski's Philadelphia Orchestra brought to Carnegie Hall a concert that included *Through the Looking Glass,* Stravinsky's *Firebird,* and Beethoven's Fifth Symphony. In his review of March 26, 1924, Taylor delayed mention of his own composition until the very end. Then he told his readers that originally he had hoped "to devote most of the available space to a shrewd and dispassionate review of the piece and its interpretation," but found it "disconcertingly difficult to be dispassionate, or even articulate." He continued: "We are to be candid, considerably overcome, and the only word of criticism we can muster regarding the evening's proceedings is that Mr. Taylor might profit by a few lessons in bowing." The last remark related to his being called out three times by the applause of the packed house, a fact noted in his father's journal.

Olin Downes, newly arrived from Boston as the *Times* music critic, was hearing *Looking Glass* for the first time: "It is the work of a man who is neither a poseur nor a mere theorist in his writing, but who writes music naturally and with pleasure in his task . . . an excellent piece of writing." Downes particularly liked the comedic "White Knight" movement, as well as the "Garden of Live Flowers," which he called "loquacious, fussy music."[19] Sergei Rachmaninoff also was in the audience that night, and the next day sent a letter to Taylor that became a treasured keepsake:

> I wish to tell you that your "Suite" made a very great impression on me. What I especially admired was the fact that you understand how to be modern, and, at the same time, keep within the limit, which is after all—not music—only color and sound. . . . [Y]our orchestration is extraordinarily beautiful, quite first class. If one has such a sound in one's orchestration, 50% of the task is accomplished and—if—besides that, one has something to say, the whole is perfect. I have, heretofore, thought, but naturally not expressed that opinion, that there were no important composers in this country, but now, I feel sure of *one* who really can show something and say a great deal.[20]

Taylor, quite pleased by the success of the suite and the critical acclaim it engendered, also learned that *Looking Glass* had been programmed for an April performance in Aeolian Hall by the two-year-old American-National Orchestra. Howard Barlow, who like Taylor was mainly self-taught in all his musical training, had founded the orchestra.[21] Barlow's one lesson in conducting had come from none other than Paul Whiteman's father, Wilberforce, the head of music education for Denver's public schools. Barlow had attended high school there in the early 1900s. After college Barlow had moved to New York and there conducted choral groups, in the process acquiring strong supporters in high society. After the First World War, "100 percent Americanism" fever struck much of the country, and he used this energy to begin his American-National Orchestra. The symphony board, composed mainly of women of means, approved of the goal of employing only American-born musicians and performing at least one work by an American composer in every concert. Naturally, the board wanted as excellent an orchestra as possible.

Taylor had never reviewed a concert by this new orchestra, so he decided to attend the March concert before hearing *Looking Glass* performed in the next. He wrote a modestly complimentary review (March 13, 1924): "The American-National, which is engaged in the pioneer task of proving that a man may be American born and still play in a band, began its spring series of concerts in Aeolian Hall with a brave attack on Brahms's Second Symphony last night. . . . The performance had encouraging qualities. Mr. Barlow's reading was intelligent and well structured, and though he could extract from his orchestra no more technical skill than it possessed, he did coax from it some effective climaxes and dynamic nuances." The following

Sunday (March 16, 1924), Taylor wrote at length about Barlow's orchestra, linking it to the need to develop more American musicians, something he considered essential for the United States to stand on its own musical feet. He stated bluntly that the reason first-desk players in most major American orchestras were foreign-born was that they had so much more training in other countries than could be provided in this one:

> The American-Nationals, technically speaking, are a second-class orchestra. But second-class native orchestras are just what this country needs. . . . The only way for a man to become an orchestral virtuoso is to play in an orchestra, and that is what the American or-chestral musician has heretofore had very little chance to do. . . . I hope the American-National will remain a second-class orches-tra. . . . If the American-National will continue its present policy and if its backers and audiences will remember to regard it as what it is, a primarily experimental organization, both for players and composers, it will eventually accomplish more for American music and musicians than a decade of "music weeks" laid end to end.

When Barlow read this, he was not particularly pleased to see his group called a second-class orchestra, but he understood the point that Taylor was making: even musicians had to learn to walk before they could run. Barlow continued preparations for the final concert of the season, which would fea-ture the *Looking Glass* suite. Taylor attended, but not as a reviewer. Two days after the concert, Barlow wrote the composer somewhat apologetically: "Just a note . . . to tell you that I enjoyed doing the 'Looking Glass Suite' more than anything else I have programmed this season. . . . Some things went wrong, as you know and we did not give you half as good a hearing as you deserve, but next time, if there will be a next time, we'll try to do it better."[22]

Unfortunately, there would be no next time, for the orchestra's board, as Barlow remembered years later, reacted to Taylor's article as if they had been "hit by an atomic bomb. . . . They would not be satisfied with a second-rate orchestra. I tried to convince them that it took years to build an orches-tra, but to no avail. They decided that they would disband."[23] The irony could not have been greater: Deems Taylor, with honest support for the group and its important mission, heard as its dying notes those of his own music.

Unaware of the damage done to the American-National Orchestra, Tay-lor finished his seasonal writings with the annual summary of the Metropoli-tan Opera's accomplishments, appearing more philosophical than before. He wondered why such great works as *Der Freischütz* and *Tristan und Isolde* had so few performances, while operas of lesser merit received so many. He told his readers (April 20, 1924) that the general policy of the Metropolitan appeared to be "producing good operas but keeping them on only so long as they draw fair audiences, and relying generally upon the sure-fire hits in your repertoire to pay your expenses. . . . It's a good working policy and a perfectly understandable one, for it puts the deciding verdict squarely up to the public. Not that I agree with it . . . [for] I believe that a great opera house ought to try to influence public taste rather than trail along in its wake." Here in not-so-subtle guise was Taylor again urging the Metropolitan to try something new, perhaps even another American opera.

Janice Meredith: A Film Score

With the end of the music season and his wife still away on tour with *In The Next Room,* Taylor spent time working on the Stamford home. He kept Mary informed of the renovations, combining facts with apparent deep emotions: "Dearest, it's very late. Mac [the Singing Policeman] and I made a chute for dumping plaster and ran it out of the eyebrow window from the top floor on the north side of the house. Then we took all the partitions out, saved the studs and lathing, and dumped the plaster in back of the house. . . . I miss you horribly, dearest love, and I wish you'd arrange to have the week shortened. I think I'll go to bed and try to imagine that you are in my arms. I love you, Mashinka."[24]

Even in summer, Taylor could not relax from the financial drain of the rental in New York as well as the mortgage in Connecticut. Though the couple still pooled their income, it never seemed enough. So when an offer arrived from Bill LeBaron to write a score for a motion picture, Taylor jumped at the opportunity. Besides money, it promised the challenge of a new medium. He and LeBaron had kept in touch after their years together at *Collier's.* LeBaron had written several Broadway successes, including *Apple Blossoms,* the Charles Dillingham operetta that introduced Fred and Adele Astaire to Broadway. In 1919 LeBaron had taken a step away from Broadway and publishing and moved into the burgeoning world of motion pictures. He'd accepted the offer of the media mogul of his time, William Randolph Hearst, to become general manager for Cosmopolitan Pictures. It was an opportunity LeBaron could hardly have refused, for few men were then as influential as Hearst. With a newspaper empire that extended from coast to coast, he had immense political and persuasive powers. Few doubted that it had been the sensationalist "yellow journalism" of his newspapers that had made the 1898 Spanish-American War inevitable.

Hearst became involved with silent motion pictures in 1914, when he introduced the first newsreels for movie-house programming. Two years later, though a married man, he became obsessed with a Ziegfeld Follies chorine named Marion Davies. Mainly because of his desire to star her in movies, he formed Cosmopolitan Pictures and sank a fortune into producing historical epics starring Davies. He knew that through his national newspaper empire he could convince the public of the greatness of the Cosmopolitan films and bring them to love his new star. At best, Marion Davies had comedic talents, and few of her many movies would make money, but Hearst didn't know that when he purchased the Harlem River Park and Casino, on Second Avenue between 126th and 127th Streets, and transformed it into the Cosmopolitan studios. It was his single-minded intention to produce epic films that would bring glory to both him and Davies, now his mistress.

By 1919, when LeBaron became the general manager for Cosmopolitan productions, the vast majority of New York film companies had already moved their studios to sunnier Hollywood. A few remained in the area, including the Mamaroneck studios of the genius director D. W. Griffith, whose *Birth of a Nation* in 1915 had opened the country's eyes to the great potential of film.

LeBaron supervised three successive spectacles that featured Davies. The first two—*When Knighthood Was in Flower* (1922) and *Little Old New York* (1923)—were modest hits, but the third, *Yolanda* (1924), a romantic drama set in the France of Louis XI, was a dismal failure. Hearst spent a fortune on this feature, even borrowing Ziegfeld's principal designer, Joseph Urban, to draw up plans for magnificent sets depicting medieval France, all built in Hearst's Harlem studios.[25] The movie opened as a road-show engagement (reserved seats and one showing per evening) at Hearst's own Cosmopolitan Theater on Columbus Circle, with an overture composed by Victor Herbert.[26]

Immediately upon the completion of *Yolanda,* the newspaper mogul set in motion plans to produce *Janice Meredith,* an epic of early American Revolutionary times based on the successful novel of the same name. Davies played the title role in the movie—budgeted at more than one million dollars, making it one of the costliest films of its time. With scenes including the Boston Tea Party, the Battle of Trenton, and Washington crossing the Delaware, it cried out for special music, an orchestral score with both drama and patriotic fervor.

It was at this point in 1924 that LeBaron contacted Taylor and asked him to supply the score for the film. Silent films needed background music, often provided by only a piano or an organ, since few motion-picture theaters could afford much more. In larger cities such as New York, however, movie palaces were emerging, each with its own symphony orchestra. *Janice Meredith* would open in such theaters as a road-show engagement, so LeBaron needed a full orchestral score.

Taylor agreed, and after completing his seasonal duties at the *World,* he turned his total attention to composing the score in a private studio provided by Hearst. He relied heavily on tunes of the era of the Revolution, from "Yankee Doodle" to "British Grenadiers." When *Janice Meredith* opened in August, the movie, as well as Taylor's score, received glowing reviews: "No more brilliant achievement in ambitious motion pictures dealing with historical romances has ever been exhibited," wrote the *Times* reviewer.[27] "We are willing," chimed in the *Musical Courier,* "to come out flat-footedly with the statement that the score which Deems Taylor has written for the film, *Janice Meredith,* is the best music for the pictures we have yet heard. . . . His contrapuntal treatment of the tunes which he borrows is exceedingly clever and he again shows himself master of orchestration. Considering the playing length of the score, nearly two hours and a half, the standard maintained is an extraordinarily high one."[28] Unfortunately, even with good reviews the movie was not a box office success, partly because D. W. Griffith's film *America,* which covered the same Revolutionary ground, had opened months earlier and stolen Hearst's thunder. As for Taylor's experience in the movies, it reconnected him with LeBaron, who, years later as production manager of Paramount Pictures, would summon him to Hollywood in an attempt to produce a film based on the opera *Cavalleria Rusticana.*

With the *Janice Meredith* score completed, Taylor, who seemed unable to rest for a minute, decided that what the music world needed was a new monthly magazine. Together with Gilbert Gabriel, the drama critic for the *New York Sun,* he gained enough financial support for an introductory issue of *Music: Illustrated Monthly Review.* An impressive editorial board included many of the top musical personalities of their day, including the composers John Alden Carpenter and Ernest Bloch, conductors Walter Damrosch and Fritz Reiner, and critic Lawrence Gilman.

Music emphasized a sophisticated humor, and its oversize-page format contained photos and drawings equal in quality to those of any other publication of its time. For publicity's sake, the first issue went free to many, including the editor of two-year-old *Time* magazine, who assigned a writer to assess the debut issue. "*Music* seems determined to be witty and gay," wrote *Time,* and then rightly identified the man behind this approach: "Taylor has been known, for the past two years at least, as both wit and musician."[29]

Indeed, even with only a cursory review of the articles, a reader could smile: Richard Child asked, "Is There a Beethoven in Hoboken?" explaining that the American Academy at Rome looked for young composers no matter

where they might be; Newman Levy wrote the fictional "My Personal Recollections of Richard Wagner" ("I explained to him my theories about the Music of the Future, and the invention that I was working on at the time, the *leit
motif.* Dick was greatly impressed"); Taylor, in more serious mode, wrote
about the emergence of jazz in the concert hall in "All Dressed Up and No
Place to Go."

That title fit the enterprise perfectly, because *Music* never got beyond the
introductory issue.[30] Why did the magazine not succeed? For one thing,
meshing humor with the serious subject of music necessitates delicate tight-
rope walking. The editors appear to have fallen off on the side of too much
humor. Also, potential subscribers were put off by the editors' self-impor-
tant challenge to the readers: subscribe to *Music,* and in so doing "identify
yourself as a true friend of music."

With all Taylor's frenetic activity, he and his wife spent less and less time
together. The Connecticut home still wasn't livable, and the summer's activities hadn't allowed Taylor to spend much time working on it. Meanwhile,
Mary had become a homebound playwright, attempting to complete the play
Mrs. Partridge Presents with her actress friend Ruth Hawthorne. The Taylors
were growing apart, and if they really took time to be honest with each
other, they must have wondered how much longer they could go on this way.

8. The World Years, 1924–1925

Seasonal Variety

Taylor entered his fourth season as a music critic contemplating the sounds of rural Connecticut. "Nature as a musician is a flat failure," he wrote in his first Sunday piece of the new season (September 28, 1924). "Life holds no more depressing experience than to sit outside a Connecticut farmhouse on a summer's night and listen to two tree toads swapping experiences— 'F-sharp, F-sharp, F-sharp'—'E-flat, E-flat, E-flat'—and so on, tirelessly, interminably, until insanity sets in." Without knowing it, he had previewed some of the grating sounds he would hear when Walter Damrosch programmed the New York premiere of *Pacific 231* at the New York Symphony's season-opening concert.

In creating *Pacific 231,* the French-trained Swiss composer Arthur Honegger had joined the makers of "machine age" music. Later in the decade, Edgard Varèse and George Antheil became the "bad boys" of this approach, ultimately employing even airplane propellers and sirens within the framework of some of their musical works. *Pacific 231* was hardly that radical; it simply depicted the journey of a steam locomotive in orchestral sounds. Taylor articulated the noisy engine's journey in his review of November 1, 1924:

> The orchestra began—a long, hissing roll on the tam-tam, over the heavy, thudding breaths of plucked double-basses, with a thin cloud of acrid violin harmonics overhead. The thing began to move. A steady, rasping, piston-like rhythm began in the low strings and

123

spread among the violins, with scraps of themes flaring among the reeds and muted brasses. The rhythm continued, gathering momentum steadily and relentlessly as the weight of the orchestra began to tell. Sometimes the noise would slacken, as though the huge engine were drifting. . . . Then back came the orchestra, with ever-increasing power and speed, until the brasses broke into a wild shout of brutal triumph—a metal giant in his cups, happily roaring and hiccoughing in a sheer ecstasy of power. Then—shriek from the piccolos, and amid a succession of huge, grinding chords, the thing came to a stop.

It was modernist music that appealed to Taylor because at its base were humor and fantasy.

Two days after *Pacific 231* ceased hissing, the Metropolitan Opera started its new season with *Aida*. Taylor, in his coverage (November 3, 1924), decided that if the opening of the World Series deserved reporting from multiple viewpoints, so should the Metropolitan's first night. The result is one of Taylor's cleverest pieces, also indicating his capacity to write in the style of other well-known journalists.

"The Facts as the Associated Press Might Communicate Them": Before a crowd estimated at 4,179, including a host of New York society notables, the Metropolitan Opera Company, Giulio Gatti-Casazza, General Manager, opened its season here tonight at the Metropolitan Opera House, on Broadway between 39th and 40th Streets. . . . The ensemble is alleged to have included 75 male singers, 75 women singers . . . and two white horses with pink eyes. . . . The performance began at 8 P.M., the estimated value of the jewels worn by the boxholders being $7,027,000.20.

"The Human Interest Story, as It Might Be Told by Frank Sullivan" (who stood in line to buy standing-room tickets): The line was rather slow in moving so I decided to move up a little—in fact, I did move up, right in front of a gentleman wearing a straw hat. I picked myself up, however, with only a few minor fractures and contusions. . . . Laughing heartily at my mistake, I strolled forward, and knocking down a little boy . . . took his place.

"The Show Itself as It Might be Reviewed by Heywood Broun" (as a sports page writer): It seems to me that the authors of "Aida" have fumbled the ball in midfield, with nothing but their own ineptitude between them and a touchdown. The piece begins as an exciting study in miscegenation, gallops brilliantly as far as the middle of the third act and then strains a tendon and staggers off into a rather

feeble and preposterous hokum story of lust and religious intoler-
ance. . . . [Giovanni Martinelli's] high notes had all the lunge and
terrific drive of a Babe Ruth going after a low one on the inside.
Elizabeth Rethberg was engaging as Aida, but the rest were only fair.
The horses were adequate.

Taylor needed this type of exercise in creative writing because his musical experiences were becoming redundant: the same orchestras, the same soloists, and the same operas. Again stretching his imagination, a month later in
a Sunday piece (December 21, 1924), he presented a "home study course"
for those aspiring to the noble profession of music critic. First, he suggested
ways to steel oneself against inevitable criticism. For example, a person
should obtain "a position as Prohibition enforcement agent and hold it for
one month, or until you no longer mind being a social outcast." He also proposed the discreet use of pet phrases, so that if the "conductor inspires in you
no comment whatsoever, remember that he 'conducted with vigor,' [and]
when a singer has no voice but is obviously doing his best, he 'possesses a
good sense of style.' . . . Do not be afraid of using these little life-savers . . .
[for] nobody will be able to prove you wrong."

Until 1924 the New York concert stage was a white person's world,
whether one was an instrumentalist or a vocalist. The ethnic breakthrough
came that year in the person of two professionally trained black singers—
Jules Bledsoe and Roland Hayes. Both had studied in Europe, a necessity then
for any American-born concert singer who hoped for critical acceptance
here. Their New York recitals preceded that of Marian Anderson by five
years. Bledsoe, a baritone, debuted in Aeolian Hall in April, but his greatest
fame came three years later, in 1927, when on the opening night of *Show Boat,*
he stepped forward as Joe, the quintessential Everyman, and sang Jerome
Kern and Oscar Hammerstein's "Ol' Man River."

The prize for being the first black singer to perform solo recitals in Carnegie Hall went to the tenor Roland Hayes, whose mother had been a slave.
By the time of his October concert, Hayes had already sung in Boston's Symphony Hall, as well as before King George V and Queen Mary in a command
performance. His recitals featured Negro spirituals, a first on the concert
stage. When Taylor reviewed Hayes's second recital (November 29, 1924),
his words made clear that what a critic saw should have no relationship to the
importance of what a critic heard:

> I tried listening to Roland Hayes without watching him last night.
> There has been so much emphasis laid upon the fact that he is a Ne-
> gro and so much rhapsodizing over his singing as expressive of the
> essential tragedy of the Negro race, that I thought it would be inter-

esting, for once, to concentrate upon the singer and ignore the man. So I sat in Carnegie Hall and watched the audience and listened to Roland Hayes. . . . If the voice could be tagged with any special racial label, one might call it Irish. . . . There is pathos in his singing, of course, in his voice and his interpretations. . . . Its effect may be enhanced by reflections concerning the lonely prophet of an oppressed race. . . . It does not matter, particularly, whether Roland Hayes is black or white or green. What does matter is that he is an artist, and a great one.

As Taylor approached the New Year, his high-profile role as a music critic took a backseat to his wife's accomplishments. On January 5, 1925, Mary Kennedy's coauthored comedy *Mrs. Partridge Presents* opened on Broadway in a production by Guthrie McClintic, Katherine Cornell's husband. The story details the emotional tussle between a mother and daughter, initiated by the unfulfilled wishes of the mother to be an actress. When the mother pushes her daughter toward the theater, the girl resists and chooses her own life's course.

The play garnered excellent reviews, including that of the *Times* critic, who called it "a jolly comedy, sweet-tempered and laughable, and not without some meat to it."[1] Sweeter to Mary than the reviews was Burns Mantle's choice of the play as one of the ten best of the year, sharing the honor with Eugene O'Neill's *Desire Under the Elms* and Laurence Stallings and Maxwell Anderson's *What Price Glory?*[2] Undoubtedly the play's success on Broadway, then later on tour, provided Mary with evidence of her writing abilities. In the years ahead she would turn less to acting and more to writing plays, children's books, and poems, though nothing would come close to the success of *Mrs. Partridge Presents.*

Portrait of a Lady and Millay's Letter

With his daily responsibilities as a music critic, Taylor could not find time to complete any new orchestral works. He dusted off *Portrait of a Lady,* the rhapsody for strings, winds, and piano that he had composed during his stay in Denver. Since it was scored for a small orchestra, he sought out Carolyn Beebe's chamber orchestra for the premiere, the same group that had initially performed *Looking Glass.* Beebe programmed it for an early February concert.

Portrait of a Lady, some eleven minutes long in performance, effectively introduces two versions of the same theme, the first played reflectively and quietly initially by strings, then by an oboe. The distinct blues quality gives way to piano scamperings that jauntily introduce the second version. The moods alternate, and the "lady" evaporates upon the vibrations of a French horn. As Taylor noted in the program, the composition had no relationship to Henry James's book of the same name: "There is no detailed program for the *Portrait of a Lady* beyond that implied by the title. It is . . . an attempt to convey the impression of a human personality in terms of music." But whose personality? In the *Lady's* two themes, Taylor most likely depicted the two virtues he sought in his ideal woman: a brisk intellect and the reflective nature of an artist. He had found these in both Jane Anderson and Mary Kennedy.

The premiere of *Portrait of a Lady* produced positive critical response, particularly from Olin Downes of the *Times,* who found it "warm in color, and sensitive in mood . . . ranking with the best writing we have had thus far from Mr. Taylor. His clear melodic style has not deserted him. . . . 'The Portrait of a Lady,' as a whole, has a fanciful, whimsical vein."[3]

As he had with *Siren Song,* Taylor again decided to review his own composition: "As one of Mr. Taylor's warmest admirers, we had looked forward with considerable interest to hearing his new work, but its performance left us rather disturbed . . . because his music set us to musing upon the wide gap that lies between intention and accomplishment. . . . The audience, probably composed of the composer's relatives, greeted the piece with what seemed to us highly disproportionate cordiality" (February 4, 1925).

Days later, the *World* published a letter from Edna St. Vincent Millay, now a reigning poet of her time, who also had been present at the concert. She briskly challenged his conclusions:

> In some indignation and no little disapproval I address you concerning your criticism in this morning's World of Mr. Deems Taylor's "Portrait of a Lady." "The audience," you say, in reviewing last night's concert given by the New York Chamber Music Society in Aeolian Hall, "probably composed of the composer's relatives, greeted the piece with highly disproportionate cordiality." Sir, I was a member of that audience. I heard with close attention and deep pleasure an unusually good program unusually well performed, not the least interesting and lovely number of which was Mr. Taylor's "Portrait of a Lady." Mr. Taylor combines as a musician two excellent attributes far too seldom found in combination: the art to expound a fine theme with power and clarity, and the good taste when that theme has been expounded, to stop. . . . I suggest in closing that last night's audience, far from being composed of Mr. Taylor's relatives, was made up of discerning and honestly delighted strangers, and that

yourself, far from being "one of Mr. Taylor's warmest admirers," represented the only relative in the auditorium.[4]

Taylor would not forget this letter, with its charm and friendliness.

Opera and Orchestra Commissions

Sometime early in the spring of 1925, Taylor received a luncheon invitation from Edward Ziegler, assistant manager of the Metropolitan. Ziegler had been one of Huneker's closest friends and had worked as a critic and writer before becoming Gatti-Casazza's right-hand man. Taylor never forgot the luncheon, recounting the story endless times in later years:

> "I want your advice," [Ziegler] said. "For years we have been looking for an American opera that we could produce with a reasonable hope of success. We tried a prize contest, and promised to produce the winning entry. We did, but we knew it would be a failure and it was. Then we tried producing the best one of those that were constantly being submitted. Nothing came in that was any good. Now we've decided to go to a composer who has had some experience in the theater and commission him to write us an opera. This is where I want your advice. Who do you think would be a good man to ask?"
>
> "Eddie, don't be silly," I said. "Commission me."
>
> "Well," he said, "that's why I asked you out to lunch."[5]

Taylor had achieved his goal; he would write an opera for the greatest company in the United States. Naturally, he had to keep quiet until Gatti-Casazza's announcement.

As Taylor closed out his final season as music critic, Debussy's *Pelléas et Mélisande* received its first Metropolitan production, with memorable portrayals of the title roles by Edward Johnson and Lucrezia Bori. Taylor had often berated the Metropolitan for never performing the masterpiece, an opera whose musical style he would attempt to emulate in the years ahead. After seeing the second performance of it, Taylor told his readers (March 28, 1925):

> There is no parallel to it in all operatic literature. In everything else . . . the composer says, in effect, "the emotional and poetic contents of this drama are thus and so" . . . but in "Pelléas" the auditor must have imagination in his own right. Debussy opens the door that sets the imagination free, but he attempts no more. Here are no big arias, no crashing climaxes. In the culminating moment of the

drama—that moment when Pelléas cries "c'est que—je t'aime!" and Mélisande whispers, "je t'aime aussi"—the orchestra falls silent; and if there be no music in the heart of the listener he will hear none at all.

In spite of what he already knew about his Metropolitan commission, Taylor decided to provide his annual assessment of their year (April 19, 1925). In it he made special note of "the sudden emergence into the limelight of Lawrence Tibbett, who has been singing minor baritone roles for the past three seasons and who suddenly electrified everybody by a brilliant performance of Ford in 'Falstaff.' . . . One role does not make a star . . . but Mr. Tibbett, with his beautiful voice and latent histrionic ability, should . . . undoubtedly become an operatic artist of the first rank." In fact, Tibbett was the first male singer born in the United States to become a star of the Metropolitan.

As to criticizing the Metropolitan Opera company, Taylor took a quieter approach than in previous years: "It may be advancing years, it may be incipient cynicism, or it may be . . . a state of corruption by the interests; but whatever the reason, I find it difficult to abuse the Metropolitan with the zest and enthusiasm of former seasons. I am afraid I am being undermined by the insidious disease that is so fatal to really hearty polemics—that growing conviction that the other fellow is doing the best he can according to his own lights." Taylor could hardly chastise the hand that was about to provide a commission. In fact, the day before his assessment of the Metropolitan season would be printed, the *Times* announced on its front page (April 18, 1925): "Gatti to Produce American Opera. Deems Taylor, Critic, Commissioned to Write One Expressly for the Metropolitan."

Taylor's four years of efforts to illustrate the need for more attention to American music and composers were paying off. Within a few days of the Metropolitan announcement, on April 22, 1925, New York papers reported a second Taylor commission: an orchestral work for Walter Damrosch and the New York Symphony. Damrosch, himself a composer, believed that he had a responsibility to help aspiring composers, for he knew the difficulties of gaining a performance. The previous January he had provided a major lift to the career of twenty-five-year-old Aaron Copland by conducting the premiere of his first major work, Symphony for Organ and Orchestra. Copland's teacher Nadia Boulanger, with whom he had studied in Paris, was the soloist. It was at this performance that Damrosch, after the symphony's tart sounds had subsided, turned to the audience and said to them jokingly: "Ladies and gentlemen, I am sure you will agree that if a gifted young man can write a symphony like this at twenty-three, within five years he will be ready to commit murder."⁶ The widely quoted comment certainly didn't hurt Copland's career.

Looking about for other composers of promise, Damrosch zeroed in on Taylor and George Gershwin, then convinced the New York Symphony board members to commission works from both.⁷ Though Gershwin's only orchestral credential at the time was *Rhapsody in Blue,* Damrosch believed in his potential and specifically contracted for a "New York concerto."⁸ The result was the jazzy and memorable Concerto in F.

Taylor's composing credentials were longer than Gershwin's, so Damrosch gave him free rein to choose the form of the orchestral work, as long as it was ready for the coming season. It didn't take Taylor long to return for inspiration to James Branch Cabell's *Jurgen.* Once again he wrote to Cabell asking his permission "to try to translate 'Jurgen' into terms of music."⁹ Cabell had no objection, so the composer began what would turn out to be a tedious struggle.

Now with two commissions, Taylor faced the dilemma of whether he should remain as the *World*'s music critic. Swope certainly felt he should, because he offered him another season at $200 per week, which included a raise of $50. Swope knew that Taylor's presence made a difference. Don Seitz, business manager of the *World,* confirmed this when he told Joseph Taylor that his son "brought the *World* more readers than any other man they ever had."¹⁰ For Deems, the decision was not made in haste. He really needed steady income, so he countered Swope's offer with another: to write only a Sunday piece, at $125 per Sunday. As negotiations continued, Taylor began to reconsider even this idea. Finally, he realized that only a clean break would allow him to focus on composing. In July he wrote to Swope and resigned.¹¹

Taylor's Impact as *World* Critic

Taylor's four years at the *World* had come at an unusual transition period for newspaper music criticism in New York. During that time, three of the four old guard had moved on: Henry Krehbiel had died; both Richard Aldrich and Henry Finck had retired. Taylor's legacy, first and foremost, was to provide a model for critical writing. The writer and composer John Tasker Howard described Taylor as one who "writes with a clarity of style, with matured authority and with disarming frankness and sincerity. . . . [H]is engaging spirit of good humor finds expression to lighten the burden of his message."¹²

As Mark Grant points out in *Maestros of the Pen,* Taylor employed "an intuitive sense of judging the merit of music by evaluating 'how it sounds' and whether it 'goes' without regard to propaganda about the music either old or new."[13] He raised the flag for melody and harmony at a time when "there was in music a definite movement from public toward private art, as there had already been in painting and literature."[14] Taylor was a populist educator who believed that concert music in the melodic tradition could be enjoyed by all, and that not only were modernists taking music to a cerebral level beyond the ken of most, but it was noisy to boot.

Perhaps no single one of Taylor's actions during his *World* years had more impact than his two-week trip to the Midwest in 1923 to hear their major orchestras. It was an imaginative venture that no other critic had even thought of undertaking. In fact, most were still preoccupied with looking across the Atlantic to Europe for their inspiration. Taylor's message—there's more across the Hudson than New Jersey—was a musical variant on Horace Greeley's "Go West, young man." Deems Taylor challenged the New England–New York musical domination, and how right he was. Just over the horizon were the United States' first great baritone, California-born Lawrence Tibbett; two composers from Philadelphia, Samuel Barber and Marc Blitzstein; and three conposers from the Midwest, Howard Hanson, Roy Harris, and Virgil Thomson. Even Aaron Copland would find populist fame for his music inspired by themes west of the Mississippi *(El Salón México, Rodeo, Billy the Kid)*.

A legacy involves paving the way for others, and it is interesting to note that Taylor's virtues of wit, clarity of writing, frankness, and sincerity also fit the music criticism of Virgil Thomson, the most famous of the twentieth-century composer-critics. Taylor's effectiveness in this same area certainly provided a good precedent for Ogden Reid of the *Tribune* (the same for whom Taylor had worked in 1916) to hire Thomson in 1940. His new employee, the irascible Midwesterner-turned-New Yorker, would stay on for fourteen years of influential music criticism.

A Summer Apart from Mary Kennedy

Taylor was now without a steady income, so he and Mary had to plan their finances carefully for the next year. As part of a money-saving strategy, they gave up their Fifty-seventh Street apartment and moved their modest furnishings to Hollow Hill, their Stamford property, which was by now livable in the summer months. Once there, they seemed emotionally stymied. Mary had put a great deal of energy into completing *Mrs. Partridge Presents,* but now she was uncertain about the next step. Her husband, with his commissions, had his next two years well defined, yet psychologically he seemed adrift. For her birthday he simply left her a note: "My dear—It's your birthday, and I haven't any money for a present. But, anyhow, I can wish it to be a happy one . . . for you are my best girl, and my wife, and my child, and my Mashinka, and I love you better than anything in the world. Your old crab."[15] By referring to himself as an "old crab," Deems clearly suggests that he and Mary were having arguments. Very likely Mary believed what affection he had for her was being replaced by his preoccupation with completing his two commissions successfully, and perhaps there was even some jealousy on her part. But there was a deeper psychological fissure: Mary wanted to have a baby and Deems continually refused to consider this. With tensions high between them, Mary decided to go to Europe for the summer and leave him to his compositions. As plans developed, she would first spend time in Paris, and then connect with her friend Emily Kimbrough, the writer, to tour the Continent. Since Deems's parents also planned a European trip, she arranged to sail with them, departing on the Fourth of July on the S.S. *Minnetonka*. Very likely she paid for the trip with the royalties from her successful play.

The sea journey began well enough. Taylor's father noted in his journal that "Mary had her breakfast in bed at 9. She had a very good night." In addition he wrote that she "has her chair in a secluded part of the deck in the sun where she is alone."[16] After only a few days at sea, Mary Kennedy's emotional state became unhinged. Her daily letters to her husband indicated a soul in torment, reaching across the ocean to regain his affection. On the fourth day she wrote: "I have been sitting out in the darkness looking at the black water and the evening star, and the pale pink and gold band that holds up the purple sky and wondering what I have done with my life that I should be so devoid of emotion." On the sixth day: "I begin to think everything is going to be all right. Do you think of me? Or am I already someone you used to know? Do you love me a little? You must NEVER say so if you don't." On the seventh day: "Deems darling, so many things divide us from that old time. Do you think we'll ever find each other again? I think life is a bad dream, in which we lose all we love. . . . Write when you can—and remember me with kindness. I love you, you know, in my own way. Mashinka."[17]

Shortly after arriving in Paris, Mary read in the newspapers that Bernard Baruch and family were in town. She had met Baruch, the financial baron and special adviser to President Woodrow Wilson, in Great Neck at the Swopes'. Apparently he remembered her very well, for when she called his suite at the Ritz, Baruch was in bed with a cold but, as she wrote to Taylor, he "came to the telephone when he heard that it was I."[18] She began socializing with the Baruchs and developed a special friendship with their daughter Renée, so much so that Mary became the family's guest as they traveled to England and Scotland in August.

Even being with influential friends like the Baruchs did not lessen Mary's sense of insecurity. She wrote to her husband and begged him not to talk about her. "Don't explain me or discuss me—I just can't bear it. Unhappy is the head about which the anecdotes gather, I say."[19] As a close friend of Katherine Cornell ("Kit"), Mary broached the deepest of her concerns: "Deems I suppose if I were as wonderful as Kit, and made as great a success, you might be able to love me as much as Guthrie [Cornell's husband] loves her—and pay attention to me in the same way. Perhaps I won't come back until I can show you that I am as good as you once thought I was."[20]

Compared with the daily letters he received from his wife, Taylor wrote less regularly and with far less emotion. His very first letter to her was chatty: "Dorothy Parker is coming here Wednesday next. . . . Mac is rebuilding the retaining wall. . . . 'Jurgen' is beginning to go faster." Then at the end, almost as an afterthought, he added: "I miss you, Mashinka darling. The house seems very large and empty without my child rampaging around. I do think, though, that this trip is the wisest move you ever made. It ought to give you rest, and beauty and leisure and peace of mind and all the other pleasant things you needed so much. Have a grand time and don't forget whose child you are. I love you, love you, dearest."[21] The house may have seemed empty, but Taylor maintained a certain ability to help assure warmth. One way was with Dorothy Parker, who found him a fascinating member of her coterie of men. The visit to Hollow Hill was more than a pleasant outing in the country.

By 1925 Dorothy Parker's marriage to Edwin Parker was in name only, and her numerous affairs fanned the gossip around the Round Table. Robert Benchley knew the psychological side of "Mrs. Parker," the name by which he always referred to her, better than anyone, and kept a platonic relationship with her throughout their lives.[22] He inevitably kept his wife, Gertrude, updated on the doings of the sharp-tongued, often suicidal Parker, so that years later Mrs. Benchley could tell an interviewer, "Dottie used to get involved with a lot of them [the Algonquin Circle men]. She was mad for Deems Taylor. *And* for Charles MacArthur."[23] Although Parker and Taylor may have dallied previously, her madness for him reached its peak while Mary was in Europe.[24]

It was Benchley who detailed the summer affair from his New York office in letters to his wife, who was away on vacation with their two boys, Nathaniel and Robert Jr.[25] On July 27, 1925, he wrote: "Mrs. P. is in better spirits, her play being quite a hit in Chicago and her emotions evidently being under better control. . . . Mrs. P. is living out with Deems in Stamford while Mary is abroad and is working on a novel." "Things around here are just about as dull as ever," began his report of July 31, 1925, "Mrs. Parker ran into Charlie [MacArthur] by accident night before last and they had dinner together. Everything was running along smoothly until quite late when one or the other of them started a little argument and Charlie bawled the life out of her and now she is up at Deems' swearing again to end it all." And on August 7, 1925: "Mrs. P. is out with Deems, and from report of people who have seen her is quite on her feet again."

While Mrs. Parker enjoyed the rural atmosphere and the company of her charming host, Taylor wrote to his wife insinuating that aside from composing, his was a humdrum life: "The business of life takes a lot of time, too, somehow. Cooking and washing dishes, and flowers, and laundry and keeping the house even vaguely clean, even with Mac to share it, eats up the hours at a fearful rate."[26] But the main thrust of the letters related to his difficulties in giving musical life to *Jurgen*.

Why had this labor of love become so tough? In the novel Jurgen is a would-be poet with an aging, unattractive wife, whose pact with the devil gives him a youthful body and interactions with some of the famed beauties of the past, such as Helen of Troy. Ultimately, Jurgen leaves fantasy and returns to the reality of home and his wife. Taylor himself had expressed his attitude to the book five years earlier when he had written to Mary that *Jurgen* "tells me everything I am, and have been, and may be, unsparingly."[27] He probably never wrote such words of personal insight again, for the story was all about fantasy and youth, major preoccupations of Deems Taylor's life.

The immediate parallel, as he attempted to put music to Jurgen's escapades, is uncanny: here was Taylor, a man searching for an artistic outlet, whose wife's insecurities signaled to him her aging, so he gave himself to another beauty, Dorothy Parker. As far as his earlier allusion to what "may be," after his eventual divorce from Mary, he sought his youth in relationships with ever-younger women. Then, in a Jurgenish finale, in old age Taylor continued to rely upon Mary Kennedy for consolation. No wonder he had such a difficult time working out the music for *Jurgen;* he was in fact attempting to write an autobiographical tone poem. After a month of struggling, he finally gave up on the idea of depicting musically some of the incidents in the novel: "I'm pretty certain now that it will be a symphonic poem in one long movement, with no attempt to follow the book literally."[28]

Paul Whiteman's Commission

The lack of a weekly paycheck sent Taylor scurrying for extra income. It was Paul Whiteman, the King of Jazz, who came to the rescue. Whiteman's Palais Royal orchestra, famed for its many recordings, concertized throughout the United States and Europe. Now Whiteman sought new compositions written specifically for his musicians, and the word went out: write something for Whiteman. "I've taken on a new commission," Taylor wrote Mary in Europe, "a definite offer from Whiteman for a piece to be ready by the middle of September. . . . I get $500 down, and $10 a performance after the first twenty. As Whiteman is booked for more than a hundred performances next season I'm reasonably sure of getting a decent return on the piece."[29] By the time he sent the letter, he already had the $500.

The Whiteman composition proved easier than *Jurgen*. Here Taylor turned to his recollections of the circus world, where fantasy and reality joined in unforgettable childhood experiences. The result was *Circus Day: Eight Pieces from Memory,* a suite of musical impressions. As he explained in program notes: "This is not one of the colossal, three-ringed aggregations that travel in special trains. . . . [I]t is a more humble circus, with one ring . . . and a tent-crew that doubles as a more or less accomplished brass band." Composing *Circus Day* took only half the time of *Jurgen,* helped by the fact that Ferde Grofé, who had also arranged *Rhapsody in Blue* for Whiteman, would orchestrate the music.

By August Mary's letters radiated a more joyful tone, and Taylor wrote to tell her so: "Baby, you don't know what you've done for me by writing such happy letters. You sound like a totally different person from the poor tired, unhappy child that started on her trip. You did need a vacation so much didn't you . . . and as I get some work done, I find myself losing the sense of frustration and guilt that has been driving me so hard for the past year. I still feel the impulse to work all the time, but it's impatience to get the work done, not desperation. I'm much more at peace, Mashinka, and I love you."[30] That peace resulted more from Parker's decision to move back to New York than from finally getting his composing motor running. Though Taylor possessed the ability to overlap female relationships when needed, in the case of Parker he must have become rather agitated by her roller-coaster emotions.

When Mary returned late in August, she had little time to bask in the refreshment of her European cure, for Taylor confessed about his summer fling with Parker, as well as a brief affair with another woman.[31] To her credit, Mary somehow summoned up all the forgiving she could muster. There is no indication that she put the blame entirely on her husband for these wanderings, for she must have known Mrs. Parker to be rather predatory. As for the other affair, she may well have blamed herself for not returning sooner.

Taylor, anxious for some peace and quiet to finish his two current compositions, convinced Mary to close up the Stamford home and go with him directly to the Philadelphia suburbs early in September. He had contacted Edith Braun, their honeymoon hostess, and she arranged for them to use the home of nearby friends. Braun's journal describes her impressions of the Taylors' visit: "[Deems] came over . . . desperate to finish 'Jurgen' and 'Circus Day.' He finished 'Circus Day' here in about six or seven days. Sometimes

he worked until 4 in the morning and started again about 10. . . . I feel that
Mary missed so many opportunities of making friends while here. All our
friends were so nice to them but [the Taylors] made no effort to reciprocate
so they lost interest. Of course Deems was working so hard on 'Jurgen,' he
couldn't do much but Mary could have. Deems dedicated 'Circus Day' to us
and we were so pleased over it."[32]

Undoubtedly Mrs. Taylor did not tell Mrs. Braun the reason for her feelings of detachment, considering the summer behavior of Mr. Taylor. Returning to New York, the Taylors rented an apartment on Forty-ninth Street.
Mary had had a long time to think about her marriage while in Pennsylvania.
She still believed deeply in the musical genius of her husband and wanted to
stand by him. She also still hoped to bring a Taylor child into the world.

Premieres of *Jurgen* and *Circus Day*

As soon as he completed *Jurgen,* and while still in Pennsylvania, Taylor informed Cabell that the *Times* had revealed the name and subject matter of his
composition: "The announcement has caused much excitement in musical
circles. The good folk here in Philadelphia, where I came to finish it, are
horrified. Two anxious friends have already begged me to change the title (to
'Little Women,' I suppose!) in order to avoid the prejudice that must inevitably be aroused by so pernicious a subject. The godless citizenry of New York,
on the other hand, show signs of inordinate delight, and appear to be looking
forward to an afternoon of unmentionable delights (a hope which, I'm
afraid, is doomed to frustration)."[33]

The musical version of *Jurgen* emerged as a one-movement symphonic
poem, some twenty-five minutes in performance.[34] Damrosch and the New
York Symphony premiered it as the final work on a lengthy November 19,
1925, afternoon program. By the time Damrosch raised his baton for *Jurgen,*
the audience and critics had already listened to the Brahms violin concerto
and a symphony by Vasily Kalinnikov, both quite long. The next day, some
critics suggested that Taylor's composition should be shortened—of course
they could not have made the same suggestion to Brahms and Kalinnikov,
since they were dead.

Taylor's *Jurgen* utilizes two principal themes and two shorter motifs. The
first theme, immediately sounded by the bass clarinet, is that of Jurgen the
Wanderer. The melody—gently descending notes in minor mode—immediately establishes a mood of apprehension, but then quickens in energy, suggesting a swaggering Jurgen. Later, the second main theme, broadly lyrical
and introduced by the cellos, brings Jurgen into the love circle of Helen of

Troy. A final musical farewell to beauty precipitates Jurgen's return to the reality of life and wife.

As to the piece's musical value, Olin Downes called the orchestration "brilliant," while the *Sun's* highly influential W. J. Henderson wrote of *Jurgen's* "splendid verve, with brilliant thematic conception." Henderson concluded his review patriotically: "There is music in every page, music that should bring gladness to the American music lover in that it was made by an American."[35] Obviously, the search for an American music hero continued, and critics saw such a possibility in Taylor because of his well-received *Looking Glass* suite. The majority of New York critics respected his talents, and Downes spoke for most: "Mr. Taylor's admirers will wish him continued advancement and await with undiminished interest his next effort."[36]

Yet, in spite of the increased interest in Taylor as a composer, *Jurgen* found no immediate acceptance. A flurry of programming activity occurred three years later, in 1928, when the Chicago Symphony and San Francisco Symphony both performed the work. The following year, Ruth St. Denis and Ted Shawn, with their modern dance group Denishawn, presented a dance version for which Taylor provided a two-piano arrangement. In 1942 Taylor revised *Jurgen* and renamed the composition *Fantasy on Two Themes*. At that time he also reflected on the difficulties of composing an orchestral opus based on a literary work:

> I once wrote a symphonic poem based on James Branch Cabell's—then—scandalous novel, *Jurgen*. What happened was that everybody who had read the book, or even heard it described, came to hear the music with a preconceived idea about what it ought to sound like. . . . I remember that one critic, in particular, went to considerable length to complain that I had utterly failed to convey a certain sense of spiritual malaise that runs through the book. Now if, instead of calling the piece *Jurgen,* I had called it "Rhapsody in D Major"—which is about what the actual form was—the critic would never have noticed the absence of that spiritual malaise. He might even have liked the piece a lot better than he did.[37]

On December 6, two weeks after the *Jurgen* premiere, the Whiteman orchestra presented Taylor's *Circus Day* in Boston's Symphony Hall to a sold-out house. The *Musical Courier* congratulated both Taylor and Grofé, the arranger: "The composer with felicitous strokes of melodic, harmonic and rhythmic invention and with ingenious orchestration has caught the essential circus day spirit."[38] What the audience heard was a lengthy suite of some forty minutes, beginning with distant sounds of a circus band entering the town with an ebullient street parade march. Musical pictures then follow: loping horses carrying bareback riders, frolicking clowns, growling lions, and galumphing elephants.

At the end of December, Whiteman brought *Circus Day* to Carnegie Hall for two performances on a program that also premiered Ferde Grofé's own composition *Mississippi Suite,* as well as the George Gershwin jazz opera *135th Street.* The first performance of Taylor's composition "set the house in a roar," according to an unsigned *Times* review.[39] In an unusual follow-up, the *Times* sent Olin Downes to review Whiteman's second performance. Downes found that the Gershwin piece, a short musical drama and a precursor in type to *Porgy and Bess,* "did not on the whole come off." However, he liked *Circus Day,* calling it "amusing and very well composed . . . a composition that accomplished what it set out to do very well."[40]

With both *Jurgen* and *Circus Day* successfully premiered, Taylor found some relief from the mental strain of composing. As for his problems as a husband, he certainly knew that his summer flings remained a cause for concern to Mary. Shortly after the *Jurgen* premiere, he gave his wife a book of poetry by the Catholic poet Francis Thompson. He inscribed it, "For Mashinka—'What else was living good for unless it brought me back to you?' Smeed, 21 November 1925."[41] We can only hope that Mary recognized the quotation as words spoken by Cabell's Jurgen as he encountered Dorothy la Désirée, "the only woman whom I ever loved." Deems relied on Mary's support to face the greatest challenge of his musical life: writing an opera that many hoped would be the great American one at last.

9. The King's Henchman, *1925–1927*

Seeking the Great American Opera

Taylor knew full well that he owed his commission from the Metropolitan Opera to two people: Giulio Gatti-Casazza, the Italian general manager of the company, and Otto H. Kahn, a New York financier of immense power and influence and the most authoritative member of the Metropolitan's board. Kahn's influence had begun in 1903, when he became a board member of the operating side of the opera, a group that leased the opera house from the owners. At that time the Austrian impresario Heinrich Conried managed the productions, but in the next few years Kahn and others became dissatisfied with his work. Kahn led the charge to find another manager. In 1908 Conried was ousted, and the operating group reorganized as the Metropolitan Opera Company, choosing Kahn as its president.[1] Now with added authority, Kahn was instrumental in luring Gatti-Casazza away from La Scala, Italy's greatest opera house, to come to the Metropolitan as its manager. A major side benefit to Gatti-Casazza's hiring was that he brought with him the already famous Arturo Toscanini to be a conductor for the company.

The desire to produce operas by American composers sat comfortably with Gatti-Casazza. "My hope, when I came to America," he wrote in his memoirs, "was to be able to discover some good American operas, which I could produce and maintain in the repertoire."[2] Kahn shared the manager's aspiration to produce American operas, and they moved quickly to find one. Their choice was *The Pipe of Desire,* a one-act work by Frederick Shepherd

Converse, for production in Gatti-Casazza's second season. Converse was one of the New England composers who had dominated American concert music in the late nineteenth century, but the three Metropolitan performances of his opera in spring 1910 received trifling acclaim.

Critics continued to pose the question "What makes an opera American?" Some argued that the subject had to be "American." If so, then *Pipe of Desire,* set in the Garden of Eden, hardly qualified. However, the argument that an American opera demanded an American story seemed completely contrary to operatic traditions, for any student knew that composers often strayed from their home grounds: Verdi in Egypt with *Aida,* Puccini in Japan with *Madame Butterfly,* and Richard Wagner in England and Brittany with *Tristan und Isolde.* Critics finally agreed on two criteria that made an opera American: the composer had to be a citizen of the United States, and the language of the libretto had to be English.

Undaunted by the unsuccessful *Pipe of Desire,* Gatti (as his staff called him) and Kahn plunged onward to find a good new American opera, maybe even a great one. At Gatti's suggestion, the Metropolitan Board sponsored a competition, with the winning composer to be awarded a prize of ten thousand dollars, quite a sum in 1912. Horatio Parker of Yale University won with *Mona,* set in Britain during Roman times, and, according to the influential critic Henry Finck, "Too Mona-tonously like an oratorio."[3] Even Gatti called it "a cold and arid thing."[4] Parker's now forgotten opera proved once again that it takes more than money to create great art.

Following the four performances allotted to *Mona,* almost every season brought another attempt at American opera, including *Cyrano* by Walter Damrosch and *Madeleine* by Victor Herbert.[5] The librettos for most of these operas scarcely held the audience's interest, and the music did little to excite the listener. The exception was the one-act *Shanewis,* by Charles Wakefield Cadman, whose melodies reached back to Native American roots and forward in the incorporation of jazz elements. *Shanewis* became the first American opera to be performed in two seasons, but ultimately it disappeared along with the others.

By 1920 Gatti and Kahn had tired of seeking the great American opera and put aside their quest. But five years later, "100 percent Americanism" and the thrill of the United States' own development in the arts renewed interest in an American opera. There was a palpable feeling that even the opera-going public wanted to steal some musical thunder from Europe, so Gatti and Kahn tried again. As the manager explained in his memoirs:

> We followed a different procedure from that of the early years of
> our American experiments. We looked for a composer who had

proved his gift, and who had knowledge of the theater. Deems Taylor seemed to us to stand peculiarly in this position. His choral works had been often performed by singing societies. His "Through the Looking Glass Suite" was one of the most popular of American compositions for orchestra, and had been highly praised by authoritative critics. He had also written, very successfully, incidental music for a number of dramas and in this way might reasonably be supposed to have a sense of the theater.[6]

Gatti himself did not ask Taylor directly, but, as described before, instead sent Edward Ziegler for that purpose.

With this commission in hand, Taylor had the opportunity of his musical life. Still, his own doubts of being able to write a successful opera must have kept him awake many a night. One person who had no doubts was Newman Levy, his friend from NYU days who knew the multiple talents of the composer. Levy expressed his belief at that time in a *New Yorker* article entitled "Versatility Personified": "Of course every one expects [Taylor] not only to compose the music, but to write the libretto, paint the scenery, lead the orchestra, supervise the lighting, and design the costumes."[7]

Taylor began his journey by seeking a librettist. He knew that creating an opera was no chicken-or-egg endeavor: music hung upon the story, so the choice of libretto was paramount. He had two choices: either write it himself or find a librettist and choose the story together. He quickly dismissed the idea of writing the libretto himself, because composing the music was challenging enough. What he needed was a librettist with a poetic command of the English language. Soon after receiving the opera commission Taylor asked his wife's advice, and she suggested Edna St. Vincent Millay as someone "extraordinary" and someone who "had something to say."[8]

Certainly Millay had said something about Taylor's *Portrait of a Lady* in the letter she had sent to the *World,* and what she had said about the music had been very positive. Of course, since Millay had won the Pulitzer Prize for poetry two years earlier, Taylor must have wondered whether he could entice her. Millay's fame now reached from coast to coast, at a time when poetry also flourished in the hands of Wallace Stevens, Marianne Moore, and Robert Frost. Light verse came from the hands of Dorothy Parker, but it was Millay whose words spoke to and for the youth of the twenties.

Edna St. Vincent Millay as Librettist

Millay had established her fame, as well as a reputation for infamous behavior, in the bohemian world of Greenwich Village during World War I. One of three brilliant and beautiful sisters from Maine, she had come to the Village to be an actress, a desire developed during her years as a student at Vassar College. She brought to the city an already growing fame as a poet with the publication of the lengthy poem *Renascence,* but in the early 1920s it was her famous quatrain about burning the candle at both ends that caused her to be the idol of those who sought to rip apart the codes and credos of life, exalting as the mores of sexuality crumbled.

For the many who met her, men especially, she was unforgettable. Taylor remembered the poet from their first meeting in Paris in 1922: "She was small, wiry, intense, almost morbidly shy. She had green eyes, set in a pointed, faintly freckled face that might have belonged to a leprechaun."[9] Shy though she might have been, she entranced and bedded many of the leading intellectuals of the Village scene, both male and female. Her multiple carousings diminished significantly, though hardly completely, when she married the rich Dutch importer Eugen Boissevain in 1923. Two years later she and Eugen left the cramped quarters of their Greenwich Village apartment for the massive outdoors of Steepletop, seven hundred acres of beautiful hills in Austerlitz, New York, near the tristate corner of New York, Massachusetts, and Connecticut. There Millay continued to write poetry, relying more and more on what she saw from the windows of her Steepletop home as inspiration for her lyricism.

Eugen took care of most of her earthly needs. He cooked, answered the phone, and wrote letters for her—all so that she could dedicate herself completely to her art and poetry-reading tours. While these tours helped to pay the mortgage, they also brought the artist's charms and intellect to many college campuses and impressionable young writers. William Shirer, one of the great journalists of World War II, recalled such an evening when he was a student in Iowa: "She had read her verses one winter evening at our college and chatted with some of us at a reception afterward. She was, I decided, the most fascinating and beautiful woman I had ever met, with flaunting red hair, a highly expressive face, rather sad eyes and a golden voice."[10] When Dorothy Parker was asked in 1966 why she no longer wrote poetry, her answer put Millay's influence in perspective: "Well you see, at that time it was fashionable—the vogue to imitate Edna Vincent Millay, and you couldn't quite do it, but you tried. Oh, *everybody* tried. All the young women in the country were writing down how they weren't virgins—whether or not they were."[11] Millay's was a life that intrigued many a biographer.[12]

In deciding to seek Millay as his librettist, Taylor recognized the value of having someone of her stature associated with him in his first operatic venture. In addition, a female librettist was something unheard of in opera. "I approached Edna Millay—with very little hope of success," Taylor later recalled. "To my immense surprise . . . she promptly agreed to give me a libretto. Whereupon I, as promptly, left it to her to find the right story for the proposed opera."[13] Exactly when he popped the libretto question to Millay isn't known, but it probably was in late spring, for by July, and with Mary now in Europe, he had been invited to visit Steepletop to begin planning. "[A] perfectly marvelous place," he wrote to his wife: "The house is rather homely and characterless, but tight and well built; but the land! About 100 acres of it is a whole side of a mountain, covered with oak and hemlock forest, and the rest of it includes two brooks and about 300 acres of rolling fields and pastures. They have acres and acres of blueberry patches."[14]

Millay insisted that no one be told of the subject of her libretto until the opera was completed. According to Taylor, he and Millay "spent many weeks, toying with the idea of a setting of *Snow White and the Seven Dwarfs*."[15] They finally agreed to proceed with the idea under the tentative title of *The Casket of Glass*.[16] By early November Millay had completed one act and showed it to Taylor, but then tonsillitis and headaches took her to the edge of a nervous breakdown. She tore up the libretto and looked in desperation for a new idea.[17] By mid-November her health had improved, and she decided on another story line for the opera, this time from Anglo-Saxon times, an era that had fascinated her during her Vassar years and studies of the language using Henry Sweet's *Anglo-Saxon Reader*.[18] Millay and her husband shared a theater box with Taylor at the premiere of *Jurgen* in November, when she very likely disclosed her new libretto idea during the concert's excitement.

Millay's choice espoused virtues that interested her deeply: integrity, friendship, and love—qualities that made the story elemental in human terms.[19] Eadgar, the widower king of England who seeks another wife, sends Aethelwold, his henchman, to determine if the reports of the beautiful Aelfrida in faraway Devon are valid. When the henchman finds Aelfrida, she is indeed beautiful and he falls deeply in love, sending a report back to the king that she is neither beautiful nor queenly, but that he will marry her himself and stay in Cornwall. After the wedding Aethelwold keeps his secret from his wife, until the day the king unexpectedly comes to visit. He then bares his soul and secret to Aelfrida, begging her to make herself as unattractive as possible. But the king arrives and a lovely, radiant Aelfrida emerges from her home. Caught in his treachery, Aethelwold kills himself with his own sword in front of his wife and his king.

Once the story line was agreed to, Millay and Taylor decided that only the sketchiest details of the opera would be released before the premiere, a way of providing the audience with the greatest dramatic impact.[20] They were aware of some similarities to Wagner's *Tristan und Isolde,* but these didn't deter them.

Before Taylor began work in earnest on the opera, an unusual opportunity came his way to bolster his ever-wavering finances. During a visit to the Brauns (probably when he was completing *Jurgen* and *Circus Day*), Edith introduced Taylor to her friend Mary Curtis Bok, who only two years earlier had founded the Curtis Institute of Music. Mrs. Bok's money came from her family's successful Curtis Publishing firm, whose *Saturday Evening Post* then ranked high in the public's reading habits. Ever a patron of the arts and thrilled to be able to help a composer commissioned by the Metropolitan, Mrs. Bok arranged for Taylor to teach a weekly composition course to specially selected advanced students: "informal discussions on orchestration, with special emphasis upon the trend of contemporary musical compositions."[21]

Every Monday during the spring of 1926, as he worked on the opera, he took the train to Philadelphia for a two-hour evening session with five students. One was Edith Braun, who wrote of the experience in her journal: "I thoroughly enjoyed it and got a great deal out of it. The talented students were Blitzstein and a young nephew of Sydney Homer, I can't think of his name, an exceedingly gifted boy."[22] Quite by accident, Taylor became one of the first teachers of two students who would later become key American composers: Marc Blitzstein and Samuel Barber. Barber was the young nephew of Sydney Homer, Sydney's wife being Louise Homer, one of the first great American contraltos. Barber, then only fifteen, would rank with Aaron Copland and Charles Ives as the most respected American composers of art music in the twentieth century, while Blitzstein's theater pieces, especially *The Cradle Will Rock,* introduced significant social themes into Broadway productions in the 1930s. Undoubtedly Taylor's interaction with such talented students only facilitated the creative process of composing his first opera.

An Opera by Mail

Years later in a written tribute to Millay, Taylor reflected on the incredible circumstances that brought his first opera into being: "'The King's Henchman' is probably the only opera ever written by correspondence. Miss Millay had been subject to recurrent and unpredictable attacks of blinding headaches. As a consequence, not daring to face a season in New York, she spent most of the year 1926 on her farm in the Berkshires, working when she was able and sending me the text in installments. As fast as one installment arrived, it would be set to music, while awaiting the arrival of the next. By a minor miracle, the result of our widely separated labors made dramatic and music sense."[23] But it wasn't just a one-way street. Taylor regularly sent his piano score installments to Millay, an excellent pianist who gained insight into the musical sense of the opera by playing the score on her grand piano in the Steepletop parlor.

The composition of the opera began in earnest in January, when Taylor received a letter from Boissevain with Millay's synopsis of the opera. She wanted "Aethelwold" to be its name, but was open to other suggestions and promised installments every few days. "Edna is not better," her husband wrote. "We cannot find out what is the trouble. It is not a nervous breakdown. She cannot use her eyes at all now, and I must do all her reading and writing. Her headache has never stopped for a single minute, and is very often dreadfully bad. Do you know of a good doctor who will give some time to find out what is the matter and make her well?"[24] Taylor's response is not known, but he may have linked Millay's love of gin to the persisting headaches.

Taylor must have wondered if the libretto would ever be finished in light of Millay's migraines, but he wrote her that he was pleased with what he received: "When I had finished reading aloud the synopsis of 'Aethelwold,' Mary remarked: 'God is very good to you, my dear,' which sums up my opinion of it better than I could do. I think it's a great libretto and find that whereas when the Met first commissioned the opera, I worried about finding a book that would be worth setting, I am now beginning to wonder whether I can possibly do justice to the book."[25]

By mid-January Taylor received a portion of the first act libretto. He was impressed by what Millay had written, but concerned about some of the words she had chosen. By letter he inquired about the specific words; her response again came via her husband: "Yes, there is such a word as diocese but it is singular, Edna says, and the plural of it would sound like a saw-mill. Personally, Deems, between you and me, I agree with you, that Bisho-pricks would sing not so good."[26] Another annoyance to Taylor was the stodginess of some of the characters' names:

> Edna, it's grand! It's so utterly Saxon in feeling, and such good poetry and good drama. . . . Couldn't Eadgar be modernized into Edgar and Aelfrida into Elfreda without doing history too much violence? A lot of comparatively literate people know Alfred the Great, who never heard of Aelfred; and all things being equal, the easier we make things for the poor dears, the better, I think. I mind Aethelwold a little, though I wouldn't interpose my dead body to keep him out. The only thing I fear is, that inasmuch as the opera is in English, the audience is going to bring contemporary English-speaking attitudes to it; and they may be saps enough to consider a

name beginning with "Ethel" too effeminate for a hero. I suppose you think that's silly. It is. But so is an audience. After all, you're violating history in your account of his deeds, so you could be forgiven for doing violence to his name, in case you did. "Wulfred" would be my choice for a hero. It has such a pleasant lupine connotation.[27]

His questioning of Millay's use of the language resulted in the high point of their correspondence: a five-page, single-spaced letter typed by Millay herself, who assigned the date as "Along in February, snowed in." She began by describing nature's attempt to disrupt the opera's creation, as snow separated Steepletop from the Austerlitz post office several miles away:

> Yours received, but not so much received as fought and bled for and wrested from the elements—five miles on snow-shoes over drifts, and into them ten feet deep, to get your letter, dearie. No, not me—him [Eugen]. There were three days the post couldn't get through from Chatham to Austerlitz, road blocked for twelve miles. . . . I am writing you from my hut, where I come every day on my snow-shoes and build my fire and work. Now to your letter. . . . "The King's Henchman" is the best title so far; so let's call it that until we hit on something better, and see how it wears. . . . I insist on using real names of the time, not making up any. . . . NO! Eadgar and Aelfrida could NOT be modernized into Edgar and Elfreda! For who-the-hell am I writing this libretto anyway, Deems Taylor or George Gershwin? Honest, old bean, nobody's going to know who Eadgar was anyway . . . Goo'-by. Love to you and Mary from me and Gene.[28]

Though the word *henchman* would later take on a negative connotation, at that time it clearly meant a "trusted follower." However, by mid-March, with the second act almost complete, the opera's name remained undecided. "Yes, 'The Saxons' *is* a good title," Millay wrote, "and looks fine on the program, you cute old thing. I don't think it is perfect but am willing to keep it till we think of a better and if we never think of a better, we'll let it stand."[29]

A month later, Taylor signed a contract with the Metropolitan that guaranteed four performances in the first season at $150 per, with two names suggested for the opera in the contract: "The Saxons" or "The King's Messenger." When Millay received his telegram with the good news about the contract, she was annoyed at the possible title of "The King's Messenger," apparently Taylor's own idea. She sent him a telegram:

KINGS MESSENGER ABSOLUTELY IMPOSSIBLE FOR THIS REASON
THE WORD MESSENGER WAS BROUGHT INTO ENGLISH BY THE

NORMANS AND I AM WRITING MY ENTIRE LIBRETTO IN ANGLO
SAXON THAT IS TO SAY THERE IS NOT A WORD IN THE LI-
BRETTO WHICH WAS NOT KNOWN IN ONE FORM OR ANOTHER
IN ENGLAND A THOUSAND YEARS AGO STOP I MEANT TO
SPRING THIS ON YOU LATER AND TO KEEP IT SECRET FROM EV-
ERYBODY ELSE UNTIL THEY FOUND OUT FOR THEMSELVES IF
EVER STOP IF YOU MUST TELL METROPOLITAN BEG THEM TO
KEEP IT SECRET STOP METROPOLITAN CAN CHOOSE BETWEEN
SAXONS AND KINGS HENCHMAN.[30]

The secret was out and now Taylor understood the basis of his gentle word
battles with the author; it was Millay at her most literary, aiming to meld music with the language of the time of the story.

Though the opera progressed satisfactorily, by mid-May the personal life
of Mr. and Mrs. Taylor had soured. After a particularly serious argument,
Mary left by train to be with her family in Florida, and Taylor immediately
penned a letter, penitential in tone: "Oh, Baby—Now you've gone out, like
Nora—and I was all dressed to go with you, too—and we've had a row, and
I'm good and wretched. And so are you, poor angel . . . and I truly DON'T
mean the rotten things you think I do. I'm truly not trying to get you off to
Florida to get rid of you."[31] Taylor certainly recognized his wife's indepen-
dent streak by referring to her as Nora, the ultimately rebellious wife in
Ibsen's *A Doll's House.*

To make matters worse for Mary, she discovered on the train that her
wedding ring was missing and telegraphed Deems to search for it. Unable to
find it, he wrote back with words suggesting he wanted to begin anew: "If it
is lost, it's probably a sign from heaven that I ought to get you a new one.
What date do you want in it—or will the old one do?" By the time she
reached Florida, she had found the ring and wired the good news, concluding: "MISS YOU BUT I AM VERY OPTIMISTIC PLEASE BE HAPPY AND DON'T FOR-
GET ME."[32]

Two days later Taylor appeared before Gatti-Casazza and Tullio Serafin,
the conductor, to preview the first portions of the opera. Edith Braun came
from Philadelphia to accompany him. The experience proved to be mildly
terrifying, as he wrote to Mary: "I played the first act and part of the second
to Gatti and Serafin today—rather, Edith did, and I sang it—and I swear I
haven't the remotest idea whether they thought it was wonderful or terrible.
Perhaps neither. At any rate, they listened in silence—Gatti walking about—
and at the end [they] burst into floods of mutual Italian with scarcely a word
of comment for me! . . . It's a bit hard to bear."[33] Before leaving, he promised
Gatti to have the piano and vocal score of the first two acts completed by

early July, so that the Metropolitan manager could take them for study as he
sailed for Italy.

The following day, another letter to Mary expressed his discouragement
and depression, which was "a hangover from yesterday's Metropolitan audition." For the first time, he cast verbal aspersions on Millay. "I know what's
the matter with Act I. The exposition is amateurish, because Edna is no dramatist. . . . I was a damned fool not to have made you write my libretto. . . .
You're a dramatist and a poet."[34]

If Taylor was on the edge of despair, so was his wife. From her mother's
home she wrote of her anguish: "I am sick and desperately miserable. My
mind twists and turns the same ugly knowledge until I think I shall die, and
find that I am much too sick to die—Where is my love? Who are you,
Deems, that should have everything, and has nothing for me not even pity?
Are there no words for me—heal me—if you cannot—I am lost—I think I
am lost anyway—Oh, love—Try to understand."[35] The tone of the letter
frightened Taylor, and he sent her daily messages of calm concern that
seemed to help, for she responded positively: "Darling, thank you for your
recent letters. They have comforted and warmed me as nothing else could. I
have been really ill I think, as you can tell by the mad letter I wrote you . . .
but I am better today than I have been in months. Dearest love I think I have
found out all about us, at last. I have jumped off the fence and I'm on your
side! I will be home soon."[36]

From his letters Mary recognized that her husband also needed support,
so she lauded him generously: "I think you are the most extraordinary musician and workman that ever lived. After all you began it when you were almost tired to death—I am proud of you my dear love, and when you hear it
you too will be proud. Now I know you haven't time for anything but work
and sleep. I think I can help you when I come back and take care of you, so
that you can finish on time. I am getting well and rested and my mind is
clear."[37]

She returned with a positive outlook, and only months later did her husband find out why his wife had seemed out of control in Florida: Mary Kennedy had discovered she was pregnant! Knowing that her husband did not
want children and might even want her to get an abortion, she at first sank
into a depression but then, in a burst of inspiration, initiated a plan that
would allow her to cover up her pregnancy until the day when she would
provide her husband with the biggest surprise of his life.

Meanwhile, the pressures on Taylor didn't let up. Millay and her husband
brought the complete final act to him in New York in mid-June. He then
worked at breakneck speed and managed to deliver the piano score of the
first two acts to Gatti as promised. With the third act incomplete and the or-

chestration yet to begin, Taylor saw great value in a trip to Paris. Considering that the city was less expensive than New York, the decision to work there was sensible. Mary, who loved Paris as much as he did, agreed.

Before leaving, they took a short trip to Philadelphia to see the Brauns, and Taylor played a portion of the last act for them. "The music is splendid," Edith wrote in her journal. She then substantiated that the Taylor finances were on the slim side: "Johnnie gave him a check for $100 to help out a little for I'm sure they're frightfully hard-up when Mary has to do the cooking. She's been plucky about it. She is witty and clever and really loves Deems I think."[38] Even the Brauns seem to have wondered about the marriage.

When Deems and Mary arrived in Paris in late July, she began a new play while he completed the opera's piano and vocal score, then began orchestrating the first two acts.[39] At the end of September they returned to New York, where his father met them at the pier: "Deems looks much better than he did when he went away," he wrote in his journal. "The orchestration is only about half done. It is a tremendous undertaking. . . . [J. Fischer & Bro.] is about ready to put the piano score on the press."[40] During their return trip, Mary had convinced her husband that it was better for her to rent a separate apartment—just for a while. In that way she could leave him alone to complete the orchestration, and she could continue work on her play. He agreed but remained a bit mystified by her desire to have her own quarters, especially since money was scarce. Of course, the plan was part of Mary's subterfuge to keep her pregnancy a secret. She chose an apartment on Beekman Place, while he remained at the Fifty-seventh Street residence.

In October New York newspapers began the long buildup toward the *Henchman*'s premiere. All that had leaked to the press about the opera was that it was similar to *Tristan und Isolde* and that it took place in England during the ninth century. In the *Times*, Olin Downes reviewed the sad history of previous attempts at American opera with their "poor librettos" and "music that lacked original invention and the sense and skill of the theatre in its arrangement." He pointed out that both Taylor and Millay "are of the young generation of creative artists in this country, and are both venturing in new and provocative fields of effort. There will be fresh curiosity and the hope that at last an American opera of value will be contributed to the repertory." Downes harbored special hopes for Millay's contribution, because "Miss Millay has long since given the public a right to expect from her verse of beauty and distinction."[41]

The Metropolitan's production plans for *The King's Henchman* were first class. For scenic designer they chose Vienna-born Joseph Urban, who had attracted the attention of New Yorkers for his glamorous settings of the *Ziegfeld Follies*. Since 1917 he had been the Metropolitan's principal designer.

His use of lighting revolutionized scene design by introducing the painting of backdrops "not in imitation of nature, but as a medium for the reception of colored light."[42]

Gatti-Casazza had also carefully selected the three principal singers. For Aethelwold he chose the young Canadian tenor Edward Johnson, whose Metropolitan debut in 1922 Taylor had lauded. For Aelfrida Gatti selected Florence Easton, English born and Canadian raised. Since her Met debut in 1917 as Santuzza in *Cavalleria Rusticana,* the company had relied on her to fill a great many roles with her excellent musicianship and incredible facility for quick memorization. Her memory reportedly caused Caruso to remark: "Her head is a music box; she lifts off the lid, takes out one record, and puts in another; that is the only way any singer could remember so many operas."[43] Johnson and Easton were veterans, but Gatti decided that the time was ripe to give Lawrence Tibbett his first major role, that of King Eadgar. Two years earlier, Tibbett's intensity and brilliant singing as Ford in *Falstaff* had generated a fifteen-minute ovation. It had been "one of the most unprecedented and certainly unpremeditated" ever heard in New York opera history.[44]

As the month of November advanced, the task of orchestration seemed overwhelming to Taylor. He saw little of his wife, communicating with her by letters and telegrams, since she had no telephone. Finances were tight for them both. After a visit to the Brauns in a vain attempt to complete the orchestration, he returned early and sent a quick note to Mary: "Mashinka darling—I thought you were probably broke, so I came back Friday night instead of Saturday morning so as to get the money into the bank. . . . The McCall check arrived, so I put in forty of that for you . . . Your account now stands at $80.00 balance in bank."[45]

Taylor had returned early for another reason: he had been asked to be the master of ceremonies at the testimonial luncheon for his father, who was retiring as administrator of the Bronx schools. Some twelve hundred people filled the ballroom of the Hotel Commodore to pay tribute to the elder Taylor, who sat next to his son on the dais, then later wrote in his journal that Deems "kept [the audience] in a roar with his subtle wit. He began by saying, 'In looking over this room, I am amazed. I didn't know there were so many people in America that had three dollars.'"[46]

After sharing some time with his family at the retirement dinner, a few days later, on Thanksgiving night, frustration and loneliness swept over Taylor. Sitting physically near but emotionally so far from the woman who had supported his musical talents so strongly, he penned words of concern and gratitude to his wife: "I wonder how you are, and what you are doing, and when I am going to see you. I've done pretty well with my work, but I haven't given you much of a life, or made much of one for myself. What I've had, you have made for me. I'd like to try to give you a little peace and happiness when this nightmare is over."[47]

While Taylor struggled with the orchestration, Millay and her husband went to Santa Fe, New Mexico, to share the sun with their friends Arthur Ficke and his wife, Gladys Brown. Ficke had been a poet friend of Millay's since the publication of *Renascence*. While the librettist enjoyed the Western air, Taylor remained in monklike seclusion, finally completing the orchestration on December 15.

The following day he dropped off the manuscript at the Metropolitan and hurried over to Winthrop Ames, his producer friend, to demand a cocktail. Both Winthrop and his wife, Beatrice, congratulated him on his accomplishment. They asked about Mary, also a favorite of theirs, whom they hadn't seen in recent weeks. Taylor passed along their puzzlement to his wife: "The general tenor of their inquiries was where the hell were you, so I told them that you had determined to finish your play before New Year's and were locked in for the rest of 1926."[48] He had not seen his wife for three months.

On the evening of December 21, Deems Taylor answered the telephone and learned the real reason for Mary's isolation. The caller was their close friend the actress Margalo Gillmore: "Deems, this is going to take all the bigness you've got. Mary's in the hospital having a baby." It was a girl.

A Nonoperatic Surprise

Mary's secret had been shared with no one. Marjorie Kummer Young, Roland Young's wife, probably came closest to expressing the wonderment of the event in a letter to the new mother: "Mary Darling! You've achieved something—to me—about as mysterious and unbelievable, as the Immaculate Conception! Not that I'm casting any reflections on Deems, but you have been so magnificently secretive! I think it's wonderful and don't quite believe it! I want to SEE it! Bless you, dear! And Deems! And the apparently impromptu babe!"[49] A similarly surprised Millay, now back at Steepletop, wrote to Arthur Ficke and Gladys Brown of the new Taylor: "Not a living soul in the world knew anything about it, not even his mother and her mother. Next day we went to see Mary for a moment, who was looking beautiful and crying for cold creams and make-up."[50] Alexander Woollcott's take on the event was short and snappy: "Dear Mary, You surprise me."[51]

Two days after the baby was born, her parents named her Joan. Joseph "JoJo" Taylor, ever the educator, promised his help in raising the child: "Your darling Baby is a complete success. It took you a long time to achieve it, but the result justifies the time of production. You will be interested now in child training—my profession. So I call your attention to [the book] 'Nine Ways of Being a Bad Parent.' . . . Outside of my own children I have never seen a more perfect child than Joan."[52] Perfect or not, the baby increased the family by 50 percent, so a larger apartment was needed. They moved to a duplex in the Turtle Bay district of Manhattan, on Forty-ninth Street.[53] Unexpected life as a father had begun, and Deems was immensely grateful that he had completed *The King's Henchman* before receiving the phone call.

Years later he would realize that two of his greatest joys in life occurred two months apart: "The first sight of his daughter, Joan, and the original orchestral rehearsal of The King's Henchman."[54] Early rehearsals went well. Taylor wrote to Millay of a rare compliment he had received from the conductor Tullio Serafin, who had been the principal conductor at La Scala in the early years of the twentieth century: "Except for leaving off the mutes in two string passages there had not been a single alteration necessary in the scoring—which, Serafin says, is a miracle. Puccini used to have to make dozens of changes."[55]

Millay could not overcome her excitement about the opera and decided to come to a rehearsal also, which proved to be providential. With the opera running too long, the director decided to cut King Eadgar's final aria. Taylor objected vigorously, as did Tibbett, who was singing the role of the king, but to no avail. The baritone recalled that Millay appeared at the next day's rehearsal, and when she realized what had happened, she openly declared war: "They won't cut that out of my opera! . . . That is the best scene in the opera. If it goes out, the entire opera goes out. We stop right now!" And, concluded Tibbett, "she was right. It turned out to be the peak of the performance."[56]

Nothing illustrated the public's interest in the opera more than the *Times* review of the final dress rehearsal. The headline read almost as if it had been the first performance: "Native Opera Sung to Society Folk." The long article identified dozens of invited friends and artists, including many from the Algonquin group, opera stars such as Lauritz Melchior and Lucrezia Bori, as well as Walter Damrosch, who was reported to exclaim after the third-act curtain, "There is real emotion in that music!"[57]

Before the premiere, Taylor wrote his assessment of its future: "If, when [*The King's Henchman*] is produced, the book and the music are found to possess individual qualities that make it something more than an imitation of something else, and if those qualities are such as to appeal to the sensibilities of an American audience—then it will be an American opera. If it is not, then it will soon be nothing at all, beyond a few hundred bound sheets of paper with black marks on them. Time and the Metropolitan subscribers will have to make that decision."[58] History has so far shown a lack of interest in

The King's Henchman's cast of creators for the Metropolitan premiere. In the center are Taylor and Edna St. Vincent Millay. Clockwise from bottom left: assistant manager Edward Ziegler, Merle Alcock, Edward Johnson, Florence Easton, general manager Guilio Gatti-Casazza, conductor Tullio Serafin, director Wilhelm Von Wymetal, Lawrence Tibbett, and William Gustafson.

(Courtesy of Metropolitan Opera Archives)

the opera, but no one could have predicted that from the highly positive response of both the public and the critics.

Premiere of *The King's Henchman*

As 8:00 P.M. approached on Thursday, February 17, 1927, members of the audience in the sold-out Metropolitan Opera House awaited the opening of the gold curtain for the most eagerly anticipated musical event of the season. Meanwhile, on that mild winter evening, the composer and librettist found themselves not inside in comfortable box seats, but outside in the long line of people waiting to buy standing room tickets. They were ticketless because of a falling-out that afternoon between Millay and Florence Mixter.

Millay and her husband were staying with Mixter, a poet friend of Millay's and a well-off society matron. She had offered them seats in her opera box. But then Mixter had done some snooping into a box of photos that Gladys Brown had given her to pass along to Edna and Eugen. The photos recorded their Sante Fe trip, and among them were nude poses of Millay and others, taken by Arthur Ficke in the New Mexico desert.

An appalled Mixter told Millay exactly what she thought of such activities. Millay, enraged, refused to have anything further to do with Mixter or her offer of box seats. She chose instead to join the outside line.[59] Just before curtain time, Metropolitan officials "discovered and rescued" the opera's creators and found a couple of empty seats for them in a box.[60] They sat down just in time to hear the brief prelude followed by the solitary voice of Maccus, Aethelwold's servant and harper, recounting battles of ages past.

The curtain rises in the great hall of King Eadgar's castle. The widowed king, eager to marry again, implores his close friend Aethelwold to go to Devon and speak with Aelfrida, the thane of Devon's daughter, who reportedly possesses the beauty and manner fit for a queen of England. Aethelwold, being shy, urges the king to send another, but his lord insists. After a pledge of loyalty, Aethelwold mounts his horse and rides off with the spirited choral finale "O Caesar, Great Wert Thou."

The second act, an extended love scene, is set in the woods of Devon among oaks and silver birches in misty moonlight. It is All Hallow's Eve, and Aelfrida has come into the forest to give the traditional incantations that will provide a glimpse of her lover-to-be. Ghostly voices support her recitations before she stumbles on the sleeping Aethelwold, who together with his harper had lost his way. Upon awakening he sees the beautiful Aelfrida and falls deeply in love, only to discover too late who she is. Caught between love and fidelity he chooses love, which is reciprocated by Aelfrida in a stirring duet. Aethelwold sends Maccus back to the king with the message that Aelfrida is plain and old, but because her father is rich and he, Aethelwold, is poor, he will stay and marry her, and he asks the king's blessing. He tells nothing to Aelfrida of his original assignment.

The third act begins the following spring with an annoyed Aelfrida, a bride of a half-year, essentially a housekeeper in her father's house. Aethelwold promises to take her to Ghent in Flanders, a city she has longed to see, and they sing of hoped-for future joy. But before they can leave, they learn that the king is on his way for a visit. The sound of the king's men singing as they approach spurs Aethelwold to disclose to Aelfrida the deception that he has harbored since they met. He pleads with her to camouflage her beauty and "be foul and bent and withered." She reluctantly agrees and goes to her room to prepare.

The king arrives and seizes Aethelwold in an embrace of friendship, then asks to see Aelfrida. He is told she is ill and unprepared. Then, in a display of unbridled vanity, Aelfrida appears before the king radiant, in her finest silks and jewels. Aethelwold recognizes only one solution to such a betrayal of friendship to his king. Advancing upon his wife with drawn knife, he tells her that it will not be she who suffers, for he still loves her. Then he plunges the dagger into his body. Powerless to stop him, the king stands by his dying henchman and ultimately urges his men to carry Aethelwold away in honor, for "this day hath he dared two kings; Myself, and Death."

At the final curtain, ovation upon ovation greeted the singers as they came forward to take their bows. Gladys Brown described the exhilaration of the event in a letter to her husband, whose illness had kept him home in Santa Fe:

> It was exciting! We had terrible seats in the front but way over at one side so that we saw about half of the stage—but were lucky to have anything and what we did see we saw well. And we heard a few words now and then. There is a great difference in singers—everything that Maccus said was clear as a whistle. . . . [T]he King almost as good and the rest nothing but blur. Aethelwold [Edward Johnson] was quite handsome but the most awful actor that ever paced the stage; to me he was utterly loathsome. Aelfrida [Florence Easton] wasn't bad but terribly fat and not very young and beautiful. But the King was swell [Lawrence Tibbett]. I didn't mind having nothing much happen in the first act since there were times when it was quite heartrending. . . . Vincent [Millay's nickname among friends] and Deems appeared at the end of each act and came again and again for prolonged applause. Vincent had a marvelous dress of red and gold but she was quite fussed and acted rather baby-girlish on the whole. But at the end of the third act people began calling for a speech and finally Vincent and Deems came forward and Deems looked at Vincent helplessly and Vincent at him. Then she spread out her hands, made a little duck of the head, and said, "All I can say is—that I love you all." Giggles and applause. Then Deems: "I— I was just going to say the same thing." Laughter and applause.[61]

In the midst of a full twenty minutes of applause and thirty-five curtain calls, attendants brought out two huge laurel wreaths: "Finally they stood alone— the scholarly musician and the girlish, frail young poetess—with wreaths of myrtle as tall as themselves."[62]

The following day's reports of the opera brought added joy to the composer and librettist (February 18, 1927): "'King's Henchman' Hailed as Best

American Opera" headlined the *Times* in Olin Downes's front-page review, with the subheading: "Millay Book Is Poetic; Composer's Expressive Music Has Beauty and Deep Emotional Appeal." Special praise was given to Taylor's orchestration. Samuel Chotzinoff, his replacement at the *World,* called it "a masterpiece," while the esteemed W. J. Henderson of the *Sun* praised it as "extremely opulent." Lawrence Gilman in the *Herald Tribune* completely approved of the libretto: "Mr. Taylor has woven a deft and often lovely sounding score about a superb poetic text, a text pithy and glamorous and full of character; rich in humor and dramatic force. . . . English words . . . sung from the stage are not only heard, but are expressive, and fitting, and often beautiful."

After the successful premiere, Gatti-Casazza announced that the Metropolitan would change the scheduled number of performances from four to seven, and that sold-out houses (the second performance had sold out before the premiere) were bringing in $15,000 each, a tidy sum in those times. As a grand finale to the joyful radiance of the *Henchman's* premiere, within the week Kahn and Gatti announced an agreement with Taylor for a second opera, to be ready in two years.

Friends and acquaintances showered praise and congratulations. Antoinette Perry sent perfumed words: "If there were roses enough to fill all the bath-tubs in this world and the next . . . they couldn't carry one millionth part as much loveliness as one little minute of the Opera! I am speechless with Happiness."

Three days after the premiere, the reigning Italian soprano, Amelita Galli-Curci, telegraphed Taylor: "Sincere congratulations on your splendid success [and] would be thrilled to have a part in your next." Taylor's response to the famed coloratura trotted out his operatic humor: "How flattered I am to have your offer to sing in the next. Now that I have you under contract I am going after Chaliapin, John McCormack and Schumann-Heink. A quartette like that could make up its own music and save me a lot of trouble."[63]

Even Alexander Woollcott sent praise: "Don't let any one tell you that you don't know how to write music." This was his clever, albeit belated, retort to Taylor's telegram to Woollcott sent years earlier: "Don't let any one tell you that you don't know how to write."[64]

Only later, when the critics of the weekly and monthly periodicals began their assessment, did some observations tilt to the negative. "After listening to two performances from various points of the Metropolitan Opera House," wrote Herbert Peyser, "I cannot confess to have grasped more than thirty per cent (at a very liberal estimate) of the words sung."[65] Another critic, recognizing that Millay had chosen to utilize only Anglo-Saxon words, called the libretto "the tortured work of a gifted woman" and asked why singers should have to sing such lines as "Now hath his Lady a bitter burthen to thole." This critic concluded, "The King's Henchman clamors for a glossary," and "One should not need a glossary in opera."[66]

Yet many others agreed that Millay had provided finely honed lines, often humorous in their content. For example, in the first act Aethelwold finally agrees to seek the lady for the king, then delineates his approach: "I climb to my saddle and I ride and I ride . . . and I say to the maid . . . if thou be as fair as men say, don thy hood and come along o' me; and sooner than a weasel can suck a duck's egg, thou shalt be Queen of England." At another point the archbishop of Canterbury stands firm to a vociferous critic: "No. The Church of God is not a candle. Blow on!"

The often sarcastic Paul Rosenfeld, by 1927 the key spokesperson for the modernist idiom, wrote negatively of both composer and librettist, saying that Taylor's music had "thoroughgoing uninventiveness," while Millay's libretto was "like so much of her work, a warming-over of the motives of past poetry." Unable to accept the success of the opera, Rosenfeld determined it was due to the "intelligence of the public which supports the Metropolitan Opera."[67] In other words, if the audience liked what they heard, that proved they were not worthy to know what true music was. For Rosenfeld, Taylor was a composer who followed the "tendency to accept the established and shrink from discovery and adventure."[68] His disdain also arose from his dislike of folksong traditions and the use of motifs à la Wagner, both of which Taylor had studiously worked into the tapestry of the opera's music.

No matter what the criticism, by writing some two hours of music, Taylor had taken a quantum leap in exercising his composing skills and playing to three of his strengths: choral writing; extensive knowledge of folksongs; and an understanding, gained from his Broadway experiences, of the need to keep the audience interested in the plot. Each act featured choral segments, with "O Caesar, Great Wert Thou" used in both the first and third acts, a special melody easily remembered. Taylor had adapted it from a folksong from Cornwall, "My Johnny Was a Shoemaker." It was the hit of the opera.[69] The choral murmurings of the ghostly voices in the second act's forest scene provided an effective surreal quality, as Aelfrida moved among the misty trees. Her song of incantation had a plaintive folksong quality, though the melody was original with Taylor.

He had resisted the use of individual arias, since they could slow down the dramatic progress of an opera. With the singer placed center stage, the results might be musically exciting but dramatically deadly. He preferred to move the opera along by providing the singers a vocal line "with natural speech rhythms, highlighting important words through pitch and duration": a modern recitative.[70] However, there were lyrical stops along the way, such as the impassioned duet between Aelfrida and Aethelwold in the murky forest, and Eadgar's lament at the end of the opera.

In addition, Taylor followed the Wagnerian approach of using musical motifs to identify characters or emotions, as well as using the orchestra to provide "tone painting": instrumental coloration to words or action. Elaine Apczynski, in her analysis of the opera, found some "sixty specific instances of true motif and tone painting" in the score: "The motifs are not always readily identifiable on first hearing, but would affect the listener subconsciously."[71] Clearly there was more subtlety to the music than perhaps even Rosenfeld was willing to acknowledge.

As for Millay, although she had never before written an opera libretto, she had written several short plays. Her libretto allowed for the conversational approach that Taylor chose for the singers, making the few arias more appreciated. According to Edmund Wilson (one of Millay's early lovers), her words evidenced her mastery of "the music of English verse," which "remains simple without ever ceasing to be personal."[72]

No matter what anyone said about *The King's Henchman,* the opera was a financial boon to the Metropolitan. At the end of the season Gatti updated Otto Kahn, then in Italy: "I want to advise you of the matters pertaining to the Metropolitan. As I already had the pleasure of cabling you since you left, everything has continued regularly and brilliantly. The old 'Mignon' has exceeded all our expectations. . . . The same may be said of the further performances of 'The King's Henchman' the success of which is indeed without precedent. . . . The season in New York closes with a profit of about $45,000."[73] *The King's Henchman* ran three consecutive seasons with a total of seventeen performances, far outdistancing any previous American opera produced by the Metropolitan.[74]

Nothing speaks to the opera's success more than the advertisement that appeared in *Musical America* six months after the premiere: "Announcing the First Transcontinental Tour of Deems Taylor's Great American Opera The King's Henchman, Last Season's Metropolitan Sensation."[75] Never before (or since) had an American opera traveled in a wide radius from New York immediately after the season of its first performances. Leading the company was Jacques Samossoud, an entrepreneurial musical director who later married Mark Twain's only surviving child, Clara Clemens. First-rate soloists (two alternating casts) included Marie Sundelius, a soprano who had been featured in the earlier American opera *Shanewis;* and the baritone Richard Hale, Heywood Broun's brother-in-law. Full staging, an orchestra of fifty members, and a chorus of the same number gave audiences a complete operatic experience.

The company initiated its tour on November 4 in Washington, D.C., with first lady Mrs. Calvin Coolidge hosting the Taylors in the presidential box in Poli's Theater for the sold-out event. "New American Opera Has Sustained Poetic Quality and Appealing Music," ran a headline the next day,[76] and the tour was on, including a week in Boston and four performances each in Columbus and St. Paul, where "English and music departments of the public schools had been made familiar with book and score."[77] Though the three-month tour of more than one hundred performances ultimately was not transcontinental, the *Henchman* made it as far west as the Mississippi.

The King's Henchman had succeeded where previous American operas had failed. William Lyon Phelps of Yale University chose amusingly accurate words when he called Taylor "an American who has written a grand opera that people who have heard it once actually want to hear it again."[78] Now Taylor had the challenge of following up a successful first.

10. *The Road to* Peter Ibbetson, *1927–1931*

Editor of *Musical America*

Two months after the *Henchman's* premiere, a frazzled Taylor sought peace and quiet. "He [is] hiding at [Hollow Hill]," his father wrote in his journal, "on the verge of nervous collapse. The strain has been too much. For a number of weeks he proposes to be a carpenter and general utility man. The social, professional and personal demands on him have been overwhelming."[1] For Taylor, the newly crowned king of American opera, pressure mounted to choose the next libretto wisely. In addition, finances continued to be an issue, and he had to come to grips with being a father. As much as he admired his wife for her support and talents, deep in his heart he couldn't be sure whether Mary had tricked him during what he later called "a one-week reconciliation."[2]

Taylor worked out his anxieties at the Stamford property, helped by Foster Kennedy, his wife's youngest brother and an architecture student at MIT. Foster did the cooking while Taylor worked on the drain boards, the front door, anything to keep his mind from the next big hurdle. "It's peaceful here and solitary," he wrote to Mary, who remained in New York with the baby. "The silence is like a hand laid on my forehead. I think of you a great deal, and wonder what you are doing and if you are happy."[3] She was, in fact, quite happy, for in addition to being a mother she had taken on a featured role in *Mariners,* a new McClintic play. Mary balanced the parts of mother and actress by hiring a nanny for Joan, a necessity throughout the next four years while she repeatedly accepted new roles on Broadway. After all, her pay helped provide some stability to the family's episodic income.

For the same reason, her husband once again turned to writing. This time he worked for two monthly magazines. *McCall's,* a popular women's magazine, paid him for a series entitled "What's Going On in the World of Music," but far more satisfying to him as a native New Yorker were the articles for *Vanity Fair,* the magazine that chronicled the twenties like no other. Its pages were populated with the works of first-rate photographers and writers, including most of the Algonquin crowd. The *Vanity Fair* pieces kept Taylor's insightful wit flowing in many directions. He wrote about "Grand Opera—Its Cause and Cure: A Guess at What Ails the Most Fashionable and Best-Hated of Indoor Recreation" (April 1928).

He even revealed the story of "The Three Immortals of Church History: The Inside Story of Kelley, McGook, and Grabbenheim, and What It Might Teach Us" (May 1929). It seems that Taylor and friends, while at NYU, secretly enrolled three nonexistent students into a church history course and managed to get them each a passing grade. In another article Taylor explored a little-known side of himself: "The Pleasant Art of Monogramming: Some Bizarre Examples, by an Incorrigible Addict, of One of the Less Familiar Indoor Sports" (February 1927).

The beauty of a verdant spring in the hills of Connecticut revived Taylor, as did the psychological boost of an honorary doctorate from his alma mater on June 8, 1927. He was in good company, for the other recipients included Secretary of State Frank Kellogg and the chairman of General Electric, Owen G. Young. In the Taylor citation, NYU chancellor Elmer Brown told the audience of a letter from the composer indicating that his goal of writing an opera "turned out to be only a milepost" now that he had a second commission.[4]

Later that summer Taylor chose the librettist for his next milepost, releasing the news to an Associated Press reporter: "I have found the most charming and compatible, the most accomplished and erudite of collaborators. We get along splendidly together. It is true that I fuss and say crude things to this collaborator, sometimes, but it is all taken in good grace. We have already concluded the first two acts of the libretto." When the reporter asked, "Who is your new collaborator?" Taylor answered, "It is myself."[5] What he didn't tell the reporter was that his libretto was based on the book *Gandle Follows His Nose,* by his friend Heywood Broun.

Before the summer was over, *Musical America,* the country's most influential weekly on musical topics, surprised the entire New York community by announcing that Deems Taylor had accepted the position of editor. *Musical America* reached out to everyone in music, from the professional to

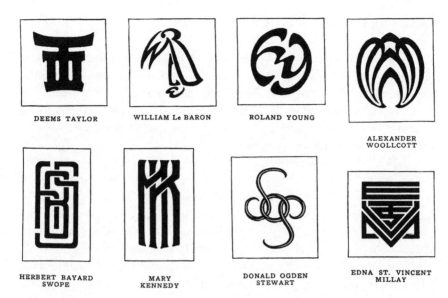

DEEMS TAYLOR   WILLIAM Le BARON   ROLAND YOUNG

ALEXANDER
WOOLLCOTT

HERBERT BAYARD
SWOPE   MARY
KENNEDY   DONALD OGDEN
STEWART   EDNA ST. VINCENT
MILLAY

Samples of Taylor's talent of monogramming. *(Courtesy of Joan Kennedy Taylor. Monograms taken from Deems Taylor, "The Pleasant Art of Monogramming,"* Vanity Fair, *February 1927, 71)*

the teacher to the amateur. But why did Taylor accept the post knowing that he had to write an opera within the next two years? It might have been the pay, but more likely he had caught a minor case of hubris: *Through the Looking Glass* was now among the most performed symphonic works by an American, *The King's Henchman* had succeeded eminently, and people still complimented him on the criticisms from his *World* days. He may have believed that as editor, he could provide the music world with lucid commentary from the unique perspective of a major figure in contemporary music. Besides, he was moving well toward his next opera, and he didn't expect the editorship to take up too much time. As it turned out, he was wrong.

On August 27, 1927, the first of his *Musical America* issues appeared, and the new editor blew a loud trumpet upon his arrival by printing "A Declaration of Intentions" on the front page, along with "Aims and Principles." He assured his readers that *Musical America* would be "Entertaining and understandable . . . Incorruptible in reading matter . . . Accurate in the presentation . . . Fearless and uncompromising . . . Patriotic . . . Hospitable to all honest criticism."[6] To the longtime reader this must have suggested that naughty things had gone on in the past, but in fact, not much had changed. The magazine continued its blend of national music coverage, concert reviews, and the eagerly anticipated columns of humor and chatty insider information.

The Opera House That Wasn't to Be

Within a month, Taylor stirred up a musical hornet's nest around the issue of building a new Metropolitan Opera House, something that Otto Kahn championed and Taylor agreed with completely.[7] Kahn had lobbied to replace the company's so-called Yellow Brick Brewery on Broadway ever since becoming chairman in 1908. Few disagreed that the production facilities were both antiquated and appallingly inconvenient.

Rehearsal space was minimal, and with no extra backstage space, sets for the operas in repertory were piled behind the building on Seventh Avenue and covered with a tarpaulin, hardly a way to improve their permanence. For the audience, the horseshoe-shaped auditorium, elegant in gold and maroon, had too many seats with terrible sight lines, which bothered the democratic streaks of both Taylor and Kahn. "To my mind," Kahn wrote, "the gravest objection [to the present building] is the fact that the accommodation for those who cannot afford to pay for expensive seats is entirely inadequate in the present house, both as to quality and as to the number of available seats. The Metropolitan was built at a time when consideration for the wants and claims of the broad masses of the people did not have that reality and meaning which, fortunately, advancing social conceptions have since brought about."[8]

By 1925, two years before Taylor became *Musical America*'s editor, Kahn had decided it was time to move forward on his quest. When the opportunity arose for him to purchase a block of property on Fifty-seventh Street between Eighth and Ninth Avenues, a block from Carnegie Hall, he didn't hesitate. Fearful of losing out to someone else, he bought the property on his own before he could meet with the board of the Metropolitan Opera and Real Estate Company, the owners of the opera house. The real estate company consisted of the fifty-four box holders in the Golden Horseshoe, all members of society's Four Hundred. They paid the taxes on the property and during the season had use of their boxes free of charge, something they treasured dearly.

Kahn offered the new property to the real estate board early in 1926 as the site for a new opera house, indicating he would sell it at cost. They listened politely and agreed to hire Benjamin Wistar Morris III and Joseph Urban as architects, then gave their approval to move ahead on the project. Kahn wanted the new building to be "plain, simple, dignified, seeking its distinction rather in being perfectly adapted to its purpose."[9] As a populist, Kahn sought to increase the number of seats; as a businessman, he wanted the building to provide rentable office space to bring extra income for the Metropolitan. "It will probably be a fifteen-story structure," *Musical America* reported before Taylor became editor, "and will accommodate approximately 1000 more than the Broadway house."[10]

By choosing Morris as the principal architect and Urban as an associate, the board unintentionally introduced a fatal flaw into the planning: the two would come to an impasse on the opera house design. Morris had been a respected architect in New York for decades and definitely had the attention of the moneyed crowd. He was particularly close to J. P. Morgan, having designed the annex to the Morgan Library. Morgan had enormous power within the opera real estate board and supported Morris. But Kahn's choice for principal architect had been Urban, whose major previous efforts had been as a scenic designer rather than as an architect. He had already provided Kahn some six different proposals.

Taylor had also favored Urban, a good friend of his since the production of *The King's Henchman.* The editor believed that Urban would do all the work while Morris, a society favorite, would receive all the plaudits. Morris and Urban went their separate ways in developing plans for the opera house: Morris preferred the traditional horseshoe, while Urban chose a three-tier, fan-shaped approach. In August 1927 both architects went to Europe, where they independently studied many of the great opera houses as well as the newest technical advances in stagecraft. On their return to New York, each was even more set in his ways.[11]

Taylor contacted Urban upon learning that his friend had developed plans after the European trip. He was invited to the architect's studios, where he studied Urban's design and made his own drawings of the plans to illustrate a major article in *Musical America.* What drove Taylor to publish the plans was his friendship with Urban, as well as his indebtedness to Kahn for having supported him in the Metropolitan opera commissions. Before the article appeared, Taylor wrote to Mary and explained the reasoning behind his decision to publish Urban's design: his friend was growing old and had expressed a concern that "if he doesn't do some big thing soon he will leave behind him nothing but a theatre, a few houses and a lot of Hearst and Ziegfeld stage sets." Taylor, who as a youngster had wanted to be an architect, concluded with uncertainty: "I don't know whether this *Musical America* piece will do any good or not, but Joe has pinned his hopes on me, and so I think the work is worth doing."[12] Qualities of loyalty and justice were part of the Taylor persona, but he had another reason to be supportive of a new opera house: he had learned the exciting news that his next work was to inaugurate it.[13]

Bold headlines greeted the readers of *Musical America* on October 8: "An Impressive Home for the Metropolitan Opera Company: Joseph Urban's

Project for the New Structure." Taylor's drawings of the proposed interior saturated the first four pages, accompanied by six thousand words of description. "I count it a duty as well as a privilege to make these plans public," Taylor wrote, "for though the Metropolitan Opera House is owned and occupied by a private corporation and financed by private generosity, it is nevertheless in an artistic sense at least, one of our great national institutions."[14] Taylor's drawings beautifully depicted the main floor and side views, and an impressive diagrammatic section cut through the entire building. He identified the highlights: the most modern stagecraft technology, seating for five thousand, greatly improved sight lines, two immense balconies, and only thirty-five boxes rather than the present fifty-four. He also stated clearly that the Metropolitan had not officially approved these plans.

Publishing the unapproved drawings proved to be a major error in judgment. The following week *Musical America* headlined: "New Opera Plans Reveal Rift in Project: Publication of Urban Plans for Metropolitan Crystallizes Situation in Which Conflict between Democratic and Conservative Elements Point to Delay in Construction of Home for New York Music Drama."[15] Mrs. Cornelius Vanderbilt II, dowager queen of the conservative element, rallied her forces against the move, and a committee of five board members, including J. P. Morgan, was appointed to seek another site. Meanwhile Kahn, taken aback by what Taylor had done, had no choice but to release a statement disapproving of the unauthorized release: "If and when plans so approved are completed, they will be placed before the public in a duly authenticated and official manner."[16]

Still, Taylor didn't give up. A week later *Musical America* headlined, "Urban Opera Plan Rouses Chorus of Praise." He had rounded up authorities in theater and scenic design for their evaluation, and phrases such as "Cannot be bettered" and "Brilliant solution" were trotted out with effective arguments.[17] But it was too late; the battle had been lost. The time was not yet ripe for opera barons and baronesses to think along more populist than feudalist lines, no matter who designed the structure or where it would be built. Taylor's entry into the fray, for all his good intentions, backfired completely. Four months later he announced that the proposed Fifty-seventh Street site had been abandoned.[18] Kahn later sold the property, and the Metropolitan Opera remained wedged between Broadway and Seventh Avenue for the next forty years.[19]

The Arrival of Radio

When Taylor took the reins of editorship of *Musical America*, most people did not realize that radio would be the greatest boon in history to music and musicians. Taylor saw its importance, though, and made sure that his readers learned about the variety of musical shows on the emerging networks.

Radio had developed quickly. In 1920, just seven years earlier, the first U.S. government–licensed radio station, KDKA in Pittsburgh, had begun broadcasting. Within a week of being licensed, KDKA created a sensation in the region by broadcasting live the results of the Harding-Cox presidential election.[20] But it was New York City that became radio's power center, with headquarters for the two prime movers: American Telephone and Telegraph (AT&T) and Radio Corporation of America (RCA).

Many individual stations began to broadcast in the early 1920s, but not until the development of networks did radio become a commercial force. The National Broadcasting Company (NBC), with its Red and Blue Networks,[21] led the way in 1926, when it beamed programs to its regional stations from New York. A year later, the Columbia Broadcasting System (CBS) came to life to challenge NBC. This ultimately brought David Sarnoff of NBC and William Paley of CBS, the two giants of radio in the twentieth century, into headlong battle.

Taylor himself had participated in the first broadcast day of CBS on Sunday, September 18, 1927. The initial sounds were light classical works in the afternoon, played by a twenty-piece orchestra with Howard Barlow conducting; next, Red Nichols and his Five Pennies played jazz. The music was transmitted through AT&T "long lines" to the network's fifteen stations stretching from Boston to Council Bluffs, Iowa. But much of it never made it, since thunderstorms temporarily knocked out the communication lines. After several hours of quiet time, Barlow's orchestra returned in the evening with a condensed version of *The King's Henchman,* narrated by Taylor and using soloists from the opera's touring company.

Taylor's presence at the creation of CBS was no accident. The network managers, New Yorkers through and through, were banking on the immense success of *The King's Henchman,* premiered earlier that same year. What better cultural jewel to dangle in front of the radio audience than a popular American opera? Unfortunately, the jewel hardly sparkled on the airwaves. Listening some hundred miles to the north at Steepletop, Edna St. Vincent Millay awaited the wonders of the new technology. Having been told only the previous day of the upcoming broadcast, she managed to get a radio receiver into her home so that she and her husband could listen. But the next day she wrote to Arthur Ficke that she had heard "only 6 notes of the opera."[22]

During Taylor's two years as the editor of *Musical America,* radio became an amazing vehicle for music distribution. By the summer of 1929, both NBC and CBS networks reached from coast to coast and provided dozens of weekly broadcasts of concert music, most without commercial sponsorship, "sustained" by the networks themselves. Each also provided its own "opera company" to present one-hour adaptations of operas. It would be another two years before the Metropolitan Opera allowed broadcasts from its stage, in 1931.

No one could have anticipated the impact that radio would have on music education in the schools. In October 1928 the *RCA Music Educational Hour,* initiated and hosted by sixty-five-year-old Walter Damrosch, began a fourteen-year run of bringing an understanding of classical music to more than seven million students weekly in its peak years. Damrosch's old-world charm permeated the four different versions of the show, each geared to a different age group from third grade through high school. Sustained by the NBC network, the Damrosch broadcasts were beamed from the Atlantic Ocean to the Rocky Mountains.[23] Concurrently on the West Coast, NBC stations carried the weekly *Standard School Broadcasts,* similar in approach but sponsored by the Standard Oil Company. The positive impact of such programs provided educators throughout the nation with arguments to their school boards regarding the need to improve music offerings in the schools.

When Taylor became editor of *Musical America,* he recognized radio's potential for bringing every type of music into people's homes for the first time, and he believed that the quality of radio concerts should be equal to those in the concert hall. From his own experience he knew that written criticism would help attain radio program excellence, so he initiated "Broadcasting across the Country," one of the first columns to supply "serious criticism of performances that are of sufficient musical importance to warrant it."[24] On December 17, 1927, David Sandow began this column with reviews of thirteen concerts, including recitals by Taylor's friend Reinald Werrenrath on the *Atwater Kent Hour* (radio's original program featuring concert artists in recital) and a one-hour version of *Der Freischütz* by the NBC Grand Opera Company.

Musical America detailed another important change in spreading music throughout the country: the development of Community Concerts. As radio advanced in importance, its impact on attendance at concerts became a concern for the managers of soloists. "I doubt if it will 'kill the concert business,'" Taylor wrote when he initiated the column on radio performances.[25] In fact, radio helped build an interest in hearing live concerts, whether the listener lived in a small town or a metropolis. When New York concert managers realized that radio was helping widen their audience, they banded together and formed the Community Concerts. More than anything else, these brought the best of musical artists to small-town America. *Musical America* alerted its readers to this new concept. To bring excellent soloists to a city, a

Taylor and John Philip Sousa in 1928.
(Courtesy of Michael W. Davis)

local group worked with the Community Concert office in New York and sold subscriptions to four performances. Depending on the amount of the resulting money pool, local organizations would be offered specific soloists, vocal or instrumental, among whom might be Lawrence Tibbett, Rosa Ponselle, the Flonzaley Quartet, or the Sinfonietta of the Philadelphia Orchestra.[26] With the development of radio and such organizations as Community Concerts, music gained a new prominence in the United States.

Another Summer in Paris

During his first year as editor, Taylor attempted to work on the libretto for his next opera while maintaining a relationship with his wife and baby, and, to a lesser extent, with his parents and sister. He was concerned about Katy, who had divorced Rowlie Davis and moved in with her parents on Loring Place. Jovial but on the heavy side physically, Katy did not have too much in common with her brother, though she did play the piano. In fact, she may have been a bit jealous of his fame, as evidenced by a comment she made at her father's 1926 retirement dinner. Katy sat with her mother and, as speaker upon speaker praised her father, Katy noted that no one, including her brother, who was master of ceremonies, had mentioned her existence. She finally turned to her mother and said: "I hope I'm at least legitimate!"[27] Though he seldom saw his sister, Taylor did recognize a familial obligation. After all, Katy had to take care of her nine-year-old son, Bill Davis, as well as operate her own kindergarten school in the Bronx. He sent her some monetary support during the first months after her divorce.

By midwinter, the Taylors had settled into an amicable relationship. Mary had completed a three-month starring role in *The 19th Hole,* a comedy about golf, so they agreed that a vacation in Paris was in order. It was a decision made far easier by a gift of five thousand dollars given him by the Juilliard Foundation "in recognition of his important musical compositions . . . [and] his career as a critic, editor and lecturer."[28] He slyly commented that the Juilliard grant was "a terrible thing to do for a lazy man," then left with Mary for France in late February on the new liner *Saturnia.* Little Joan remained with a nanny.

In Europe they both worked on their writings, she on a new play and he on his *Vanity Fair* articles and *Musical America* editorials. In April they received a telegram from their daughter, suspiciously articulate for a one-year old: "PLAYED IN THE PARK TRIED TO GATHER ARMFUL PIGEONS SMELLED FLOWERS WITH GREAT WRINKLING OF NOSE HAVE NEW DOUBLE TEETH MANY NEW WORDS LOVE TO REVERED PARENTS."[29] Mary, apparently moved by the message, decided to return home earlier than planned.

With his wife gone, Taylor spent the rest of spring in France hoping to get his writing and composing juices flowing, but socializing kept intruding. Among the highlights was a glorious party in honor of the Gershwin brothers, who also had been in Paris that spring of 1928 so that George could complete *An American in Paris.*[30] In Taylor's letters to his wife, he spoke of dining with Paul Mowrer, his poet friend from the war days, as well as with Elizabeth Hadley Richardson, the recently divorced first wife of Ernest Hemingway. He also mentioned meeting with F. Scott Fitzgerald, who told him that he was "sick of America."[31]

"My father did mention several drinking sprees with Scott in Paris," Joan Kennedy Taylor mentioned years later.[32] Fitzgerald felt a special gratitude to Taylor for a letter the composer had sent him three years after they had met at the Swopes'. "It's just four o'clock in the morning," Taylor's letter began, "and I've got to be up at seven, and I've just finished [reading] 'The Great Gatsby,' and it can't possibly be as good as I think it is. . . . You've got [H. G.] Wells' gift of going after the beauty that's concealed under the facts, and, Goddammit, that's all there is to art."[33] Fitzgerald, who had read many negative comments from critics about his novel, wrote him his thanks: "I was deeply touched by your enthusiasm by your writing to tell me of it. . . . Thank you more than I can say both for the thought and, especially, the act."[34]

Throughout his Parisian stay, Taylor wondered whether he and Mary should move permanently to the Stamford home, which would save a lot of money. He advanced the idea in letters to her, mentioning the two main expenses that would be involved: winterizing Hollow Hill, and the many train trips they would be making back and forth to New York as they continued their professional lives. A week before returning, he telegraphed her: "THOUGHT IT OVER. LETS TRY THE FARM."[35]

Apparently she agreed, because back in the States, he spent time working to make the Connecticut house completely livable. Before that chore was completed, Taylor the editor suffered another psychological trouncing. Throughout 1928 *Musical America* had continued with its weekly large-page format, but Taylor, who had been around his literary friends too long, decided that what the magazine needed was a touch of class, especially features by well-known names. To provide these articles, he went after Ernest Newman (whom he believed to be the greatest writer on music then living) as well as Aldous Huxley, Edna Ferber, Millay, and many others.

So it was that longtime readers found two other surprises in the first issue of February 1929: the beginning of biweekly publication, and a change of format to an oversize pamphlet. To most readers these changes meant that the something-for-everyone policy had been overturned. The resulting rumble of opposition soon changed to thunder, and in August *Musical America* announced that ownership had returned to those who had been associated with the publication under its founder, John Freund. It was a journalistic palace revolt, and Taylor was out of the editor's chair. The publishers rehired former editor A. Walter Kramer and promised their readers to "make *Musical America* again the outstanding publication in its field, a distinction which it enjoyed for many years."[36] It was one of Taylor's saddest moments. Earlier he had lost a battle fought for his friend Joseph Urban, and now he'd lost a war.

The September edition printed many huzzahs extolling the return of the "old" *Musical America*. Letters of thanks for the return to the former format came from diverse members of the music community—teachers of piano and music, directors of music schools, music clubs—the people who had found themselves disengaged from the *Musical America* of Deems Taylor and friends. It was a lesson that he remembered and applied years later, as the intermission commentator for the New York Philharmonic broadcasts. He learned to speak in a way that appealed to everyone who listened, from classical music neophytes to composers.

False Starts for a Second Opera

On top of his turbulent final months at *Musical America,* Taylor had been struggling at the same time to complete a libretto for his second opera. The decision to be his own librettist—"the most accomplished and erudite of col-laborators"—was not working out too well. Attempting a transformation of Heywood Broun's novel was proving to be a mistake. *Gandle Follows His Nose,* like *Jurgen,* was a fantasy. It crossed the Arthurian legend (knights and battles) with the Arabian Nights (genies and sorcerers), worlds highly complicated for opera. He did not look forward to having to disappoint his friend, who, when Taylor had told him he had chosen *Gandle* for his next opera, had been elated and generously told Taylor: "This is sheer luck for me, so don't let's mention money. I will be perfectly satisfied if I get a gold cigarette case out of this."

"A gold cigarette case?" the composer answered incredulously. "I guess you have some misconception as to the rewards of music."[37]

But the months of work on the *Gandle* libretto had brought only frustra-tion, so much so that he again reached out to Millay:

> I've been laboring for about a year on an opera which, I have just re-alized, must have two or three more years of toil before it can be finished satisfactorily. Meanwhile the Met is hollering for an opera to be ready about a year from now. Could you, would you, can you, will you, *won't* you join the ball? You've had a year for the pursuit of health, and that's enough. . . . Assuming everything, what I'm dying to do is something about medieval Paris—something with 14th cen-tury inns and night watches, and wooden bridges with little houses on them, and city gates. . . . This is a hell of a lot of nerve, but there's no harm in asking. Speak, speak, thou fearful guest.[38]

Millay quickly responded that she couldn't help; she was too busy, but she had time to murmur a prayer for him: "That some colossal good luck will drag you by the hair out of this purgatory before you get ill or go mad or beat Eddie Ziegler's head in with a baton."[39]

Taylor plunged ahead, completing the first draft of the *Gandle* libretto in December 1928 and never having revealed to the press the subject of the op-era.[40] Then two months later, almost two years to the day of the premiere of *King's Henchman,* Taylor announced that he was throwing in the musical towel on his still-undisclosed opera subject. The reason he gave to reporters was that he had gotten caught with "too much thought. You can't have too much thought in an opera. It goes by emotion."[41]

For a man who thrived on fantasy, Taylor's second choice—Elmer Rice's *Street Scene,* the rousing hit of the early 1929 Broadway season—was strange indeed. Emotion pulsed through every fiber of the play, which was a naturalist portrayal of life in the tenements of New York. It was a story of jealousy, murder, and survival. Taylor saw it twice in early January and received Rice's permission to adapt the play into an opera. Two possible reasons for Taylor's leap from fantasy into realism come to mind: first, the play dealt with his native city; second, he had worked with Rice on *The Adding Machine* and respected him as a playwright.

This time Taylor kept no secret of his plan, releasing the subject to the newspapers before he even began the libretto. Olin Downes, in a lengthy Sunday piece about the choice of *Street Scene,* found "difficulties of all sorts" facing the librettist-composer, especially in "the profoundly tragic essence of the drama and its fearless reflection of reality." Downes observed, "What makes his new creative adventure so interesting and indeed momentous is the nature of his theme and its wholly American character."[42]

Taylor, who at this time was still editor of *Musical America,* had been unable to complete winterizing the Connecticut house, so he and Mary remained in New York. When they looked financial reality in the face that spring, they knew they didn't have the resources to maintain both an apartment and a country home any longer. Early in May 1929 they moved permanently to Hollow Hill, where they put up with assorted plumbers and electricians for another five months. Taylor's construction skills did not extend beyond carpentry. By the end of the summer, he wasn't an editor either.

Now disengaged from *Musical America* and settled in Stamford, his struggle with *Street Scene* continued. Because of the false start on *Gandle,* he asked for and received a two-year extension from Gatti-Casazza for the opera's completion. Then in October a rather surprised Taylor read that his friend George Gershwin also had been commissioned to write an opera for the Metropolitan, choosing for his subject the classic Yiddish drama *The Dybbuk.* If anything, this announcement awoke Taylor to the fact that he had better produce something, and soon.

The turnabout came quickly. A month later he made it known that he had shelved *Street Scene* and would now base his opera on *Peter Ibbetson,* a book by the Englishman George Du Maurier.[43] This time the reason he gave for the change was that *Street Scene* had become "increasingly difficult to prepare for the lyric stage as he progressed on the music";[44] he simply could not complete it in time. The *Times,* after previous first-page coverage of his choices, by now had tired of Taylor's indecision, so the *Peter Ibbetson* announcement was placed deep inside the paper. However, three days later a *Times* editorial congratulated him on "a selection full of enchanting possibilities."[45] (He later learned that the Gershwin opera would never be written, because the rights to *The Dybbuk* had already been given to an Italian composer.)

Choosing Du Maurier's *Peter Ibbetson*

"I'd always had 'Peter Ibbetson' in the back of my head for an opera subject," Taylor revealed quite surprisingly in his announcement to the press. This mental bookmark had been reinforced when he'd met the English actress Constance Collier at a party at Katharine Cornell's home. Collier, who now called the United States her home, had brought an adaptation of Du Maurier's novel to the Broadway stage a dozen years earlier, in 1917.

In it she played the female lead, while the brothers John and Lionel Barrymore, both major Broadway stars, took the male leads. The acclaimed production brought an appealing story to the audience. *Peter Ibbetson* tells of a young man, Gogo Pasquier, whose father was French and his mother English, who grows up near Paris. After the tragic accidental deaths of both parents, he is taken to London by his arrogant, self-centered uncle Colonel Ibbetson, where Gogo's name is changed to Peter Ibbetson. When the mature Peter meets Mary, the Duchess of Towers, at a party, he comes to realize that the married duchess is in fact the grown-up Mimsey Seraskier, his French childhood sweetheart whom he has never stopped loving. Mimsey had taught Gogo to "dream true," a way of entering and sharing each other's dreams. As the story evolves, Peter accidentally kills his uncle after a violent argument, and he is sentenced to life in prison. There nightly he joins the duchess by dreaming true until their mortal lives end.

In *Peter Ibbetson,* Du Maurier fashioned one of the first novels to deal with the unconscious and the world of dreams and reality; his concept of dreaming true even entered the vocabulary of the literati. For example, Alexander Woollcott wrote to his sister from Europe, toward the end of World War I, expressing his wish to be out of the army and back home: "Of late, almost for the first time, I have taken to dreaming myself back in America, but I am no Gogo Pasquier, and I cannot dream dreams worth while."[46]

Peter Ibbetson fascinated Taylor as a modern fantasy with autobiographical overtones, since Du Maurier himself was half French and half English and had grown up in Passy, near Paris. It was Du Maurier's first novel, written when the author was fifty-seven years of age, an accomplishment later in life that amazed Taylor, who wrote: "If *A Farewell to Arms* had turned out to be written by Charles Dana Gibson [the famed American illustrator of the Gibson Girl], we should all probably feel much as George Du Maurier's contemporaries must have felt when *Peter Ibbetson* appeared in 1891."[47] Du Maurier,

blind in one eye, gained early success with black and white drawings, particularly as an illustrator for the English humor magazine *Punch.* His captions often pricked the pretentious behavior of high society; one cartoon, for example, depicted a well-dressed society threesome chatting about the music that
a pianist has just finished playing:

> *Mrs. Gushington (aside to her husband):* What a long, tiresome piece of
> music that was! Who's it by, I wonder?
> *Mr. Gushington:* Beethoven, my love.
> *Mrs. Gushington (to hostess):* My dear Mrs. Brown, what heavenly mu-
> sic! How in every bar one feels the stamp of the greatest genius the
> world has ever known![48]

Taylor must have felt a kinship with Du Maurier himself, since they both had
talents for drawing and writing, and also were natural wits.

After deciding on *Peter Ibbetson* for his subject, Taylor needed to gain
Constance Collier's permission to use the work, since she owned the rights
to it. He requested her approval to prepare the libretto himself. She happily
agreed, being "honored and delighted to have the privilege of being associated with you in this venture."[49] He would officially share the authorship of
the libretto with the actress, though he alone wrote it. He explained this ra-
tionale to Edward Ziegler: "Since I've got to give Constance credit anyway
(she owns the rights and did part of the play) I've agreed to put her name on
the libretto."[50]

Before secluding himself at Hollow Hill to begin *Peter Ibbetson,* Taylor
agreed to a second historic whirl with the microphones as host for the first
Puccini operas ever broadcast. This reinforced his growing fame as the major
U.S. spokesman for opera. Two years earlier, in 1927, NBC had presented a
radio first, a national hookup of live broadcasts from the Chicago Civic Opera. Only one or two acts of an opera had been broadcast, none by Puccini
because Ricordi, his publisher and copyright owner, had refused. Naturally
they believed, and quite rightly, that "radio could not do full artistic justice to
the music."[51]

But when radio's importance as a disseminator of music became evident,
the Ricordi organization slowly relented. Finally, in November 1929, the
first of six condensed Puccini operas was presented over NBC, with Taylor
providing commentary where portions were omitted. Frances Alda, the
Metropolitan singer who also happened to be the ex-wife of Puccini's friend
Gatti-Casazza, was the featured soprano.[52]

Aside from the Puccini broadcasts, in early December Taylor cleared
himself of all other obligations and began composing *Peter Ibbetson.* He
worked in an upstairs study in the Connecticut home, while a governess

Taylor and three-year-old Joan at Hollow Hill, their home in Stamford, Conn.
(Courtesy of Michael W. Davis)

cared for three-year-old Joan. Mary answered all phone calls and did everything she could to keep visitors to a minimum. John Vansant, a cousin, did
stop by and described the composer in action: "He was home alone and was
writing some music; we sat and watched for about half an hour. He would
rush upstairs for a few minutes and then come down and play a few notes on
the piano, and then rush upstairs again and repeat and repeat this performance."[53] Taylor worked straight through to mid-July to complete the piano-
vocal score, and by the time he set down his musical pen, he had spent
233 days composing *Peter Ibbetson.* The opera understandably had taken two
months longer than *The King's Henchman,* since this time he was both composer and librettist.[54] The orchestration took the remainder of the year.

As was the case with *The King's Henchman,* the Met decided on a February
premiere for Taylor's second opera, with rehearsals beginning after New
Year's Day. Another exceptional cast had been assembled: Lawrence Tibbett
as Colonel Ibbetson, Edward Johnson as Peter, and a longtime Metropolitan
favorite, the Spanish-born Lucrezia Bori, as Mary, Duchess of Towers. Bori's

best years were behind her, but her voice still sparkled and she had excellent diction. For scenic design Gatti turned once again to Joseph Urban, and for orchestral direction to Tullio Serafin. This time the publisher made the piano-vocal score of *Peter Ibbetson* available well before the opening.

Taylor himself drew the beautiful cover for the score, a depiction of two children, hand-in-hand in silhouette, looking toward a fantasy castle framed in a pastel blue sky. The dedication page had three words, "To Walter Damrosch," an early acknowledgment of Taylor's indebtedness to the man whom years later he cited as "the greatest force in my musical life [because] he played my music and commissioned works from me."[55]

Another Successful Opera

For critics, the anticipation of Taylor's second opera included questions as to whether the composer would venture into more modernist zones than he had with *The King's Henchman*. Before the opera's premiere, Olin Downes, having previewed the piano-vocal score, told his readers that *Peter Ibbetson* would be "pre-eminently melodic, lyrical," with no surprise digressions into modernism. The critic also cited the libretto's "unique value . . . its concentration upon emotions, the life of the spirit, and not upon theatrical claptrap."[56] As the day of the first performance approached, press coverage was not as extensive as it had been for Taylor's first opera. Nonetheless, the first two performances sold out rapidly, with scalpers asking (and getting) as much as one hundred dollars per pair of tickets, a small fortune in Depression days.

On the afternoon of February 7, 1931, Taylor sat with his wife and three-year-old daughter in Golden Horseshoe box seats. Luminaries abounded throughout the audience of 3,600: the Spanish ambassador, honoring Lucrezia Bori by his presence; Walter Damrosch and his wife; Constance Collier, Antoinette Perry, Charlie Chaplin, William LeBaron, and the Irving Berlins; and Algonquin group members Edna Ferber, Donald Ogden Stewart, Harold Ross, FPA, and Harpo Marx. His parents were in attendance as well. During the time before the curtain rose, Taylor must have thought back on that night four years earlier, when he and Edna St. Vincent Millay waited outside to buy tickets. Unhappily, Edna would not be with him for this premiere; two days earlier, her beloved mother had died at her home in Camden, Maine, and Millay had gone there to bring her mother's body back for burial at Steepletop.

Peter Ibbetson opens with only a brief orchestral prelude. As the curtain rises on Act I, waltz music permeates the English country home of Mrs. Deane during an elegant ball for her friends. The annoying Colonel Ibbetson arrives and insists upon reading a poem that he has written in French. His nephew Peter, an architect, arrives and accidentally reveals to the assembly that the poem was written not by his uncle, but by a French poet. The colonel is furious and berates Peter, who then seeks out Mrs. Deane and tells her how much he hates his uncle, especially for taking him away from Passy after the death of his parents.

Finally calmed down, Peter shares with Mrs. Deane the memories of his boyhood days as Gogo Pasquier, and his childhood love for Mimsey Seraskier, who taught him how to dream true. The Duchess of Towers is announced, and soon after her entry she chides Mrs. Deane and others for their materialistic concerns: "Time passes, and with it, the world and its wonder." She leaves without speaking to Peter, but they both sense a strange communion, for they are indeed Gogo and Mimsey.

At the beginning of Act II, Peter returns to an inn in Passy to savor the days spent there in his boyhood, but even his old friend Major Duquesnois is too aged to remember him. Glancing outside, Peter notices Mary, the Duchess of Towers, passing in a carriage. Puzzled, he sinks into a comfortable chair, falls asleep, and dreams of the duchess, who appears and leads him back to their happier days. "Why am I here?" asks Peter.

"I do not know," answers Mary. "This is my dream; and never before has any living creature entered."

Peter, observing the dream's characters, watches as the colonel appears and attempts to seduce his mother, only to be stopped by Gogo rushing to help her. Peter awakens to find that the duchess has come to the inn to escape a storm. They begin to talk and soon realize that they've just been in each other's dreams, dreaming true as Mimsey and Gogo. Immediately she draws the line, for she is married and insists they cannot see each other again: "It is too late. I am not free. I shall think of you, always. . . . Dear Gogo, farewell."

Act III finds an agitated Mrs. Deane and her mother coming to see Peter at his uncle's home to inform him that the colonel is claiming that he, the colonel, is Peter's father. Peter shows the women a photo of his real father and convinces them that the colonel's statement is a villainous falsehood. After they leave and his uncle returns, an angry Peter demands he retract the lie. The colonel's laughter drives Peter into a fury; he strikes his uncle with a stick and accidentally kills him.

The scene changes to Newgate Prison, where Peter, condemned to death, awaits execution, refusing to reveal to the chaplain the reason for his homicidal anger. Mrs. Deane excitedly comes to tell Peter that through the duchess's intercession, he has been given a commutation to a life sentence. She brings him Mary's message: "Tell him . . . his life has just begun." A chorus sings several French children's songs as a dream sequence finds Mary and Peter dreaming true, looking upon their days as children with their families.

In the final scene, Mrs. Deane visits Peter in his prison cell thirty years later. She tells him Mary has died, but he already knows because on the previous night, Mary did not appear in his dream. Peter dies, Mary appears, and "out of the dead body on the cot rises Peter Ibbetson, the young Peter of Act I. He goes slowly to Mary. They meet, and stand enfolded in each other's arms" as the curtain falls.[57]

For twenty-one-year-old Lehman Engel, the *Peter Ibbetson* premiere remained etched in his memory: "It was during the 1931 season when a group of us unwashed young avant-garde 'composers' attended the matinee premiere of Deems Taylor's (we referred to him privately as Damn Stealer) opera *Peter Ibbetson* (renamed by us *Peter Rabbitson*), overseeing everything from our standing room vantage point. Of course we hated the opera. It was too conventional, too 'vanilla' and dull; everything was beneath our youthful contempt, but we kept our places to the bitter end." The "unwashed" modernists heard the deafening applause accompanying curtain call after curtain call, and then they saw Taylor appear on stage, "a tiny man outsized in every way by all others around him . . . [He] extended his arms, palms outward, and there was instantaneous breathless silence. After a very long pause, he spoke, simply and tastefully, and we, with our snobbishness, were annihilated because we were deeply moved. 'When you go to your homes this evening,' Taylor said, 'please remember that you have just seen one completely happy man.'"[58]

The day after the premiere, the *Times* again provided Taylor with front-page prominence: "Great Ovation Won by 'Peter Ibbetson' at World Premiere. Deems Taylor's Native Opera Is Greeted with 36 Curtain Calls at Metropolitan."[59] Olin Downes wrote half of the review, which filled six columns, and confirmed his prediction that emotions would be central to the opera's impact: "Strong men actually wept. They did." High praise went to the lead singers, especially Edward Johnson as Peter Ibbetson, a role cited by several critics as his best ever. Taylor echoed this assessment in a note of appreciation: "Thank God for dreaming up Edward Johnson when He was creating tenors."[60]

One critic found the composer's "method of writing vacillating between that of Puccini, Wagner and Debussy."[61] Resemblances to Wagner seemed to gain most mentions by critics, even though Taylor denied that the form was Wagnerian. "I started writing it," he told an interviewer, "in the expectation that the score would contain the usual assortment of leit-motifs, developed in the accepted way. But the music did not work out that way."[62] Indeed, where in *The King's Henchman* he had used many motifs à la Wagner, there were few in *Peter Ibbetson*. Taylor confessed to the same interviewer that in composing the opera, he realized "two minor ambitions of his life: First, to write a waltz in the Strauss style, and second, to make thematic use of French folk songs."[63] The waltz was the underpinning to the ball in the first act and provided thematic unity. Even FPA liked "the tuneful waltz," though he didn't like the character of Peter, believing him to be "afflicted with a mother-fixation as well as galloping-infantilism."[64] Critics praised the libretto and folksongs, both French and Taylor-made, sung by invisible choruses in the dream sequences.

In the first act, both Colonel Ibbetson and the duchess are given significant set pieces. Her aria—"I could never dedicate my days . . . to your solemn ritual of fashion, your litany of trifles that pass the time"—has a memorable lyrical surge toward an impassioned high note. Similarly, the recognition scene in the second act, where Peter and the duchess realize they are the Gogo and Mimsey of the past, provides a central emotional force in the opera; and in the third act, an impressive dirgelike sound from the orchestra prepares Peter for an execution that does not come to pass. Overall, in a manner modeled on Debussy's *Pelléas et Mélisande,* Taylor used the orchestra to paint the emotional scenery.

Though most first-night critics were gently positive in their assessments, Lawrence Gilman of the *Herald Tribune* unexpectedly proved rather severe by noting that only the most inspired composers could build on the music of the past immortals and metabolize it into something new. "Mr. Taylor has not yet shown us that he can accomplish this sort of creative imaginative transmutation," Gilman concluded.[65] Actually, the Gilman scowl could have been anticipated, for in the past Gilman had joined Paul Rosenfeld as an exponent of the belief that if a composer does not change his musical stripes from past traditions, he is not worthy of acclaim. A week later, Walter Damrosch protested Gilman's criticism: "The article seems to me more like the effort of a district attorney who is determined to convict Deems Taylor at all cost as a criminal for having composed an opera. It takes so little cognizance of its many beauties."[66]

Taylor did not battle Gilman's assessment, but about a year later he wrote to him about what he had "tried to do in 'Ibbetson,' and, imperfectly, but in at least a small part, accomplished." He was not referring to "the quality of the music [because] that is God's gift or curse, and can't be helped." What he had attempted was "a vocal line for the English language." Taylor was convinced that melodies are closely intertwined with the composer's native language, an understanding he had gained through his translation of folksongs from so many different languages. "A musical theme," he explained to Gilman, "is a vocal and a language theme. Its rhythms, its phrase endings, the rise and fall of its line, are an expression of the accents, quantities, and rise and fall of the spoken tongue of the composer." He had determined that for the languages long associated with opera—Italian, German, French, Russian—the relationship of the words to music had been worked out over centuries. "What I know about 'Ibbetson'—and up to now it has been my secret—is that the singers are singing English. In all the voice parts there is not, I think, one false quantity, one misplaced accent." Taylor proudly told Gilman he had "[tried] to do for his own tongue what centuries of musical tradition have done for others."[67] Unlike Millay, who had chosen to prepare a libretto that essentially was an academic exercise in the Anglo-Saxon language, Taylor had attempted an amalgamation of words and music.

In general, critics believed that though there were moments of intense musicality and emotion in *Peter Ibbetson,* it did not add up to a satisfactory whole. To some the libretto outweighed the music in quality. "George Du Maurier did much more for Taylor than Taylor was able to do for Du Maurier," wrote Oscar Thompson in *Literary Digest.*[68] The modernist supporter Paul Rosenfeld again provided the nastiest jabs: "In the end, for all the hubbub in the orchestra and on the stage, in spite of the harmlessness and even brightness of certain individual passages, one sits bewildered by the sense that nothing has been said at all and nothing of any sort taken place."[69] By this time Rosenfeld had no patience for the romantic, impressionistic past. He wanted newness. Several years previously, he had spotted that commodity in the young Aaron Copland. Speaking of Copland's music, which was then more dissonant than his later works, Rosenfeld said simply: "We do not know where it came from. We merely know that we had not met it before. . . . [I]t places us immensely alertly in the stream of metallic, modern American things."[70]

No matter what the critics wrote, audiences loved *Peter Ibbetson* not only in New York but in Chicago, where the Ravinia Festival produced four sold-out performances the summer following the premiere; Johnson and Bori sang their original roles, and Wilfrid Pelletier conducted. Taylor, without his wife, went there for the first performance and wrote her of his joy at the Ravinia success: "The performance was extraordinary. . . . The audience was very thrilling and the papers—thanks, I believe, to the fact the New York critics had roasted it—fell over themselves."[71] Even the young Claudia Cassidy, who became one of the most feared music critics of her time, was positive and found that the "'Peter Ibbetson' score is a refreshing glimpse of what the brilliant modern may do to restore grand opera to the contemporary scheme."[72] To her, Taylor was a modern composer. Fortunately, she would never meet Paul Rosenfeld in a dark alley.

Peter Ibbetson remained in the Metropolitan repertoire through five seasons (but was performed in only four). Its twenty-two performances outdistanced the seventeen of *The King's Henchman,* the previous record holder for an American opera.[73] In 1933 the Metropolitan honored the work by making it the first American opera ever to open a season. To Taylor's further satisfaction, one performance in 1935 featured nine-year-old Joan in the nonsinging role of Mimsey in the dream sequences. In previous years that part had been taken by June Lockhart, whose father had been the cowriter with Taylor of the ill-fated *Heigh Ho.*[74]

Popular as the opera was, a tragic event would lead to its premature removal from the repertoire. In 1935, upon the retirement of Gatti-Casazza, the Metropolitan chose as his successor Herbert Witherspoon, director of the Chicago Opera and formerly a bass with the Metropolitan. Edward Johnson agreed to be his assistant, but only if he could also remain as a singer. Then, just one month into his new job, Witherspoon died of a coronary thrombosis. Johnson received the news in Detroit, where he was singing in the city's Civic Opera production of *Peter Ibbetson.* Between rehearsals he returned for Witherspoon's funeral, at which time the Metropolitan board made it clear to Johnson that they were considering him for general manager. After going back to Detroit for the next day's performance, he received a telegram from the Metropolitan board offering him the position. Deciding to accept the offer, he left the hotel to sing what would be his final performance on any opera stage. The Detroit audience, unaware of the drama behind Johnson's performance, "thundered its applause, and composer Deems Taylor, as well as Pelletier, Johnson and Bori received curtain calls too numerous to count."[75]

Johnson felt very possessive of the role of Peter Ibbetson. Even at rehearsals for the premiere, Bori commented to the singer: "I do believe, dear Edward, that you have forgotten Edward Johnson and really 'become' Peter Ibbetson."[76] No one else had sung the role of Peter, so in the same way that great ballplayers have their "number" retired, Johnson, now the Met impresario, apparently decided to retire Peter from the Metropolitan as his own personal number. Why else would such a successful opera leave the repertoire? Johnson himself later acknowledged the opera's unusual financial achievement: "Peter Ibbetson made more money than any other single opera during the past twenty years—more than $150,000. For an American opera this is either a miracle or else it indicates a renewed public interest in opera, and I prefer to think it's the latter."[77] In view of the Metropolitan's be-ing over a million dollars in debt at the end of the 1934 season, Taylor's opera provided significant financial help. It also brought more fame to the com-poser than any other work he had created. Perhaps too much. What could he possibly do for an encore?

11. Rough Times after Peter Ibbetson, 1931–1934

A Return to Journalism

On February 16, 1931, *Time* featured a cover photo of a serious-looking Deems Taylor composing at the piano, fresh from the success of his second opera. The magazine's cover story, in assessing the importance of *Peter Ibbetson,* raised the old question of what constitutes "a good native U.S. opera" and concluded that it "will probably remain a matter of debate until it arrives." The writer passed no judgment on Taylor's opera, except to say that "the audience had evidently liked it."[1] Nonetheless, by putting Taylor on its cover *Time* recognized his unusual achievement of two successful operas in a row. He was only the second American-born composer to have the honor of being on the cover of *Time;* George Gershwin had been there six years earlier, in 1925.

Taylor certainly deserved the honor, but honors didn't bring money. Though the ten performances of *Peter Ibbetson* during its first season garnered an additional $2,500 for him, operas alone would not pay the bills. Fortunately, William Randolph Hearst's *New York American* needed a music columnist. Within a month Taylor signed on to produce three columns a week at an annual salary of $20,000. The pay was enormous, considering that the average individual income at that time was about $500. Hearst obviously remembered Taylor's wit and upbeat criticism in the *World*.

On March 9, 1931, the *American* published Taylor's first column in a city that had changed dramatically since his *World* days in the early 1920s. The

Great Depression had spread its economic pall across the land, while New York had grown up and out with developments such as Radio City, the Empire State Building, and the George Washington Bridge. Movies now talked and radio was becoming the entertainment vehicle for the masses. In music, the modernists—Aaron Copland, Roger Sessions, Alban Berg, Arnold Schoenberg—were in the ascendancy in many quarters, particularly among the literati. It was an exciting time to be a critic, and during the following year Taylor wrote about all these subjects and many others, some with little relationship to music.

He reported on the breadlines of the unemployed, after a visit to an American Relief Free Lunch truck dispensing food to hundreds: "You see, I didn't really believe that men were starving in New York. . . . Go up to Seventh Avenue and 47th St. some night, and see it for yourself. . . . I can guarantee you a spoiled evening. . . . If you do go, take all the cigarettes you can carry. Give them out. A man doesn't feel so forlorn if he has something to smoke" (January 3, 1932).

On naming the George Washington Bridge, he wrote (May 4, 1931): "It must have been very difficult to arrive at the final decision. . . . The name chosen was probably the best—safe, conservative, agreeable to Wets and Drys alike, easy to remember. Besides, what nobler duty could a bridge perform than to rescue from oblivion the name of one who, thus far, has had practically nothing, beyond a state, a city, another bridge, an avenue, a pie and an instantaneous coffee named after him?"

In the only column he ever wrote about a family member, Taylor told his readers on November 13, 1931, about twelve-year-old Bill Davis, his nephew, whose birthday had been celebrated two days before: "He is somewhat above the average, physically and intellectually. . . . I make this statement with confidence, as it is based on the testimony of his mother, his grandmother, and—with reservations—his grandfather. . . . He is fond of swimming, tennis and football, has a flair for carpentry and mechanics, and is a voracious and impartially omnivorous reader. . . . About three years ago he horrified his mother by announcing that he and some of his intimates had founded a nightclub. The enterprise, however, proved to be a harmless one, its nefarious title being merely the result of a misunderstanding; the members were, as Bill explained, knights—like King Arthur's Knights." Deems clearly saw in his nephew many of his own traits! (Bill would attend NYU in physics and become a pilot in the Air Force during World War II.)

Of course, he also covered the music world thoroughly. He observed of the Stokowski-conducted U.S. premiere of Alban Berg's *Wozzeck,* one of the most lauded twentieth-century modernist operas (March 23, 1931):

The school of Schoenberg has produced a dramatic composer of the first order. . . . The score of Wozzeck is an extraordinary contrapuntal achievement. It is not, perhaps, the sort of counterpoint that would appeal to a German musical scholar of the old school. . . . Bach, however, while he might have made a wry face over it, would have rendered its creator a grudging respect . . . [f]or the voices in Berg's orchestra are manipulated with great skill. Their progressions have little to do with accepted notions of concord and key-relationship; but they are real progressions. His canons are canons, and his fugues are real fugues.

His view of critical attempts to categorize American music was that "[p]eople seem to be worrying almost continuously because they can see no sign of an American 'School' of music. . . . Apparently composers, in their opinion, are something like flying fish, and can get nowhere unless they are moving in a body" (September 27, 1931).

On the revival of the opera *Lakmé,* in which the highly popular French soprano Lily Pons, standing a mere five feet tall, exhibited a bare midriff, he lauded her courage: "Certainly no prima donna in my memory could have dared to dress it as she does. Her costume . . . an authentic Indian dress that is two hundred years old [suggests] the old joke about its certainly being small for its age. . . . [E]ven aside from the risk of catching cold, there have been few operatic coloraturas . . . who could have risked the experiment. In Mme. Pons' case, it was a complete success" (February 24, 1932).

For a Sunday morning Dollar Concert, he guest-conducted a hundred-musician orchestra performing his *Looking Glass* suite at the Roxy Theatre, then New York's largest and grandest. "Guest-conducting is easy," he reported. "It consists merely of beating time and giving cues, with an air of complete authority, to players who know them anyhow. In order to create a really satisfactory illusion, the guest-conductor should endeavor to keep up with the orchestra as nearly as possible" (March 16, 1931).

Ten years earlier, Taylor had announced to his *World* readers an event that was quite amazing: the Capitol Theater orchestra would play Richard Strauss's epic tone poem *Ein Heldenleben* for a Sunday morning audience. This had suggested to him that linking such "intricate" music with popular entertainment put "the musical destinies of America . . . in the hands of the motion picture orchestras."[2] Here was an unusual prediction, yet logical enough as spectacular movie palaces arose in large cities everywhere. To provide the needed background music for silent films, theater owners installed massive pipe organs and often employed their own orchestras. Music pervaded almost every minute of a person's escape into fantasy before the silver screen.

Of course, the fantasy began when people left their workaday worlds and entered the theater's architectural wonderland: vast, rococo pillared lobbies, elegant, sweeping staircases, and auditoriums that simulated Oriental temples, Spanish courtyards, or simply gilded throne rooms. These entertainment palaces, first built by independent exhibitors, soon were erected by production companies with names that appeared on the facades in brilliant lights: Paramount, Fox, Warners, Loews, RKO.

In 1927 the Roxy Theatre opened in New York, the supreme example of such architectural opulence. Referred to as the Cathedral of the Motion Picture, the 6,214-seat auditorium was the product of the supersalesman of theatrical presentations, Samuel L. Rothafel, nicknamed Roxy. Five years earlier, when Roxy had managed the Capitol Theater, he had initiated concerts by the theater's orchestra with "heavy" works such as the aforementioned *Ein Heldenleben*. These proved so successful that when Rothafel opened his Roxy, he carried on the tradition of concerts with the largest theater orchestra ever assembled: one hundred musicians, with four conductors to cover the entire daily performance schedule.

The Roxy's Sunday morning concerts started at 11:30 A.M., thereby obeying New York City's strict ordinance forbidding movies during Sunday morning church time. As the historian Ben M. Hall wrote: "It was quite an experience to settle down for a pre-noon concert of Brahms and Borodin with the delicious knowledge that when it was over there awaited the complete Roxy deluxe performance . . . [including] the Russian choir, the Roxyettes and all. And a movie too."[3]

By the time Taylor conducted the Roxy Orchestra, such productions were fading fast for the simple reason that sound had been added to movies. In fact, the profits of Taylor's Sunday morning concert went to unemployed musicians, many of whom would soon take the road to Hollywood to join studio orchestras seeking musicians.[4] With the talkies gaining rapidly in popularity, the era of live music at the movies came to an end. But Taylor had once again been in the right place at the right time to participate.

The Metropolitan Opera on Radio

In 1931, when he was working for the *American,* Taylor received a call once again from the Metropolitan Opera—but not for another opera; they wanted him to be commentator on their soon-to-be weekly national broadcasts, beginning on Christmas Day. The Metropolitan was joining NBC in broadcast wedlock, something that surprised Taylor, who was well aware of

From left: Fritz Reiner, George Gershwin, Taylor, Robert Russell Bennett. August 1931, Lewisohn Stadium, New York City. *(Courtesy of Photofest)*

Gatti-Casazza's longtime resistance to carrying operas over the radio. The manager did not believe that radio could produce the quality of sound to do justice to the Metropolitan's singers. But with a relentless NBC pestering him, Gatti finally gave in and approved a test broadcast.[5] The result proved positive to his ears, not only musically but also financially. NBC's offer of $120,000 per season for weekly programs gave monetary solace to the Metropolitan board, because the Depression had affected attendance and initiated an ever-descending fiscal spiral.

Taylor accepted the role of radio host, and on Friday, December 25, 1931, assisted by the young announcer Milton Cross, he welcomed the afternoon audience to the broadcast of *Hänsel und Gretel:* "This Christmas afternoon marks an epoch in the career of the oldest permanent operatic organization in America. For the first time in its history an opera is to be picked up by microphones from the stage of the Metropolitan Opera House, in New York, during an actual performance by the Metropolitan Company, and broadcast to American listeners wherever they may be."[6] As he continued, he explained that Hänsel is diminutive for Johann and Gretel for Margaret: "The English equivalent of the title would be 'Johnny and Peggy.' Perhaps," he concluded, "we had better stick to Hänsel and Gretel."[7] The next day, Saturday, December 26, the Metropolitan also broadcast the last two acts of Bellini's *Norma,* thereby initiating the Saturday opera program that would become the longest-running series of live broadcasts in radio.

Except for *Hänsel und Gretel,* the first Metropolitan presentations were only portions of an opera. Taylor's role was to describe the action of the opera—not when there was singing, but when the orchestra played. For some this was unsatisfactory, as NBC discovered when one woman called to tell them that she couldn't hear what was going on because "some idiot keeps talking."[8] But when all the listener comments were in, compliments outweighed complaints. Taylor disclosed this to the audience two weeks later:

> We have received several thousand replies, of which fewer than one hundred were opposed to being told what was going on upon the stage. It was interesting to notice that of those opposed to my speaking during the performance, the great majority came from listeners in and about New York City and other large musical centers—in other words, from people who had, and still have, ample opportunity to attend performances of opera. . . . [However], they are not primarily the public for whom these broadcast performances are intended. The people we want to reach, and I am happy to say seem to have reached, are those who have never seen opera.[9]

Though Taylor's populist approach made sense, the Metropolitan in the end sided with the purists. He was replaced at the end of the first season by Milton Cross, whose distinctive voice provided commentary for the next forty-three years—only when the houselights were on.

Biting the Hand That Fed Him

Taylor's unique relationship with the Metropolitan Opera fired up again in March 1932, when he informed his *American* readers of the opera company's severe financial difficulties. Perhaps it was a foolhardy thing for him to do, because at the time he was the voice of the Metropolitan Saturday broadcasts. However, he knew that his two operas had helped greatly to add to the coffers, so he felt he had a right and a responsibility to tell the public "the truth." From his point of view, the board members of the Metropolitan Real Estate Company—the Vanderbilts, Astors, and even the Kahns—talked a good line, but beyond paying the taxes on the building, they were really poseurs regarding opera support. To underscore his point, he disclosed that board members could (and did) sublet their free boxes for personal profit.

The financial situation had reached a crescendo for the Metropolitan, because it had ended its season a half-million dollars in debt, with all reserves exhausted. Commenting on this, Taylor lauded Gatti, who had managed to accumulate backup funds "by performing prodigies of management and economy." He therefore concluded that it was Gatti's frugality, not the largesse of the board, that had "built the Metropolitan into the greatest single institution of its kind in the world." Taylor's appraisal ended sarcastically: "A backer, if I understand English, is someone who backs something up. The only direction in which the Metropolitan's backers do any backing is down" (March 30, 1932).

The column had spunk. Here was the side of Taylor that, once he saw an injustice, was willing to make it public. He shared his feelings about the column in a letter to Mary, who was in Florida with Joan to help cure the child's whooping cough: "Everybody at the Met was terribly excited about it and said that at last somebody had had the courage to tell the truth, etc. I saw Eddie Ziegler and Gatti, and they both were very stern and surprised, and wondering how I got the facts—with broad grins on their faces."[10] But the members of the Golden Horseshoe, reading the *American* that day, must have wondered about Taylor and his second broadside in five years, the first being the contretemps about the Urban plans. Perhaps they didn't realize he was attempting to make the board members view the Metropolitan as a national institution, now that it was on radio.

Otto Kahn contacted Taylor and asked for the opportunity to respond in the earliest possible column, to which Taylor happily agreed, for he still had high regard for Kahn. "Each box holder pays annually a certain sum," Kahn wrote to *American* readers, "which goes to pay the taxes on the building (from which burden the Metropolitan Opera Company—the operating Company—is thus entirely relieved) and other expenses of a minor character. That annual payment of late years has been $5,220 for each box owner, i.e. a total annual outlay of $182,700" (April 5, 1932).

Kahn then sent a confidential letter to Taylor disclosing that he had contributed at least two million dollars "in one way or another, to aid the cause of the Metropolitan Opera."[11] Taylor immediately sent back a response: "Naturally, it is no particular surprise to me to learn that your efforts on behalf of the Metropolitan have cost you the enormous sum you name. My 'blast' was, as I imagine you realize, quite impersonal, and directed against the Directors and the Real Estate Company as corporate bodies." Taylor realized, though, that in fairness he should have excepted Kahn from this attack: he told Kahn this, explaining that his "fury" was at those of the board who "accepted credit as disinterested patrons of art," then disclaimed "any particular obligation now that a crisis in operatic affairs has arisen."[12]

As the Metropolitan's monetary woes worsened, some believed the city should take over the company. Such a suggestion was put forth in all sincerity by one of the Metropolitan's reigning sopranos, Rosa Ponselle. Taylor decided to agitate the board a bit more by appearing to support Ponselle's suggestion. He identified precedents in Europe for such an approach and suggested that not only could Tammany Hall produce wonderful operas, but it also could help solve some of the unemployment problems caused by the Great Depression (April 6, 1932):

> I can read even now the newspaper accounts of the opening night. They would run something like this: "Last evening the Mayor's Municipal Opera Company began its first season in the Metropolitan Opera House. The building had been completely renovated (various leaders of districts doing construction) and the lobby was finished in orange and blue, the traditional colors of the city. . . . The orchestra had been augmented to 225 members. . . . The chorus, of 362 registered voters, was present, but did not sing. . . . At the request of a committee of Italian citizens, tomorrow night's performance will be L'Italiana in Algeri. There was talk of producing [Richard Strauss's] The Egyptian Helen on Saturday but it was found that the number of Egyptian voters in the city was insufficient to warrant the expense.

Taylor knew that his words, combining the experience of both a journalist and a composer, would reach the inner sanctum of the board. And his relentless picking away did have results.

On the positive side, the board welcomed its first female member, Eleanor Robson Belmont. She convinced the others of the value of an Opera Guild made up of people who, upon joining, could be brought closer to the stage through attendance at rehearsals and social events. Once initiated in 1935, this populist organization became a key financial support. The guild also reached out to radio listeners to send in pennies and dollars to help the Metropolitan. The response was gratifying, and the support base multiplied.

And what of the negative side to the Taylor snipings? One might think that, despite two successes, he was never asked to compose another opera for the Metropolitan because of an angry board, but that was not the case. There were many reasons. One was the success of The King's Henchman. With that opera, Gatti and Kahn had realized their hope of producing a winning American work, which spurred them on to seek further possibilities. Of course, they first turned to Taylor with a second commission. Since he took four years to complete it instead of two, Gatti and Kahn continued to expand their search. Their timing was good, because many more American composers were now finding a voice.

Otto Kahn remained positive about future American operas, and in 1929 put his imprimatur on *Merry Mount,* an opera then being written by thirty-three-year-old Howard Hanson. The native of Wahoo, Nebraska, had gained special recognition in the music world with his successful Symphony No. 1 ("Nordic") and his directorship of the new and increasingly influential Eastman School of Music in Rochester, New York. *Merry Mount* was adapted by Richard Stokes, a Midwestern music critic, from one of Nathaniel Hawthorne's *Twice-Told Tales.*[13]

The Metropolitan's financial troubles delayed production until the spring of 1934, even though the previous year it had produced the one-act opera *The Emperor Jones,* based on the Eugene O'Neill expressionistic play, as Guzski notes, "a radical departure from the traditional operatic conventions observed by . . . Taylor."[14] Louis Gruenberg, the composer, had gained a reputation as a modernist, and what caught the fancy of the audience was his hypnotic use of tom-toms throughout the opera. Tibbett again was called on to star in both *The Emperor Jones* and *Merry Mount.* Both operas brought to the Metropolitan stage the essence of two of the greatest U.S. authors, Hawthorne and O'Neill. After more than a dozen attempts, Gatti and Kahn had finally succeeded in bringing American stories to the Metropolitan.

When Otto Kahn died in 1934, Deems Taylor lost his strongest supporter and the Metropolitan Opera lost a unique visionary. Along with Gatti-Casazza's and Tullio Serafin's departures in 1935, the troika of positive support for American opera disintegrated completely. The Metropolitan did produce some new American operas during the next decade, when Edward Johnson took over as the new manager, but most were one act in length, and thus less expensive to stage. For example, in 1938 the production of Gian Carlo Menotti's *Amelia Goes to the Ball* used the sets from its Philadelphia premiere the previous year (at the Curtis Institute of Music), sets described by one critic as "shabby."[15] Financial issues remained paramount.[16] Bread and butter still came from Verdi, Puccini, and Bizet.

However, it would be wrong to indicate that the reason for Taylor's disappearance from Metropolitan commissions had only to do with the departure of Kahn and Gatti and the appearance of other composers to take Taylor's place. As he moved more and more into radio, his life as a full-time composer had, if not ended, certainly hit a major detour. Money remained his main concern, a preoccupation that drove him into another divorce.

The Death of JoJo and the End of Another Marriage

When Taylor's criticism of the Metropolitan's board appeared in the *American* in spring 1932, he had only several months left on his contract. With the

Hearst newspaper in financial difficulties, the editor asked him to take a cut in salary, which he agreed to do. But when he was asked to take another cut to renew his contract, Deems Taylor said good-bye.

Taylor now faced a bleak economic future without the $20,000 per year he had earned with his *American* contract. His contribution to the family's income came from a potpourri of sources: $1,500 from the six performances of *Peter Ibbetson* in its second season; a similar amount from hosting a weekly series on NBC on the history of opera; and a few hundred dollars in performance fees for the increasingly popular *Through the Looking Glass.* Fortunately, the Taylors had not invested in the stock market in the 1920s, nor had they lost savings in bank failures, so at least they had not suffered a major decline in their assets. What they continually faced were mortgage payments for Hollow Hill, as well as hotel bills for lengthy seasonal stays in New York. While Taylor had been writing his *American* column, his wife had taken a role in the long-running *Barretts of Wimpole Street,* but she left the cast when Joan became ill with whooping cough. It was Mary's last appearance on a Broadway stage.

While Taylor had been in Chicago the previous summer viewing the successful productions of *Peter Ibbetson* at Ravinia, he had written to Mary with a heavy heart: "I miss you . . . I've been in such a rotten, paralyzed state of mind and heart. I feel as if I'd been dragged out of something or other. Maybe I'll be better. I wish you'd give me another try. I love you."[17] Deems's words indicate he and Mary had had a severe break. The couple had shared a dozen intense years fueled by the theater and their theatrical and literary friends, by his success as an opera composer and hers as a playwright and actress, by his infidelities and her loyalty, and by the surprise arrival of Joan. They knew the marriage was unraveling, but they decided to give it one last try with a summer in Paris, the city they both loved and still an inexpensive place to live. Since Taylor had to complete the NBC series on the history of opera, he sent Mary, Joan, and a governess ahead to Paris in May 1932. Soon after arriving, Mary received a letter from an apparently rudderless husband:

> Where are you, and how are you? Let me know. So smart I am, and know all about everything except anything worth knowing. I wish, for instance, I knew something about myself—why I throw my life out of the window all the time and what the hell it is that I want. At the moment I haven't even the skimpy satisfaction of being able to look with pride even at my work. I've been going over the proof of "The Portrait of a Lady" and I hate it. Nothing that hasn't been said a million times. The Looking Glass music is pretty good, and my own. Nothing else is really worth all I've wasted for it. I think I'm tired.

I hope so, God knows. Give my love to Joan. Her life, at least, I haven't yet spoiled. Let her think well of me. I'll try to deserve it of her. Deems.[18]

Another sadness was in store for the dejected composer before he again saw Paris.

On June 28, Taylor's parents started for Greensboro, Vermont, their favorite summer spot, to spend several weeks of vacation with longtime friends. They planned to leave early in the morning, but when they took their luggage out to the car in front of their Bronx home, they were shocked by what they found, as Taylor's father noted in his journal:

> We had five flat tires. [Spares were on the back of cars in those days.] On inquiry we found that every car on our block was in the same condition and there were at least a score. Later we learned that the entire neighborhood from Sedgwich Avenue to the Concourse and northward to Kingsbridge Road had been visited by racketeers and some 500 cars had been ruined. Our tires had been punctured by an ice pick, usually twice but in some cases the tires had been slashed. The crooks even left their visiting cards with the name of a garage where we might find "protection."

Fortunately, they were able to purchase new tires that day and belatedly started for Vermont, traveling north on U.S. Route 7 through Connecticut, only to have another flat tire north of Danbury. They finally arrived at their vacation site the next day, and JoJo, as he always did, summed up the cost of the trip: "The repairs for the day (including new tires) totaled $28.24; gas and oil $6.33; meals and night lodging $10.90."[19]

It was the final entry in his journal. Six days later, he died of a heart attack. The *Times* ran an obituary: "Dr. Joseph S. Taylor, Educator, Dead at 75: Retired District Superintendent of Schools Here—Father of Deems Taylor, Composer." His body was sent back to the Bronx for a funeral service to be held in the family home on July 5.

What impact his father's death had on Taylor is unclear. In his letters and essays he kept silent on the feeling he had for his parents, a silence consistent with his lifelong pursuit of keeping his emotions well below the surface. His sister, Katy, later acknowledged this trait in her brother in a letter to Mary: "[Deems] is pretty apt to keep his deep feelings to himself and for that reason I am sure that there is much he has left unsaid that he really wanted to say."[20] Father and son shared intellectual pursuits, a need for personal achievement, and a work ethic, but apparently little else. "Your only trouble is the same as mine," JoJo had once written to Deems. "You are inclined to do more than the letter of your contract calls for. I am doing twice as much work as many of my colleagues because I simply do not know how to do superficial or dishonest work. Like father, like son."[21] Golf, which was JoJo's summertime passion, held no attraction for Deems. In fact, he once told a biographer that he had "tried golf exactly twice in his life, the first time breaking a man's jaw in the act of driving, and on the second occasion playing another's ball, with even more distressing results."[22]

Whatever can be known of the father-son relationship must come indirectly. As a youth, young Deems had a model of perfection in his father. Recall the statement made by JoJo when he returned from an 1890 trip to the Midwest: "Never made a single mistake of any sort. . . . I have more than realized my highest expectations." Years later Deems told his daughter that his parents had expected "100 percent" in all his school tests. He also revealed to a biographer that after graduating from NYU, "the lack of a Phi Beta Kappa key on [his] watch chain was always a source of annoyance to his father."[23] Deems would have both the Mennonite work ethic to prompt him and a father who expected the very best.

But achievement alone was not sufficient to satisfy his father, for in none of JoJo's detailed annual journals of the family activities is there praise for either his son's NYU varsity shows or his later Broadway accomplishments in musical revues. Neither is there mention of Deems's "coveted time-piece" awards from FPA for exceptional contributions to "The Conning Tower." Praise for Deems's successes came for achievements of the higher realm only—orchestral works and operas.

A sense of humor does not appear to have been among JoJo's attributes. Again one recalls Deems's explanation of the wit of W. S. Gilbert: "the almost inevitable reaction against the father's solemnity and morbidity."[24] *Morbidity* may be too harsh a word to pin on JoJo, but solemn he must have been. He was a man to be respected by a son, but perhaps not warmly loved. With no record of Deems's behavior at his father's funeral, it is reasonable to assume that a stoic stance reflected whatever he held in his heart.

Deems and Katy must have helped with the multitude of details amid the "bustle of the house, the morning after death."[25] Katy at the time was in the final year of a three-year course at Mills Training School on Fifth Avenue to gain a diploma as a kindergarten teacher and follow in her father's footsteps. At Katy's commencement, Deems provided the keynote address and announced a scholarship fund he would provide in the name of his father: each year one member of the entering class would receive one hundred dollars. This was a goodly sum during the Depression. Joseph Schimmel Taylor's son had honored his father in the right way. Following JoJo's funeral, Mummie sadly learned the depth of her dependence on her husband after nearly fifty years of marriage. Deems recognized his responsibility to help maintain the family home, which still had a mortgage, and he began a monthly ritual of sending checks to his mother. As it developed, JoJo had not provided well for his wife, who for the rest of her life had to maintain a home that relied on rent from boarders.

Three weeks after his father's funeral, Taylor finally sailed for Paris on July 28, 1932. Mary had already been there more than two months. A self-imposed pressure to compose another opera continued to press on his mind. In spite of an apparent lack of interest from the Metropolitan, a comment in an earlier letter to Mary suggested he still had hopes for the Yellow Brick Brewery on Broadway: "I've been reading, looking for an opera story . . . I'm rather tempted by 'The Dragon' [an Irish fantasy by Lady Gregory] . . . [I] fear that the charm of the actual dialogue will be swamped by a musical set-ting and . . . I can't quite see it in the vast spaces of the Met. Also, I reread the Gandle libretto and still yearn over it a bit."[26]

During their Paris stay, the Taylors evidenced a continued respect and support for each other's creative talents. Mary completed the text of her first book, *A Surprise to the Children,* the story of a fairyland entered into by a small girl and boy; Deems composed four songs for the book. Its dedication, "To Joan," was no surprise, for she had become the center of Mary Kennedy's life, the main reason she had decided to withdraw from further stage work.

Yet Paris apparently did not help the marriage, for after they returned to the States, what emotional bonds remained were further stretched in early 1933. Taylor still had not found a stable income and knew full well he would never survive only on earnings from his music. Naturally, the Depression continued to exert its psychological strain on anyone who was not employed full-time, so when NBC and the Kraft Company came to Taylor with a lucra-tive offer to host a new radio variety show, the Kraft Music Hall, he suc-cumbed to the strains of tinkling dollars.

Variety shows had become big hits on radio; they were initiated in 1929 by the extremely successful *Fleischmann Yeast Hour* with Rudy Vallee, whose nasal tenor caused many a female's heart to flutter. Vallee also had a knack of bringing onto his show new entertainers who became great successes on their own, such as Alice Faye, Milton Berle, and Edgar Bergen and Charlie McCarthy. The Kraft Music Hall's weekly two-hour program would feature music played by the highly popular Paul Whiteman and his orchestra, with singers performing both semi-classical and popular music. Al Jolson, then recognized as one of the greatest entertainers of the era, also made periodic appearances. With such a lineup and format, Taylor must have known the show would be a success.

But when Mary learned of the Kraft offer, she became indignant. She couldn't understand how her husband would allow his reputation as a composer to be compromised by his mixing with the popular entertainers of the day. She perceived that Deems would become just another merchandiser, since the Kraft program had been designed to promote their new mayonnaise replacement, Miracle Whip. Mary urged him to turn down the offer, but he did not agree with her. First of all, he had a broad view of what good music was, and he believed the songs of a Jerome Kern or a George Gershwin were something special in the development of American music. Most important, he realized that his radio voice, not his composing pen, would provide what he needed to support his family and allow for a vital social life. He politely told Mary he had no choice but to take the offer.

When Taylor walked up to the microphone for the first Music Hall program on June 26, 1933, he began a dozen years in radio that made his among the most listened to and recognizable voices of his time, but it also ended a dozen years of marriage. The husband Mary wanted was a composer, not a radio star; she decided that divorce was now her only option.[27] She and Joan moved into the Frank Gillmore home on Beekman Place, from which Margalo Gillmore, Frank's actress daughter, had called Taylor eight years earlier to surprise him with the news that he was a father.

Communication between Mary and Deems now became spotty, though in one letter "Deems the Repentant" showed his colors: "I thought of you a great deal last night—of how much bravery and patience you really have and how completely selfish I am. I'm sorry."[28] Taylor's confession may have come closest to a view of his inner person, someone consistently concerned with advancing himself and his many talents. His apology notwithstanding, Mary contacted Curtis Bok in Philadelphia to initiate divorce proceedings.

Bok, the son of Mary Curtis Bok, founder of the Curtis Institute of Music, proved to be both an adviser and a friend. He recommended going to Nevada for its well-known quickie divorce. Three years earlier, the state had reduced residency for uncontested divorce from three months to six weeks, giving further impetus to an already bustling industry. In addition, for a divorce the state required only such "vague but generous grounds like 'incompatibility' or 'mental cruelty,'" at a time when New York State still stuck to adultery as its sole grounds.[29] Mary agreed to the plan, and Bok made a reservation for her at the first of the Nevada "divorce ranches," the T-H Ranch near Sutcliffe. Joan would remain with a nanny.

Mary wanted no publicity whatever while she was in Nevada, so Bok advised her to use "the name of Mrs. Joseph Taylor of New York City. I doubt whether it will cause any attention. I am suggesting to Judge Brown that when he files the papers, which must be filed, he use Deems's proper name of Joseph D. Taylor. . . . As I have told you, you cannot avoid the papers getting news of the fact that legal papers have been filed but these contain only your names and the general charge of cruelty. Beyond that nothing will be known of the facts or details."[30]

Before leaving, she listened once more to her husband on a radio program. In a journal meant to be read years later by her daughter, she expressed her restless, yet generous feelings about him: "They are introducing Deems now—and now he is speaking . . . very crisp, very decided, very sure of himself—very important—all the things that he has worked for. I remember Abigail Adams's sigh for her 'untitled husband' with whom she began life so happily but who soon disappeared when the honors began to crowd upon him. I wonder what you will be? Clear-eyed wondering child—you can be proud of your father and his fine accomplishment, for him you have . . . but I sigh a little for the lover I have lost—do not mistake me though. I am glad you have such a distinguished father."[31]

Still, Mary could never forget the times when he showed his unfeeling side. A classic example occurred one evening after she had opened in a Broadway play: "As she and Deems were in a taxi preparing to leave the theater, a rather pretty young thing came up to speak with them. Gallant Deems, obviously impressed by the young lady, turned to Mary and said, 'Give her the flowers!' then took one of Mary's opening night bouquets and presented it to the young woman."[32]

On May 15, 1934, the *Times* reported the Taylors' divorce with the subhead, "Cruelty Charged by Actress, Author Wife of Composer, Who Refuses to Comment." A week later Mary received a letter from Katy, her sister-in-law. Six years earlier, Katy had also found divorce her only answer, leaving her, like Mary, with one child to raise. "Mary dear, Somehow this doesn't seem at all like a permanent step to me. I have said 'Deems and Mary' so often together that it is hard to separate them in my mind. I am hoping that after you have lived apart for awhile that what is really true about both of you will draw you together again. . . . Deems has written us that it is his fault. He has never spoken a word of anything that was unkind about you since he has known you."[33]

Years later, a grown-up Joan recalled an episode that identified the irreconcilable differences in the personalities of her parents. At a boarding school where her mother had sent her, there was a prize. "If you win the Tidy Prize," her mother said, "I'll give you $50.00—not to spend, of course." Her father, listening to this, retorted: "If you win the Tidy Prize, I'll give you $100.00—provided you spend it at once."[34] Such opposites had lived their allotted years together. Mary's stay in Nevada provided time for reflection on what they

A formal portrait of
Deems Taylor, 1934.
*(Courtesy of Michael W.
Davis)*

had meant to each other. She asked Deems to remember their good years together. He responded graciously: "I do remember, Mashinka. I shan't forget
it. It was a lovely life."[35]

The divorce settlement gave Mary custody of their daughter, and much
more. To assure Joan's education until she reached the age of eighteen, Taylor
would provide his ex-wife with one-half of his gross income, taxes prepaid.
In addition, he would pay the mortgage on the Stamford property, which she
and Joan would occupy. For years, he complained to anyone willing to listen
of the heavy financial burden placed on him, but it did not prevent his maintaining a loyal, friendly relationship with Mary throughout his life.

Taylor at Fifty

The summer of 1934 gave Taylor plenty of time for reflection, much of it occurring as he stared at New York hotel room walls. He knew that in one year
he would be fifty years old, and he had no permanent residence; the Stamford home, which he had filled with examples of his carpentry talents, was
now Mary and Joan's principal residence. His marriage scorecard read "two
marriages, two divorces": hardly a successful personal life. On the other

hand, his operas, cantatas, and especially the *Looking Glass* suite had provided him great success, something his peers had recognized ten years earlier by electing him to the National Institute of Arts and Letters, the prestigious group of authors, composers, and artists that became "the first enduring literary and artistic elite in America."[36] He was now also one of the twenty-four directors of the influential ASCAP. In both of these organizations, he rubbed elbows with the powerful in music and literature.

Two honorary degree hoods hung in his closet, one from NYU and the other from Juniata College in Pennsylvania, where his father had taught for a year in the pre–apple butter days of New York City. At the Juniata ceremony, Taylor had spoken to the students and provided some tips for success, especially emphasizing the need to be improvident: "Do the things you most want to do first. Then save your money. If John Keats and Henry Purcell had worked to make money and save it, they may have had more money, but the world would not have had their poetry and their music; for both died young."[37] Without a doubt, Taylor practiced what he preached, for he had done what he wanted to do: compose operas and other music. However, he had not saved money, and now, with all his financial obligations, his checkbook became the center point of his life.

Taylor's Kraft contract ended in July 1934, and in August *Newsweek* reported: "Mr. Taylor has retired to his farm . . . and given up radio work to concentrate on composing." The story arose because Mary, no longer his wife but willing to be his librettist, had tried to convince him to develop an opera based on "The Story of Ming-Yee," a Chinese fantasy from a story by Lafcadio Hearn.[38] But in fact Taylor was not in Connecticut concentrating on composing; he was in New York signing a contract with Chase and Sanborn, the coffee company, to host a weekly one-hour program of condensed operas to begin in December. Mammon won out again.

With the Chase and Sanborn contract hardly dry, Taylor received a summons from William LeBaron to go to Hollywood for a few months. LeBaron, now a major producer at Paramount Pictures, had a high-paying project that was perfect for his longtime friend: helping to prepare the script for the first filmed opera since the advent of sound in the movies. It took little time for Taylor to pack his clothes and head west. Filming an opera sounded exciting, and now, with both radio and movie contracts, his financial future seemed bright indeed. His socializing future had possibilities also, for he had already fallen head over heels for another woman, Colette d'Arville, whom he had met while Mary was in Nevada. When he returned from California, Colette would be waiting for him with open arms.

12. Hollywood, Colette d'Arville, and Ramuntcho, 1934–1936

The *Chivalry* That Was Not to Be

On the train to Los Angeles in late August 1934, Taylor undoubtedly thought back on his long friendship with Bill LeBaron, and the heights that his *Echo* cowriter had scaled since they had worked together in 1924 at Cosmopolitan Pictures. After completing *Janice Meredith,* LeBaron left his position as general manager of Hearst's Cosmopolitan productions and moved to a similar position at the Astoria, Long Island, studios of Famous Players Company, producers of Paramount Pictures. But the lure of Hollywood was great, and three years later LeBaron, a man described as "next to impossible to dislike,"[1] moved to California as a producer for RKO, a fledgling studio seeking to enter the big leagues. By hiring LeBaron RKO chose wisely, because in 1931 the LeBaron-produced Western epic *Cimarron* brought the company its first (and, as time would tell, only) Academy Award for best picture. Over at Paramount, studio chief Adolph Zukor, who had known LeBaron from his Astoria days, saw what LeBaron had accomplished and in 1932 lured him back to Paramount with a yearly salary approaching a quarter-million dollars.

By this time Hollywood was producing the second generation of musical films. The first had begun in 1927, when Warner Brothers' *Jazz Singer* created a craze for both talkies and musicals, and every studio rapidly responded to draw audiences. The resulting films had little plot, even less memorable music, generally overweight chorines for the dance numbers, and camerawork that proved static and boring. Audiences soon tired of these attempts, and musicals almost disappeared. As the Great Depression deepened, imaginative choreographers such as Busby Berkeley saw ways to give movement and panache to singing and dancing spectacles, and the second generation of musicals emerged to boost the morale of dispirited viewers.[2]

Hollywood's musical net had been cast broadly: even opera singers became stars. Two years after *The King's Henchman* premiered, the movie industry discovered that the good-looking and energetic Lawrence Tibbett "could act [and] was relaxed before the camera, and he could pull off a bravura grand manner without seeming ridiculous."[3] In 1929 Metro-Goldwyn-Mayer studios released *Rogue Song,* starring a dashing, sometimes bare-chested Tibbett in one of the first all-Technicolor sound films. Good reviews propelled Tibbett into several more pictures. On the female side, the beautiful Grace Moore, who had first sung on Broadway before becoming a Metropolitan diva, turned *One Night of Love* into one year of cash for Columbia Pictures in 1934. With musicals in resurgence, Paramount decided to take them to a higher plane; they would film an opera, something not attempted in Hollywood since movies had learned to talk. It was at this point that LeBaron sent for the obvious man to help bring the project to completion.

Taylor had never been to Hollywood, though he certainly knew many people there. Some, like his old friend Roland Young, were transplanted Broadway actors, while others—including Robert Benchley, Dorothy Parker, Marc Connelly, and Donald Stewart—were Algonquin comrades who had migrated in hopes of getting rich as screenwriters. When Taylor's train arrived in Los Angeles, Roland Young met him and gave him the run of his house in Beverly Hills. Taylor met LeBaron to sign the contract and then returned to the Young home to write Mary Kennedy and explain why he was in California: "It's a grand job, and not a hard one. Paramount is going to try an experimental production of a grand opera as a picture. . . . They're beginning with 'Cavalleria Rusticana' and my job is to fit the score to the spoken parts of the continuity. My contract calls for four weeks, with an extra optional week if I need it." Then he confessed that there might be even more gold in the Hollywood hills: "Paramount has also taken out options with me for two more pictures to be made within the coming year if this one goes over. . . . For the present picture I get five thousand dollars, for the second, seven thousand five hundred, and for the third, ten thousand. Isn't that rather pleasant?"[4] The letter was the beginning of his lifelong commitment to inform Mary Kennedy of his doings, motivated perhaps by both loyalty and guilt.

LeBaron believed that an audience existed for opera on film, especially because the public's consciousness had been raised by the Metropolitan broadcasts on Saturdays. But which opera to choose? Movie audiences could not be expected to sit through a lengthy work no matter how interesting, so he astutely chose the one-act *Cavalleria Rusticana* (Rustic chivalry), whose success had been without question. Pietro Mascagni's opera pulsed with Sicilian passions, great tunes, and a juicy story of unfaithfulness. For a working title the studio chose *Chivalry,* and Taylor was given the challenge to shape the music and script into a cohesive whole. Each morning he worked diligently in an office provided by LeBaron, then in the afternoon and evening he took time to appreciate Hollywood's social life in its sparkling variety, including lunch with Irene Dunne, the actress whom LeBaron had discovered and starred in *Cimarron;* then tennis and dinner with the financier Bernard Baruch, Mary's friend and already twice on the cover of *Time.*[5]

But between the cocktails and after only a week of work, he began to hear rumors that everything was not going well for *Chivalry.* Indeed, any thoughts he had for film glory were fading, all because of Hollywood's problems with censorship of sex and violence. What *Chivalry* was up against was another battle to keep the silver screen "pure." With the emergence of sound movies, religious groups had increased the pressure on the motion picture industry to decrease the brutality and overt sexuality in films. A dozen years earlier, during the silent film era, Hollywood had met such demands for reform by establishing the Motion Picture Producers and Distributors of America, headed by Will Hays, a Presbyterian elder. The Hays Office, as it came to be known, sought to stave off governmental action by self-policing. It adopted a Production Code in 1930, which extolled the philosophy: "Wrong entertainment lowers the whole living condition and moral ideals of a race."[6]

Two years after the code's implementation, some movie scenes still hummed with sexuality. In *Night After Night,* the 1932 film produced by LeBaron that introduced Mae West to the screen, an admirer of West ogles the scintillating jewelry flashing all over the undulating star and remarks, "Goodness, what beautiful diamonds!" West's classic reply—"Goodness had nothing to do with it, dearie"—strongly suggests that the code still wasn't working, and Will Hays knew it. In 1934 Hollywood paid its penance for perceived immorality when Joseph Breen became head of the Production Code Administration.

As religious groups urged federal action to reduce the sinfulness on screen and the newly founded Catholic Legion of Decency entered the fray, Breen demanded that all screenplays be submitted to him for approval. After reading a script he would send suggested changes, which, if carried out, assured approval to proceed filming. One result of such prudery was the on-screen separation of married couples into twin beds for the next thirty years.

Special dispensation was needed even for what would become one of the most quoted responses in movie history, Rhett Butler's answer to Scarlett O'Hara's question about her future: "Frankly, my dear, I don't give a damn!"

Five days after Taylor began work, Paramount submitted its *Chivalry* script to Joseph Breen.[7] The opera's love triangle remained central in the script: Lola, though married, has an affair with Turiddu, her old flame; then Turiddu's current girlfriend, the jealous Santuzza, fans the passions of the village, prompting Lola's husband to murder Turiddu. Breen read the script and, by return letter, identified serious problems: "First is the definite portrayal that Turiddu has seduced Santuzza. Second, the further definite portrayal that after Turiddu has seduced Santuzza, he goes back into adulterous relations with his first love, Lola." Breen had two recommendations: "In the first instance, we are of the opinion that there should be no inference of a seduction and pregnancy, and in the second, we recommend that Turiddu's relations with Lola be only an infatuation which motivates his serenading her."[8] A week later, Breen informed Hays about the proposed *Chivalry:* "We have advised the studio that it will be necessary to eliminate the illicit sex and a good deal of the brutality of the original operatic version."[9]

LeBaron, Taylor, and others recognized that if the script followed Breen's suggestions, the heart of the opera would be ripped out. With the code in charge, *Chivalry* wound up on the log pile of never-produced films. At least the experience gave Taylor a taste of Hollywood, something he would enjoy much more four years later, when he returned at the request of Walt Disney to participate in the production of *Fantasia.* But this time, after six weeks in California, he had to pack his bags and return to New York, where Colette d'Arville awaited.

Colette d'Arville

The twenty-nine-year-old d'Arville, a petite French soprano from the Basque country, had arrived in New York in 1931 to sing the title role in *Carmen* with the French-Italian opera company in Trenton, New Jersey. She must have quickly made political and social connections, for when Marshal Pétain, the great World War I hero, arrived in New York that October as an official visitor, d'Arville sang the "Marseillaise" at the public reception.[10] During the next few years she sang with small opera groups, then made her New York recital debut in January 1934, at a concert that garnered a brief *Times* review: "Although some of [her] mezzo-voce performance in the Debussy and Ravel groups delineated the vocal line with a pleasant timbre and commendable flexibility, her effective voice seemed too small for even Town Hall."[11]

Though the circumstances of Taylor's meeting d'Arville are not known, the day certainly is, for in his appointment book on April 24, 1934, for the first time he used red ink to emblazon the phrase "Met Colette this night." In the month that followed they met almost daily, which he noted carefully in his appointment book, sometimes with an intriguing red dot after an entry, suggesting that Taylor's passion for things French had found another outlet. Their intense socialization broke when d'Arville left in late May to visit her family in France for several months, an ocean voyage she would take every summer throughout their relationship. On Taylor's return from California they resumed their frequent meetings.

Early in 1935, some six months after beginning his involvement with Colette, Taylor decided to confess to Mary his newest interest:

> There is—how does one say it?—someone else. I don't want to write her name, because no one knows anything about it. There have been rumors, but no one knows or is likely to know. . . . Mashinka, I would like you to know. It is not an "affair." I am not her lover. I am very much in love with her, and the chances are a hundred to one against my being able to marry her. I wish I could tell you more about it, but I cannot. It is not my secret to tell. Forgive this awkward way of putting things. I had to tell you, somehow.[12]

If we add together all that became known about d'Arville, the likelihood that they were not lovers is close to zero, but what exactly did he know about Colette? No letters are known to exist between them. His appointment books provide the only information of their extensive commitments together, books that also indicate that often there would be late dinners at which d'Arville and Taylor were joined by Giovanni Martinelli, then one of the reigning Italian tenors of the Metropolitan Opera. Taylor had known him from the days of *The King's Henchman,* having even inquired of Martinelli if he would consider taking the role of Aethelwold in the opera for the 1928–29 Met season.[13]

But neither Martinelli's nor Taylor's interest in d'Arville was operatic. Rosa Ponselle, the great American soprano who had often sung with Martinelli, years later in an interview spoke of the tenor's affair with Colette: "I met her and got to know her a little, but I don't think she was singing much around that time. I don't know what she was doing, really. I guess the polite way to say it is that she was an 'international consort.' She was a pretty girl, and Martinelli was head over heels about her. Everybody knew [about] it, and some of us thought it was affecting his singing. I never thought he was quite the same [vocally] after that."[14]

Taylor was no less smitten than Martinelli. That both Martinelli and Tay-

Colette d'Arville, soprano from the Basque area of France. She caught Taylor's eye after his divorce from Mary Kennedy.
(Courtesy of Yale University Music Library)

lor were d'Arville's lovers would be confirmed several years later by, of all people, Arturo Toscanini.

Taylor and Radio: A Deeper Commitment

Taylor's hosting of the *Chase and Sanborn Opera Guild* every Sunday night on NBC began in December 1934. The coffee company had become one of the earliest commercial sponsors in radio and had tried a variety of approaches to gain an audience. As early as 1929, Chase and Sanborn had paid Maurice Chevalier five thousand dollars a week, a record at that time, to star in a musical variety show. Two years later their radio hour featured Eddie Cantor, the banjo-eyed Ziegfeld star.[15] When they lost Cantor to Hollywood, the company decided to go "high class" and sponsor weekly adaptations of famed operas. Apparently they believed that the same people who laughed at the humor of Cantor would also happily spend an hour listening to opera, especially if hosted by Deems Taylor, the well-known American opera composer.

Taylor's pay of six hundred dollars per broadcast was well earned: he had to cut the opera score down to an hour's length, revise translations, rehearse, direct, and run the show on the air. "I spend from twenty to thirty hours a week at the typewriter," he wrote his agent, George Bye. "At the moment I scream if anyone speaks loudly to me. After the holidays I'll either be dead or not working so hard."[16]

Presenting the condensed operas in English gave special pleasure to Taylor, for, as he told his audience, "Since we are, after all, in America, we present these performances in the language of America." And Chase and Sanborn spared no expense. *Newsweek* reported that for *Rigoletto,* the first of the operas presented, "John Charles Thomas and 100-odd singers and musicians tried their best to make listeners forget Cantor's songs and remember Verdi's."[17] Wilfred Pelletier conducted the top-flight orchestra, and the great singers featured in following weeks included Elizabeth Rethberg, Giovanni Martinelli, Frederick Jagel, Lucrezia Bori, Richard Crooks, Jan Peerce, Rose Bampton, and the great Wagnerian tenor Lauritz Melchior.

"The broadcast is rather successful—with the public and the sponsors, that is," Taylor wrote to Mary, "not so much with the grocers. They hate it."[18] Years later, Taylor told the story of a district representative for Chase and Sanborn who had heard *Madame Butterfly* (with musical wings clipped) and thought it was lousy. When the sales manager asked why, the man replied: "'Poor Butterfly' is my favorite song and they didn't even sing it."[19] The *Chase aud Sanborn Opera Guild* would be Taylor's final program as a spokesman for opera. Though originally slotted for one year, it ended after four months for two simple reasons: the cost of supplying an orchestra and first-rate soloists was too great, and, far worse, Eddie Cantor returned after two months and opened a new show on CBS at the same Sunday hour.

Taylor, in his post-divorce days, lived in the Barbizon-Plaza Hotel. His gross income for 1934 topped $30,000, but because of the divorce agreement and taxes, what he had left was about one-third of that. Considering that the average personal income at the time was only about $400, Taylor was doing fine with his net of $10,000. He was concerned, however, that Mary was exerting too much control over little Joan's life and was keeping her away from him. Apparently he complained of this to Margalo Gillmore and the charge got back to Mary, who challenged him on the point. Taylor's emotional doors flew open in response:

> Did I tell Margalo that you were keeping me from seeing Joan? I don't remember putting it in quite those terms—but haven't you, just a little bit, made it at least difficult for me to see Joan? I think you don't quite realize how much I love Joan, nor in what way. . . .

If she must have a single parent, you are the one that is essential for her. . . . But I do terribly want to see her. If I honestly thought that she would be better off, happier, and more complete, not seeing me under even these unhappy circumstances, I would never see her again—and you will not believe what that would cost me. But I can't believe so. I think I have something for her, too.[20]

The letter must have touched Mary, for Joan's visits with her father increased—but not for long, because from April 1935 to June 1936, Mary took Joan on a round-the-world trip. They started with several months in the Orient, where Mary's interests in those customs and religions deepened. She financed the trip easily, since in 1935 alone the portion of Taylor's income that Mary received was $18,000, taxes prepaid. One benefit of this trip pleased Taylor: for almost a year he had access to Hollow Hill at any time.

With the unexpected early conclusion of the *Opera Guild* program, Taylor had no permanent radio income until the fall of 1935. At that time he began a season-long series as host of the *Swift Studio Party,* another of the variety shows by then commonplace on radio. The "party" took place in the fictional studios of Sigmund Romberg, the famous composer of *The Student Prince* and *Desert Song.* Taylor introduced guests and bantered with them, while Romberg conducted the orchestra and sometimes joined in the fun with his rather heavy Hungarian accent.

Taylor and variety shows were natural partners, and when such programs needed a splash of musical culture, the producers often summoned Taylor as a one-time guest. One call came from Rudy Vallee's *Fleischmann Yeast Hour,* the first and most important of the big-time radio variety shows. Vallee, with his crooning style, had reached extreme heights of popularity through recordings and radio. He introduced Taylor as "the leading radio commentator on musical events and personalities" and gave him six minutes to describe the evolution of different orchestral instruments.

Taylor always insisted on writing his own script. In this case he gave the listener a six-minute survey course, concluding with the slide trombone:

This instrument is of great antiquity and probably invented by the Egyptians, inasmuch as carvings on certain Egyptian tombs show the King of Egypt with his foot on the neck of a trombone player. . . . And now that we have taken our little trip through instrument land, let us hear Mr. Vallee's orchestra in a composition that makes brilliant use of all the instruments whose private life we have just been discussing—a work by the famous Jugoslavian composer, Emile Schlemiel: the "Water Music" from the sixth act of his opera, "Dov'è il Gabinetto?"[21]

Ramuntcho, Taylor's Third Opera

In 1935, busy as he was in radio work, Taylor could not put out of his mind his personal need to write another opera. As noted earlier, in the three years after the *Peter Ibbetson* premiere, the Metropolitan had produced two more works by American composers, Louis Gruenberg's *Emperor Jones* and Howard Hanson's *Merry Mount.* With the death of his champion Otto Kahn the previous year, Taylor realized the likelihood of a third commission had dimmed considerably. Nonetheless, he had had two successes. Besides, few of the modernist composers appeared to have much interest in writing operas. The one exception was Virgil Thomson, whose ultimately successful *Four Saints in Three Acts* Otto Kahn had effectively turned down in 1930 without even listening to it.[22] So, with few American competitors, Taylor determined to put his time-limited creative powers into composing another opera.

The idea of using Pierre Loti's novel *Ramuntcho* as a subject came from movie director Jean Negulesco. While in Hollywood for the ill-fated *Chivalry,* Taylor had told Negulesco of his frustration at not finding a good opera subject. He most likely also confessed his current infatuation with the Basque-born Colette. This would explain Negulesco's suggestion that Taylor consider *Ramuntcho,* a story of unrequited love set in the Basque region. The more Taylor thought about the suggestion, the more he realized this subject would enable him to integrate his personal life with his composing life. When Taylor sought the rights to the story of Ramuntcho, a pelote player, he must have discovered that two composers had already composed music based on it, neither with particular success.[23] This should have been a warning to him, though he might have also taken it as a challenge to succeed where others had failed.

What is particularly puzzling is why Taylor did not consider writing a comic opera as his third venture. With his innate wit and interest in fantasy, this would seem to have been a natural. Walter Damrosch, perhaps his strongest supporter, wondered the same thing; he wrote to Taylor indicating that he hoped to live long enough "to shout my loudest bravo at the first performance of your comic opera (words and music) which until now you have refused to write."[24] If Taylor had followed his original temptation to use Lady Gregory's *Dragon* as the basis of an opera (instead of waiting twenty years as he did), his creative powers might well have produced a fantasy with comedy. As it turned out, his obsession with d'Arville supplanted his musical inspiration.

In May 1935 d'Arville sailed for her annual five-month visit to her family, and on her return learned that Taylor had begun work on an adaptation of *Ramuntcho,* with a libretto already sketched out, as well as some of the music.

What may have inspired him to move forward was a call that summer from George Gershwin, who wanted to go to a baseball game at Yankee Stadium and invited Taylor to join him. No sooner had Taylor arrived at Gershwin's apartment than he found himself listening to a private performance of his friend's score for *Porgy and Bess,* months before the opera's pre-Broadway opening in Boston. Taylor's wholeheartedly positive reaction so impressed Gershwin that he wrote about it to DuBose Heyward, the librettist and coauthor of the play *Porgy:* "I played some of the music for Deems Taylor, whose judgment I respect highly, and he was so enthusiastic and flattering that I blush to mention it."[25]

Taylor, hearing the gorgeous melodies spinning out one after the other, must have reflected on the incredible gift that Gershwin possessed, something he did not have in any similar measure—the gift of memorable melody. For the modernist composer, melody was not an issue, but Taylor, with his reliance on the virtues of romanticism and impressionism, needed tunes. He knew that the melodies in his operas that persisted in the listener came mainly from adapted folk tunes, melodies that had stood the test of time. Gershwin's melodic gifts permeated not only popular songs, but also his serious works, such as *An American in Paris* and the Concerto in F. One also wonders if the astute Taylor, in listening to *Porgy and Bess,* might not have recognized that the great American opera had been written, though generations would pass before many critics would admit this.

Whether what he heard discouraged him or not, Taylor saw that the stories of *Porgy and Bess* and *Ramuntcho* had one major similarity: they were about poor people living a simple life. He decided that like Gershwin, who had gone to South Carolina to compose and hear some of the native Negro traditions in song, he would go with Colette to the land of the Basques the following summer and collect some folk tunes for use in the opera.

During the winter radio work kept him busy, but with the end of the Swift series in March 1936, he had to let Mary Kennedy know that finances were a little tight. She still had not returned from her round-the-world trip. "This is the year's low tide for me financially," he wrote. "Both my radio accounts have gone off the air. . . . Of course there's an ASCAP check due about the 15th of this month. I don't know what it will come to, but it ought to be somewhere around $2000. What with income taxes and the money I'm sending mother every month, the treasury is a bit anemic at the moment. . . . This sounds silly, but *I am* broke at the moment. I had to lend Edna and Eugen $1500."

In the same letter he told Mary his current feelings about Colette, while once again seeking forgiveness from Mary for both major and minor peccadillos: "I shall marry her if I can—and if she can. Not this spring, nor this summer. In the fall, perhaps. Perhaps never. . . . I *have* to take the path that I see ahead of me, Mashinka, and yet I cannot deny that I shall always feel accountable to you. I shall never be able to be happy while you are not. And still I must stumble ahead. I know much of what you have suffered through me. Believe me, I know now. And forgive me. Give my dear love to Joan."[26] The words "I shall always feel accountable to you" are revealing. Deep in his heart, Taylor must have realized that his best composing years had passed, and always they had been with Mary's continual encouragement.

Colette sailed for France in June 1936, and Taylor planned to meet her a month later. But before he departed he left Mary a letter, to be read upon her return the following month. In it he explained how things stood with his new amour: "Things between us are still unsettled and I'm not particularly happy over them, but I'm very well. [Colette] is in great difficulties, which I wish I could explain; but they're not my secret. I still hope and wait—a funny role for me, isn't it? But I MUST put all my eggs into one basket, even if the end is disaster. I learned that from you, Mashinka. And thank you."[27]

What disturbed him is unknown. Several facts unearthed in the research for this book lead to speculation. The first is that Colette d'Arville was a stage name: her real name was Marie Marthe Cescosse. The second, and far more important, was that Colette had a son in France with the family name of Cescosse. With no evidence of a previous marriage for the French singer, one must assume the boy was illegitimate.[28] How Taylor would have reacted to such news is unclear, but more than likely he would not have been pleased to discover more secrets about his "international consort."

Once aboard the *Ile de France* on his way to meet Colette, he again wrote Mary: "I decided last Monday that a search for local color for the opera was as good an excuse as any for going myself on a trip. So I'm off for a look at the Pyrenees. It won't be a long look—I stay a day or two in Paris, then go to Biarritz, from which I'll probably visit some of the Basque towns."[29] Though he had worked on the *Ramuntcho* libretto already for more than a year, Taylor sought melodies that would bring an authentic flavor to his opera.

He rendezvoused with Colette in early August in the Basque port town of Saint-Jean-de-Luz and watched the Sunday fiesta, which was highlighted by energetic fandango dancing. As he described later, "The climax of the evening is reached by the arrival of the *toro del fuego,* an artificial bull, worked by two of the boys, who chases the dancers, spouting fire from the sparklers and Roman candles that are stuck in his hide."[30] In Taylor's mind, the fiesta provided the idea for the beginning of the opera's third act—a ballet utilizing the fandango rhythm and melodies of the region. Later, in a local bookstore, he discovered exactly what he needed: a Basque songbook with folksongs of the area. Satisfied, he and Colette spent their final days in Europe "acquiring local color and inspiration on the beach, at the pelote games, and on the terrace of the Bar Basque."[31]

Back in the States, Taylor learned that some earlier discussions with CBS had borne fruit: he would be their first music consultant and adviser, at a salary of one thousand dollars per month. A major part of the assignment made him the intermission commentator for the New York Philharmonic Sunday broadcasts. It was a golden opportunity, and it would bring his greatest fame in radio. For the next six years, Deems Taylor would be the friendly guide for millions, escorting people gently along what to many were the mysterious paths of classical music.

13. The Philharmonic Intermissions Begin, 1936–1938

The New York Philharmonic on Radio

By the mid-1930s radio broadcasting had entered its golden age, bringing the American public a variety of entertainment hardly dreamed of when Pittsburgh's KDKA had first beamed its signal sixteen years earlier. In 1936 radio shows that would entertain for decades were well under way: comedians such as Jack Benny, Fred Allen, and Fibber McGee and Molly; *Lux Radio Theater,* with its host Cecil B. DeMille; the *Breakfast Club* with Don McNeill; the *March of Time* news documentary; the soap opera *Ma Perkins;* the *Jergens Journal* with Walter Winchell, a national reporter with incredible influence. Yet with all the new entertainment venues, the four national networks—Mutual (begun in 1934 with New York's WOR as its flagship station), CBS, and the Red and Blue networks of NBC—continued to give special prominence to live concerts of classical music, providing the nation its most widespread contact ever with such forms of art.

Once the networks went national in the late 1920s, and continuing throughout the 1930s, they believed that part of their responsibility was to be music educators, to bring live concerts to every nook and cranny of the United States. One study in 1937 found that the four networks together averaged almost thirteen hours of live symphonic music per week, principally on weekday evenings and on Sundays.[1] CBS, NBC, and Mutual, in addition to sponsoring live broadcasts of the best orchestras in the country—including those of Boston, Philadelphia, and Cleveland—had each developed its own studio orchestra. To the listener these concerts projected an image of quality programming, but for the networks the concerts were not inexpensive to produce. With no commercial sponsors, the concerts were sustained with funds from other advertising sources.

These sustaining programs came from a variety of sources. For example, in 1932 Howard Hanson saw an opportunity, as director of the Eastman School of Music, to emphasize the music of American composers. He initiated a decade of weekly broadcasts of the school's symphony orchestra. Also in 1932, Radio City Music Hall opened in New York and for the next ten years presented its orchestra, conducted by Erno Rapee, in midday Sunday radio concerts. The Radio City orchestra's 1937 cycle of the seven Sibelius symphonies was described as a "marathonic undertaking never attempted previously in radio."[2] Sponsors ultimately surfaced to attach their names to such programming. Automobile manufacturers, with symphony orchestras of their own, became the first sponsors: the General Motors Concerts began in 1929 over NBC, and the Ford Sunday Evening Hour started in 1934 over CBS. In the latter case, Henry Ford hired the Detroit Symphony Orchestra and disguised it as his own.[3]

From the earliest network days of radio, the New York Philharmonic, of all the nation's orchestras, had the greatest radio exposure, for two reasons. First, it had become the sole orchestra in New York, the nation's radio capital, and was therefore the easiest to get in front of microphones. The second reason was that William Paley, who had come from Philadelphia in 1928, a year after the birth of CBS, saved the network from bankruptcy. Engaged in a battle of egos with NBC's David Sarnoff, in 1930 Paley signed a contract with the Philharmonic to broadcast their Sunday afternoon concerts nationwide. An astute businessman, Paley went after the contract with the Philharmonic because he believed it would "draw more upper-class listeners to radio."[4] He had good reasons to believe this, for not only was the Philharmonic the nation's oldest and best known, but its conductor at that time was the celebrated—and controversial—Arturo Toscanini. In addition, the orchestra pérformed in Carnegie Hall, the most famous concert venue in the nation. Paley's conviction proved correct, and the radio public did indeed accept the New York Philharmonic as if it were the United States' own orchestra. (Paley had also tried to gain the Metropolitan Opera broadcasts, but lost out to Sarnoff.)

CBS maintained the Philharmonic's national broadcasts as sustaining programs. Without a sponsor, the network decided to fill the concerts' fifteen-minute intermissions—the "hole in the musical donut"—with musical commentary, another way to enlighten listeners who were new to symphonic music. Olin Downes, the preeminent *Times* critic, was the first intermission commentator, but he quit after three seasons. Lawrence Gilman, a well-known critic and longtime Philharmonic program note writer, then took over as a permanent commentator. But his intermission talks proved heavy-handed and dull to many of the new generation of listeners, who sent letters of complaint to the Philharmonic.

A month before the November start of the 1936–37 season, Arthur Judson, the Philharmonic's powerful manager, informed the board chairman, Marshall Field, of the complaints about Gilman. Judson reminded Field that the Philharmonic contract with the network called for a commentator to be hired by CBS "subject to the approval of the [Philharmonic] Society." Then Judson added: "I assume that . . . the Society shall not unreasonably withhold its approval." Judson then informed Field that the network had hired Deems Taylor as its musical consultant, "to take charge of its important musical broadcasts and is desirous of having Mr. Taylor make the comments . . . in the intermission." Judson concluded by requesting that the Philharmonic board approve Taylor's appointment quickly, "so that I may act with reasonable promptness."[5]

Judson's careful phrasing suggests that he already knew CBS had promised Taylor the job. After all, Judson held a major interest in CBS as one of the network's original founders. The decision to dismiss Gilman annoyed some members of the orchestra board, which necessitated that Douglas Coulter of CBS send Judson an apologetic letter: "I can't begin to tell you how unhappy all of us are over this misunderstanding in the Deems Taylor matter. . . . We, of course, should have checked more definitely with you and your board before, rather than after, committing ourselves to Mr. Taylor."[6] The shrewd and masterful Judson had every reason to minimize the difficulty, so he ended the minor contretemps by a straightforward response: "I do not think there is anything we can do but to consent to Mr. Taylor making the radio comments, although our Directors do not accept this with very good grace."[7]

Taylor entered the intermission world unaware of the ill temper of some of the board members. However, a far bigger problem faced the Philharmonic than who would provide the intermission talks; it had lost Arturo Toscanini, its star attraction of ten years, when he had resigned and returned to his native Italy at the end of the previous season. As Joseph Horowitz shows so clearly in *Understanding Toscanini,* the Italian maestro had dominated the New York music scene as no one ever had. Toscanini's popularity manifested itself on the evening of April 29, 1936, when he gave his final Philharmonic performance. Some 140 standing-room tickets became available before the concert, and when those sales were "announced closed, a throng estimated at five thousand bore down on Carnegie Hall. A police detachment

of over sixty men, including five on horses, struggled to liberate the main entrance."[8] Such was the intensity of the Toscanini adulation.

Nevertheless, within two weeks of his resignation announcement, the
board brought great news to Philharmonic audiences: beginning in November the great German maestro Wilhelm Furtwängler, recommended by
Toscanini himself, would be on the podium. Furtwängler was not unknown
to New York, because ten years earlier he had been a guest conductor of the
Philharmonic. At that time, music critics had melted in the heat of the German's baton movements. Olin Downes spoke of communicative fire in everything Furtwängler conducted: "The performance of the Brahms C Minor
Symphony was perhaps the most thrilling in this writer's experience." Another critic at those 1925 concerts was Taylor himself: "[Furtwängler] closed
the concert with a performance of Beethoven's Fifth of such conviction and
blazing intensity of feeling as I have seldom heard. Some of the commentators hear echoes of Beethoven's unhappy love affairs in this work, but there
was nothing bereft in last night's Fifth. It was a pagan poem, hymning the
fierce joy of sheer living, ringing with the laughter of happy gods. No wonder
the audience cheered."[9]

When the Philharmonic contacted the tall, wiry-haired Furtwängler, he
agreed to split his conducting year between New York and Germany. The
"Prussian Disciplinarian," as *Newsweek* labeled him,[10] would conduct the first
half of the season. The announcement of the Furtwängler appointment first
brought applause from music lovers, but the enthusiasm dampened quickly
as the conductor's possible involvement in the Nazi regime raised concerns
that radiated back to him. In response Furtwängler claimed that only one
thing mattered to him: music. But the hue and cry in the United States, particularly from the Jewish community, was too great. Within a month of the
original announcement, Furtwängler withdrew as the Philharmonic's conductor, sending a cablegram to the board: "I propose postpone my season . . .
until the public realizes that politics and music are apart."[11] The postpone-
ment was permanent.

Now the board had a real problem. Whom could they appoint to replace
the incredibly popular Toscanini? Because of financial difficulties, they first
cut back the season by six weeks and chose five guest conductors, including
Toscanini's local favorite, Artur Rodzinski, then conductor of the Cleveland
Orchestra. In a big surprise to everyone, they selected John Barbirolli to lead
off the season with ten concerts. Barbirolli, an Englishman of Italian and
French parentage, was hardly known on this side of the Atlantic and certainly
did not have the glamour and fame of a Toscanini or Furtwängler, something
desired by New York society. How was it that he gained the leadoff position?

Joseph Horowitz sees the powerful hand of Arthur Judson in this decision. Judson, as Philharmonic manager, had a strong need to control. Of course, with Toscanini he had to be totally hands-off. But with Toscanini now gone, Judson pushed for a "less expensive, less troublesome, less independent principal conductor."[12] Judson was no fool, for he knew from his contacts that Barbirolli was an excellent conductor with broad experience. In fact, by mid-December Barbirolli had a three-year contract as musical director and permanent conductor of the Philharmonic.

Taylor Begins His Intermission Commentaries

Deems Taylor began his radio talks on November 8, 1936. Years later, in a radio interview with his daughter, he explained why he would never forget that first experience:

> *Joan:* Did you find it different writing criticism for a newspaper and these intermission talks or were you using basically the same approach?
>
> *Deems:* I was using basically the same approach. I'll tell you, those intermission talks were what to a newspaper man, the music critic, would be the Sunday piece.
>
> *Joan:* In other words you wrote your intermission talks, you didn't just speak them.
>
> *Deems:* Oh, on the very first one I decided I would ease things up, just sit down and chat and so I made some notes. Well, brother, that was one of the most disastrous intermissions in the history of music. So while I was waiting to be fired, I tried another one, except this time I wrote it and called it "The Monster."[13]

The radio audience responded enthusiastically to "The Monster," an essay that became Taylor's most famous, and later was the first chapter of his book *Of Men and Music.* To the Philharmonic's listeners he described the monster as "an undersized little man, with a head too big for his body—a sickly little man, . . . a monster of conceit. . . . [H]e had the emotional stability of a six-year-old child, . . . almost innocent of any sense of responsibility [and] . . . completely selfish in his other personal relationships. . . . [He had] a genius for making enemies. . . . The name of this monster was Richard Wagner." But Taylor didn't leave Wagner painted as a Frankenstein fiend, for he asked in conclusion: "What if he was faithless to his friends and to his wives? He had one mistress to whom he was faithful to the day of his death: Music. Is it any wonder that he had no time to be a man?" (November 15, 1936).[14]

In contrast to the larger-than-life Wagner, two weeks later Taylor spoke about an almost reclusive Franz Schubert, whose Symphony No. 2 the Phil-

harmonic was playing that Sunday: "At the time he wrote the symphony . . .
he was an instructor in his father's school. His salary was the equivalent of
eight dollars a year . . . and I'm afraid he couldn't have been worth much
more than that as a schoolteacher. For by 1815 he was completely obsessed
with music and had written two symphonies, a mass and 147 songs. He
couldn't have had much time for school work" (November 22, 1936).

The public quickly accepted Taylor as the Philharmonic's intermission
commentator. His clever style appealed to most listeners, along with his
ready wit and reassuring voice, which altered the impression of many who
thought classical music was too highbrow. Taylor had the gift of choosing the
right words; they neither put off the uninitiated nor made the scholar blush.
Alton Cook, the radio editor for the *World-Telegram,* gave his opinion of Taylor's intermission talks after hearing only four of them:

> Hurrah for Deems Taylor! Deems Taylor has provided the solution
> of what to do during the long intermissions of talk on . . . Sunday af-
> ternoon Philharmonic-Society broadcasts. You can just leave your
> radio on and listen now. Aware that most of us don't care whether
> music is legato, rubato, or tomato, Deems doesn't tell much about a
> sudden change of key after the crescendo in the piccolo. . . . He
> talks about composers as though they were actual men with human
> frailties, such as stealing, lying, cheating, . . . as well as musical
> geniuses.[15]

Though Taylor knew that John Barbirolli was no genius, he became aware of
the injustice of the perception of the conductor as second-rate simply because he was unknown, so he sought to help listeners better understand his
strengths. He lauded the Britisher on one of his first broadcasts: "Mr.
Barbirolli's growing popularity is due, I think, not only to his gifts as a conductor, but also to his extraordinary talent for building interesting programs.
If you'll forgive the sacrilege, I think that a well-balanced symphonic program is rather like a well-balanced dinner. Neither should consist entirely of
appetizers, nor entirely of sweets" (December 13, 1936). Taylor probably
didn't know that one reason for the success of the programs was that Judson
worked very closely with Barbirolli in developing them, giving him advice as
to which works had been successful or unsuccessful on past Philharmonic
programs.[16]

What pleased listeners most about Taylor's intermission talks was the
variety of approaches he took, including interviews with orchestra members. As questions from the public poured in, he cleverly began to develop
intermissions based on these, many of which opened fascinating musical
doors. "Isn't it possible," one listener asked, "that one reason why the great-

ness of certain works by the earlier composers failed to be recognized at once was the fact that they were badly played?" Taylor responded after explaining that so many of the modern musical instruments were so much better than those of previous centuries: "The great masters of the past, whatever they may have heard in imagination as they wrote their scores, never lived to hear the perfect performances of their works that we now take so for granted" (February 7, 1937).

Another listener opened the inevitable discussion on modern music: "I am unable to appreciate the modern composers. Such music seems to me to be without melody, harmony or form, and literally gives me a pain. . . . Could you say a few words on this subject?" Taylor's answer was both logical and sage. He cautioned that even before hearing a new composition, the first issue a listener needed to address was a fear of the music. Concerning the music itself, he provided one of his wisest pieces of advice ever: "Make it a point to hear a piece of new music at least twice before you make up your mind about it. Because your first impression is only a reaction, and a reaction is not an opinion" (March 7, 1937).

Taylor attempted to be fair in his commentary about the sounds of ultra-modern music. His remarks proved both illuminating and restrained; he had undoubtedly mellowed since his days as music critic at the *World:* "Atonality, polytonality, liberated counterpoint, and all the other ities and isms are, when you boil them down, efforts to arrange combinations of tones such as have never been heard before." At another point he explained, "Composers today are experimenting with a new musical language. There is as yet no dictionary for it, and no way of studying it except to listen to it without panic and without mental reservations. And the more we listen, the better able shall we be to weigh and estimate the value of what present-day composers are saying. Some of them are just talking pig-Latin; but others may be saying something that we may all, some day, be grateful to hear."[17]

Without a doubt, it was the music of Arnold Schoenberg and his modernist school to which Taylor was referring. As luck would have it, Schoenberg himself often listened to the intermission commentaries from his home in Los Angeles, where he had settled as an émigré composer. He was teaching at the University of California, Los Angeles, and wrote to Taylor in 1939 indicating that he found the talks "very interesting." Schoenberg also found the one-way conversation frustrating, since "very often have I violently desired to fortify some of your statements with my own experiences."[18] Ever the moody person, the modernist perpetually sought greater acceptance of his music.

Schoenberg understood completely the unique power that Taylor wielded as the only person on radio consistently presenting to millions opinions about concert music, as the following episode illustrates. Dika Newlin, a student of Schoenberg's, heard the Philharmonic broadcast of December 3, 1939. She wrote in her journal that Taylor "happened to say something slighting about Schoenberg."[19] Because the script of that broadcast has been lost, what the slight was is not known. However, a month later Schoenberg drafted a letter: "Mr. Taylor, why do you think so little of us composers? . . . Radio is a very strong weapon—this you should not forget when you announce definite decisions about disputable questions. He who possesses a different opinion, as for instance one of those modernistic composers whose thematic inventivness [sic] you belittle—such one is not able to tell your audience whether and why his opinion is better than yours."[20] Perhaps the letter was never sent, for only a draft exists in the Schoenberg archives, but the modernist composer believed his music needed a more balanced critical approach than what Taylor was providing.

Taylor opened the door again for Schoenberg a year later, when he returned to the subject of modern music. Though Schoenberg did not hear the discussions, students such as Newlin brought them to his attention. Again he quickly penned a letter to Taylor, referring to his commentaries involving "technical and esthetic questions of modern music":

> It has occurred to me that you might be interested in certain considerations of modern music, and especially mine. I have just finished my lecture, an honour bestowed upon me by the University of California at Los Angeles as its Annual Research Lecture. Its subject is "The Composition with Twelve Tones" about which much nonsense has been spread by both knowing and unknowing persons. I think it might be of some assistance to you to know my viewpoints, whether you approve of them or not, and being a writer myself, I know how comforting it is to quote exactly.[21]

Taylor did indeed recognize the importance of the information in Schoenberg's lecture, and on his March 9, 1941, broadcast, he explained to the radio audience the Viennese composer's twelve-tone approach:

> Now we come to the element in modern music wherein it differs most conspicuously from the music of the past—its unorthodox harmony, its persistent use of dissonances. . . . According to Dr. Schoenberg, what distinguishes dissonance (or discord) from consonance is not a greater or lesser degree of beauty, but a greater or lesser degree of comprehensibility.
>
> . . . What the Doctor is saying is, in short, that when you hear a series of chords that are strongly dissonant, whether or not they

sound beautiful to you depends on whether or not they make sense to you. If your ear finds a certain degree of musical logic in that progression of chords, you like it. If not, you don't. . . . Dr. Schoenberg points out that his invention of repeated sets of twelve notes is closely allied to Wagner's invention of the system of leading motives. In both cases the idea is to convey a sense of unity and balance in a composition that otherwise doesn't necessarily possess any definite form. Whether or not the hearer is conscious of where that sense of unity comes from is not important.[22]

Dika Newlin heard the broadcast. "I thought [the intermission talk] a very good job," she wrote in her journal, "eminently fair and unbiased and perfectly understandable. He called the old man 'Doctor' all the way through, which should please him much."[23] Indeed it did: Schoenberg telegraphed Taylor the following day: "GREATLY ADMIRING YOUR INTERPRETATION OF MY THEORIES. I THANK YOU VERY CORDIALLY."[24] It was a graceful end to an exchange exemplifying the fairness of Taylor in providing his listeners with the means to make up their own minds about modern music.

At the end of Taylor's first season, the cartoonist-humorist Don Herold spoke for many listeners when he wrote of his reaction to listening to Taylor: "Of all the musical people that I hear discussing music Deems Taylor comes nearest to winning my confidence. For me, he offsets thousands of the bluffers and poseurs that I believe to exist in the world. Sometime I'm going to visit Deems Taylor for two hours and give him $50 and have him psychoanalyze me musically, and see if he can find out if my mother was, just before I was born, frightened by a long-haired Chautauqua piano-player."[25]

Helping the American Composer

As a composer Taylor knew how difficult it was for Americans to gain performances of their works, so throughout the Philharmonic years he focused attention on them. On the afternoon when Artur Rodzinski conducted Symphony No. 1 of twenty-seven-year-old Samuel Barber (April 4, 1937), Taylor couldn't help bragging a bit:

Eleven years ago I conducted a sort of criticism class among the best composition pupils at the Curtis Institute. They'd bring me original composition . . . and then we'd sit down and criticize the pieces, not for form or technique, but . . . were they any good as music? And there was a sixteen-year-old boy named Sam Barber in that class; and I pride myself that I must have been one of the first few who said, "Watch that kid. He has something." And I still think he has something, a very brilliant and important future among the world's composers.

But Taylor's pride changed to anger as he assessed the opportunities for American composers:

> No, the American composer decidedly does NOT stand on the same step with his European contemporary. The attitude of his own countrymen is hardly one calculated to make him feel like an important or even moderately useful person. He knows that among you—and by you I mean YOU—not one in a hundred honestly cares a tinker's dam about American music. You get up committees, and you give lunches, and you make speeches, and you give prizes. . . . [I]n fact, you do everything except the one thing that would give him a little hope and self-respect: arrange matters so that a new piece of American music could be heard more than once by the same audience.

Taylor's commitment to help American composers rested not only in words, but in actions. With his national fame, he could have made lists of promising Americans and published them, as did young Aaron Copland in his article "America's Young Men of Promise."[26] Instead, Taylor chose to act by providing incentives for any composer to write a new work.

Five years earlier, in 1932, Merlin Aylesworth, then president of NBC, had informed Taylor that the network "would like to do something practical and substantial toward discharging radio's great debt to music, toward the stimulation of musical composition in America and the encouragement of American composers."[27] When Taylor suggested a contest, Aylesworth jumped at the idea and told him that if he organized the competition, NBC would provide a generous ten thousand dollars in prize money.

Taylor did his part, spreading the word for composers to submit pieces no longer than twelve minutes in performance. NBC received 573 entries! An eminent jury of conductors—Leopold Stokowski, Frederick Stock, Walter Damrosch, and Tullio Serafin—chose the top five without knowing the identity of the composers, then an NBC orchestra played them on a national program. A "National Committee of Awards, some 150 distinguished Americans," chose the winners. It was musical democracy in action. The top prize of five thousand dollars went to Philip James, head of the NYU Music Department, for "Station WGZBX."[28]

Another instance of Taylor's advocacy for American composers occurred in 1934, when, in honor of his late mother, Paul Whiteman established the Elfrida Whiteman Scholarship: a four-year award to a music school for a young composer. Whiteman asked Taylor and George Gershwin to be two of the four judges of the works submitted. The winner was nineteen-year-old David Diamond, who definitely justified the judges' choice by becoming an eminent and respected American composer. After Diamond was awarded the scholarship, he learned that his greatest supporter among the judges had been Deems Taylor.[29]

As the musical consultant at CBS, Taylor had another idea to help boost Americans. Even before beginning his intermission broadcasts, he had convinced Davidson Taylor, director of CBS's music division and no relation, to provide commissions to six composers for works up to forty minutes in length, ready to be performed in 1937 on *Everybody's Music,* the summer Philharmonic replacement concerts that featured Howard Barlow and the Columbia Symphony. "Radio has a duty to American composers," Deems Taylor said. "It is the only institution in America today which is fitted at the present time to give the musician a 'break.' . . . It can become the greatest patron of the living art of music ever seen in the world."[30]

This time he undoubtedly had a hand in the choice of the six for the 1937 commissions, and they were already among the leading American composers: Aaron Copland from Brooklyn; Louis Gruenberg, a Russian immigrant; Roy Harris and Howard Hanson, two Midwesterners; Walter Piston, a New Englander and Harvard professor; and William Grant Still, an African American who had moved from arranging for jazz orchestras to composing symphonic music. In fact, he had been the arranger for Red Nichols on the first day's broadcast of CBS.

Since the compositions were to be written for a radio premiere, Taylor and Barlow aired a special program illustrating how such diverse effects as mutes on trumpets and trombones, and the glissando effects of strings, and even timpani, added tone color in radio music. Copland, in writing his twelve-minute piece *Music for Radio,* acknowledged Taylor and Barlow's advice: "I decided to use several special effects in the orchestration: a muted trumpet ('felt hat over bell'), . . . flutist standing at the microphone, bassoons and saxophones for jazz effects, and a vibraphone."[31] Copland also agreed to allow CBS to run a contest to rename *Music for Radio,* with the prize being the original manuscript. Of the thousand suggestions received, *Saga of the Prairie* was the winner, an appropriate choice since Copland used a cowboy tune in one section, but the name never stuck. Still, such a large response was indicative of a large listening audience for the performances of these new compositions.

The Copland work and all the others proved to be of high quality: Hanson's Third Symphony; Still's atmospheric *Lenox Avenue,* for narrator, chorus, and orchestra; Gruenberg's opera *Green Mansions;* Piston's *Concertino for Piano and Orchestra;* and Roy Harris's *Time Suite.* CBS commissioned a second group of composers the following year, then dropped the concept. Nonetheless, supporting and encouraging a dozen composers was no mean accomplishment at that time.[32] Radio gave them a special opportunity to be heard.

Colette d'Arville, as usual, departed in May 1937 for her five-month sojourn in France and provided Taylor with the opportunity to complete *Ramuntcho,* which he accomplished by the end of August. Because hope still sang its siren song, he decided to contact Edward Johnson, now general manager of the Metropolitan, to request a meeting to come and play through the score for him. Though Johnson put him off until later in the year, good news arrived from the West Coast that the important German conductor Otto Klemperer had programmed both *Through the Looking Glass* and Ballet Music from *Casanova,* Taylor's composition for the Broadway play, for concerts with the Los Angeles Philharmonic.

Family happiness was also now at a new high. With Mary and nine-year-old Joan back from their round-the-world trip, Deems was able to spend more time with Joan than ever before. He took her out to lunch, or just walked with her around the streets of New York. Deems was also pleased that his sister, Katy, had found happiness in a marriage with Robert Stranathan, a college professor.

But not everything that summer was pleasant, especially when he learned on July 11 of George Gershwin's death in Hollywood from a brain tumor. This jolted Taylor. Theirs had been a special relationship. Gershwin, as noted earlier, held Taylor's musical opinions in very high esteem. Not only had he called Taylor to his apartment to give him a special run-through of *Porgy and Bess,* but years before that he had previewed *An American in Paris* for Taylor on the piano, then asked him to write the program notes for the premiere. Taylor had promptly accepted, and his notes are still quoted today.

Though the two did not socialize, they had a special bond: each had learned orchestration on his own, rather than in an academic setting. For better or worse, both had an independent spirit, a sense of being different. Gershwin's biographer Edward Jablonski identified a key reason that the man from Tin Pan Alley thought so highly of Taylor: "[He] was one of Gershwin's earliest champions and completely free of the snobbery that most critics of the time expressed."[33]

Of Men and Music: A Best-Seller

The summer of 1937, full of both music and sadness, also set Taylor off in the direction of becoming a best-selling author. Often feeling chronically overextended, he had for years continued to refuse his agent's request for a book. "Much as I'd like to write such a book," he had indicated to George Bye, "I really don't believe I'd ever get around to doing it, simply because of the hideous amount of research work that would be necessary in order to turn out a critic-proof job."[34] What changed his mind was the success of the Philharmonic intermission talks. When he realized that the fifteen-minute talks could be tailored relatively quickly into essays, he gave his agent the go-ahead to accept a contract from Simon and Schuster, who had been after him for years. At the end of the Philharmonic season, Taylor gathered together some of his best intermission efforts, supplemented them with material from newspaper columns and magazine articles, and published *Of Men and Music;* it became one of the 1930s' best-selling books on music, going into thirteen printings.

The book opened with "The Monster," his commentary on Richard Wagner. This second of his Philharmonic intermissions is still cited today in collections of essays as an example of conciseness and clarity. In the second chapter he honored his music theory teacher, Oscar Coon. In the other fifty-seven short essays, Taylor's subjects meandered about the music world. For example, in one he urged a listener to have a "Tolerant Ear" for modern music. In another he wisely noted that among composers, "the truly great ones survive without explanatory footnotes." Of these he extolled John Philip Sousa, whom he cleverly summarized in eight words: "Sousa was no Beethoven. Nevertheless he was Sousa."[35]

Reviewers praised the book's literate, informative, and witty style. "It is so engagingly written, so full of general intelligence, humor, and miscellaneous information," wrote George Stevens in *Saturday Review,* "that it ought to be enjoyed even by those who can't tell 'The Flying Dutchman' from 'Pomp and Circumstance.'"[36] The *Times* asked Paul Rosenfeld, who had been so critical of Taylor's operas, to review *Of Men and Music.* The assignment may well have arisen when an editor remembered that in 1920, Taylor had reviewed Rosenfeld's first book for *Dial* magazine. Taylor had concluded that Rosenfeld's book, *Musical Portraits,* had merit: "A well-written, interesting, sincere, exasperating book. In other words, a book worth reading."[37] Rosenfeld was even more generous in his assessment of Taylor's first book: "In point of form alone, this bright little volume . . . ranks highly amid the recent American literature of music. The author is one of those composers whom fortune has blessed with the ability to express themselves aptly about their art in words."[38]

After a summer of hard work, Taylor returned to radio in a double capacity, for in addition to his Sunday Philharmonic responsibilities, he now served as the master of ceremonies for the Wednesday evening *Chesterfield Show,* resulting in a doubling of his radio income. Tobacco companies had begun to link their names with quality music, in this case featuring a sixty-five-member orchestra conducted by Andre Kostelanetz, with guest artists such as Jascha Heifetz, Kirsten Flagstad, and Lawrence Tibbett.

As for the Philharmonic intermission commentaries, letters to CBS expressed high satisfaction with them, so in his second season Taylor continued to build many intermissions on listeners' comments or questions. During an October 1937 broadcast he spoke about "musical plagiarism," a topic close to his heart. He introduced the subject with a personal account of the many critics who, after the premiere of *Peter Ibbetson,* accused him of stealing from Puccini, Massenet, Wagner, Debussy, and any of the Strauses you might name. Taylor's thoughts wafted by radio waves onto the lightly populated Canadian plains of central Alberta. There, the young teacher Fraser Macdonald heard the broadcast. Macdonald always listened avidly to the Philharmonic programs, and this time he reacted passionately to Taylor's comments. Years later Macdonald recalled the international event: "[Taylor's] talk inspired a letter from me in response, which I composed in my head in my walks between home and school but didn't get around to committing to paper with my typewriter till the following Sunday. Our mail was picked up only twice a week, so it wasn't until Tuesday that it left for New York. You can imagine my utter astonishment when I heard it being read on the air the following Sunday."[39]

Taylor devoted his entire intermission to discussing the uncommon insights in the Canadian's letter:

> [Mr. Taylor,] you were saying, in effect, that we tend to worry too much about the originality of a tune, and that we are quick to shout "plagiarist" over the shadow of a likeness between two melodies. I not only agree with you, but I would go even further. Don't you think there is too much attention paid to the composer and not enough to the composition? That is to say, do we not too often listen to the man who wrote the music instead of to the music he wrote? In other words, do we not make too much of so-called originality? Instead of saying, "Is this good?" we say "Is it original?"[40]

Taylor concurred strongly, for one of his constant missions in life was to have the listener seek out the "good" in "good music."[41]

Unlike Macdonald, many listeners made requests of Taylor, often ones that he was hard pressed to fulfill. He explained this six months after the death of Gershwin (December 5, 1937):

> My heartfelt thanks to those of you who have been kind enough to write to me so generously this year. But please don't ask me to set

tle arguments as to whether So-and-so is greater than So-and-so, and PLEASE don't ask involved questions and send money for a reply. Someone wrote last week, asking me to write a short essay on George Gershwin's place in American music and sent twenty-five cents to pay for it. Please don't tempt me beyond my strength. I don't mind stealing an occasional two-cent stamp, but up to now I've managed to resist stealing a quarter.

A month before this, Taylor had had occasion to wonder about his own place in American music. He had gone to the Metropolitan Opera to play the complete score of *Ramuntcho* for Edward Johnson and an assistant. In the ledger kept by the staff, which identified the manager's reaction to every new opera put forward to the Metropolitan, the entry for *Ramuntcho* was short and fatal: "Old fashioned music and weak libretto. Some very effective spots, notably 'O Pirenees.' In general falls below Mr. Taylor's previous operas."[42] It is not known when Taylor learned there would be no third opera at the Metropolitan, but he must have wondered why Edward Johnson wasn't more supportive. After all, Taylor had provided the tenor with two of his best roles at the Metropolitan. Then again, perhaps *Ramuntcho* wasn't very good. In either case Taylor did not give up. He knew he would find someone to produce it.

Broun's *Connecticut Nutmeg*

Whether downhearted or not, Taylor now found an opportunity to exercise his writing talents in two unusual ventures. The first came about when Harold Stearns asked him for an updated chapter on U.S. music culture for *America Now,* the book Stearns planned as a follow-up to *Civilization in the United States.* Stearns, after ten years of self-imposed exile in Paris, returned to the States with desires of identifying what changes had occurred since 1922. He suggested that in Taylor's update, he should emphasize radio's impact on music, something completely unforeseen in 1922. Taylor agreed and wrote a chapter about two-thirds the length of the earlier one. Much of it dealt with how radio had become an educational force, far more significant than the phonograph had ever been. He also saw promise in the federal government's continuing support for artists and musicians, especially through the Depression era's Works Progress Administration (WPA). Both concerts and plays were produced through the WPA, not to mention the miles of murals painted in a variety of public buildings.

Taylor revisited the topic of the American composer, who "is infinitely better trained than he used to be," the result of the growth of conservatories such as Curtis and Juilliard, as well as university departments of music. The populist side of Taylor reemerged as he urged the American composer "to find an idiom that is intelligible to the people around him, worry more about what a Kansas masonry contractor thinks of him . . . and worry less about whether or not Béla Bartók would approve." If the composer cannot find such a voice, "Mozart and Kern and Gershwin will leave him hopelessly outdistanced."[43] In the end Taylor's chapter was more like one of the Sunday pieces from his journalistic days, an overview with some clever ideas, but ultimately superficial. He certainly did not put as much thought into it as he had sixteen years earlier for the music chapter in *Civilization in the United States.*

Taylor's writing adventures continued nevertheless. In May 1938 a brainstorm of Heywood Broun's emerged full-blown. Broun, along with his wife, Ruth Hale, now spent summers on a ramshackle farm near the Taylor home in Stamford. Breathing the rural air, Broun decided to initiate an old-style country newspaper entitled *Connecticut Nutmeg.* He convinced Taylor and nine other members of what was loosely seen as the Stamford–New Canaan writer's colony to provide one thousand dollars each to initiate the venture; for this investment, Broun guaranteed, every member would be both publisher and writer: no editor would darken their door, and no advertising sully their pages. As George Bye, the literary agent and president of the corporation, explained to a *Newsweek* reporter, the *Nutmeg* was not in business to make money: "We expect to emphasize the more purely spiritual values."[44] John Erskine, a writer and the head of the Juilliard School, wrote the first editorial: "We are a group of human beings who think we have serious things to say to other human beings equally serious. . . . We promise to supply at least two problems where you had only one before."[45]

Spiritual though they aspired to be, among the ten was one of the more down-to-earth individuals of his time, the ex–heavyweight champion Gene Tunney, who found Shakespeare more to his liking than any ring opponent. He had actually lectured on the Bard of Avon at Yale in 1928, at the invitation of the highly respected William Lyon Phelps. In Tunney's first *Nutmeg* column, he revealed "that in the minutes before his first fight with Dempsey he killed time reading Somerset Maugham's 'Of Human Bondage.'"[46] One can't be sure whether this revelation helped the sales of the Maugham book.

The idealism espoused by the ten editors soon fell upon the hard rocks of financial reality, but the gallant crew wrote on, mainly concerned with the deliberate world of Hitler's Europe and the dynamism of Roosevelt's United

States. Their camaraderie extended to populating a "Nutmegger's" softball team, managed by George Bye. Known as "Bye's Prehistoric Sluggers,"[47] players included Broun, Taylor, the famed columnists Westbrook Pegler and Quentin Reynolds, as well as Harold Ross of the *New Yorker*. Their enemies came from "across the border" in New York: "Lowell Thomas and His Nine Old Men," among whom was the young prosecuting attorney Thomas E. Dewey, a few years before he became governor of New York. But neither softball nor good intentions paid the bills, and after a year and a half Broun briefly took over the complete financing of the venture, then allowed it quietly to expire.

About the same time Taylor helped begin the ill-fated *Connecticut Nutmeg*, he completed four years of calling the New York hotels his home. Now he wanted something more permanent. By 1937 his net annual income had reached the handsome level of $16,000 (very good for the time), out of a gross of $38,000. It was time to think upscale. In June 1938 he moved into an elegant four-room apartment on the corner of Fifth Avenue and Sixtieth Street. Through his enormous seventh-floor windows, he had panoramic views of Central Park from both the living room and the master bedroom, each of which had its own fireplace. He arranged the living room to be a center for music, with his Steinway grand piano in a place of prominence. On sunny days he could lounge on the apartment-wide balcony, overlooking Fifth Avenue and Central Park. It was here, in the Hanover Bank Building at 2 East Sixtieth Street, that Deems Taylor made his home for the next twenty-two years.[48]

Taylor's emotional involvement with Colette d'Arville had continued into its fourth year. Early in 1938 the soprano planned her second Town Hall recital, and Taylor composed the song "Tandis qu'amour dormait" specifically for her. But the *Times* reviewer suggested that in addition to having a small voice, Colette's stage mannerisms tended toward the kinetic: "Miss d'Arville was happiest, artistically, in those [songs] . . . that could be submitted to musical liberties and assisted by assorted histrionics not possible, for example, in Scarlatti, Schubert or Wolf."[49]

Before Colette left for her annual trip to France, Taylor made plans to meet her for a tour together on the Continent. Then, late in June, now comfortably set in his apartment and packing to leave, Taylor received an unexpected phone call. The caller was Walt Disney, who sought an immediate meeting to present an exciting proposal that would involve Taylor. A luncheon was arranged, and Disney, considered the king of animation since the success of *Snow White and the Seven Dwarfs* two years earlier, asked Taylor if he would be interested in appearing in a film among cartoon characters.

14. *The* Fantasia *Years, 1938–1940*

Fantasia: The Groundwork

When Taylor returned from Europe in mid-August 1938, he found a letter from Disney with disappointing news: "I am up to my neck in *Pinocchio* and with *Bambi* just getting started and the new studio underway, I do not believe I am going to have much time to devote to the musical feature that I discussed with you while in New York."[1] Taylor probably reflected on his previous experience in Hollywood and wondered whether, as with *Chivalry,* all would come to naught.[2]

But early in September, Disney changed his mind. An excited Taylor wrote to Mary Kennedy, his loyal listener, to tell her he was again on his way to Hollywood:

> I'm leaving tonight for the coast! Saturday [Disney] called his [New York] office frantically to get hold of me and have me come out at once. . . . The job is for four weeks now and another week some time within the year. I'm not entirely certain just what I do, except that I'm to consult with Disney and Stokowski and do a certain amount of commenting in the film. I told you the idea, didn't I? A program of orchestral music, illustrated with Disney cartoons. I get $1440 a week ($1600, less Columbia's 10%), which makes it worthwhile to have an agent![3]

By 1938 Walt Disney was the talk of Hollywood. He had brought animation to a level of artistry hardly dreamed of when Winsor McCay's *Gertie the Dinosaur,* the pre–World War I cartoon, had first flickered on movie screens. Mickey Mouse had become an internationally beloved rodent, and *Snow White and the Seven Dwarfs,* the studio's first animated feature, had filled the Disney coffers to overflowing. With this money he built the greatest movie animation studio in the world, in Burbank.

Disney's vision of a feature film meshing colored animation with classical music had developed from his earliest cartoon successes, the *Silly Symphonies.* In these short pieces Disney had sought to link animation, story, and music in unusual ways, originally with the imaginative touch of Carl Stalling, the studio's first music director. Stalling had been an organist for silent films and used many classical themes as part of the background music. Not surprisingly, the first *Silly Symphony,* the 1929 black and white *Skeleton Dance,* used the sinister *Danse Macabre* of Camille Saint-Saëns, among other works, to accent the jangling of the skeletons' bones. But the *Skeleton Dance* proved a hard sell to theaters. After Stalling left in 1930, eventually to develop the highly successful Looney Tunes cartoons for Warner Brothers, the *Silly Symphonies* turned mainly to original music from Disney composers.

The ultimate idea for *Fantasia,* according to Disney archivist David R. Smith, came from Disney's perception that his *Silly Symphonies* had to be taken to a higher level.[4] To reach it they would star Mickey Mouse in a version of the story of *The Sorcerer's Apprentice,* using the music of the French composer Paul Dukas. The *Fantasia* historian John Culhane states the issue clearly: "Essentially *The Sorcerer's Apprentice* sprang from Disney's desire to go beyond the usual animated cartoon with its combination of comic strip graphics and slapstick. . . . Indeed the most important factor carrying the animated film beyond its roots in comic strips and slapstick film shorts was music."[5]

Paul Dukas had composed his tone poem *L'Apprenti sorcier* in 1897, basing the music on the legend in Goethe's ballad poem "Der Zauberlehrlin." Dukas's music—pungent, atmospheric, and dramatic—satisfied Disney as the musical means to bring Mickey Mouse into the rarefied air of great animated art. The perceptive Disney knew that animation was still considered "lowbrow" to many people, and that animated features could benefit artistically by blending with well-known concert music. To use the analogy of the Ginger Rogers–Fred Astaire dance team, cartoons had the sex appeal, and concert music would give them class.

In order to transform Mickey Mouse into a sorcerer's apprentice, Roy Disney, Walt's brother and business manager, first acquired the rights to the Dukas music. Then the Disney artists began their work, using a Toscanini recording to prime their imaginations. Later Disney chanced upon Leopold Stokowski, who remembered years later, "One night I was in California, and I had dinner in a restaurant and a man walked in and looked at me and came over and said, 'I'm Walt Disney. May I talk with you?' So I said, 'Yes, of course.' And we sat down and talked. He said, 'I have the idea of Dukas' *The Sorcerer's Apprentice.* I would like to make a short. Would you like to do the music and I'll do the pictorial part?'"[6]

At the time Stokowski was as famous as Toscanini, perhaps more so because of his central role in the movie *100 Men and a Girl,* the men being Stokowski and his then all-male orchestra, and the girl being the teenage singing star Deanna Durbin. Disney, of course, knew of Stokowski's fame. "I am all steamed up over the idea of Stokowski working with us," he wrote to Hal Horne, his Eastern representative. "We could stretch a point and use his hundred men as well. . . . [I] believe that the union of Stokowski and his music, together with the best of our medium, would be the means of a great success and should lead to a new style of motion picture presentation."[7] With encouraging enthusiasm from the showman conductor, Disney arranged for Stokowski to go to California and record the Dukas music with an orchestra of Hollywood's best musicians. Since both Disney and Stokowski loved to experiment with recording mediums, they agreed to record the score in six-track stereo, a feature-film approach unheard of at the time.

But after the Disney animators had completed the transformation of Mickey Mouse and all the bills were in, Roy told his brother the sad facts of movie life: the cost of preparing *Sorcerer's Apprentice* was four times greater than that of any previous *Silly Symphony;* they would never recoup their money if they released the film as a short subject. Knowing that his brother was correct, Disney took what would be one of his greatest mental leaps: he asked Stokowski to join him in producing a feature-length film, which he first named *Concert Feature,* incorporating the already completed Mickey Mouse segment as well as "a group of separate numbers, regardless of their running time, put together in a single presentation."[8]

Once on their way, Disney and Stokowski agreed that *Concert Feature,* whose name was soon changed to *Fantasia,* should have a concert format and use a commentator. The choice for that role was obvious. Both Disney and Stokowski had heard Taylor on the Philharmonic broadcasts and knew he had all the necessary components to be the on-screen host for *Fantasia:* the voice, the whimsy, and the capacity for clear explanations. It was at this time that Disney contacted Taylor, with the eventual result that the composer once again headed by train for Hollywood.

Taylor especially looked forward to working with Stokowski, whom he admired deeply as an orchestra builder. He had expressed this admiration in typical Taylor fashion in his review of a Philadelphia Orchestra concert in 1923: "There must be something wrong with the Philadelphia Orchestra, for no orchestra in the world could possibly be as good as Mr. Stokowski's men sounded last night. . . . A couple of handsprings and three rousing cheers are about the most comprehensive expression of opinion we can think of at the moment."[9]

In preparation for his monthlong stay in the Los Angeles area, Taylor contacted Roland Young, who once again invited him to stay at his home. Expecting to see Young when the Santa Fe Superliner pulled into Los Angeles' Union Station, Taylor instead found a Disney car waiting to take him directly to the studios. The staff's story conferences had begun the day before, and Disney didn't want to waste time. Taylor quickly learned that Disney developed story ideas through meetings with as many as a dozen people in attendance, often spending three continuous hours in brisk discussions. After stenographers recorded conversations verbatim, transcriptions were made and distributed to all participants for their review prior to the next day's gathering.

Taylor plunged into a month of such conferences. Except for *Sorcerer's Apprentice,* no decisions on music for the animated segments had yet been made. Taylor learned that Disney wanted the "battle of good versus evil" to be the subject of at least one segment, while another should feature mythological creatures such as centaurs and fauns. The great animator also desired a humorous satirical piece. During the meetings, Disney relied almost entirely on Taylor and Stokowski for suggestions of appropriate music for the cartoon segments. As specific compositions were suggested and considered worthy, a staff member ran out to locate a recording to be played at the next meeting.

During the rapid exchange of ideas among the dozen or so participants, some of Taylor's ideas clearly influenced decisions made about the music. Remarks he made at his first story meeting helped plant the seeds that would grow into the prima ballerina Hyacinth Hippo and Ben Ali Gator, her partner in dance:

> *Disney:* Put the Dance of the Hours down. That could be treated comically.
> *Stokowski:* I'd like to see you do it. It's a real, old Italian "enjoy-yourself" number.
> *Taylor:* You could "horse" it all you like, and nobody would feel annoyed. You'd be at liberty to kid Dance of the Hours.[10]

At another point in meetings, Taylor said, "I would like to see you do [Mussorgsky's] Night on the Bare Mountain. It is a 'witches' sabbath' sort of thing."[11] Disney had once noted that "[g]ood and evil, the antagonists of all great drama in some guise, must be believably personalized."[12] He heard the struggle between these elements in the Mussorgsky composition, and the conjoining of the "witches' sabbath" with Schubert's "Ave Maria" became the final segment of *Fantasia.*

Just five days after arriving at the studios, Taylor suggested what would become the most controversial segment of the movie. Disney asked, "Was there ever anything written on which we might build something of a prehistoric theme—with prehistoric animals?"

> *Taylor:* Le Sacre du printemps would be something on that order.
> *Disney:* There would be something terrific in dinosaurs, flying lizards and prehistoric monsters. There could be beauty in the settings.
> *Joe Grant* [one of two story directors on the film]: A "dawn of creation" theme.

They listened to a recording of the Stravinsky work, after which Disney exclaimed: "This is marvelous! It would be perfect for prehistoric animals."[13] Indeed, it became the basis for a Disney version of the tumultuous birth of the planet Earth, the evolution of the first living creatures, followed by spectacular dinosaur battles. Taylor's suggestion of *Rite of Spring* was hardly surprising, as he had reviewed its New York premiere in 1924, calling it "as stark and primitive in outline as the wall pictures of a cave-man."[14] Some of Disney's staff rebelled at the composition's dissonance, but Taylor cogently countered their argument: "After all, the people who think it's too strong, too dissonant, are not taking into consideration the fact that you are going to have pictures with it." He then gave a contemporary example: "[T]he music that Werner Janssen wrote for the General Dies at Dawn, which is just an ordinary motion picture, . . . sounded just as dissonant, even more than the Rite of Spring, but the audience is looking at something and they don't hear dissonant harmonies when they are looking at a picture. There is all the difference in the world."[15]

The story meetings continued. "It's like working in Santa Claus's workshop," Taylor wrote to the ever-interested Mary: "We've been meeting daily, listening to records, planning the program, and discussing picture possibilities."[16] Within a month of Taylor's arrival, agreement had been reached on the music for the film: Tchaikovsky's *Nutcracker Suite,* Bach's Toccata and Fugue in D Minor, Stravinsky's *Rite of Spring,* Pierné's *Cydalise,* Ponchielli's *Dance of the Hours,* Debussy's *Clair de Lune,* Mussorgsky's *Night on Bald Mountain,* Schubert's "Ave Maria," and Dukas's *Sorcerer's Apprentice.* Members of the animation and story staffs were brought together to listen to the various compositions and discuss the type of visual activity that might be appropriate.

But the order of the musical segments strained the group's thinking. Some argued for placing *Rite of Spring* last because of its powerful images, while others believed that viewers should leave the film on an upbeat. And what about the opening? Taylor made the suggestion, ultimately carried out, to begin the film with an empty stage slowly filling with orchestra members who tune up in advance of the introductory comments, after which Stokowski himself mounts the podium.[17]

And what should be the first animated portion? The creative Disney staff, capable of bringing the strangest objects to animated life, made a wild suggestion: present the sound track as something alive, a vertical stripe that cautiously would take center stage after Taylor wheedled it from the edge of the film. Disney liked the idea, for he was determined to advance animation's potential by displaying imaginative abstract forms in at least a couple of segments. He agreed that both the sound track and the Bach segments should be presented with abstract art forms. What his imaginative artists finally devised were colorful kinetic Rorschach forms blossoming from specific sounds: dainty filigrees from a flute, bulbous enlargements from a tuba, and finally eye-popping horizontal fireworks from a crashing cymbal. Story meetings continued as Taylor had to return to New York for the Philharmonic broadcasts, and he delivered to Disney a script of his proposed introductions for each of the musical segments.

The month had not been all work; Taylor had numerous friends in Hollywood. As did so many Californians, he developed a case of Anglophilia in his choice of new acquaintances, for in addition to Roland Young, he became friends with the British actors Reginald Gardiner, Ronald Colman, and Douglas Fairbanks Jr.[18] He didn't overlook women either, but here he remained true to the United States. Kay Francis and Mary Astor showed up in his appointment book, as does Ginger Rogers, with whom he shared nearly a dozen dinners during his first month, and who loved classical music. She had met the composer, "an encouraging friend," years earlier through Harold Ross, the editor of the *New Yorker* and one of Rogers's first boyfriends.[19] Without a doubt, on either coast Taylor knew how to live the good life.

He returned to New York just in time to begin the Philharmonic broadcasts, and, with Martinelli and d'Arville, to continue a most unusual threesome. Whether Taylor realized what was happening, others certainly did, as is made clear in a letter that Arturo Toscanini sent to a mistress in Italy. It happened that d'Arville returned from her 1938 summer trip on the *Normandie,* the same ship that was bringing Toscanini back to the States for

A Disney artist's interpretation of Taylor as a centaur, drawn during the preparation of Disney's *Fantasia*.
© Disney Enterprises, Inc.

(Courtesy of Walt Disney Archives)

his second season conducting the NBC Symphony. That November, Toscanini sent a letter to Ada Mainardi that contained, among other items, the information that he had met "aboard the Normandie—one Colette d'Arville, who they say is simultaneously the lover of Martinelli (tenor) and Maestro Deems Taylor. Well, she's really a pretty little lady who . . . took a fancy to me." An annoyed Toscanini then describes how a friend of his brought d'Arville to his cabin, then "disappeared, leaving me alone with her. My Ada, at that moment, I felt nausea—I'll say no more—and when you feel nausea *every other appetite goes away*" (emphasis in original!).[20] The international consort was living up to her reputation, having set her maritime sights on the Italian maestro, a man well known for dalliances.

How could Taylor have been blind to this side of d'Arville? Perhaps it was simply a serious case of denial, but even denial has its wake-up call. This may well have happened when, as he told his daughter years later, he learned that d'Arville reserved the weekday hour of 4:30 P.M. for the financier and womanizer Solomon Guggenheim, a man who reportedly told his nephews: "Never make love to a woman before breakfast. . . . You might have a better offer before lunch."[21] Taylor, with his need to be wanted by a younger woman, must have cared for d'Arville a great deal, but either he heard the whispers or he came to his senses. For whatever reason, in the year ahead Colette d'Arville's name appeared fewer and fewer times in his appointment books.

Mixing Disney with Philharmonic Intermissions

Now in his third year with the Philharmonic, Taylor revealed to a reporter the extensive preparation needed for his intermission talks: a twelve-minute script could take some five hours to complete, including the research and drafting the remarks. After that "he starts talking to himself. He may repeat a sentence forty times before he is sure it sounds completely natural." Being a perfectionist, Taylor made every effort to make no mistakes, because "the minute one makes a slip over the radio, there are thousands who don't wait a minute to write in about it."[22]

Searching for new ideas for his radio year, Taylor decided that teaching the listener something about musical structure might be worth a try. On one broadcast, he explained the sonata form using portions of César Franck's Symphony in D Minor as the example. Afterward he asked his listeners to send him their evaluations of his teaching success, and the following Sunday (January 22, 1939) he reported on the response: "Of the hundreds of letters that I've had from you, the verdict is in the ratio of fifty Yes to one No. By the way, among the noes were several who suggested that I not only refrain from discussing a symphony, but that I refrain from discussing anything on the air. Well, I know how you feel. I often feel that way myself on Sunday mornings."

Taylor's sense of humor and cleverness helped build the Philharmonic's listening audience. At the end of his third year a CBS advertisement stated, "The Philharmonic's Sunday afternoon audience has grown from 2,760 [in 1930] to 10,000,000 listeners each week. And 45,000,000 people now hear one or more of the Philharmonic broadcasts each season!"[23] Among them were members of honorary degree committees from Dartmouth College and the University of Rochester. Both institutions offered Deems Taylor an honorary doctor of music degree, to be awarded at their 1939 commencement ceremonies. He accepted both, even though the ceremonies were on succeeding days. First he took the train to New Hampshire and the Dartmouth ceremony, where he was cited for being "music's minister plenipotentiary to the world at large,"[24] and then, taking advantage of the developing commercial airlines, he flew the next day to Rochester. At that ceremony, the citation honored another side of Taylor: "Your belief in the promise of American music has helped to make that promise come true."[25]

In May, before receiving his honorary degrees, Taylor returned to the Disney studios for a month, the first of two summer trips to review the progress of the animation and refine his commentaries for each segment of *Fantasia.* Two significant changes had occurred in the choice of music since his previous summer's involvement. The first was the deletion of *Clair de Lune,* and the second was the replacement of the little-known *Cydalise and the Faun,* by Gabriel Pierné. Disney's mythological creatures—centaurs and fauns—now would gambol about to the music of Beethoven's Sixth Symphony, the *Pastoral.* Taylor had not been left out of this decision: Stuart Buchanan, a Disney story man, had written him for his opinion of the change. Taylor responded that he thought the idea "a stunning one," explaining that of all of the Beethoven symphonies, the *Pastoral* alone was program music, for Beethoven himself had written descriptions of the sounds of nature he mimicked in it. "I can see no possible objection to it," Taylor wrote.[26] At one point Disney even suggested that Taylor be outfitted in a centaur costume, for his appearance "when he comes up to the mike after the Pastoral."[27]

Before the Disney artists could begin their animation, the sound track had to be completed, so the crew went to Philadelphia in April 1939 to record the music. Stokowski and his Philadelphia orchestra were ready, and the engineers set up their equipment in the Academy of Music, the orchestra's home. Since the engineers had to fulfill Disney's desire that the music be transmitted to the audience in stereophonic sound—a first in commercial films—this was no simple task. Thirty-three microphones on nine different channels were used to create Disney's "Fantasound."

In July, Taylor returned to Hollywood to complete his introductions. His two-month stay was made special by a two-week visit from his daughter. Joan, now twelve, had shared only occasional days with him during the past years, because Mary had not permitted lengthy visits. This time she relented, perhaps remembering her own entrancement with films as a young girl in Jacksonville, and her appearances in several of the Hearst epics that starred Marion Davies. By giving in on this occasion, Mary gave Joan two weeks that she would relish for a lifetime. This time in Hollywood would also solidify Joan's growing desire to be an actress.

Deems met Joan on the morning train, settled her into rooms at Roland Young's home, then took her to lunch at the famed Hollywood restaurant Chasen's, where they were joined by Reginald Gardiner, a suave English character actor. The next evening Joan was in the throng who cheered seventeen-year-old Judy Garland at the premiere of *The Wizard of Oz.* In the days that followed Joan enjoyed lunches and dinners with the English crowd, and

parties by the pool at Ginger Rogers's home.[28] Joan, whose smile and dim-
pled cheeks left few uncharmed, also impressed Lillian Gish, one of the
queens of silent films, who happened to be visiting Hollywood for the first
time in sixteen years. Gish later told a reporter "the most wonderful day in
her two months on the Coast was the one she spent in the Disney studios
with Deems Taylor and his young daughter, Joan." While with Disney, Gish
congratulated him for producing "the only really new thing in pictures," but
she did have one complaint for him: "It's an awful thing you've done to us
poor actors. We couldn't hope to be as good as Mickey Mouse, Donald
Duck, Pinocchio or any of the Seven Dwarfs." Disney's response was a classic: "Actors are all right but you can't leave the ground—you cannot soar,
you cannot fly."[29]

In early September, a few weeks after Joan had returned by train to New
York, her father followed. The year ahead would severely test his work ethic,
for in addition to the Philharmonic broadcasts, he had committed himself to
writing a sequel to *Of Men and Music;* hosting a major new radio program,
Musical Americana; and doing what was needed to complete *Fantasia.*

When Taylor sat down to prepare for another season of intermission
broadcasts, he acknowledged that while he had been in California enjoying
the sunshine, the world had changed: Hitler had invaded Poland and started
what many feared would be another world conflagration. In one of his first
broadcasts (October 15, 1939), Taylor reflected upon his brief foray into
France during World War I:

> There's one advantage—if you want to call it that—in having lived
> through a war and that is that when the next one breaks out you can,
> to a limited extent, predict the course of events. I remember that in
> 1914 . . . theatres in London, Berlin, and Paris were all closed
> down. . . . You may not believe, for example, that in this country, in
> 1918, while you could eat sauerkraut, you had to order it under the
> name of "liberty cabbage"; that German police dogs became Belgian
> police dogs almost overnight, that people hesitated to be seen on
> the streets leading a dachshund, and that Wagner's music could not
> be played in the Metropolitan Opera House. . . . To refuse to listen
> to music because you don't happen to care for its composer is rather
> like beating a child because you dislike his father.

Taylor was calling for fairness toward the music, even if people were unjust
to the composer.

Taylor seldom allowed his emotions to show in public, but he came close
to shedding tears on the Philharmonic's Christmas Eve 1939 broadcast,
when he told the radio audience of the death of Heywood Broun on Decem-

ber 18: "I lost a friend this week, a man who had been my friend for nearly a quarter of a century. He died last Monday morning at the age of fifty-one." Taylor followed with comments very much in the spirit of the season:

> For Heywood Broun, more than any man I have ever known, was the embodiment of that phrase that is so closely associated with the Christmas season: . . . "and on earth peace, good will toward men." About this time each year we recall that phrase, for about twenty-four hours. But Heywood lived it. He covered many subjects in his writing, and he was a hard fighter. He hated unfairness, and oppression, and stupidity, and greed, and the ideas for which some men stand. But he was one of those rare persons who know that you do not defeat ideas by hating men. I have never heard him say anything unkind or ungenerous about anyone; and I don't believe he ever disliked—let alone hated—any person. And that is why I should like to turn over part of today's intermission to my dead friend to let him speak to you, through me, about Christmas.

Taylor then read Broun's "A Shepherd," the story of a young man named Amos who lived near Bethlehem at the time of the first Christmas. Broun's beautiful tale told of older shepherds who asked Amos to accompany them to see the Christ child. Amos refused and told them he would find God just where he was: shepherding.

When they returned from Bethlehem they asked him if, in their absence, he had found anything of God in his heart. "Amos told them, 'Now my hundred are one hundred and one,' and he showed them a lamb that had been born just before the dawn. 'Was there for this a great voice out of heaven?' asked the eldest of the shepherds. Amos shook his head and smiled, and there was in his face that which seemed to the shepherds a wonder even in a night of wonders. 'To my heart,' he said, 'there came a whisper.'"[30] The requests for a repeat of this reading were so great that the following Christmas, Taylor once again brought the story to his listeners, this time read by his teenage daughter, Joan.

The musical topics for intermissions after Christmas ranged widely, from orchestras in small communities to the difficulties of composing. Taylor's commentaries now received the ultimate compliment: they became the subject of a *New Yorker* cartoon. In it a salesman is showing an oversize record player to a wealthy couple: "Now this model not only plays fifty records, but it changes them, turns them over, and gives a brief comment on each by Deems Taylor."[31]

For the final concert of the 1939–40 Philharmonic season (May 5,

1940), Taylor became reflective and philosophical, determinedly aware of what was happening on a global scale:

> What are the lasting things in the world, the things that are of final importance? Science, philosophy, religion, and art. . . . I do believe that of all the arts, music is the one most essential for the spirit, the most intangible, the least sophisticated. If music is closely allied with all religions, the fact is not without significance. . . . Music has no politics, no race, no loyalties or treasons. Every composer that ever lived or lives, no matter when or where, is your friend and brother. Remember that. Hold on to that friendship. If you do, it will outlast this madness.

Musical Americana Helps Young Musicians

Always looking for another outlet for his radio talents, starting in January Taylor added a weekly journey to Pittsburgh, to serve as master of ceremonies for the new program *Musical Americana*. Few commercial radio music programs ever surpassed this Westinghouse presentation, with an orchestra of more than one hundred members (mostly from the Pittsburgh symphony) and a choral group of twenty-four. Westinghouse also hired the two most recognizable voices on radio for music commentary: Taylor to be the master of ceremonies, and Milton Cross, already well known for the Metropolitan Opera broadcasts, to be the announcer. For six months, every Wednesday Taylor, Cross, and the conductor Raymond Paige took the train to Pittsburgh. After a morning rehearsal, the Thursday evening program was broadcast from the massive Syria Mosque Theater. As was common in the days before radio transcriptions, the program was performed twice, each time before four thousand people: first at 8:30 P.M. for the Eastern and Central audiences, then again at 10:30 P.M. for the NBC Western audiences. A late evening train took Taylor, Cross, and Paige back to New York.

On the first broadcast of *Musical Americana,* Taylor waved the flag for American composers: "We have an idea that Americans tend to undervalue their own composers. We do give our popular composers a hearing. But we also have a large number of composers who write more or less serious music that we would undoubtedly like . . . if we gave ourselves a chance to hear it. And we propose to give you that chance. This, then, is going to be a program of American music, both frivolous and serious."[32] Then listeners heard music by Jerome Kern, Edward MacDowell, Henry F. Gilbert, and a few others of Deems's compatriots.

Musical Americana gained special applause for a unique concept in radio, because each program featured a performance by a music student from one of the country's leading schools. This had never been done before. The idea had most likely been Taylor's, and, as he explained to his audience: "I think we tend to take orchestral musicians much too much for granted, forgetting the obvious fact that the very existence of our great orchestra depends upon their talent and training. And so . . . Musical Americana is inviting our leading conservatories to send us their most gifted students of orchestral instruments."[33] *Newsweek* applauded this approach as a break from "radio's endless chain of baritones, tenors, and sopranos."[34]

Over the weeks, seventeen conservatories sent their best to Pittsburgh—pianists, violinists, cellists, trombonists, trumpeters, twenty-one instrumentalists in all—talented musicians who were frightened, yet thrilled beyond belief, to be making a national debut.[35]

(Sixty years later, five of them recounted their memories of that experience and how it influenced their lives. Nathan Stutch, a member of the cello section of the New York Philharmonic from 1946 to 1990, recalled representing the Curtis Institute as an eighteen-year-old: "The appearance convinced me that my life would be that of a cellist." Reminiscing about Taylor ("I see his face before me"), Stutch recalled a charming man, knowledgeable and whimsical, "a major force in the music world at that time."[36]

(Harry Herforth, a trumpet player from the New England Conservatory and a native of Pittsburgh, remembered that the appearance "crystallized a belief in myself as a musician," a belief that carried him into the trumpet sections of the Boston Symphony and the Cleveland Orchestra.[37] The performance of Sidney Mear, a trumpeter from Eastman School of Music, was heard by Carlos Chavez, Mexico's foremost composer, who invited him to play in the Symphony Orchestra of Mexico. Afterward he spent most of his professional life as a teacher at Eastman.[38] Elis Ronbeck, a violinist from the University of Southern California, chose variety: he became a substitute in orchestras and played in venues from the Copacabana nightclub to Radio City Music Hall, then performed for decades with the Metropolitan Opera orchestra.[39]

(David Falway, a trombonist from the University of Michigan, had been recommended by William Revelli, the university's famed bandmaster. Reflecting back, Falway stated simply, "Music has been good to me." He went into the insurance business, but a dance band on the side kept his trombone sliding through the years. His gratitude to music continues in the concerts he sponsors today to provide scholarships for young musicians to attend the National Music Camp at Interlochen.[40])

Taylor's Westinghouse connection ended in June when, in a cost-cutting mood, the company moved *Musical Americana* to New York studios, reduced the size of the orchestra, and changed musical offerings from fairly serious to lighter fare. The program's director now also substituted as host. For Taylor this really didn't matter, because he wouldn't have been able to continue anyway. Disney had summoned him to Hollywood to complete *Fantasia*.

Fantasia Comes to Life

"You'll need your full dress clothes for the live action shooting," Disney wrote, "and with good luck we should be completely finished by the middle of September."[41] Taylor arrived in early August 1940, reported to the studio in white tie and tails, and met James Wong Howe, a preeminent cinematographer in Hollywood whom Disney had hired to film all the live-action shots, principally Taylor's introductions to the animated sequences.[42] Howe was famed for deep-focus camera work and later won Academy Awards for *The Rose Tattoo* and *Hud*.

Fantasia's live-action beginning shows orchestra members assembling for a concert against a blue background. To provide more visual energy to the scene, Howe briefly flashes color spots on various instruments as they tune up. Taylor appears from center rear, climbing a few steps to the upper level of the orchestra. In a long shot, the formal-looking Taylor is seen standing, bespectacled and with balding pate. The camera slowly moves toward him and he introduces himself: "How do you do. My name is Deems Taylor." He then speaks of Disney, his artists, and "this new form of entertainment, *Fantasia*," then alerts the audience to the three types of music to be enjoyed in the next two hours: music telling a definite story, music painting a certain picture, and "music for its own sake . . . which we call absolute music."

His introduction became so famous that three years later, in a *Looney Tunes* satire of *Fantasia* entitled *A Corny Concerto* (for "Corny-gie Hall"), a narrator emerges climbing stairs from behind the orchestra: a formally dressed, bespectacled and bald Elmer Fudd. The lisping Mr. Fudd also welcomes the audience with a folksy salutation: "Gweetings music wuvvuz!" and then introduces two animated "Stwauss" waltzes.

In every one of the introductions to the seven different musical segments, a non-lisping Taylor speaks to the audience from next to a music stand. Howe provides variety by changing hues of the side lighting. Also, a few animated moments draw attention away from Taylor, including a brief "spontaneous" jazz episode by some of the orchestral musicians. Most of the introductions are short, except for that to *The Rite of Spring*. Here Taylor explains that the visualization of Earth's beginnings is based on the latest scientific understanding available to Disney and his staff. To bring some levity to this portion, just as he begins declaiming about the Earth and dinosaurs, a

Leopold Stokowski and Taylor during the preparation of *Fantasia. (Courtesy of Photofest)*

jarring, clanging sound à la Stravinsky emerges from the orchestra, and the camera reveals that the entire set of chimes has accidentally tipped over.

It took several weeks longer than expected to complete the live-action footage, and Taylor took advantage of the time to socialize. On one occasion he accepted an invitation from his former paramour Dorothy Parker to a tea at her Hollywood home in late September. She and her husband, Alan Campbell, still seeking satisfaction as screenwriters, had remained in California. Among the other guests was F. Scott Fitzgerald, who wrote to his wife, Zelda, that he had spoken to Taylor, "whom I hadn't seen twice since the days at Swope's."[43] Undoubtedly the two reflected on those Great Neck days, when the Algonquin crowd had been at its heartiest. They probably lifted a glass to bygone days, and for Taylor this would be a bittersweet memory: Fitzgerald died three months later.

Back in New York Taylor received a letter from his mother, who still maintained the family home in the Bronx: "I am excited about 'Fantasia.' All accounts say it is Disney's best. I'll be anxious to see you even in one scene in anything. As a boy you had a good deal of histrionic ability and why not now?"[44] It is likely that then and there, he decided to escort his mother to the *Fantasia* premiere.

Disney's animators produced the two-hour film in less than eighteen months, a monumental task considering that every second of the animation took twenty-four separate drawings, making a total of more than a hundred thousand for the complete movie. (Computer-generated animation was decades away.) Disney won the race with time on the very morning of *Fantasia's* premiere in New York City, December 13, 1940, when the reel of the final "Ave Maria" sequence arrived by chartered plane with only four hours to spare.

The drizzle that had persisted throughout the day ceased in time for the guests to enter the Broadway Theater. What they experienced in the next hours they did not soon forget: music that seemed to come from every part of the theater, brilliantly colored thistles dancing to a Russian trepak by Tchaikovsky, dinosaurs fighting to their death accompanied by Stravinsky's savage music, and Mickey Mouse, the quintessential adolescent, seeking the power of the universe in the *Sorcerer's Apprentice*. Disney had even provided a theatrical intermission to the movie as a musical breather.

After the premiere, arguments began between the purists and the entertainment-minded. Movie critics loved it. "Simply terrific," wrote Bosley Crowther, the *Times* critic, "as terrific as anything that has ever happened on a screen."[45] Others were not so kind. Contrary to Taylor's belief that no one would object to seeing mythological creatures gamboling to the music of Beethoven's *Pastoral* Symphony, music critics particularly disparaged that sequence. They could not stand the centaurs, with their lack of manliness or the Disney-invented "centaurettes," whose makeup and hairdos sprang from the 1930s rather than mythology. Nor did they like the abstract violin bows and undulating waves, all pulsating to Bach's Toccata and Fugue in D Minor. *Fantasia* even caused a psychological trauma in Dorothy Thompson, a nationally syndicated columnist of immense popularity. She abhorred the thought of superimposing animation upon the music of such "musical gods" as Bach and Beethoven: "I left the theater in a condition bordering on nervous breakdown . . . [seeing] a caricature of the Decline of the West."[46] At the very least, *Fantasia* did not leave its viewers unmoved.

Otis Ferguson may have written the best summary of *Fantasia*: "Dull as it is toward the end, ridiculous as it is in the bend of knee before Art, and taking one thing with another, it is one of the strange and beautiful things that have happened in the world . . . something never thought of and not soon forgotten."[47] This was certainly the feeling of Taylor's mother when the evening was over. In her diary she recorded the event in simple words: "Dec. 13, 1940. 'Fantasia' in the evening. Deems sent car for me. Then orchids, Stork Club for dinner. Deems came home in car with me. A wonderful show."[48]

Throughout most of 1941, *Fantasia* was presented in road-show engagements in some twenty theaters around the country, with a full year's run in New York City. The initial release lost money because of the expense of installing Fantasound equipment in each theater. In addition, the European war curtailed both foreign distribution and the availability of the needed stereophonic equipment, so the road show ended. In April 1942 a shortened nonstereophonic version opened, cleared of all but the first of Taylor's introductions.[49] Not until a 1956 reissue did interest in *Fantasia* increase considerably, for by then almost all movie theaters had stereophonic sound equipment. In 2000 the Disney Company produced a DVD version of *Fantasia* equivalent to the original road-show version, with Taylor once again introducing every segment to the viewer. The masterpiece was again whole.

As he had developed it, Disney had had great hopes for *Fantasia*. In fact, he believed that if it was successful, he would be able to release new versions every few years. Taylor had even prepared introductions for a half-dozen other compositions, "to have them for the future in case we decided to make any one of them."[50] Unfortunately, the original release was not financially profitable. It was only *Fantasia 2000*, released sixty years later, that belatedly realized Disney's hope.

15. Radio Daze, 1940–1942

A New Girlfriend

In the midst of his successes with the Philharmonic intermissions and *Fantasia,* Taylor's relationship with Colette d'Arville had broken down, and he solidified a special friendship with Giuliana Taberna, a minor actress in radio dramas at CBS whom he had met in 1937. Though he was unable to make a clean break and continued to see Colette after she returned from France in the succeeding months, his appointment books register increasing meetings with Taberna until, by the end of 1940, d'Arville disappears completely and Taberna reigns supreme.[1] What made the change unusual was the reversal of roles; this time Taylor was not the pursuer, but the pursued, for Taberna had a penchant for famous men.

Taylor's new girlfriend had dark hair and Mediterranean features from her Italian parentage, and she often dressed flamboyantly. Money came from her family in Italy, plus the little she made from acting. But her real joy was appearing to be the possession of a celebrity, deriving her identity from his personality.[2] At CBS Giuliana had minor roles in some of Norman Corwin's *Columbia Workshop* radio plays, and Corwin remembers meeting Taylor through her after she presented herself as Taylor's girlfriend.[3] Taylor accepted the role of celebrity of choice, and Taberna clung to him like Velcro. Although she was thirty years younger than he, she happily accompanied him—a lovely, vibrant woman on the arm of a charming and witty man.

Giuliana Taberna, radio
actress and successor to
d'Arville. She clung to
Taylor like Velcro.
*(Courtesy of Yale University
Music Library)*

Intermissions Turn Serious

By early 1940 Taylor had produced his second book based on his intermission
talks: *The Well-Tempered Listener.* Like *Of Men and Music,* the new book achieved
unanimous praise on publication, going into six printings. Some reviewers,
such as Howard Taubman of the *Times,* now recognized something special in
the author: "Mr. Taylor might be regarded as the modern version of the wise,
homely philosopher who illuminated the conversations around the hot stove
in the general store of a dull Winter evening."[4] *Yale Review's* R. D. Welch pictured Taylor as a musical Franklin Delano Roosevelt, referring to the author
as "fireside commentator to musical America (and the world at large)."[5]

As the fireside commentator began his fifth year with the Philharmonic
the following fall, his talks covered more serious issues. The previous summer in Hollywood he had met many refugee composers and writers, most
notably Igor Stravinsky, Italo Montemezzi, Arnold Schoenberg, Erich Korngold, and Thomas Mann. Taylor explained to his listeners why these artists
had fled Europe (November 10, 1940):

> This war is different from all others in history in that the threat of
> death is continuous and present everywhere. Bombers have seen to

that. . . . You see, the war of nerves is an uncannily clever device. It has its origin in a realization of the fact that the most shattering test of anyone's endurance and self-control is not danger, but suspense. It faces the defender with an enemy against whom there is only one defense: luck. And luck is not a very dependable shield . . . and those are the conditions under which hundreds and thousands of artists must try to work today. The war is not only killing some of them; it is killing the initiative and the creative powers of the survivors. . . . And so it is up to us, here in the Americas, to produce that music.

Taylor also continued to use letters from listeners to enliven his intermissions. One high school student wrote with a definite purpose: "We are studying in our music class about music and the American Democracy. I would appreciate it very much if you would give me your opinion on what music does for our American Democracy, and, if it would not be too much trouble, send me a picture of yourself." Taylor responded factually (March 30, 1941): "Well one thing it does, apparently, is to encourage mass action. That same day's mail brought identical letters from six other students in that high school. As far as my picture is concerned, I'd love to send it but I warn you that it isn't likely to influence the cause of American democracy one way or the other."

After the Philharmonic season concluded, during the summer of 1941 Taylor turned briefly to composing, still his first love, and completed a half-hour musical score for a Norman Corwin radio play. Corwin's genius had made the *Columbia Workshop* radio's best weekly program of experimental drama, and an appreciative CBS provided him twenty-six consecutive weeks on the *Workshop* for original half-hour productions. Among these were his biblical trilogy: "Samson," "Esther," and "Job." Corwin wanted an original musical score for each.

When he approached Taylor to write the score for "Job," the composer had been in the artistic doldrums for months, and the request lifted his spirits considerably. (Bernard Herrmann and Lyn Murray were the composers for the other two parts of the trilogy.) The completion of the music for the August 24 production, which starred Charles Laughton, called for a party at the Stork Club with Taylor's new girlfriend. It was only one of many times during the year that the couple and their friends boosted their spirits in either the Stork Club or "21," two of New York's famous upscale drinking establishments. As an indication of his extensive partying in those years, though Taylor netted only about ten thousand dollars in 1941, his bills for the two nightclubs amounted to some one thousand.[6]

Taylor's Busiest Year on Radio

Commercial radio had hit its stride by 1941, a year that would be Taylor's busiest ever in the medium. Throughout the 1930s radio had served mainly as free entertainment, with a variety of programs—comedy, drama, music—that helped Americans to forget the difficulties of the Depression and the war building in Europe. But by 1941 listeners appreciated another of radio's capabilities: it brought World War II into their homes with an unexpected immediacy. Those who heard the shortwave broadcasts from England by Edward R. Murrow listened to the actual sounds of war in the background.

Meanwhile, the U.S. government knew that the future was dark, so they began to sponsor radio programs to convince the audience to purchase Defense Bonds and Stamps. The U.S. Treasury Department asked Taylor if he would volunteer his services as the master of ceremonies for *America Preferred,* which would be produced live every Saturday evening for a year. He didn't hesitate to say yes to a program that would feature live performances by great concert artists.

As the host, Taylor revealed the program's agenda on its first broadcast: "A tribute to those musical artists of foreign birth who have elected to make America their homeland—America Preferred: people who are Americans *by choice* because here that most precious gift, human freedom, still survives."[7] It was a spectacular lineup, including Arthur Rubinstein, Ezio Pinza, Lily Pons, Jascha Heifetz, Gregor Piatigorsky, and Lauritz Melchior. At the beginning of every broadcast, the announcer informed listeners that Taylor and all guest artists were donating their services, thereby assuring that the radio audience would recognize them as role models of patriotism.[8]

Though Taylor received no salary for *America Preferred,* another new weekly broadcast filled his pockets very nicely when Prudential, the New Jersey–based insurance company, decided to move from sponsorship of the successful soap opera *When a Girl Marries* to the *Prudential Family Hour.* This program featured the popular mezzo-soprano Gladys Swarthout, an orchestra, and Taylor as commentator. The show became immensely popular, and, like all successful programs, it had a gimmick: the radio audience selected the music to be played by sending in their requests by mail. For Taylor it was a minor gold mine, bringing him thirty thousand dollars per year at a time when CBS paid him only eleven thousand for his Philharmonic intermissions.[9] It also made for a very busy Sunday: the *Family Hour* was broadcast only an hour after the Philharmonic intermission talk, so Taylor had to make a mad dash from the Carnegie Hall radio room to the CBS studios at 495 Madison Avenue.

Taylor had achieved a unique place in radio by 1941, known both for his championing of music and for his wit. He was a popular guest on many programs, especially *Information, Please,* the most sophisticated, yet often wildly funny, radio quiz show. Clifton Fadiman, the book critic for the *New Yorker,* read listeners' questions to a four-person panel who provided the answers. Audiences loved Fadiman, whose voice and manner conveyed the sense that he was intellectual as well as a "regular guy." Within a year of its start in 1938, the Tuesday evening program was one of the most popular on radio, with some ten million listeners.

The panel had two permanent members—FPA, Deems's old friend and donor of the celebrated timepieces, and John Kieran, a somewhat laconic sports columnist with multiple interests. Guests of every type—politicians, authors, comedians—filled the other two slots, with Taylor a particular favorite. Years later Fadiman recalled why: "[Deems] possessed a natural light touch. He could be witty without effort, and his charm was never tainted by self-exhibitionism."[10]

It was largely the program's spontaneity that appealed to listeners. For example, on one program with Taylor and Edna Ferber as guest panelists, Ferber answered a question that required her to sing a portion of "Sweet Adeline." As she began tentatively, Taylor, FPA, and Kieran eagerly joined in to give the audience the worst rendition ever heard of the old barbershop ballad. The studio audience roared its approval. In another program, the author John Gunther was a guest panelist and identified Reza Pahlevi as the Shah of Iran. When Fadiman pressed him with the question, "Are you shah?" Gunther quipped back, "Sultanly."[11]

In his exceptional *On the Air: The Encyclopedia of Old-Time Radio,* the author John Dunning shows that *Information, Please* was the first program that NBC allowed to be prerecorded for release to the West Coast at a later time. The reason was simple: "being spontaneous, it was impossible to repeat. . . . For the first time listeners heard the phrase 'This show has been transcribed from an earlier network presentation, for release at this more convenient time.'"[12] *Information, Please* opened the floodgates for other programs to be transcribed, instead of having to be repeated hours later for the West Coast.

For Taylor, neither guest appearances nor new programs touched the importance of the Philharmonic intermission broadcasts to which he returned in mid-October 1941. Many times his commentary reflected on the international conflicts and their horrors, from Hitler in Europe to the Japanese invasion into China. Yet always he urged his listeners to keep music apolitical, as he did in this broadcast of November 16, 1941:

Information, Please quiz show panel, October 22, 1940. From left: John Kieran, Herbert Bayard Swope (*World* editor when Taylor was music critic), Taylor, Franklin P. Adams. Both Kieran and FPA were regulars. *(Courtesy of Photofest)*

A high school in California had a school song set to the old Austrian National anthem. You'll notice that I say "had." For now, it appears the song has been banned because it also happens to be the tune of "Deutschland Über Alles." First of all, I'd like to remark that it seems pretty silly to me to forbid the singing of an air because some people you don't like happen to have put some words to it. The original words to Haydn's tune began "Gott erhalte Franz den Kaiser"—"God save Emperor Francis"—and refers to Francis the Second of the Holy Roman Empire, who became Francis the First of the Austrian Empire after Napoleon had formed the Rhine Federation in 1806. And whatever else Francis I might have been, he was certainly no Nazi.

Early that December, Taylor hosted two *America Preferred* concerts by Arturo Toscanini and the NBC Symphony. The Treasury Department had eagerly sought the maestro's appearance because few in music had made their opposition to fascism clearer than Toscanini. The first of the two concerts aired the evening of December 6, 1941. During that broadcast, Taylor urged his listeners to buy Defense Bonds and Stamps and help the government build an "arsenal for democracy." In words that now seem eerily prophetic, he told the audience that "Yesterday is dead; tomorrow is as yet unborn. The past cannot be regained, but the future can be saved by free men and women."[13] The next day, as he prepared to deliver his Philharmonic intermission talk, the broadcast was interrupted to announce the attack on Pearl Harbor.

During the following week's intermission, Taylor reflected on the Day of Infamy in nationalistic terms typical of the times (December 14, 1941):

> One thing about last Sunday's happenings struck me as a perfect bit of symbolism. And that is the fact that the news of the attack on Pearl Harbor by the Japanese reached us as approximately 7 percent of the population of the United States was listening to the weekly broadcast of the Philharmonic-Symphony Orchestra. Both peoples were doing what they had been brought up to do: the one to work, and then to rest and enjoy that rest: the other, to invade and destroy and try to conquer.

It was only natural that on succeeding Sundays, Taylor focused on the wartime crisis. On January 18, 1942, he read portions of a letter by the American composer and pianist Abram Chasins, who beautifully identified the role of the creative artist in war. "He will render his greatest service," Chasins wrote, "not by ceasing his creative activity, but by fulfilling it; not by patterning his world after the art-killing world of our enemies, but by affirming, in art, the world we are fighting for. . . . Democracy is something that one does, and does not *stop* doing; that one affirms by action, and not by inaction."

Ramuntcho Comes Alive

By the beginning of 1942, with three radio series to host and write scripts for, Taylor needed daily massages to drain the tension from his body. In addition, a production of *Ramuntcho* was finally on its way. He had completed the orchestration in 1938, the same year in which the Philadelphia Opera Company was organized. This professional organization was different because of its young singers who performed all operas in English. Taylor had attended some of their productions and found that not only could they sing, but they could also act. He brought *Ramuntcho* to the attention of the company's artistic director, Sylvan Levin. The four-year-old organization had never had a world premiere, and, after Levin studied the score, he informed Taylor that they would be honored to present it.

As preparations advanced for the premiere, Samuel Barber wrote from Philadelphia to his former mentor to tell him of his high anticipation: "I look forward to hearing your newest in Philadelphia. From all reports the company is preparing it with greatest enthusiasm."[14] During the final rehearsals in January 1942, Taylor himself shuttled back and forth from New York. "I heard the first orchestra rehearsal yesterday," he wrote to Joan, by now attending a private high school in Maryland, "and nearly died of joy. It's a *wonderful* score, and let me be the first to say so."[15]

On Tuesday evening, February 10, 1942, Taylor escorted his mother to the Academy of Music in Philadelphia for *Ramuntcho*'s world premiere. It was a black tie affair, with music critics from major Eastern newspapers, as well as *Time* and *Newsweek,* among the crowd. When the curtain rose, the audience was treated to what *Time* called "an old-fashioned opera of love, misunderstanding and renunciation."[16] In Act I, Ramuntcho, an excellent player of the centuries-old game of handball called pelote, has joined a group of smugglers in a Basque village on the Spanish border. As he tells them of his love for the village girl Gracieuse, the approach of customs officers sends them fleeing. Later, at a pelote game in the village, Ramuntcho and Gracieuse's meeting is observed by her disapproving mother. Ramuntcho tells Gracieuse that after his obligatory army service, he will give up the life of a smuggler and become a pelote champion. When he asks her to marry him upon his return, she replies: "You know I will, my Ramuntcho."

In the first scene of Act II, at a picnic just before his regiment's departure, Ramuntcho expresses concern that Gracieuse spends too much time in church or with the nuns. Is this a life she might choose over him? "I love to enter the old church at twilight, with the sound of bells dying into silence," she admits to him, but insists that she will be waiting for his return. But the second scene opens two years later, and a sad Gracieuse sings of her puzzlement at never having heard from Ramuntcho. She does not know that her mother has been destroying his letters; a postman arrives in the girl's absence and gives the mail to her mother. At the end of the scene, the Mother Superior comes to tell the mother that Gracieuse has decided to become a nun.

Another year has passed when Act III opens. Young people are dancing the fandango and singing folksongs during a Sunday celebration in the village. Ramuntcho arrives and learns that Gracieuse is a nun, and also that her mother destroyed all his letters upon receipt. He visits Gracieuse at the convent in the second scene, reveals the mother's deception, and tells of his continuing love.

Gracieuse is saddened by the action of her mother, but tells Ramuntcho that she has given herself to God and cannot break her vows. "Think of me always as a lovely dream that never came true," she sings, "This is not the end, Ramuntcho. We shall meet again in another world when God permits." With a defiant Ramuntcho raising a clenched fist at a crucifix and a sobbing Gracieuse kneeling in prayer, the final curtain falls. Then "manifestly spontaneous applause . . . brought the composer, as well as the cast, before the curtain to take a bow."[17]

Taylor later wrote his impressions of the performance to his daughter, who had been unable to attend because of the private school's rules against leaving on weekdays. "The audience was really enthusiastic. They broke into several scenes with applause, and at the end they stood up and cheered. When I came out, with the conductor, they began to shout 'author!' and 'speech!' I held up my hand for silence, and when I had it, said, 'Pardon me just a moment,' kissed Levin on both cheeks, and walked off. Then they did holler!"[18] Of all the singers, critics singled out Dorothy Sarnoff (Gracieuse) for praise, especially for an effective "Ave Maria" in the final scene.[19] The orchestral introduction and ballet music at the beginning of Act III, the portion of the opera that had been previously published and played by the New York Philharmonic, also got heavy applause.

Henry Pleasants, a highly respected Philadelphia music critic, lauded the company in its presentation but was not pleased with the opera: "Measured against the old standards, it is not a great opera, hardly even a very good one. . . . The music falls pleasantly, chromatically, familiarly and sometimes a little monotonously upon the ear." Pleasants placed major blame on the story, whose simplicity Taylor had seen as a virtue: "But simplicity, admirable as it may be in an opera book, is no substitute for dramatic suspense and emotional tension. Excepting the relatively uncomplicated experience of a fully requited love, nothing happens emotionally to Ramuntcho, on the stage at least, until he returns at the end of the opera to find Gracieuse is a nun. Gracieuse, with the same exception, experiences nothing save the anxiety of unanswered letters and the despair which prompts her to take the veil."[20]

New York critics generally gave positive comments, such as those of Howard Taubman of the *Times*, who praised the lush instrumentation and indicated that there were "frequent outbursts of approval for singers and music."[21] Francis Perkins of the *Herald Tribune* emphasized Taylor's special talent for choral writing. However, *Variety*'s critic believed the trip to Philadelphia was a waste of time: "The opera drags interminably and resembled operetta, or bad musical comedy."[22]

One week after the premiere, Linton Martin, another well-spoken Philadelphia music critic, identified the opera's difficulty: "Deems Taylor, the librettist, let down Deems Taylor, the composer, to the extent of giving him a book virtually devoid of dramatic value and equipped with characters no-body could care much about—characters that were, indeed, not even so much cardboard cutouts as made of pastel tinted tissue paper."[23] This indeed had been a mistake. Years earlier, Taylor had written about poor librettos: "Go over the list of works that hold the operatic stage today and you will find that almost all of them possess dramatic interest." As examples, he listed *Rigoletto, La Traviata, Tosca,* and *La Bohème,* among others. "In all of these works," he pointed out, "one finds the dramatic essentials of character, mo-tive, suspense, and conflict."[24]

Taylor should have heeded his own words, but in this case his emotions had overwhelmed his logic. His relationship with Colette, more than any-thing else, had led him into the world of *Ramuntcho.* But, by the time of the Philadelphia performance, Colette was no longer a part of his world.

An Argument with a Mann

Throughout the *Ramuntcho* preparations, Taylor carried on with his Philhar-monic broadcasts. Now that war had been declared, old arguments linking music and politics arose from the ashes of World War I. He created a furor over comments he made regarding a letter that Erika Mann wrote to the *Times.*[25] Erika was the daughter of Thomas Mann and detested the Nazis. She argued in her letter that Richard Strauss represented Hitler's abhorrent re-gime, and therefore his music was abhorrent. In his Philharmonic rebuttal, Taylor chided Mann's daughter for arguing quid pro quo: just because the Nazis had banned the literary works of her father did not make it right to do the same to the music of Strauss. "There is no enemy music," he said. "[But] there may be enemy words, set to music. Ban the songs, if you like. But mu-sic, by itself, is neither hostile nor friendly" (February 22, 1942).

Letters poured in, and the following Sunday, March 1, 1942, Taylor shared some of them. One listener chided Taylor: "Consciously or uncon-sciously you talk like a fifth columnist. Such words give comfort to the en-emy." Others suggested he should stick to music commentary: "It would be pleasant and inspiring to feel that occasionally the public could hear a pro-gram like the Philharmonic without the intrusion of preaching or a buy-a-bond talk."

Three weeks later the *Times* published a letter from Katherine Anne Por-ter, the author whom Taylor had met and befriended in Denver years earlier. Porter ardently supported Erika Mann's concern and concluded her letter by saying: "[Strauss and Walter Gieseking] are our enemies not as artists but as Nazis, and as Nazis they have forfeited any right to profit of this country."[26] Here Porter waved her flag much too vigorously, for history would show that

Richard Strauss was no friend of the Nazis. In addition, as Taylor had previously pointed out to his listeners, "Of the orchestral tone poems upon which [Strauss's] fame will probably rest, the five greatest were written between 1888 and 1898. . . . There was no Fuehrer in those days" (March 1, 1942).

With the Philharmonic season coming to an end, Taylor must have realized he had tilted his musical remarks too far into politics, so he returned to issues of American music with a plea to give the American composers wider hearing (April 19, 1942): "I wish you'd make a little effort to hear music by American composers. . . . In a survey of music played in 1940–41 by sixteen major orchestras, less than 6 percent was from American composers. . . . A number of you get very angry and excited about the playing of so-called 'enemy' music. We composers would like it better if you got a little angry and excited about the non-playing of American music."

Listeners of the intermission talks, which now had less of the wit and musical insights Taylor had previously provided, may have started to tune him off. Evidence of this comes from the eminent San Francisco music critic and commentator Alfred Frankenstein. It was about this time that San Francisco radio station KSFO lost its CBS affiliation. As a result, the Philharmonic now aired over a new CBS affiliate. To be competitive, KSFO brought in Frankenstein to host a program of recorded classical music at the same time that the Philharmonic aired on the rival station. When Frankenstein reviewed the Hooperatings for his show, he discovered something very curious: "During the first hour the Philharmonic usually had a bigger audience than we did," he wrote, "but during the last thirty minutes we always had twice the Philharmonic's hearers. This happened regularly and consistently, regardless of programs, and the only explanation can be that people switched to us as soon as Deems Taylor began his intermission commentary."[27] Of course, this was only one audience, San Francisco, but the fact remains that it was a much more serious Taylor who now spoke on Sundays. And times were indeed difficult, as the war effort consumed the nation.

16. ASCAP Fades In and Intermissions Fade Out, 1942–1945 (Part 1)

The ASCAP That Taylor Inherited as President

Within a week of the closing of the Philharmonic season, in a surprise to most in the music industry, the board of ASCAP (American Society of Composers, Authors [lyricists], and Publishers [of music]) elected Deems Taylor its president. The previous year had been the rockiest ever for the board, as will be described. As a result, the job description might well have read: "Must have calm demeanor, great tact and diplomacy, and experience in music, theater, and radio." On the board's second ballot Taylor was elected president, only the third in ASCAP's twenty-eight-year history. For the next six years, in addition to his other responsibilities, Deems Taylor would lead the most powerful music organization in the United States.

Deems loved ASCAP. He had been admitted as a member in 1927, thirteen years after its founding, and had become one of the twenty-four board members in 1933. He believed wholeheartedly in the mission of the society—collecting royalties for the use of copyrighted music, then distributing the monies among members by a preordained method of sharing. France had established such a society as early as 1851, but not until the U.S. Congress passed the Copyright Law of 1909 could one exist here.[1] Congress had long resisted giving composers collection rights. "[There is] enormous respect for the man who takes out a patent," Taylor wrote, "but none for the man who takes out a copyright. That difference in attitude comes, I suppose from the fact that a patent usually involves something tangible [like] a hairpin, for instance—whereas the man who writes a symphony or a ballad has produced something that is, fundamentally, nothing but a lot of sounds."[2]

The part of the 1909 law that "established minimum damages of $250 and costs for the unauthorized performance for profit of copyrighted music" made ASCAP not only possible, but also a necessity.[3] No songwriter or composer could spend time running from restaurant to theater collecting royalties; someone had to do that for him—a performing-rights organization, which was really a collection agency for songwriters and composers.

The seeds for ASCAP had been planted in 1907, when Giacomo Puccini visited the United States for the first time. One evening while he was at dinner with George Maxwell, his publisher's agent in this country, he heard the restaurant's small orchestra playing selections from his operas. He inquired of Maxwell what royalties would be forthcoming from this use of his music. When Maxwell informed him that there would be no royalties, just the pleasure of applause, Puccini told Maxwell "that if he were in Europe he would damn well be getting paid."[4]

After the passage of the new copyright law, Maxwell remembered Puccini's comment and urged Victor Herbert, then the most respected songwriter in the United States, to lend his considerable weight to establishing such an organization. Herbert did just that, and on February 13, 1914, the first general meeting of ASCAP was held. George Maxwell was elected as its first president. Herbert then sent an open letter to composers and lyricists urging them to become ASCAP members and thereby receive their fair share of the licensing fees that ASCAP would collect.

Many legal questions still had to be resolved at the beginning. For example, did music played in a restaurant profit the restaurateur and therefore require payment to the composer? Herbert became the central figure in resolving this major legal issue when he filed a suit against Shanleys, a Times Square restaurant, for playing his music without proper payment. The case received several rebuffs in lower courts, but then ascended to the U.S. Supreme Court, where it gained a unanimous favorable decision. This decision, written by the highly respected associate justice Oliver Wendell Holmes, stated that "music contributed to the profit-making ability of an establishment and, therefore, constituted a performance for profit, even if no special admission was charged."[5] The landmark case gave ASCAP all the legal clout it needed to move forward as the songwriter's best financial friend.

As ASCAP organized, resentment emerged from all the groups that now had to reach into their pockets for licensing fees: elegant restaurants with orchestras, vaudeville theaters with their insatiable need for new songs, and motion picture exhibitors using background music for silent films. It took the first ten years of ASCAP's existence to develop an effective national organization, as well as an equitable method for distribution of fees. While this was going on the playing field changed, and radio emerged to become the most voracious music user of all, forcing ASCAP to add the licensing of all stations to its responsibilities.

In 1931 ASCAP's income approached two million dollars: half from radio license fees; a third from motion picture fees; and the rest from dance halls, restaurants, hotels, parks, carnivals, circuses, and steamships.[6] When Taylor became a member of the board, he soon learned that the radio industry, with its ever-increasing advertising revenues, saw ASCAP as a monopoly. Broadcasters pestered the federal government to bring a suit against ASCAP, which the Department of Justice finally did in 1939. "If you have been an observer of current events during the past half a dozen years," Taylor wrote to members, "you could have enjoyed the grotesque spectacle of a national government, which grants copyrights, trying to destroy, via a monopoly suit, the only effective mechanism that copyright owners have devised for protecting those copyrights."[7] Nonetheless, as holder of all popular music rights in the country, ASCAP did seem to fit the definition of a monopoly. Still, as Taylor indicated, it was within the law.

As the 1930s came to an end, monopoly suits did not prevent ASCAP from announcing fee increases of 100 percent for all contracts up for renewal by 1941. From the society's perspective, since the expanding radio industry used more and more ASCAP music, the broadcasters should pay more. But the networks and the National Association of Broadcasters (NAB) were not sleeping. In 1939 they had established Broadcast Music Incorporated (BMI), an ASCAP-like organization with its own catalog of composers and publishers. BMI attracted new and younger composers with a payment method different than that of ASCAP. BMI's was based on the actual number of performances of their songs over radio. ASCAP instead had a complicated payment hierarchy providing unusually generous payments to the "old boys," including Taylor.

BMI had had a problem just getting started. ASCAP corralled the vast majority of composers, so whom could BMI attract to build its own catalog? Astutely, the managers started by seeking out the composers of cowboy, hillbilly, and "race" music, a group that ASCAP's membership turned its nose up at. BMI also enlarged its ranks by urging music publishers to leave ASCAP and come to them with their catalogs of songs. When the important publisher E. B. Marks agreed to such a transfer, BMI received fifteen thousand songs in one lump, a great help in building a significant catalog in a short time.

In early September 1940, at an NAB meeting in San Francisco, the radio industry looked ASCAP boldly in the eye and told the society to lower the proposed new license fees significantly. And if it didn't, station owners would remove all ASCAP songs from the air after January 1, 1941. Many in ASCAP scoffed, since they didn't believe that stations could subsist without the music of George Gershwin, Cole Porter, Irving Berlin, and all the other great songwriters in the ASCAP catalog. Lines had now been drawn in what became known as the radio war.

One of the first skirmishes of the war occurred at the Golden Gate International Exposition, on San Francisco's Treasure Island. This exposition was the West Coast's successful equivalent of the 1939–40 New York World's Fair, and, like it, ran for two seasons. On September 24, 1940, just five days before the end of the Treasure Island fair, ASCAP presented tens of thousands of fair goers with a full day of ASCAP music. This attempt at a show of strength began in the afternoon with symphonic music and followed with an evening of popular music. ASCAP wanted Taylor, who at the time was in Hollywood finishing work on *Fantasia*, to host the afternoon event. He found this a pleasant duty and flew up to San Francisco to spend the two-hour program listening to the works of five American symphonists, including his own *Circus Day*, performed by the San Francisco Symphony.

For the evening program, ASCAP's "power hitters" performed. In the words of W. C. Handy, it was "a program that was never before nor can ever again be duplicated this side of Kingdom Come."[8] A crowd of twenty-five thousand roared with delight as Gene Buck, then ASCAP's president, introduced a seemingly unending number of famous songwriters, all of whom played or sang (or both): Harold Arlen accompanied Judy Garland in "Over the Rainbow"; W. C. Handy played "St. Louis Blues" on his cornet; Hoagy Carmichael played and sang "Stardust"; Sigmund Romberg and Jerome Kern played some of their songs on the piano; George M. Cohan and Irving Berlin sang, with Berlin closing the evening in an emotional version of "God Bless America." The entire concert was recorded, but never broadcast. It was released commercially sixty years later.[9]

The next day an article in the *San Francisco Examiner* identified the undercurrent below the music: "ASCAP Brings Its Radio War Right to Enemy, Scores Victory of Varying Degree." But ASCAP's victory was short-lived, for its mightier-than-thou attitude did not faze the radio broadcasters; they simply left the contracts unsigned. And when listeners tuned in to hear music on January 1, 1941, they heard only BMI songs. ASCAP music was gone. Taylor was among those who couldn't believe that the public would put up with the songs of "second-rate" BMI composers. In conversations with friends, he said the initials BMI actually stood for "Bad Music Indefinitely."[10]

While ASCAP looked to the public to put pressure on radio stations, BMI representatives continued gathering composers for their catalog, and found a treasure trove in Latin American music. Soon Americans swung shoulders and hips to the rhythms of Brazilian sambas and Cuban rhumbas. It seemed the public didn't care whose songs they heard, or whether they were so old as to be in the public domain. Especially popular were the strains of Stephen Foster—a suitably ironic touch, since Foster had died in the charity ward of New York's Bellevue Hospital, reportedly with only "thirty-eight cents in coin and scrip" to his name.[11]

As ASCAP music vanished from radio, so did the major source of revenue for its members. When their income dropped, members became disgruntled, but calmer heads prevailed. By the end of 1941, new contracts had been signed without the increases originally demanded, and ASCAP music returned to all networks.

The tough year finally ended, and the ASCAP board wondered if Gene Buck, its president of twenty-one years, might not have served a bit too long. Buck had been the right-hand man of Florenz Ziegfeld and had written twenty editions of the *Follies;* he was the lyricist for many of the songs that accompanied elegantly costumed chorines as they descended the staircases in those opulent productions. A larger-than-life individual, Buck was the quintessential Broadway know-it-all with legions of friends. He entertained them in a massive Great Neck mansion, with a "cavernous living room," which his neighbor Ring Lardner referred to as "the Yale Bowl—with lamps."[12] Buck, with his connections, had been the perfect president for ASCAP after George Maxwell had set the society on its way.

However, during the radio war, in the eyes of many board members he became a bit too independent. *Variety,* ASCAP's unofficial chronicler, described the problem: "Intense publisher-director antagonism toward Buck [had] been accumulating since early 1941 when he undertook to treat with go-betweens in a U.S. Department of Justice situation without first consulting ASCAP's board of directors."[13]

Though the board determined it was time for a leadership change, it also recognized the perception in the music industry that ASCAP's popular music composers were generally a greedy lot. Since composers for the concert hall made far less money, a new president from that group would help temper criticism. Taylor was the obvious choice, with his longtime association with the group and the respect he had gained in the concert hall, in the opera house, on Broadway, and on radio. On April 23, 1942, the ASCAP board, with the necessary two-thirds vote, elected him president for the usual one-year term. Buck's dramatic ways would now be replaced with Taylor's quieter manner. The new president even agreed to serve without salary, quipping that his goal was "to get the presidency to the point where I will earn my salary."[14] Buck, on the other hand, was kept on as consultant at a salary of

$25,000 per year. Taylor's decision not to be paid was more pragmatic than generous, for he realized that 1942 would be a peak year of earnings, half of which still went to Mary Kennedy; added income would only be swallowed up in taxes.[15]

The First Three Presidential Years

One thing and one only headed Taylor's list of ASCAP tasks as he began his presidency: fences had to be mended both within the radio industry and with the U.S. Department of Justice. The federal agency actually had become annoyed with both sides in the radio battles. Meanwhile, many in Congress still did not believe lyricists and composers should maintain copyrights for two terms of twenty-eight years each. To help change these attitudes, Taylor and his public relations head, Richard Frohlich, as well as songwriter friends such as Irving Berlin often headed for Washington to talk to members of Congress about the function and value of ASCAP. The entertainment and drinks that followed at the Washington Press Club brought many a congressman into a more amicable relationship with the organization.[16]

Taylor also had some fence-mending to do within ASCAP itself. Gene Buck's supporters seldom disguised their annoyance at losing him as president. Especially vocal in this regard was Billy Rose, who, like Taylor, was a New Yorker of multiple talents. Unlike Taylor, he had parlayed his into financial success, first as a lyricist ("Me and My Shadow," "It's Only a Paper Moon"), then as a Broadway producer (Jumbo), and finally as a nightclub owner (Billy Rose's Diamond Horseshoe). Soon after Taylor was elected president, Rose invited him to address a meeting of his Songwriter's Protective Association.

"When speechmaking time rolled around," Taylor recalled years later, "Billy . . . had a few words to say concerning myself. They were to the effect that Buck had had a raw deal, and that while I was admittedly there with the quips, it remained to be seen whether a wisecracking highbrow could make a good president of ASCAP. I did my best to give an imitation of a man suddenly stone-deaf; just the same, it was hard to take."[17] Rose and many others soon found out that the new president possessed diplomatic ways to achieve what he wanted, and what he wanted was a unified ASCAP that better served its members. About six months later, at a general meeting chaired by Taylor, Billy Rose asked for the floor. In front of five hundred ASCAP members he publicly apologized to the president for making unfounded assumptions and criticisms.

In Taylor's first months as president, what needed healing most were the ill feelings of the radio broadcasters toward the society. With his innate sense of positive communication, Taylor convinced the board to invite representatives of the networks, and even the chairman of the Federal Communications Commission, to be the society's special guests at its annual dinner at the Hotel Astor. As *Variety* reported, "The bickering and acid exchange of personalities which used to mark the tail end of such events was absent. Instead, the assembly went nostalgic and reveled in old time writers playing and singing their old tunes." Before some seven hundred members and with the invited radio dignitaries on the dais with him, Deems urged the special guests to look at the ASCAP members and observe closely that "we are not equipped with horns and tails. . . . This is a sort of after-the-war dinner. It gives us an opportunity to bury our hatchets elsewhere than in each other's heads."[18]

As was often the case, Taylor's wit covered over some of his real intentions, which were revealed in a letter to his daughter: "As president, I invited most of the radio big shots—CBS, NBC, Mutual, et al.—and to everybody's astonishment, they all came and had a good time. Everyone hails it as a masterstroke of diplomacy. For your private ear may I say that I tried it for the fun of seeing how they would squirm out of it? So I'm very faintly disappointed."[19] The fact remains that probably no event during Taylor's six years as president had such positive ramifications as this dinner of *bons amis*.

By giving more attention to improving services to its members, Taylor's leadership helped define what *Variety* labeled "the new ASCAP."[20] Of special concern was a proposed change in the classification system by which members received their share of the license fees. The newer, younger members had long decried the ASCAP hierarchy. They hated the system that "would permit an Irving Berlin or a Hoagy Carmichael to draw a huge revenue in a year when they had not written a tune while some unknown—whose first hit may have made a fortune for the publisher—drew only a few hundred dollars."[21] Taylor himself had certainly profited from this approach, for he had gained the top rank. As a result, about one-quarter of his total annual income now came from ASCAP royalties.

In the fall of 1942, a committee presented a new payment system for member consideration. It looked to BMI's approach and introduced "frequency of performance" into the equation. For the new members this made sense, but it did not play well for the older members, many of whose songs were no longer popular. ASCAP's income had now topped six million dollars. In the unique vocabulary of *Variety*: "The boff 1944 take is largely due to ASCAP's ability this year to steer clear of drawn-out, expensive legal maneuvers."[22] The calming hand of Deems Taylor had helped bring some peace and quiet to ASCAP and had helped swell the pot of money to be distributed.

ASCAP provided solace of another kind to composers and lyricists. With the spirit of Stephen Foster hovering about, the society from its very beginnings had established a relief fund to be available to "a sick, infirm, needy or deserving member or his widow, infant children or indigent parent." The annual dues of the members provided the fund's monies.[23] To this day ASCAP, a private organization, does not reveal this side of its responsibilities, but those who are the recipients of such generosity often tell others. In this way it was known that with Taylor at its head, ASCAP provided for the health needs of the final years of the émigré composer Béla Bartók, as well as those of one of the great friends of American composers, Mrs. Edward MacDowell.

Béla Bartók arrived in the United States in 1940 from his native Hungary, fleeing from the German intruders. In his first two years here, he found support transcribing a collection of Serbo-Croatian folksongs on a Columbia University grant. Afterward, with little income and ill with leukemia, Bartók desperately needed medical help. As a noncitizen, he could not be a member of ASCAP. A prescient friend recommended that the family contact the society, with the result that "[a]fter approaching ASCAP, there was no need to seek any farther, for they instantly took up Bartók's case, assuming full responsibility."[24]

ASCAP's beneficence toward Bartók had a definite cheerleader in Taylor. As he had made clear in his Philharmonic talks, he knew the difficulties that European émigré composers faced in the United States. He had heard Bartók's music and shared with the Hungarian his great interest and joy in the folk music of many lands. To help Bartók, ASCAP arranged for him and his family to spend the summer of 1943 at a private sanitarium at Saranac Lake, in the Adirondack Mountains of northern New York State. Later ASCAP maintained a level of support for both medical and other living expenses, including two more summers at Saranac Lake, before Bartók died in 1945.

Taylor definitely took a hand in assuring that ASCAP provide for the health needs of Edward MacDowell's widow during her long years of illness. Taylor showed empathy for Mrs. MacDowell as early as 1928, when he wrote an editorial about her in *Musical America:* "For many years, Mrs. MacDowell has given her life to an unselfish project, the MacDowell Colony at Peterborough, where creative people of all branches meet, rest and work. . . . Those who have heard Mrs. MacDowell's lecture-recitals remember her bright enthusiasm and earnestness for this cause. Fighting always against ill health, she has always managed to earn enough through these to support the Colony from year to year."[25]

Early in the Taylor presidency, Mrs. MacDowell suffered a life-threatening illness, an event she recalled years later in a letter to her attorney: "I must refer once more to ASCAP and what it meant to me through those sixteen months when I was in a Los Angeles hospital with three private nurses for all those weeks. When I was taken so desperately ill . . . from an infection of the kidneys, nobody imagined that I would live long . . . but the moment [ASCAP] heard of my desperate condition Deems Taylor . . . telegraphed to Miss Richardson saying 'Leave nothing undone for Mrs. MacDowell's comfort and health.'" Marian MacDowell concluded her letter in good humor: "They didn't realize I was going to live so long!"[26]

Olin Downes, with the extensive network of insider contacts expected of a key *Times* music critic, wrote to Taylor in 1946: "I have just discovered that in Mrs. MacDowell's long illness you, through ASCAP, rendered the assistance which took care of her in this most serious emergency. . . . I think this is one more tribute to the work you do and the man you are, and also to the breadth of the assistance that ASCAP is giving to worthy musical causes."[27]

Pleased with Taylor's leadership, ASCAP returned him to office for what would be a total of six years. However, for the first three he continued to refuse a salary, so the board insisted that he accept several tokens of their appreciation. In 1944 he was presented with a rather large, flat package. Under the wrapping paper was a 1905 Claude Monet painting of water lilies—*Les Nymphéas*—then valued at $7,070. The following year the token consisted of Honoré Daumier's *Insurgent on the Barricade,* at a value of $12,625.[28] Taylor hung the water lilies in his Fifth Avenue apartment in such a way that the lakes in Central Park could look up and be inspired.

Taylor's Final Intermissions

In 1942, the year Taylor began his presidency of ASCAP, he also began the last year of New York Philharmonic intermission talks, with American-born conductors one of his subjects. He alerted listeners to the many he considered excellent, while American orchestras continued to place European-born conductors on their podiums. As an illustration of the difficulty facing good American conductors in mounting a podium, Taylor pointed out that "for the first time in seven years a native-born American has been conducting the New York Philharmonic in Carnegie Hall" (November 15, 1942). This was not Leonard Bernstein, but rather Taylor's old friend Howard Barlow. (It would be another year before Bernstein's famed "last-minute" debut in place of the ailing Bruno Walter.)

In the December 20, 1942, broadcast, Taylor followed up with an explanation: "American-born conductors find themselves with insufficient training and knowledge to compete with the thoroughly trained Europeans. . . . No matter how promising a young American conductor may appear, the members (both Board and performing) of an established orchestra are going to accept or reject him by comparison. . . . Most of the European conductors went through long and thorough training in European opera houses." A week later, in his tireless quest to bring attention to American musical talent, he continued by naming names: "I happen to know four native Americans whom I consider absolutely first-rate conductors . . . Howard Barlow, Frank Black, Edwin McArthur, and Alfred Wallenstein." As it would turn out, the next year Wallenstein would be the first American-born conductor to be appointed head of a major symphony: the Los Angeles Philharmonic.

But even apolitical statements brought political commentary. One listener saw fascism in Taylor's promotion: "Your broadcasts about American-born conductors and their chances and fate are more than strange. Are you advocating an American policy of chauvinism, which almost has a Nazi smell?" Taylor responded in a later program (January 10, 1943):

> Perhaps the question of nationality should never come up. As a matter of fact, I'd say that it shouldn't if the odds were even. But they're not. They're against the American. I don't blame the public for the prejudice that he encounters. . . . I believe that if the candidates for the conductorship of a typical American orchestra were each required to conduct a concert anonymously with a screen between himself and the audience, in more than a few cases the successful candidate would turn out to be an American.

Taylor, of course, was pointing out that talent should transcend nationality.

The world war wore on, and many letters to Taylor were from soldiers or sailors who wrote of their joy in listening to music on records or radio. Taylor hadn't told his listeners that fifty thousand copies of each of his books—*Of Men and Music* and *The Well-Tempered Listener*—had found their way to soldiers and sailors in paperback Armed Services Editions, a size just large enough to fit into the breast pocket of a uniform. After the war ended, he told a reporter about the impact of these books: "[They] brought me letters from soldiers in Bataan and Japan and all sorts of places. They never asked for anything; just expressed appreciation or went to the bat with me about something I had written. I recently received a letter from a German POW in Germany who asked my permission to translate [*Of Men and Music*] into German."[29]

But no letter from the war stirred Deems more than the one he received from Egypt in December 1942, written by Caleb Milne, a young ambulance corpsman in the African theater with the American Field Services. He remembered Taylor and "the Philharmonic concerts of happier days when the magic of music had enriched so many Sunday afternoons at home." Milne then described a time when he and other American volunteers drove their ambulances behind the advancing Eighth Army in Egypt: "We made many a trip to carry not only our own wounded troops but the hurt and dying of Italy and Germany to the near-by hospitals. . . . We lit cigarettes for all of them, padded pillows against the jolting cars and rendered what little comfort as was possible under these war-clouds." Early the previous November, one of Milne's passengers had been a severely wounded German. By the time the ambulance arrived at the field hospital, the soldier was dead. Milne then described what the soldier had left behind:

> From the dusty, torn knapsack of the soldier a book had fallen to the floor. In the shielded ray of my flashlight I could read the title in that curious German script—"An Introduction to Mozart." . . . I took the book back to the front with me that night, for written in the fly-leaf by my unknown passenger were two words, that like music and medicine, were above enmity. They were Goethe's last words— Mehr Licht—More light! And I am writing you of this incident not as a sentimental episode, but to send to the Philharmonic the gratitude and the hungry welcome that will always greet music wherever, and whenever, civilized men are listening.[30]

Taylor later described the letter as "one of the most deeply felt and profoundly moving communications that the war has yet inspired."[31] Months later came the news that Caleb Milne had joined the German soldier in death.

Taylor never read Milne's letter to his audience, but it may well have been on his mind when he bid farewell on April 11, 1943:

> This is the last time that you and I shall meet this season. . . . Millions of young Americans in uniform are eagerly listening to music in any way they can get it—by radio, in concert, on records. And they don't seem to care who wrote it. I haven't heard "enemy music" mentioned for months. Perhaps we have all come to realize that it isn't the name on the cover that counts. It's the music that matters. Well, the train is pulling out. I'm glad to have known you. Thank you for your letters. May we meet again. Good-bye.

Between the lines Taylor was bidding a permanent adieu, for he knew that CBS had reined in the U.S. Rubber Company as sponsor for next season's Philharmonic broadcasts. Musical commentary and the Philharmonic were now to part company. Never again did a national broadcast regularly offer the insights and educational flavor that Taylor provided to help the invisible audience become comfortable with music through the ages. Five years

later, Taylor's voice reappeared for one season during Philharmonic intermissions, but the words he spoke were not his: they were those of Standard
Oil of New Jersey.

Taylor's Philharmonic intermission talks were a unique part of radio's
golden age. He and Walter Damrosch could take credit for educating the
public about the fine points and joys of concert music. Damrosch's role was
that of music education in the schools; Taylor's had a broader sweep. As the
musical encyclopedist David Mason Greene stated forty years later: "A generation of American music lovers owes . . . its introduction to the art to his
[Taylor's] genial, informal, laid-back radio commentaries."[32]

Over the Radio Hill

During his last year of intermission broadcasts, Taylor reached his peak as a
featured radio personality. His earnings for 1942 came to $63,000, the sec-
ond highest annual income he ever made. In 1943 he remained the host on
the *Prudential Family Hour,* at $1,000 per broadcast, and maintained the right
to prepare his own script for introductions. Sometimes he took advantage of
this; he arranged to have two portions of the *Ramuntcho* ballet music played
on successive programs. Since the program prided itself on following the
wishes of the listeners, he introduced the second part in a folksy way: "You
may remember that last week I announced that if you liked the first part of
the ballet, we'd play the second part today. Well, the returns aren't all in, but
my mother and my sister said they liked it, and a lady in Oklahoma wrote in
to say that she didn't. So I'm happy to announce that by a popular vote of two
to one, you have elected to hear the rest of the music."[33] It was typical Taylor
patter, but it got some of his music on the air.

Meanwhile, advertising agencies continued to expand their influence
over radio programs, which included control of the script. This did not sit
well with Taylor. He had always demanded to write his own material. "My
radio horizon seems a bit clouded at the moment," he wrote to his daughter
during his second year with *Prudential*. "Mr. Craig, the new radio head of
Benton and Bowles, is talking of sending me to the showers after November
21, and Gladys [Swarthout] is threatening to walk out of the program if I'm
fired."[34] Indeed, Taylor did receive his pink slip in November, though
Swarthout remained for the rest of the season.

Nonetheless, Taylor's name recognition among radio folk remained
high, and in December 1943, a month later, he signed on as the host for *Radio
Hall of Fame,* the most extravagant variety show radio ever broadcast. Sponsored by Philco, a company then synonymous with excellence in radio manu-

facturing, the show's package of comedy, music, and drama cost $50,000 in its premiere performance alone. According to the *Times,* this was "probably a record for a sixty-minute commercial presentation."[35]

Billed as "a listener's digest of the entertainment world," the first show featured Paul Whiteman's orchestra; Bob Hope in a monologue from Hollywood; the inimitable Jimmy Durante and his unique humor ("I had an uncle who played two instruments at the same time. With the left side of his mouth he played 'Life is just a bowl of cherries'; with the right side of his mouth he played 'Don't sit under the apple tree'; and with the middle of his mouth he blew out the seeds"); songs by Hildegarde, the "French chanteuse" from Milwaukee; a report from the war front by Quentin Reynolds; and the final scene from Moss Hart's *Winged Victory,* presented by two unknown actors, Lee J. Cobb and Edmund O'Brien. For Taylor's part, he received $1,000 per broadcast, but the script was written for him.

Philco maintained its costly all-star approach every week. Though Taylor found the salary very nice, what concerned him most was his loss of control of the words that came out of his mouth. "I've finally persuaded them to let me at least rewrite the stuff I'm supposed to say," he wrote to Joan. "They can't quite seem to get it through their heads that this 'easy, conversational style' that they go on about is as much a matter of the writing as of the delivery."[36] The battle with the scriptwriters continued until the untimely demise of the *Radio Hall of Fame* six months later. It is said that the stars in the heavens glow brightest before they burn out; Philco's extravagant program was such a star in the world of the radio variety shows, intensely luminous as its genre was dying out for lack of listener interest.

Taylor, no longer having a weekly program of any sort, kept his voice before the public in special ways, including memorial broadcasts for significant musical figures. He had done this for John Philip Sousa at his death in 1932, and at the one-year anniversary of Gershwin's death in 1938. Deems Taylor's ability to speak simply and eloquently was evidenced in his tribute to Jerome Kern on the very evening of Kern's death. He considered Kern one of the greatest songwriters ever born and wanted his memorial words to make that clear. At the end of a program featuring Kern's songs, Taylor spoke while the orchestra softly played his beautiful "The Touch of Your Hand":

> You will hear his music played for many and many a year. Think sometimes of the man who created this, who created it for your enjoyment and refreshment, and sometimes consolation. He brought us one of the rarest of gifts—happiness. . . . You know, in a way it's foolish to think of death in connection with the composer of *Very*

Good Eddie, The Cat and the Fiddle, Music in the Air, Showboat, and so many others, for as long as his music lives, he will live. And so, long life to you, Jerry, old friend. Good night.[37]

Sad events weren't the only occasions for Taylor's appearances on radio. In fact, he was welcomed as a guest by most of the comedians, including Fred Allen and radio's favorite husband and wife, George Burns and Gracie Allen. In one show with Fred Allen, the comedian asked Taylor's help in writing a sequel to the then current Broadway sensation *Oklahoma!* Allen's musical was called "South Dakota." As Taylor listened to the songs, he noticed that the melodies sounded a bit too much like those of Rodgers and Hammerstein, so he donned his hat as ASCAP president and humorously deflated Allen's alleged hopes for Broadway glory.

Taylor even appeared on *It Pays to Be Ignorant,* the often hilarious spoof of quiz shows such as *Information, Please.* During the program, questions were answered by a permanent panel of "three nitwits who made up the 'board of experts' [and] spent most of the time trying to figure out what the questions were."[38] Famous guests asked such questions as "Who came first, Henry the Eighth or Henry the First?" This led only to rambling monologues and personal attacks on the guest for attempting to trick them. During Taylor's visit, a question about the musical scale led to a massive misunderstanding:

> *Taylor:* The first note of the scale is do, the second is re, and the third is mi.
> *"Expert":* You mean the third note is you?
> *Taylor:* The third note is not you, it's mi.[39]

The confusion took five minutes to straighten out.

One of the first programs on which he appeared was the very popular *Duffy's Tavern,* nine months after completing his Philharmonic job and while in the midst of his *Philco Hall of Fame* work. The writers, knowing that Taylor had been supplanted on the New York Philharmonic broadcasts, worked that into the show's comedy. The program began, as always, with Archie, the tavern manager, receiving a phone call from Duffy, the ever-absent owner: "Hello—Duffy's, where the elite meet to eat, Archie the Manager speaking, Duffy ain't here—Oh, hello Duffy. Tonight?—Deems Taylor—Deems, Deems. No, Duffy, you don't say what are they, you say who is he? Yeah, it's different from Yonkers. He's a guy used to be in Carnegie's Hall—A guy that talks about music—yah—just talks. Sure, for that he gets paid. They have to pay him, otherwise he wouldn't stop talkin'." Later, Archie's helper Eddie alerts him to a guest.

Eddie: Mister Archie, there's a man over there complaining.
Archie: Why is he complaining?
Eddie: Cause we ain't got no *Peter Ibbetson* records in the juke box.
Archie: Who else could it be but Deems Taylor! [Applause]
Archie: Well Deems, it's good to see you again. Are you still working at the Philharmonica?
Deems: No, I'm now on the Philco Radio Hall of Fame.
Archie: O, no more Philharmonica huh? When'd they can you?
Deems: I wasn't canned Archie; the engagement was terminated by mutual consent.
Archie: Are they still paying ya?
Deems: No.
Archie: Don't let 'em kid you, Deems; you was canned. Boy the way you kick around—Carnegie's Hall, Hall of Fame—always in a hall.
Deems: Well you know me Arch, hall or nothing at all.
Archie: Hmmm. Same old corny Deems.[40]

Perhaps at times he was corny, but it was Taylor's wit and literary talents that had carried him through a decade of broadcasting to become one of the most recognized voices on radio. He had successfully straddled the world of sustaining programs and commercially sponsored ones, but by the mid-1940s, little remained in radio without sponsors. Along with them came the advertising agencies and their scriptwriters. Taylor had been "canned" not by the wishes of the public, but by the legitimate desire of commercial networks to increase their profits. But not far down the road was television and the end of the golden age of radio.

17. Taylor as Author, Father, and Composer, 1942–1945 (Part 2)

Pictorial History of the Movies: A First

During his first three years as ASCAP president, Taylor's radio commitments slowed down and the presidency speeded up, but he still found time to be an author. After two successful books of musical essays, Taylor turned to a unique undertaking. His agent, George Bye, had become aware of "one of the finest collections of photographs of motion pictures from the earliest days to the present that have ever been assembled." He explained his idea: "Each picture has a lot of documentation. What is wanted is a piquant writer like your charming self to take these captions and rewrite them—and organize the pictures and take credit as editor. . . . If I got a pretty hefty publishing advance and good royalty terms do you think you might be interested?"[1] He found the idea fascinating, terms were arranged, and in 1943 Deems Taylor emerged as a movie historian with *A Pictorial History of the Movies,* a book that went into six printings.[2] It had particular influence among the young.

The lives of at least two people—the movie director Martin Scorsese and Richard Lamparski, the author of the series *Whatever Became Of*—were changed by Taylor's book. Scorsese explained how he came under its spell: "When as a small boy I first fell in love with the movies I discovered a book by Deems Taylor entitled *A Pictorial History of the Movies* at our local branch of the New York Public Library. It was the only film book that I knew about, and I borrowed it time and time again. . . . It was the first course in my film education."[3] In a documentary about his film world, Scorsese spoke again of

Taylor's book, which "cast a spell on me 'cause back then I hadn't seen many of the films shown in the book, so all I had at my disposal to experience these films were these black-and-white stills. I'd fantasize about them and they would play into my dreams."[4]

Richard Lamparski as a teenager discovered *A Pictorial History of the Movies* on the shelves of Grosse Point Park Library, in Michigan, and succumbed to the glory, glamour, and mystery he found in the photographs. Forbidden to bring books into his home by his "Maryland Irish" mother, a "professional Catholic," Lamparski visited the library regularly. His questioning mind concentrated on the unusual, such as one photo from the epic film *The Birth of a Nation,* in which a soldier gazed longingly at Lillian Gish. In the caption, Taylor wrote that the director, D. W. Griffith, had "ordered his assistants to discover the man's name and address . . . [but] he melted into the horde of Hollywood extras and was never heard of again." Young Lamparski wondered what did happen to the extra. Other photos raised similar questions; it was the "absolute beginning" to his very popular series of books about Hollywood's forgotten people, *Whatever Became Of,* a series that ran to eleven editions.[5]

In the 1940s Taylor and his daughter began a deeper, more satisfying relationship. He admitted to Joan that he hadn't wanted to be a father, and that she had resulted from "an ironic twist of fate and his own weakness," but he stressed that he had "fallen in love" with her after seeing her for the first time.[6] By 1942, owing to a peregrinating mother, Joan had attended eight different schools, in such far-flung spots as Peking, Paris, and Ellsworth, Maine, as well as New York. Now in her high school years, she was settled into St. Timothy's in Catonsville, Maryland, a strict boarding school where parents were permitted visits only on specified weekends. Mary Kennedy was traveling and taking courses at Radcliffe College during those years, so it was Joan's father who came to visit and take Joan and her friends out to lunch and tea.

Little by little Joan began to feel more comfortable with her father, as the layers of her mother's control peeled away. Certainly the two weeks together with him in Hollywood during the making of *Fantasia* had helped, as did another rare two-week stay with him in New York during her last Christmas vacation from St. Timothy's. Joan was supposed to remain only briefly in Manhattan on her way to spending Christmas with her mother in Cambridge, Massachusetts, but once settled into Deems's apartment, she wanted to stay a few extra days to attend Manhattan parties with her friends. "Stay with Deems," a miffed Mary urged. "It will be my Christmas present to you."

Joan asked her father what to do. "Call her bluff and stay with me," he said, and she did live with him for two weeks and did not go to Cambridge, much to Mary's annoyance. When she returned to St. Timothy's, Joan ended up in the infirmary. "I suppose I ought to feel very guilty about having sent you to bed for a week," Deems wrote to his daughter, "but I can't seem to manage it. Those two weeks with you were among the best times I've ever had, and if they stretch you on a bed of pain . . . I can bear it."[7]

The bright and cheerful Joan appealed greatly to her father, and they established an easy flow of letters during her Maryland years. Though "Dearest" was his typical salutation to her, he began one letter: "Best of off-springs—to date." When he wrote to indicate pleasure with her grades, he also revealed something of the difficulties he had had with his own parents: "As one who has considerable difficulty in balancing a check book, we note with awe your 86 in algebra and 94 in geometry. The proper parental attitude . . . is to inquire testily why you failed to get 100 in all subjects; but remembering the pain in the neck that such an attitude caused us in our own adolescent years, we refrain."[8] The father-daughter relationship now was firm.

The Composition Juices Flow Again

After completing *Ramuntcho* in 1937, Taylor no longer seemed to have the self-discipline and inner spark of a composer. Mary Kennedy's support and encouragement had disappeared; in fact, his life now seemed to revolve around producing sufficient money to assure his daughter's education, while maintaining his own social commitments. He needed a prod to get him to compose music; radio work and writing books—his current means to financial security—had almost completely taken over his life.

If Taylor had an Achilles heel, it would have been his fondness for the good life. Once he turned to radio with its financial rewards, he no longer grew as a composer. In 1940 he received a letter from David Strauss, a writer and opera lover, who had seen nine performances of *Peter Ibbetson* at the Metropolitan and berated Taylor for not continuing to compose operas. "Look at Wagner," wrote Strauss. "At a time in his life when money was a grave need, he was able to turn his thoughts to such a long and difficult task as the Ring, knowing it meant divorcing himself from public attention for a number of years. Why not tell CBS to get someone else, Mr. Taylor?"[9] Though Taylor considered himself a composer first and foremost, he simply could not do what Strauss suggested. Twenty years earlier he had written to Mary Kennedy that "Art doesn't tolerate bigamy,"[10] and now he had proven the truth of his own words.

In fact, from 1937 to 1942 he composed only three pieces: the aforementioned "Job" for Norman Corwin, music for a *Cavalcade of America* program, and *Processional,* composed for the first-ever public ceremony of the National Institute of Arts and Letters.[11] When Howard Barlow and the Baltimore Symphony had given the first public performance of *Processional* in 1941, the composer had been present. The words of one reviewer indicated more about how people felt about Taylor than about the composition: "The composer was given a rousing reception, both in the official box, and on the stage, where he eventually emerged—a warmth enhanced by his popularity as a radio commentator."[12]

In 1942 two people jolted Taylor into a return to modest composing efforts. The first was Eugene Goossens, the British-born conductor of the Cincinnati Symphony and an adventurous programmer fascinated with the form of fanfares. With the war raging, Goossens wrote to Taylor and a number of mostly American composers, requesting that they compose patriotic fanfares for the symphony's 1942–43 season. The subject could be either an Allied country or a specific group participating in the war. The idea excited Taylor, especially when he learned that his was to honor Russia. He remembered a particular Russian folksong, "Dubinushka," from the years when he had worked with Kurt Schindler on translations. The song had become the anthem for the first Russian Revolution, of 1905–6, such that czarist troops were commanded to arrest anyone heard singing it. Taylor decided to compose his fanfare around "Dubinushka," explaining his thinking in the program notes for his "Fanfare for Russia": "[It] reflects—to me at least—something of the primitive toughness of the Russian fibre, the thing that has enabled them to put on the magnificent show they staged outside of Moscow and—now—Stalingrad." Goossens played Taylor's fanfare in October, the second in a sequence of eighteen.[13] The following March, Goossens premiered the one that has since echoed through more concert halls than any other: Aaron Copland's "Fanfare for the Common Man."

"Fanfare for Russia" proved to be Taylor's warm-up for a larger-scale work that was requested by Howard Barlow, long an admirer of Taylor's music. In August 1942 a euphoric Barlow contacted the composer, for he had been offered a two-week stint in November as guest conductor of the New York Philharmonic. Since the first day of CBS, Barlow had been the conductor of the network's symphony orchestra, but there had been few opportunities to conduct "big league" orchestras. Now he was to be one of eight guest conductors of the Philharmonic—in fact, the only American—and from these the board would choose a successor to the departing John Barbirolli. Among the others were Bruno Walter, Fritz Reiner, and Artur Rodzinski. Knowing the reluctance of orchestra boards to hire American-born conductors, Barlow held little hope of being selected; nevertheless, he wanted to provide something special for the first week of his concerts.

Barlow loved Taylor's *Through the Looking Glass.* Not only had he conducted it with the ill-fated American-National Orchestra, but also in 1938 with the Columbia Symphony Orchestra he had made the first recording ever of the suite. Now Barlow requested something of similar flavor, which provided the opportunity for another fantasy to stir Taylor's blood. This time he turned to a Dr. Seuss story, *And to Think That I Saw It on Mulberry Street,* composing a theme and variations entitled *Marco Takes a Walk.*

Marco is an overimaginative little boy who regales his father with embellished stories based on a simple observation, "a horse and wagon on Mulberry Street." Taylor described the little boy's elaborations: "[Marco] decides to make the story better by saying that a zebra was drawing the cart. No, he'll make it a chariot—no, a reindeer, pulling a sled—no, better yet, an elephant, a blue one. Still better, there will be a Rajah riding the elephant, and the steed will be drawing, not a sled, but a bandwagon, with a big brass band aboard."[14] He dedicated *Marco Takes a Walk* to Joan.

This charming work's theme, with the horse's clip-clops provided by Chinese woodblocks, is followed by six variations: (1) a zebra pulling the cart (muted violins in glissando "stripe" effects); (2) a charioteer driver (scherzo-like); (3) the zebra replaced by a reindeer (xylophone "hoofs"); (4) a sleigh and an elephant (brassy heaviness); (5) a rajah on an elephant's throne (Oriental sounds); (6) a brass band, followed by a return to the "plain horse and wagon on Mulberry Street." Barlow's Carnegie Hall premiere performances included a Sunday Philharmonic broadcast, during which Taylor told the listeners that Barlow "telephoned me last August, demanding it, and hounded me so . . . that I had to finish it, if only to shut him up."[15]

Noel Straus, the *Times's* second-string reviewer, covered the November 14, 1942, premiere: "Some of the music is saccharine, but all of it is humorous, imaginative and skillful in an unpretentious way, if none of it is particularly original." After this dollop of snideness, the reviewer admitted that the work "definitely appealed to the large audience, judging from the large hand it received, which brought bows from the composer who was in one of the boxes."[16]

Four months later, John Barbirolli returned to guest-conduct the Philharmonic and programmed *Marco Takes a Walk.* This time Olin Downes reviewed the concert and praised Taylor for the sentiment and whimsical quality of the music, reminding his readers that the little boy on Mulberry Street had within him the quality of a Don Quixote, "great in his visions, pathetic in his resignation before reality."[17] Both Barlow and Barbirolli found *Marco* a

crowd pleaser. Barbirolli took *Marco* to Canada and England for several concerts, and Barlow conducted it with both the Chicago Symphony and the Baltimore Symphony. Taylor attended the Baltimore concert, where something
special happened. "I wish that you could have heard the Baltimore Orchestra
last week," he wrote to Joan. "Barlow conducted 'Marco Takes a Walk,' and
had to play it twice. Nice, huh?"[18]

The success of the Dr. Seuss–inspired work made Taylor think that Walt
Disney might find *Marco Takes a Walk* intriguing as the basis for an animated
film. He sent him a copy of the off-the-air recording made of Barlow's
Sunday broadcast, but it proved to be a dead end. "I have your records of
'Marco Takes a Walk,'" Disney responded, "and liked them very much although I do not see how I could use them."[19] Disney's response is perplexing,
since the Marco story was exactly the type of fantasy with which his animators could have soared, but perhaps it was simply that Disney didn't want to
pay Dr. Seuss for the rights. *Marco Takes a Walk* was never commercially recorded and has never taken its rightful place in children's concerts. This is
sad, for there are few works in the symphonic repertoire so capable of enliv-
ening a child's imagination.

The following year, the Philharmonic offered Barlow another guest appearance. By then the orchestra board had chosen Artur Rodzinski as its permanent conductor, which led the realistic yet disappointed Barlow to tell his
nephew: "Too bad my name isn't Barlowski."[20] With the success of *Marco
Takes a Walk,* Barlow again asked Taylor for a short work for his next Philharmonic concert, even offering the composer the honor of conducting the first
performance himself.

Since this concert was to take place just before Christmas, Taylor chose
to write a concert overture, featuring a tune that had a Yuletide connection.
In his operas he had used folksongs from other countries, so now he decided
that for the overture, he would use an American folksong as the central
theme. He settled on "I Wonder as I Wander," a song from the mountains of
the South. He dedicated the work to Giuliana Taberna.

Two days before Christmas, Taylor conducted the Philharmonic in his
"Christmas Overture." Olin Downes reviewed the short work, noting the
composer's emphasis on the folksong's simple melody. First the piece used
the "rich but pastoral tone" of the English horn, then ended with the theme
in a brass chorale, "all in the Christmas mood." In a puzzling approach to programming, Barlow also premiered another holiday-related composition,
"Christmas Festival Overture," by the Russian-born violinist-composer
Nicolai Berezowsky. Downes found Berezowsky's use of Ukrainian folksong
themes more appealing than Taylor's use of "I Wonder as I Wander."[21]

The competition in Christmas overtures had an accidental winner when, after its premiere, Taylor withdrew his work from further performances. His reason could not have been more embarrassing to someone who was president of·ASCAP: he had forgotten to check whether "I Wonder as I Wander" might be copyrighted. And it was. He learned of his mistake from the copyright owner, John Jacob Niles, a well-known compiler and troubadour singer of American folksongs.

Niles had developed it in 1933 after hearing a few lines of verse and a fragment of melody sung by the daughter of revivalists in Murphy, North Carolina. He had taken out the copyright on "I Wonder as I Wander" and was willing to give Taylor permission to use the melody, but the composer decided that his fee was too high. He shelved his composition permanently.

It is ironic that Taylor had this experience the first time he chose an American rather than a European folksong to incorporate into a composition. His contemporaries—Aaron Copland, Virgil Thomson, and Roy Harris—established a good deal of their composing fame by utilizing American folksongs or hymns in their creations. This provided them à more homey identification as American composers than it did Taylor, who couldn't seem to disengage himself from the European romantic traditions.

At about the same time, Alfred Wallenstein came to Taylor with a request for a short new work he could perform with the Los Angeles Philharmonic. Wallenstein knew Taylor's music, for he had conducted an abbreviated version of *The King's Henchman* as well as the *The Highwayman* when he had headed the Mutual network's New York studio orchestra. Taylor agreed to the commission, and after fitful jabs at composing something, he wrote Joan and expressed his complete frustration: "I've just had to write to Alfred Wallenstein to tell him that I can't finish the new piece he asked for in time. . . . I don't know just what happened. . . . Maybe I sat up too many nights working on the Christmas Overture. In any case, I started the thing and then got completely and hopelessly stuck—hated what I had written . . . firmly convinced that I never was a composer and never will be."[22]

A week later, he wrote his daughter about an insight he had had, which to others already was obvious: "Whenever I write music that is better than pretty good, it always turns out either to have a definite program or to be for the theatre. That's my racket, and I must stick to it."[23] Wallenstein premiered Taylor's "Elegy for Orchestra" almost a year after that minor epiphany. It was a short orchestral threnody for an Egyptian princess who died at age twelve. Taylor again dedicated the work to Giuliana Taberna, perhaps because their relationship of a few years was now approaching rigor mortis. The reviewer of the *Los Angeles Times* quickly dispatched "Elegy for Orchestra" as "a slight bit of sentimental romanticism, charming to hear but definitely old-hat and within the possibilities of any arranger on a Hollywood lot."[24]

A Shadow from the Past: Jane Anderson

In April 1943, during Taylor's relatively modest creative surge, he received a call from the Federal Bureau of Investigation. The FBI needed him to listen to some recordings of German shortwave broadcasts, full of anti-American propaganda. In so doing, he was forced to relive a part of his past that he preferred to forget; they believed one of the voices was that of Jane Anderson, his first wife, and wanted his opinion about their hunch. That Jane's shadow would again fall across his path was probably no surprise to Taylor, for a year earlier *Time* had pinpointed her as "Lady Haw-Haw,"[25] the female version of "Lord Haw-Haw," the American-born William Joyce, then broadcasting pro-Nazi propaganda to England from Germany. Taylor listened to three recordings but could not absolutely identify the voice as that of his former wife: "Inasmuch as I have neither seen Jane Anderson, nor spoken to her since 1928, and also allowing for the distortion of the voice that is almost inevitable in short-wave transmission, I cannot conscientiously make a positive identification. However, I feel justified in saying that there is a very strong probability that the voice recorded on record number eleven is that of Jane Anderson."[26] By July a grand jury in the District of Columbia had reviewed evidence and indicted Jane for treasonous activities, along with seven other American citizens.

Jane's road to near-treason had started in Spain in 1934, when she had married the Marqués Eduardo Alvarez de Cienfuegos, whose family was said to be well connected to Spanish royalty. With the outbreak of the Spanish Civil War, Jane, now a Catholic, sided with General Francisco Franco's nationalist armies and once again became a journalist, reporting on the war for the London newspapers of Lord Northcliffe. Her stirring articles of "the atrocities of the anti-Franco Loyalist troops—of seeing defenseless prisoners brutally slaughtered . . . and of unspeakable excesses against the church," hardly sat well with the Loyalist government, which captured and imprisoned her.[27] A trial led to a verdict of treason, and execution appeared imminent. After American intervention, the Spanish government released Jane "on condition that she leave the country immediately."[28] Returning to the United States, she began several years of public speaking, particularly to Catholic groups. Obsessed with her belief that communism was sweeping the world, she told her audiences that it was the "Reds," not the Fascists, that the country should fear.[29]

In 1939, with the Spanish Civil War over and Franco's Fascist government in power, Jane visited Spain and ultimately entered the world of propaganda broadcasting from Berlin.[30] After World War II, she and her husband were apprehended in Innsbruck, Austria, in 1947. The Spanish government "engineered their release . . . [while] the Justice Department publicly declined to prosecute."[31] Jane was, after all, a Spanish citizen by marriage, and the U.S. government was reluctant to annoy the Franco regime. In 1948 Jane and the marqués appear to have returned to Spain, and then disappeared forever. Taylor never learned more about the woman who had been his first wife.

Bittersweet Elements of Life

Taylor maintained his relationship with Giuliana Taberna from 1940 to 1945. More often than not they found their enjoyment at the Stork Club, which originally had been a speakeasy during Prohibition days. Sherman Billingsley, the owner and himself a former bootlegger, had transformed it into the place to be seen in New York. There Walter Winchell, Gotham's top radio tattler, held court and passed along information of all the comings and goings of the "beautiful people" who frequented the popular site: the Duke and Duchess of Windsor; every Hollywood star of importance; and authors such as Ernest Hemingway, who in machismo style "had grandiosely tried to pay his bar bill . . . with a $100,000 royalty check he had gotten for the screen rights to *For Whom the Bell Tolls*."[32] Giuliana, with her eyes on celebrities, thrived in this ambiance; Taylor also had found fame enjoyable and liked having people stop by his table to say hello.

But there was a sad side to Taylor's life at this point: the loss of friends. In November 1944 Mac the Singing Policeman died. Taylor hadn't seen much of him after the Stamford house had been renovated, so he was stunned to read in the *Times* of his friend's death. What Taylor appreciated in Mac was the effervescent, heart-on-your-sleeve man that he himself could never be. Mac had not married and spent most of his life either in hotels or as a guest in the home of a friend. According to Heywood Broun's son Woodie, who had grown up with Mac always around the house, the genial singer "had studied the art of 'guesting' with the painstaking care that other artists give to the violin. . . . He could make himself indispensable within an hour of his unexpected arrival at your house."[33]

Though Taylor had tried to help Mac improve his naturally beautiful voice, the baritone had no interest in a singing career. Instead, the barrel-chested ex-policeman found himself playing the quintessential Irish cop in many Broadway plays. After joining New York's key theatrical group, the Player's Club, he established a close bond with James Cagney, who insisted on taking him to Hollywood and featuring him as an Irish politician or a cop in practically every Cagney movie.

Mac collapsed and died in Boston's South Station while supervising the transport of Cagney's racehorses from the star's ranch on Martha's Vineyard back to Los Angeles.[34] The next day Taylor sent a check for fifteen dollars to the New York Knights of Columbus in Mac's memory. The amount may seem small, but it was a rarity for Taylor to contribute to any charity, so the money did come from the heart.

Then forty-two-year-old Colette d'Arville died a month later, at her Park Avenue apartment "after a long illness."[35] One can only guess what went through Taylor's mind at that time, because his relationship with her remains an enigma. Among his recollections must have been the fact that Colette had been the spur to his writing *Ramuntcho,* an opera of which he remained proud, even though many critics had not been kind. Nonetheless, if he contrasted his friendship with Mac to that with Colette, he would have recognized that Mac's life had been an open book in friendship, while Colette's had been more of a locked diary.

The deaths of Mac and Colette emphasized for Taylor the psychological pain of approaching sixty years of age. Though Giuliana was young and beautiful, he found her less and less satisfying intellectually. Perhaps Giuliana sensed that something was wrong, because she presented him with something very special for his fifty-ninth birthday: a scrapbook of greetings and photos from some one hundred of his friends, including Leopold Stokowski, Richard Rodgers, Frederic March, Lillian Gish, Norman Corwin, and Lawrence Tibbett. Gathering and assembling the messages had taken Giuliana months. On the first page of the impressive achievement she printed a reflective thought in Italian, a saying by Saint Francis of Assisi: *Tanto é il bene che aspetto; ch'ogni pena m'é diletto,* So great is the good I await, that every pain I count a delight.

Giuliana chose the quotation all too correctly, for pain would soon outweigh the good in her life with Taylor. He needed a woman with talent and youthful artistry to inspire him; Giuliana was no longer that woman. For this man whose love of fantasy had led him from the *Looking Glass* to *Jurgen* to *Circus Day* to *Peter Ibbetson,* it would be the fiction of the circus world and "Alice" that would bring him his next special woman.

18. More Beginnings and Endings, 1945–1951

The Third Mrs. Taylor: Lucille Watson-Little

When Robert Ringling contacted Deems Taylor early in 1945, he hardly knew he was setting the scene for the composer's third marriage. Ringling now headed the Ringling Brothers and Barnum and Bailey Circus and was at the winter quarters in Sarasota, Florida, preparing the 1945 season. As Ringling met with his staff, one unspoken thought was constantly in their minds: the horror of the July 6, 1944, performance in Hartford, Connecticut. The circus tent had erupted into a catastrophic fire that killed 168 people, mainly children. Subsequent lawsuits almost brought the most famous circus in the United States to financial collapse,[1] but Ringling was determined to produce as grand a show as he could muster for the new season, in the great tradition of "the show must go on." He concentrated especially on the "spec" (spectacle), the colorful pageant that had always opened the performance but was now to precede the intermission.

Ringling had chosen "Alice in Circus Wonderland" as the spec's theme for the new production. To make this one extra special, Ringling's staff applied new gilt to grand old circus bandwagons that would accompany the Alice characters, the elephants, clowns, and bareback riders as they paraded around before the applauding audience. The spec, as stated by a literarily nimble public relations man, would be "A Peerless Pantomimic Parade through the Piquant Periphery of Childhood's Happy Memories . . . A Glittering Pageant Embellished by the Reappearance of Priceless Circus Wagons Restored to Former Grandeur."[2]

The spec also needed special music performed by the circus band, and it was for this reason that Robert Ringling, who once had sung with the Chicago Opera as a baritone, contacted Taylor. Very likely he had met Taylor during his operatic years, and he certainly knew of the successful *Through the Looking Glass* suite.

Taylor, then still ASCAP president, hardly hesitated before accepting Ringling's invitation to go to Florida. First of all, with income from his radio appearances slackening, the circus contract for four thousand dollars would help keep the checkbook balanced. Second, as he saw the approach of his sixtieth birthday, a distinct sign of mortality, a visit to the land where Ponce de Leon had searched for the fountain of youth seemed most appropriate. It also provided an opportunity to focus on the unusual sideline he had once revealed to an interviewer who asked about his hobbies: "I have one hobby. I look under beds for beautiful blondes."[3] In Florida he wouldn't have to look under a bed, for blonde-haired Lucille Watson-Little, nearly forty years his junior, was sitting on a chair waiting for him in Sarasota.

Lucille was a talented designer who had learned her trade with the noted Broadway designer Howard Bay. Her friend Billy Livingston, then one of the top U.S. designers, had been signed by Ringling to develop the spec costumes for 1945, but while in Sarasota, Livingston had fallen seriously ill. Lucille received an urgent call to take the next train to Florida and complete the costuming designs, particularly the fabric-covered wings that flip-flopped as the elephants walked, giving the illusion that they were gigantic butterflies.[4]

The blonde, blue-eyed Lucille arrived before Taylor and joined the artistic staff in listening to a pompous Robert Ringling pontificate about the "famous" Mr. Taylor, whom he expected them to treat with "extreme respect and deference." Lucille had often heard Taylor on the radio, particularly on *Information, Please*. "So the Deems Taylor I appreciated was not the 'stuffy version' pushed down our throats," she later recalled. "When Deems arrived at the round luncheon table, we were introduced to him [by Ringling], one by one, which started with 'You know, of course, Deems Taylor,' followed by our names and qualifications. When it was my turn, I heard myself saying, 'No, I don't know Deems Taylor. What does he do?' Robert Ringling turned into a huge bowl of Jello, red with indignation, while Deems and myself roared with laughter. . . . Deems and I made 'sparkles' right away."[5] The emotionally unexpected had happened once again to Taylor.

After finishing the musical arrangements for Ringling, Taylor returned to New York looking forward to more meetings with his new girlfriend. A few weeks later the circus arrived and, as usual, started its national tour at Madison Square Garden. With the war still on and the Seventh War Bond Drive about to begin in April, the circus did its part: each of the fourteen thousand audience members purchased a war bond as the price of admission.

To further show his gratitude to Taylor for the music, Robert Ringling provided him the use of his private box for the premiere, allowing the composer to host Katy, her husband, and their young son, Bob Stranathan Jr., to an up-front view at center ring.[6] What they saw and heard, the critics lauded. "Alice's Wonderland came to life last night," wrote the *Times* reviewer the next day, "and the wonders of Alice's Wonderland paraded to a lilting score by Deems Taylor."[7] *Billboard* called the spec "really . . . something to behold. All thru the show the costuming was such that it rated the superlatives tossed about by reviewers for the New York dailies. . . . Few were sitting on their hands when the intermission was announced, and as an added attraction Deems Taylor, the eminent composer and music critic, took the baton from Merle Evans to direct his own composition for the extravaganza."[8] Audience response proved that both Taylor and his soon-to-be wife had done their work well.

Several weeks later, on April 18, Mary Kennedy answered the phone at Hollow Hill to learn that there was more to Taylor's circus world than fantasy. The reporter on the other end of the line asked to speak to Deems Taylor about his recent wedding. A puzzled Mary asked what he was talking about, and when he told her that Taylor had eloped with a girl some forty years his junior, she slammed down the phone. Why hadn't her former husband, who always confided in her, told her about his newest venture?

In fact he had, but unfortunately he had chosen a slower means of communication. Several days later, Mary received his announcement in the mail: "Dear M—I am leaving town for about a week because I am marrying Lucille Watson-Little, whom I met in Florida. I am telling no one, but I do want you to know at first hand, in case the news should break. I know that you wish me well. Love, Deems."[9] When Mary found out that even Joan had known of the marriage before she had, she forbade her eighteen-year-old daughter ever to see her father again. Joan obeyed the dictum for one year.[10]

The wedding of the well-known Taylor to such a young woman caught the fancy of New York reporters, with the *Daily News* headlining, "Deems Taylor in Big Top Elopement,"[11] while the *Times* simply reported, "Deems Taylor Weds." "The press really went to town on us," Lucille later remembered. "A lot of bad clichés such as 'in and out of tune.' And of course our age difference."[12] The newlyweds needed to escape, so Taylor enlisted the help of his friend Jean Dalrymple, the ebullient press agent and manager of the popular pianist José Iturbi. Dalrymple had a Connecticut retreat named

Taylor and his third wife, Lucille Watson-Little, at the Stork Club five days after their 1945 marriage. They were married for eight years. *(Courtesy of Photofest)*

Pinafore Farm in Danbury, only some seventy miles north of Manhattan. Here in a modest summer cottage on a rocky outcropping that overlooked a large pond, the newlyweds spent a quiet few days away from reporters.

Apparently something was in the air that month, because within the week Gloria Vanderbilt married Leopold Stokowski, who also was forty years older.

When the Taylors returned to New York, friendly greetings awaited them. Millay and her husband announced a feast in their honor if they would drive up to Steepletop: "I have a fatted calf who is longing to [be] veal," wrote Eugen.[13] George Bye asked what Lucille's circus specialty happened to be: trapeze artist, gymnast, or aerialist. But then he decided it didn't matter: "One or the other, I think she will make a fine addition to our neighborhood and we look forward to some exhibitions this summer, you old rascal, you!"[14]

Not everyone expressed congratulations. Giuliana Taberna also received a letter from Taylor and went into shock. Years later Taylor wrote to Leila Hadley Luce, who was a friend of both Taylor and Giuliana, expressing his sorrow at Giuliana's reaction: "A shame that such happiness should cause such pain," he wrote, perhaps an unconscious reference to Giuliana's preface to the birthday scrapbook.[15] According to Joan, her father gave Giuliana a fur coat to help ease the hurt.

The newlyweds settled quickly into Taylor's Fifth Avenue apartment. Lucille, or Lou, as she preferred to be called, possessed all the virtues her husband sought in a woman: she was young, pretty, talented, and a fine conversationalist. The age difference didn't seem to bother him at all, as he told friends at a party shortly after his marriage: "Everyone is saying of me that I have married a girl young enough to be my granddaughter. Well, it's true. And what of it? I'm having a wonderful time, and I love it."[16]

In August 1945, four months after his marriage, Taylor's high spirits joined those of the rest of the nation as World War II came to an end. He was also pleased that Bill Davis, who had married during the war, had come through unscathed. (Davis would continue a career in the Air Force, first gaining a Ph.D. in physics, then becoming part of atomic energy research and other military scientific projects.)

Another reason that Taylor had apparently reached the apotheosis of happiness at this time was that financial freedom had arrived for him: Joan had reached eighteen years of age; he no longer had to provide half of his income to Mary Kennedy. During every year of the divorce agreement—1934 to 1944—Taylor had earned from $30,000 to $63,000. He rarely netted more than one-third of his gross because half went to Mary, and he had to pay taxes on her half.[17] Now, because he no longer had the obligation, he cleared $37,000, a jump from just under $14,000 the previous year. Grateful to be free from the financial burden, he generously gave Mary his half of the Stamford property, yet agreed to continue to pay the property taxes and monthly utility bills. Still, that left quite a lot of money for the newlyweds.

Their love for the theater created a special bond as they began life together. Lucille recalled how her husband once again put his carpentering skills to work:

> Deems built a first-rate theater stage, as good as the Metropolitan's. It had a very elaborate lighting system, lifts, and turntables. All in an inch scale. I designed the sets and costumes. We would choose our plays or opera and we had weeks of hobby-fun together. . . . One Christmas I gave Deems a welding set for model workers. He was overjoyed and played with it all day. He welded everything he could find together, including the key into our front door. We had to get help to unweld ourselves from the apartment.[18]

Of course there was more to the marriage than playing theater. Taylor, in spite of his love for his daughter, had no interest in being a father again, so in case the youthful Lucille got any ideas, he laid down the law: "No children!" As she recalled years later, "He was not made for fatherhood, or for old age."[19]

Lucille's youth certainly helped him to banish the thought of advancing years, as did socializing with friends. Unfortunately, many of these acquaintances had spent too many years imbibing. Lucille recalled the evening in November 1945 when they expected Robert Benchley to join them at a dinner party at "21": "We waited and waited for Benchley to arrive. I think it was Marc Connelly who thought to call his hotel. They told him he was taken to the hospital with a very bad nose bleed that was impossible to stop."[20] Five days later, on November 21, 1945, Benchley died as the result of a cerebral hemorrhage, with cirrhosis of the liver a fateful helper.

Benchley's death occurred just when Taylor was summoned to his final live network radio program. Competition for the broadcasting dollar had grown during 1945, with the arrival of the American Broadcasting Company (ABC). The new network was, in fact, NBC's Blue Network: the Federal Communication Commission had viewed NBC's Red and Blue networks as a monopoly and forced them to sell one. As competition increased, networks searched for new concepts to lure the radio listener. NBC finally bought an idea that Raymond Paige, now the conductor of the Radio City Music Hall orchestra, had tried to sell producers for years: *A Battle of Music*, pitting classical music versus jazz. RCA-Victor, whose recordings featured both, agreed to be the sponsor, realizing that the program could be a great advertisement for recent releases.

The battle began to rage in December 1945. As its knight protecting classical music, RCA turned to Taylor, with the jazz expert Leonard Feather as his foe. Paige's radio orchestra attempted to be both symphony and "rugged rhythm ramblers." Taylor was introduced as having "the armor of authority, the ammunition of an expert and the flaming sword CONVICTION," while Feather was to uphold "the honor of the hepcat clan . . . as advocate and keeper of the whisker-frisking flame."[21] The script tended toward the corny, yet a *Times* review of the first program noted that both Taylor and Feather "tossed off the quips with considerable aplomb, keeping tongue well in cheek and not being too cute too often."[22]

No matter how trite the script may have been, at least Taylor was again in a position to be a convincing booster for classical music, a role he had played for decades both in print and on radio. As far as his feelings about jazz, those had been explained in the *Well-Tempered Listener:* "Anyone can understand jazz, chiefly because there's nothing to understand. All you have to do is expose your ear to it. That is nothing against jazz; when it is mildly stimulating your nervous system, and doing things to your feet, it is doing all its creators ever intended it to do. But serious music takes serious listening."[23] According to his daughter, Taylor didn't like the improvisational aspect at all. She recalls becoming enamored of recordings of Dixieland music, to her father's dismay.

While the *Battle of Music* progressed during spring 1946, Taylor was pleased to find that Joan had become a regular visitor. She was a student at Barnard College, and though her mother had forbidden her ever to speak to her father again, Joan decided that one year was enough. Besides, she wanted to get to know Lucille; after all, they were about the same age. What Joan learned in her visits was that her father and Lucille were a very happy, busy couple: she with costume designing for Broadway, he on several projects, including music for the next Ringling extravaganza.

After the great success of the "Alice in Wonderland" spec, Robert Ringling turned to Taylor again for the 1946 show. The fit appeared perfect, since the theme was "Toyland" and musical fantasy was Taylor's forte. This time the contract called for "an original piece of music of the Spectacle and . . . an original short overture to the performance."[24] Unfortunately, what Taylor composed didn't fit the world of peanuts and cotton candy. *Billboard's* assessment of the Madison Square Garden April 1946 opening night told it all: "Toyland hits despite dreary musical score." The review lauded the entire production except for one aspect: "[The] only sour note in the Spec was the music, conceived and directed personally . . . by Deems Taylor. It was much too long-haired to build the carefree spirit of Toyland-age. . . . It is entirely possible that Robert Ringling and Taylor were the only two people in the building who enjoyed the music." After some attempts to perk it up with new arrangements, the Taylor music was replaced by melodies from Victor Herbert's operetta *Babes in Toyland.*[25] Predictably, Robert Ringling never called on Taylor again.

The Death of Mummie

Taylor's mother died in her Loring Place home on March 25, 1946, "after a week's illness."[26] She had lived just long enough to celebrate her ninetieth birthday at a party given by Katy but unattended by her son, who had been busy completing the ultimately aborted music for Ringling. The years after JoJo's death had not been happy ones for her. In spite of her husband's penchant for details and careful spending, he had left little money for her support. In fact, he had saddled her with the fourteen-room Bronx house, which necessitated a housekeeper at all times, and her only income was the rent from boarders and the monthly checks that Deems sent her.

Clues to Taylor's relationship with his mother come from a variety of sources, including her letters to him from 1938 to 1943, which have been preserved. Unfortunately, none of his written communications to her are known to exist. There probably were few to begin with, since telephone calls were the major source of communication between mother and son. But she expressed frustration at being unable to reach him: "I can't get you on the phone very often. I know you are very busy but I could have a list of questions ready and you wouldn't have to take time to read my long letter."[27] Here was a mother reaching out, but knowing full well that fame had taken her son from her.

Taylor did find time on certain holidays, such as Christmas, to visit his mother, and he made her Mother's Day of 1940 extra special when he presented her with an album that documented his life in photographs. He signed it, "To My Beloved Mother, Katherine Moore Taylor, from a Grateful Son." The album shows his growth from a two-year-old into a handsome college youth with a beguiling smile. Glasses became an integral part of his life at age twenty-two, as evidenced here, and the journey to baldness was a long one. Photos highlight Taylor's music years; there is the NYU honorary degree ceremony and a radio broadcast with John Philip Sousa. Interestingly, aside from several photos that include Mummie, the only woman to appear is three-year-old Joan, suggesting that Taylor believed his two greatest gifts to his mother were his fame and his daughter.

Mummie had anticipated her son's fame. "From the day you were born," she wrote him, "I felt that you would have a career and create something superior to the general run of people. I think it was just because you were my own."[28] What she had recognized at his birth, she now had to live with. His infrequent visits were the price she had to pay. Her letters also identify the key Taylor trait of keeping emotions well hidden. "I'm proud of your career," she wrote in 1938, "and I know the work you have to do. I believe I know the part I play in your life even if you never tell me so."[29] After she had gone to Philadelphia with Deems for the premiere of *Ramuntcho,* she wrote, "People are constantly saying to me, 'You must be proud of your son.' I am such an inarticulate person that I cannot put into words the reply I would like to make," which of course would have expressed so much more than pride.[30]

She also suggested that Deems possessed an innate shyness when she wrote about thirteen-year-old Joan, whom she had seldom seen: "I wish I knew her better. I am somehow so shy of youngsters. You know the feeling, being just like me."[31] Taylor's mother provided the stability in his life, challenged as he had constantly been by a perfectionist father. Yet his emotions had remained stifled.

Moll Flanders

In the months after his mother's funeral, Taylor again heard the siren song of Broadway, as did Lucille. Her friend James Carhart brought them a script he had developed based on Daniel Defoe's eighteenth-century novel *Moll Flanders*. The heroine seemed a spicy subject indeed, with her many roles—lady, thief, prostitute—played out among both royalty and scoundrels. Deems and Lucille, composer and scenic designer, decided they had the combined background and talent to create a *Moll Flanders* that producers would want on Broadway, something far different from *Oklahoma!, Carousel, Carmen Jones,* and *Annie Get Your Gun,* musicals that had wowed audiences during the preceding few years.[32]

They worked on their *Moll Flanders* project late into every night, Lucille on one side of a divided living room designing costumes and sets, Taylor on the other side working on the score. He liked the musical challenge, for in addition to the requisite songs, the work provided opportunities for many dance sequences. He was able to envision these for everything from a bacchanal to Bartholomew Fair. He even needed fire music, to accompany a spectacular first act conclusion depicting the Great London Fire of 1666.

By April 1947 the Taylors were satisfied that they had something special and arranged to present a piano-vocal run-through for the Theatre Guild's chief administrators, Theresa Helburn and Laurence Langner, the Guild's founder. Perhaps Taylor thought the Guild owed him a favor, since some twenty years earlier he had provided them the incidental music for *Liliom* and *The Adding Machine.* But days after the run-through, Helburn wrote the composer a thanks-but-no-thanks letter: "You've certainly conceived a musical play rich in the grace and charm of the period. . . . But it really is a tremendous production—one that could not possibly be taken up lightly, and I am afraid that with our musical commitments for the Fall, it would be far too much of an undertaking."[33] The Guild was in fact committed to *Allegro,* Rodgers and Hammerstein's next musical.

The Taylors did not give up. They contacted William Hess, who had sung the lead in *Ramuntcho,* to help them with other presentations in seeking "angels" to back the show. "I think we sang about 20 auditions," Hess recalled in an interview, "and it never got off the ground. Even then in '46 or '47, it would have cost about $800,000 to mount."[34] On the surface the cost of the production seemed the key issue, but Taylor's music, as well as the subject itself, also had problems, as a critical analysis of the score shows clearly even today. The Taylors' *Moll Flanders* includes few, if any, songs with the tuneful-ness necessary for a successful Broadway musical. Unfortunately, Taylor did not have the gift of a Broadway tunesmith.

At that time, good and memorable songs were the essence of Broadway musicals, not spectacle. In addition, successful works looked to America for their subjects, as evidenced in the landmark musicals before 1947: *Show Boat* deals with the South and miscegenation; *Of Thee I Sing* concerns American politics; *Pal Joey* is a New York heel; and *Oklahoma!* involves the settling of the West. It is odd that Taylor did not recognize this fact.

The Taylors finally had to admit that their *Moll Flanders* appeared doomed to life in a drawer. Still, like any good composer, Taylor did not let all his music go to waste. Some years later he returned to the score, review-ing what he had written for the dance sequences and scene changes. These possessed a period tunefulness, so he extracted portions and organized them into *Restoration Suite,* later renamed *Three Centuries Suite.* In addition, some of the songs became part of *The Dragon,* his fourth and final opera, and the work that would end his life as a composer.

Taylor and Free Speech

In the spring of 1946 Taylor again was elected president of ASCAP. It was his fifth year, and the coffers were overflowing. In previous years the board, in lieu of salary, had provided him with tokens such as the aforementioned paintings by Monet and Daumier, as well as fur coats for his ladies, including one for Joan. But in 1946, as Taylor reviewed his financial situation, he real-ized that radio no longer provided a major source of his income, so he may have dropped a few broad hints to his fellow ASCAP board members. In-deed, he was offered an annual salary of $25,000, which he accepted grate-fully. But with it came the added restriction that any future president could serve only two successive one-year terms.[35] Meanwhile, Taylor was still far from the poorhouse: in 1946, helped by the ASCAP pay, he hit his all-time high in annual income: $84,000.

Taylor had helped calm the legal waters of ASCAP, but as he began what would be his final two years as president, another battle loomed with the emergence of commercial television. The board saw the potential for a struggle similar to that of the radio war. To provide some time to come to agreements, ASCAP allowed telecasters to use its music without charge until the end of 1948. The expectation was that during this time an initial satisfac-tory decision on licensing could be worked out. This actually happened, a major achievement on Taylor's concluding watch.[36]

On April 8, 1948, Taylor announced to the annual general meeting of

ASCAP that his final months as president were at hand. He had served the two one-year terms the board now allowed. *Variety* reported that in spite of Taylor's announcement, "for weeks there was considerable indecision as to whether the limitation rule would be bypassed this year and Taylor retained."[37] The indecision led to an "old boys" group pushing hard to reelect Gene Buck, but that effort went nowhere. Finally the board chose Fred Ahlert, author of its newest rating system.

Even with the two-term rule, the real reason that Taylor was not pressed to stay on as president may have had to do with something completely different: the anxiety that prevailed at the time regarding communism in the United States. *Variety* saw this as a distinct possibility: "There was the general dissatisfaction among high ASCAP-ites over Taylor's assent to the use of his name as one of a committee formed to defend the rights of 10 Hollywoodites cited for contempt of Congress a while back."[38]

The stand that Taylor took in support of the group, later known as the Hollywood Ten, caught the attention of the FBI, which wrote the following into its file on Taylor: "In the December 1, 1947 issue of the 'Daily Worker,' an east coast Communist newspaper, Deems Taylor's name and picture appeared as being one of sixty-five leaders in the arts, sciences and professions who denounced the motion picture producers in an open letter for discharging the ten writers and directors who were cited for contempt by the House on [*sic*] Un-American Activities Committee."[39]

Taylor's stand may have been surprising to some, because throughout his life he had kept his political profile low. For example, when his daughter told him after the presidential election in 1940 that she had heard he'd voted for Wendell Wilkie and not Franklin Roosevelt, he responded with a deflecting question: "I thought there was a curtain on the voting booth?"[40] Yet issues of injustice and free speech gnawed deeply within him, accentuated by the Mennonite traditions handed down from his father's family.[41] Though he may have seemed soft-spoken on the air, Taylor employed the power of the written word when the cause moved him. When the Daughters of the American Revolution denied Marian Anderson access to Constitution Hall in Washington for her 1939 concert, Taylor sent a telegram that didn't mince words: "This action subverts the clear meaning of the U.S. Constitution, in particular the Bill of Rights, and places your organization in the camp of those who seek to destroy democracy, justice, and liberty."[42]

In 1948 ASCAP board members may well have been tuned in to whispering campaigns that tainted Taylor with the red of communism. Such stigmatization was common in the days of the House Un-American Activities Committee and its cohort, the FBI, which had also written into its Taylor file that he had been a sponsor for several music festivals hosted by organizations "cited by the Attorney General of the United States as Communist."[43] Board members may also have known of the petition signed by Taylor and sent to the attorney general in mid-December of the previous year, which demanded that an extradition order for the composer Hanns Eisler be canceled. Eisler, a German who had studied with Schoenberg, had distinct left-wing leanings, but the fourteen artists and scientists who signed the petition believed he was being railroaded. Along with Taylor, signers included Thomas Mann, Albert Einstein, Aaron Copland, and Leonard Bernstein. And finally, one may wonder whether some musically savvy board member remembered Taylor's "Fanfare for Russia." Those were the days in the United States when, in some minds, such connections had the ring of minor treason.

Since Taylor did not wear his politics on his sleeve, the ASCAP board would not have known that his belief in fairness and free speech was matched by his anticommunist feelings, something later made clear in a letter to his Algonquin friend of many years, Donald Ogden Stewart. From the late 1930s and into the 1940s, Stewart became a major screenwriter in Hollywood. Taylor apparently discovered that Stewart had become sympathetic toward the communist line, or the Movement, as it was then referred to. "I got a long, serious well-meant letter from Deems Taylor," Stewart writes in his memoirs, "telling me what a fool I was as an artist to get mixed up in any political activities, especially Communist ones. It was really very decent of Deems. . . . It surprised me, though, that Deems was so violently anti-Communist; he was the first of my old friends to react that way."[44]

No matter how the board came to its decision, it is unlikely that Taylor wanted to continue as president anyway, for he confided to a friend, "Getting out of the Papal chair of ASCAP is a great relief. Six years is enough."[45] When Louis D. Frohlich, a longtime general counsel for ASCAP, returned to New York from a West Coast trip to learn that ASCAP had selected a new president, he wrote to Taylor of his belief "that over the years you were most cooperative, loyal and devoted to ASCAP's cause and that your incumbency of the office was a great help to the society, perhaps more than they will ever realize."[46] ASCAP apparently did come to realize how well Taylor had served, because in 1955 *Variety* reported that the ASCAP board was again considering him for president. "[H]is administration from 1942–1948 was generally regarded as a success."[47] Taylor never served again as president of ASCAP, but he remained on its board.

The Creative Arts Call Again

With the ASCAP presidency behind him, Taylor turned to a continuing love: spreading the good news about music, this time as the nation's first longhair disc jockey. With television revolutionizing the media, many radio stations looked for new ways to attract listeners. Chicago's Radio Features, knowing that Taylor remained an eminent spokesman for classical music, asked him to initiate a syndicated program of recorded music, augmented with his usual witty commentary. With the prospect of excellent income, he accepted.

By September 1948 transcriptions of the half-hour-long *Deems Taylor Concert* were airing on independent stations from coast to coast. The format was simple: Taylor played portions of recordings that people could buy at nearby music stores, and he commented briefly on them. Within a year, one hundred stations around the country carried the weekly program. John Crosby, the era's major radio and television commentator, approved. "[Taylor's] own style," he wrote, "is perhaps best typified by one introduction which went as follows: 'It may seem strange that George Gershwin and the 18th Century composer Arcangelo Corelli had something in common. Yet both left, at their deaths, estates of over a quarter of a million dollars and a collection of paintings. There the resemblance ends.'" Crosby had found a recent survey that indicated "all age and all income groups listen to serious music. . . . It's a very heartening picture and should be especially so to Deems Taylor, who has done as much as anyone to popularize great music."[48] The program lasted several years and was Taylor's last word to the radio public about the joys of concert music.

He also returned to writing when Simon and Schuster urged him to publish a third book based on his Philharmonic intermissions. The resulting *Music to My Ears* had all of the usual Taylor insights and wit. "Part One: Prologue" contained the highlight, a satisfying explanation of what it takes to compose a symphonic work. As an example of the mere physical effort of composing, he asked the reader to consider the time it takes to put notes onto the musical staves. "I counted the number of notes on the last page of the score of Mozart's Jupiter Symphony," wrote Taylor. "There are 284 of them." He compared that to a page of Richard Strauss's tone poem *Ein Heldenleben,* a musically denser work in which he found 714 notes: "Try copying—not originating, just copying—one page of a full orchestral score sometime, if you want to understand why composers can't afford to spend all of their time in a frenzy of inspiration."[49]

Taylor reviewed for the reader all the musical instruments a composer had to consider, along with the peculiarities of each. He reminded any neophyte that if a trombone is in the score, the composer must "know the seven positions of the trombone and avoid writing fast passages that make the player look like a sword swallower."[50]

In 1949, the year that *Music to My Ears* appeared, Taylor showed that his fanciful world still functioned exquisitely with the publication of *Moments*

Mousical, a mouse's view of music history. The book had brilliant full-page drawings by Walter Kumme, who portrayed major events in the history of music as if carried out by mice, whether in ancient Egypt or on the stage of Carnegie Hall. Taylor revved up his punning engine to explain Kumme's drawing of ancient mouse hieroglyphics; he wrote, for example, of the "Mousetta Stone . . . found in the basement of an old mousqe by a Mous-lem."[51] Of course, Richard Wagner's operas found a special place. One draw-ing showed the three Rhine Maidens in "Wagner's great Nibblungen Trilogy . . . Mouselinde, Mousehilde, and Mousegunde."[52] After reading the book, Gladys Swarthout, his longtime friend from opera and radio, wrote to ask that he "analyze for us 'Ballo in Mouschera' and 'Mousphistofeles,' each of which mousterworks should be scrutinized."[53] Though *Moments Mousical* was a one-joke book, Taylor's short and pithy commentaries and Kumme's charming drawings pointed out to any reader that classical music didn't have to be serious all the time.

The Deaths of Boissevain and Millay

From the time of their collaboration on *The King's Henchman,* Taylor had deeply admired Edna St. Vincent Millay. A warm friendship had developed between them, which was carried on even after he had married for a third time. Visits to Steepletop occurred with some regularity, times fondly re-membered even by Lucille:

> Steepletop was truly a poet's creation. . . . For instance, in the woods one would suddenly come across a fence and a gate between two trees, with a bench in the middle. Edna explained she liked to go and sit in her "green rooms." The woods were another house for her. . . . Edna woke up every morning at the crack of dawn. She would walk through the woods around the house [and] go through the gates she had placed between some of the trees . . . then move on up to the highest point of the land, a rose garden where she would either curse out God, or compliment God for the good news of the day. She would then go back to the house and sip a pink gin for breakfast. Eugen however would always manage to get some food into her. He was madly in love with her, and she with him.[54]

Eugen Boissevain also found Taylor a friend who, with his experience in rural Connecticut, knew how to cut down a tree. Such knowledge was a ne-cessity for Boissevain's plan of a most unusual birthday gift for his wife. He made sure that the Taylors came to Steepletop the day before Millay's birth-day, so that the gift could be prepared. It seems that every morning when the poet awoke, she would go to her bedroom window, throw open the shutters, and absorb the beauty of the plants, the woods, and the hills in the distance. But one tree annoyed her; it cut off her view, and she grumbled about it every morning. The night before her birthday, after she had fallen soundly asleep, the birthday project took place as Lucille described: "Eugen and Deems sawed down the 'damnable tree.' Their poor hands were full of blisters. The next morning they waited until Edna threw open the shutters to shout 'Happy Birthday' under her window."[55]

Taylor admired Boissevain's complete dedication to Millay. Though he knew that Eugen had lost his importing business during the war, he still believed that Edna and Eugen had set aside sufficient funds to maintain their quiet life of Steepletop. Consequently, it surprised him to receive a letter in mid-August 1949 in which Eugen requested that $1,500 be sent as soon as possible: doctors had discovered cancer in his right lung. "They must operate immediately," he wrote Taylor. "Before I go to the hospital . . . I must get some money to pay for nurses and things."[56] Taylor sent the check on August 20. The apparently successful operation was performed in Boston, but soon afterward Boissevain suffered a stroke. He died on August 29.[57]

Her husband's death so stunned Millay that she entered a hospital to recover. When she returned to Steepletop, she had her telephone service changed to permit only outgoing calls. "If it rang," she said, "I would hear his footsteps as he ran to answer it."[58] Through the dismal winter and the following summer, Millay remained alone, interacting only with the neighbors who helped her maintain Steepletop. Though she had been addicted to morphine for some years, with the help of Eugen she had broken from that. Now only alcohol provided solace. Sometime in the evening hours of October 18, 1950, Edna St. Vincent Millay fell down the narrow staircase and lay crumpled at the base of the stairs, her neck broken. The following morning her groundskeeper found her there in peaceful death.[59]

When Taylor learned of Millay's death, he did not waste a lot of time in sadness or in wondering about the great beyond, for he believed God to be a "Total Mystery."[60] He preferred to remember the beautiful days at Steepletop with Edna and Eugen, swimming in the forested swimming pool, or designing and installing a new lintel for their living room fireplace. Still, he could not escape the fact that Millay's death meant that the one great artistic partner of his life had departed.

Another Marriage Ends

Not only had Taylor lost Millay, but he was in the process of losing another wife. Two months earlier, Lucille had flown to Paris to further her painting ambitions. She had saved some money from her Broadway designing activities, as well as advertising fees for endorsing Fatima cigarettes in major magazines as "Mrs. Deems Taylor, Famous Painter and Theatrical Designer." Taylor had supported her decision to go to Paris; he had also promised to send monthly checks, always with the hope that her ambitions and their marriage could remain viable.

But for the youthful Lucille, ambition alone had not initiated the separation. Taylor's years of excessive drinking were beginning to show, which made her realize that a life with a much older man had its limitations. "We all drank too much," Lucille remembered years later. "We had a lot of close chums such as Robert Benchley and Dottie Parker. Just a couple of examples. That's one of the reasons we separated. [Deems] was beginning to have 'blackouts.' It scared me and reminded me of the Irish side of my family. The English side held out, but the Irish side had big problems. It was a repeat show for me. I was perhaps too young to handle the situation."[61]

Five months after Lucille had left for Paris, her husband wrote of his intention to come to be with her for the remainder of the year. Not only did he miss her, but he also wanted to escape what was now obvious: no one was playing his music or performing his operas. He shared this frustration with William Grant Still, a friend and a major black composer. Like Taylor, Still had not followed the modernists, and thereby suffered a similar fate: there were few performances of his work. Still and his wife, Verna Arvey, admired Taylor and especially appreciated his spearheading the drive to elect Still to the National Institute of Arts and Letters, an effort that ultimately proved unsuccessful.

Arvey wrote to Taylor asking his opinion of why neither her husband's nor his own compositions were played any longer. His answer suggested more than a little annoyance at having become a disregarded composer: "I no longer bother even to try to get my own stuff played by organizations such as the Philadelphia, Boston, or Philharmonic. The performances I do get are by the smaller fry, like Indianapolis and Los Angeles, or even Harrisburg, Pa. They don't feel that they're doing me a favor, and they haven't signed up with the Inner Circle boys." Very likely he referred here to some of the composers with left-leaning politics, such as Aaron Copland and Leonard Bernstein. Taylor concluded his letter: "It may interest you to know that my wife is apartment hunting in Paris. If she finds one, we're going to get out of here— maybe for good."[62]

An escape to Paris must have seemed a step toward heaven for Taylor, but when he added up his assets, he found he could hardly even get out of New York. To improve his bank account, he sold the Daumier painting for nine thousand dollars (it had actually decreased in value) and left in April

1951 for a two-month visit to Paris. The usual joy of being in Paris was tempered by discussions with Lucille about their future. Did life together remain a possibility? Did she want to remain permanently in Paris? Lucille wasn't sure, but she asked Deems to look for a little shop in Greenwich Village when he returned to New York. If she followed him, she would sell art objects from Paris.[63]

Lucille came back to New York a year later, but by that time she and Deems had decided that although fondness remained, to continue the marriage was to live a lie. They agreed to seek an annulment, which necessitated Lucille's returning in the fall of 1952 to give depositions that would convince the courts that some aspect of their union had not fulfilled the marriage contract. Whether that claim was true or simply manufactured, by March 1953 the annulment was granted, and they said their legal good-byes. Lucille went back to the Paris art scene, bolstered by a commitment from New York's Ward Eggleston gallery to provide a major exhibition of her paintings in 1954. Every month she also received a six-hundred-dollar check from Taylor in yet another manifestation of his generosity mixed with guilt, since annulment precluded his having to pay alimony.

After Lucille's successful New York show of May 1954, she invited Taylor to Paris to get to know her friend Borrah Minevitch, the harmonica virtuoso who, as leader of the Harmonica Rascals, had been famous in the United States in the 1930s and 1940s. He was now settled in Paris as a French film producer. "Borrah threw a big party in Deems's honor," Lucille recalled. "They enjoyed each other in spite of a certain jealousy. Borrah was a very funny man. Irresistibly funny."[64]

Lucille had fallen in love with Borrah, and together they planned to open a restaurant. In June 1955 they married; three weeks later he died of a stroke at age fifty-two. When Taylor learned of the tragedy, he asked Lucille whether she would consider remarrying him. But for Lucille the answer could only be negative: "One can't go backwards, it seldom works," she later remarked.[65] In spite of what appeared to be a rebuff, Taylor's fondness for Lucille persisted. Four years later she married Alain Térouanne, also a French film producer, but until then, he continued to send funds to help her through difficult times, a simple example of the innate loyalty that endeared him to her.

For Taylor, the state of marriage needed to be reconsidered. Twenty-five years earlier, in the middle of his second one, he had expressed his opinion about the institution to Charles Shaw: "Marriage . . . like all other human institutions, offers grave grounds for complaint, although . . . no fitting substitute for it has, as yet, been devised."[66] Now having ended his third, he decided that there was a fitting substitute after all: long-term friendships.

19. A Life with Friends, the 1950s

Taylor as Bachelor

The word *moderation* aptly describes Taylor's first years without the effervescent Lucille. In the daytime apartment life was shaped by Lilly, his housekeeper, who cleaned and cooked, or called Casserole Kitchen to bring up some steaming hot dinner by 6 P.M. Days were filled with meetings of the ASCAP board, counting money (as treasurer for the American Academy of Arts and Letters), stabs at composing, and lunches with friends. Appearances on radio were now rare, except for Saturday afternoons during opera season, when often he would be a guest on the Metropolitan Opera broadcast's intermission opera quiz.

Never one to remain long without the companionship of a female, Taylor had found a new friend only a month after Lucille left for Paris in 1950. He discovered her just where any red-blooded American male would like to look: the Miss America Pageant. During that summer he had committed himself to be a judge at the Atlantic City spectacle, part of a nine-person panel that had to recognize not only beauty but also talent, since the pageant now provided a variety of scholarships to winners and runners-up. Taylor knew beauty and certainly had an ear for musical talent, so when he heard Yolande Betbeze—five-foot, five-inch, brown-haired Miss Alabama—sing the coloratura aria "Caro Nome" from *Rigoletto,* both his eyes and his ears were pleased. He looked at her and must have remembered what he had said to Mary Kennedy before their marriage: "I worship talent and brains, you know."[1] Apparently Betbeze also impressed the other judges, for she became Miss America of 1951.

The judges could hardly have suspected that by choosing Betbeze as a beauty queen they also chose a maverick. She had studied first at Spring Hill College in Mobile, a Jesuit institution heavy on theology and philosophy, then at the University of Alabama. With such a background, as well as her singing talent, she saw herself as more than just a body to be paraded about in a swimsuit. After becoming Miss America, she refused to tour the country modeling the swimsuits of the Catalina company, one of the pageant's main sponsors. Catalina withdrew and initiated both the Miss USA and Miss Universe Pageants. Years later Betbeze stated quite simply, "People can thank me—or blame me—for that."[2]

Such an independent spirit and agile intellect appealed enormously to Taylor, so after the pageant's conclusion he invited Betbeze to contact him if she came to New York. As fate had it, when Taylor returned from his spring visit to Lucille in Paris, Betbeze came to New York to study music and acting. It was the beginning of a long social engagement. "He was the father I never had," she recalled years later.[3] When they met at his apartment for dinner, usually a Casserole Kitchen entrée, they would often dine alone on the apartment balcony, look out over Central Park, and talk of philosophers and music.

While Taylor socialized with Miss America, in the winter of 1952 he welcomed another young woman to stay with him in his apartment: his daughter, Joan. During the mid-1940s, Joan had completed four years at Barnard College on Manhattan's Upper West Side, across Broadway from Columbia University. While at Barnard, through her father's connections, she gained a role or two in radio dramas, advancing her interest in making acting a lifetime career. At the same time, she began dating Donald Cook, a psychology major at Columbia, and during her senior year, in fall 1947, they became engaged. Once Mary Kennedy found out about the engagement, she employed a variety of stratagems to break up the romance for a highly personal reason: she believed an actress first had to establish herself in the profession, and only then consider marriage.

First she began to create chaos with Cook's parents. At the time, Donald was living in Manhattan and Joan was still living with her. So, when Donald did not get Joan back in time after a date, Mary would call Mrs. Cook at her Long Island home late at night and complain, suggesting that she had better rein in her son. When that didn't work, Mary refused to attend Joan's graduation. She left it up to Deems and Lucille (not yet gone to Paris) to represent the family.

In spite of this defiance, Donald summoned up courage to face his future mother-in-law and ask her approval. Mary resisted, but Joan, who wanted very much to get out from under this control, recognized her mother's intentions to scuttle the impending marriage. Finally Joan took a stand: either her mother agreed to the marriage or she and Donald would elope. Mary relented; she would pay for the wedding and have the reception in her apartment.

The marriage took place in September 1948 at a Unitarian church in Manhattan, with Deems and Lucille present along with Mary. The newlyweds first rented a room in a boardinghouse near Columbia and Joan began a series of odd jobs, while Donald remained at Columbia as a teaching assistant pursuing graduate work. For several months they interacted pleasantly enough with the unpredictable Mary Kennedy. But then the inevitable happened, for though on the surface she had approved of the marriage, deep down she wanted it ended. At Thanksgiving, a minor misunderstanding about why Mary did not attend dinner with the Cooks was the catalyst that precipitated a three-year silence between mother and daughter.

Within the year Joan became pregnant. She wrote the news to her mother, but never received an answer. In January 1950 Michael Cook was born and the couple rented an apartment near Columbia. Donald now had become a part-time instructor there while continuing graduate studies, and Joan gained some supporting roles on live television series, such as *I Remember Mama,* but the marriage wasn't working. Most likely both had entered marriage as an escape, and now, with precarious finances and the added pressures of a baby, the stark reality of their situation became all too clear. After two and a half years, on Thanksgiving weekend 1952 (a holiday that was becoming fateful for Joan), they agreed to an amicable temporary separation. Needing time to work out the arrangements, Joan asked her father if, for a few weeks, she could sleep on his living room couch. Without asking any questions, Deems said yes.

The troubled couple finally determined they had sufficient funds for Donald to keep two-year-old Michael and take him to a day nursery on weekdays. For Joan, whose early years were often spent with a nanny, such an arrangement probably did not strike her as unusual. She agreed to come on weekends and take care of Michael, clean the apartment, and cook for the week ahead.

The "few weeks" that Joan thought would suffice to clarify her marital problems (she would ultimately get a legal separation, then a divorce in 1955) turned into a year and a half of sleeping on her father's couch. During that time, she and Deems became more than daughter and father; they became the closest of friends.

Having the company of both his daughter and Miss America renewed Taylor. He found time to reconsider some of the incidental music he had composed for *Moll Flanders* and shaped it into *Restoration Suite,* a group of dances typifying the rhythms of eighteenth-century England: a pavane, a saraband, a rigadoon, a jig, and a waltz. He appropriately dedicated the work to Lucille, without whose help he would never have composed it. Knowing that his friend John Barbirolli had introduced *Marco Takes a Walk* to Great Britain, he sent the score to him in England for possible programming.

Barbirolli agreed to conduct the work but questioned why Taylor had written a waltz for the suite, since there were no waltzes during the Restoration era of English history: minuets, yes; waltzes, no. Caught in an anachronism, the composer agreed to replace it with a minuet for later performances. But he never did, and no evidence exists that Barbirolli ever conducted the work. Years later Taylor found a way out of the dilemma, thanks to a suggestion by the controversial author Ayn Rand. She told him simply to change the title to *Three Centuries Suite* and keep the waltz. The tuneful piece sat on Taylor's shelf until the summer of 1961, when a student orchestra of the National Music Camp at Interlochen, Michigan, gave its first performance in the United States.

Taylor's Payback to Billy Rose

The loyalty that Taylor showed to his women he likewise extended to men who had done him favors. During his years with Lucille, he had developed a firm friendship with Billy Rose. It was an attraction of opposites, for while Rose found the cultured wit of the composer much to his liking, Taylor admired Rose's brashness and businesslike demeanor. The friendship came about only after Rose publicly apologized for having openly challenged Taylor's potential as ASCAP president. Taylor never forgot Rose's kindness in so generously acknowledging his inappropriate comments, and he looked for an opportunity for positive payback. He found it ten years later, when Rose's mistress, Joyce Matthews, slit her wrist in an attempted suicide. The half-hearted attempt occurred after Rose had told her he had no plans to divorce his wife, the former Olympic swimming champion Eleanor Holm, also the star of Rose's immensely successful Aquacades at the 1939–40 New York World's Fair.

The New York and national presses played up the attempted suicide, Rose's philandering, and finally Holm's divorce suit. The courtroom spectacle played itself out in a journalistic frenzy that became known as the War of the Roses. The public couldn't get enough of the saga, so in late summer 1952 the *New York Post* pandered to its readers' interest with a twelve-part series on Billy Rose, his life, and his women. According to the *Post,* five reporters had spent eight months researching the accused adulterer. Before the series began, Rose sought and was granted daily rebuttals of the *Post'*s previous day's comments, a "last word" column, as he called it.

Reporters interviewed many of Rose's friends, including Taylor, who was touted as Rose's cultural authority. When Taylor was asked to explain Rose's well-known art collection, he simply said, "Billy is very interested in culture, and goes at it the way he goes at anything else. He spent a year acquiring knowledge of painting." Taylor also revealed Rose's naïve side. While planning *Carmen Jones,* an updated version of Bizet's *Carmen* with an all-black cast, Rose needed to hire a conductor. "[Billy] asked me one day," wrote Taylor, "if Toscanini would be interested in doing the musical direction of 'Carmen Jones' and, if not, how about Stokowski."[4]

At the end of the two-week *Post* saga, Rose asked his friend Taylor to present the readers with the "final word" about Billy Rose; it was the perfect opportunity for a Taylor payback. He entitled his story "My Friend Billy," but began rather negatively: "My first impression of Billy Rose was not a pleasant one." He continued with the previously noted story of how Billy had questioned his aptitude for ASCAP's leadership, then, in a dig at the *Post,* suggested that Rose's later apology had been "bigger than the little dogs that bark."

Taylor continued in a way that made it clear he was holding his journalistic nose: "This series is a pretty odoriferous example of yellow journalism at its yellowest. It is 'news' only in that it is printed in a newspaper." To prove his point, he gave examples showing that "the Post never directly charges Rose with anything. Anything nasty to be said about him is put in the mouth of some anonymous accuser." He pointed out that the series projected the belief "that Billy Rose's chief crime is that he was born on the lower East Side and grew up to be a millionaire—an achievement that for some reason seems to have infuriated The Post."[5] What angered Taylor was, of course, another case of injustice.

Rose deeply appreciated what Taylor wrote about him and invited him to spend as many weekends as he wanted at Roseholm, his country mansion named for his marriage. Most of the time Betbeze accompanied Taylor to the Mt. Kisco, New York, home. For Miss America 1951, these weekend visits to Roseholm were part of the "last of the great salons—fabulous years with fabulous people," during which Hollywood stars such as Marlene Dietrich, James Stewart, and Orson Welles often visited.[6] Rose's financial advisor and friend Bernard Baruch once even dropped in with Winston Churchill.[7] It was a world that charmed not only Betbeze, but her gallant companion as well.

Two More Books, but So Different

For Taylor there was more to life than Joan, Miss America, and Billy Rose, of course, for bills still had to be paid. Now the only radio revenue came from infrequent appearances. Book royalties had the capability of providing effective and consistent income, so with the help of his agent, Taylor found two more opportunities as an author. The first took advantage of his talents with the French language. On one of his trips to Paris he had acquired the *Anthologie libertine,* a book of some two hundred pieces of light verse about *l'amour,* that subject so dear to the Gallic heart. Millay had also loved the book, as Taylor would later write: "Some years ago, I lent my volume of Anthologie Libertine to Edna St. Vincent Millay—and had a hard time getting it back. She was as enchanted with the poems as I was, and we both agreed that it was a pity there was no English translation."[8] A man not unappreciative of a sexually suggestive verse or two, Taylor decided to translate some of the poems. The resulting book, *The One-Track Mind: Love Poems of Seventeenth and Eighteenth Century France,* became his ultimate tribute to his late poet friend, with the dedication "In happy memory of Edna St. Vincent Millay who was amused."

The decision to publish each French poem and its English translation side by side provided a special spicy exercise for young students of the language; take, for example, this one by Bernard de la Monnoie (1641–1728):[9]

"La Pénitente"	"The Penitent"
Une fille accorte et finette	A pretty creature went alone
Se confessant à père André,	To Father André, to confess;
Il la trouva forte à son gré,	Who, taken with her loveliness,
Et lui dit d'une voix doucette:	Assumed a confidential tone:
—Mademoiselle, ne peut-on	"My daughter, tell me—have no shame—
Savoir comme l'on vous appelle?	What are you known as, by your kin?"
Mon Père, excusez-moi, mon nom	"Pardon me, Father, but my name
N'est pas un péché, lui dit-elle.	Is hardly what you'd call a sin."

At the same time that Taylor was translating naughty French verses for publication, he took on a far more difficult task, the biography of not one person but two: Richard Rodgers and Oscar Hammerstein. He had known both from his earliest days with ASCAP, and they were, as he would write in the introduction to *Some Enchanted Evenings,* "two talented people of whom I am very fond and whom I admire inordinately." He saw the duo as his era's equivalent to Gilbert and Sullivan, another pair whom he deeply admired.[10] At an award dinner honoring Rodgers and Hammerstein, Taylor predicted that they would become as immortal as the Savoyard pair: "Dick Rodgers' music is so simple, we often forget how good it is. Oscar Hammerstein has brought to the lyric theater something that Gilbert never did—poetry. . . . So I'll lay eight-to-five that if Gilbert and Sullivan have lasted seventy-five years, 'Oklahoma!' will be playing in A.D. 2050."[11]

Taylor's active admiration also translated into his championing their admittance into the prestigious National Institute of Arts and Letters, "the first enduring literary and artistic elite in America."[12] He had been elected into the 250-member institute in 1924, shortly after the success of his fully orchestrated *Through the Looking Glass* suite; ten years later he had become one of the 50-member Academy, the inner circle of the institute, emulating the centuries-old French Academy. At the 1921 groundbreaking of the Academy's own building on Manhattan's West 155th Street, Marshal Ferdinand Foch of France, commander of the Allied forces in World War I and a member of the 40-member French Academy, "wielded a ritual trowel . . . as an emissary of French cultural prestige."[13]

The institute members were highly conservative in their selection process, so it was no surprise that by 1944 they still had not acknowledged the extraordinary talent of some composers of Broadway musicals, or of any composers of African American origin. Taylor's sense of injustice focused on the musicals, and he initiated a plan. He would first try to gain membership for Jerome Kern, whose lineage extended back to the classic 1927 musical *Show Boat*. For his initial assault he sought help from his longtime friend Julian Street. Street was a member of the writer's group of the institute, one of the original members of the Dutch Treat Club, and, along with Taylor, a recipient of one of FPA's timepieces.

"I have been carrying on a vigorous one-man campaign to have Jerome Kern nominated for membership in the Institute," he wrote to Street in 1944. "If you'll propose him, I shall certainly second the proposal and get another seconder." Handwritten at the bottom of the typed letter, Taylor announced his next crusade: "I also want to nominate Oscar Hammerstein II and Richard Rodgers."[14] Street cooperated, and Kern was admitted in 1945, months before he died. A saddened Taylor later wrote: "[I] shall always consider it a disgrace that we didn't elect him soon enough for him to enjoy it."[15] But Kern's membership opened the Broadway gates; Hammerstein was elected to the institute in 1950, and Rodgers in 1955.

Taylor and Lucille had often visited the Park Avenue apartment of Dorothy and Dick Rodgers, and gone on weekends to Rockmeadow, their forty-acre Connecticut estate in Southport. During these visits Linda Rodgers, the teenage daughter, became especially devoted to Taylor because he paid particular attention to her. In her estimation he was, unlike many other visitors, full of humor. Linda had studied piano since age four, and many of her conversations with Taylor built upon common musical experiences at the keyboard. She also observed the warmth and affection between her parents and the Taylors. Yet below the surface there existed several dark sides of Richard Rodgers, including a propensity for alcohol and a penchant for spearing persons with a hostile humor often brought on by overindulgence. Taylor shared his fondness for excessive imbibing, and he never had to feel the sharpness of Rodgers's sarcasm because Rodgers thought too highly of him as a friend.[16]

Trusted completely by both Rodgers and Hammerstein, Taylor began the interviews and research necessary to tell their story. As he wrote in the introduction: "To write the biography of a living person is to tell an unfinished story. The sitter for your portrait doesn't hold still. By the time your book goes to press he may be dead or in jail. . . . It is even more nearly impossible to write a satisfactory biography of *two* living persons." Taylor's charm and writing abilities overcame many of these difficulties as he emphasized their professional lives, beginning with their musical experiences before joining as a team. Hammerstein had worked with many composers, such as Jerome Kern and Sigmund Romberg; Rodgers only with Lorenz Hart. Taylor then turned to the musicals, the joys of *Oklahoma!* and other hits; the sorrows of *Allegro* and *Me and Juliet*.

Just before the book was put on sale, Taylor hurried over to the Rodgerses' apartment with presentation copies. When he gave Linda her own copy, she was somewhat taken aback at the kindness, so she hesitated. "Why don't you open it?" the author asked. She flipped quickly through the pages, looking first at the many photographs of her father and Hammerstein. Then she turned back to the beginning and saw why Taylor insisted on her opening it in his presence, for the dedication read: "To Linda Rodgers from an elderly admirer." It was one of the nicest things that ever happened to the youngest of the Rodgers daughters.[17]

Throughout the time that he worked on *Some Enchanted Evenings,* Taylor continued socializing with the beautiful and perky Betbeze. He cared for her deeply, and she, recognizing his emotions, continually reminded him that "he was never to cross the line."[18] Still, his essential kindness and loyalty impressed her deeply. Though marriage was definitely in Betbeze's plans, the groom would not be Taylor, for she had found someone else. On a lovely spring night in 1954, after she and Taylor had attended a New York City Opera performance of the Prokofiev fantasy opera *Love for Three Oranges,* Yolande Betbeze informed him of her impending marriage to Matthew Fox, an executive in Hollywood at Universal International Pictures.[19] Taylor took the news hard, yet he realized that marrying Betbeze would have been truly a fantasy: a nearly seventy-year-old man marrying Miss America.[20] If his marriage to Lucille had caught the attention of the *Daily News,* this one would have made the front page of the *National Enquirer!*

As his social engagements with Betbeze ended, he found that the years brought less and less income: only about $15,000 in 1955, his lowest net in many years. In addition, the postwar inflation concerned him. His income now relied mostly on ASCAP royalties, diminishing book royalties, and program notes for the Book-of-the-Month classical record club. The year 1955 did bring some financial alleviation, because Mary Kennedy had sold the Stamford property and he no longer had to pay her utility bills and taxes. In addition, Lucille had remarried, and he did not have to send her his self-imposed monthly checks.

Though Taylor had not been blessed with a gene for saving money, nonetheless he found ways to avoid social expenditures. His friend Lyn Murray, a well-known composer and music arranger for radio, pointed out one of these ways in his daily journal: "Monday November 14, 1955: I am in New York seeing some shows and looking up old friends. Saw Deems Taylor. . . . Deems is always a pleasure to see, although he hews to his rule of never picking up a check, but who cares? He's always been so supportive of me and I am truly glad I know him. He lives in a beautiful apartment on Fifth Avenue . . . and is still bitching about the rent—$250."[21]

The beautiful apartment now had no woman in it aside from Lilly. The previous year Joan had moved into her own apartment, taking her son, Michael, to live with her. She now worked in an editorial capacity with Library Publishers, the publishers of *The One-Track Mind.* In spring 1955 she and Donald decided to proceed from separation to divorce. Joan followed her mother's lead; she went to Nevada to establish the necessary six-week residence. Mary agreed to pay for the entire process, mildly satisfied that her prediction had come true. But when Joan returned from the West and went back to work, she found her desk at Library Publishers empty. They had not honored her leave of absence; instead they had fired her. However, she quickly found a better job, as publicity assistant at the Knopf publishing house.

Having enjoyed being with her father for a few years, Joan made sure to stop in often. But she began to observe in Deems signs of memory loss and increased difficulty in walking. Joan worried, but Taylor admitted only that he had slowed down considerably. In the summer of 1957 he insisted on going to Paris to see Lucille once more, and he asked Joan to come with him. He had never lost his fondness for his former wife, and had found a clever way to see her again: by agreeing to do an ad for Air France in exchange for two round-trip tickets. They arrived in time for Bastille Day and, at Lucille's suggestion, stayed at a charming hotel on the Left Bank. Her restaurant had just opened, and she appeared to be her happy self again. This was the memory that Taylor took back with him from his final trip to his beloved Paris.

The Dragon, Taylor's Final Opera

On their return, Joan saw her revivified father tackle the completion of *The Dragon,* a lengthy one-act opera on which he had been working for years. The fictional beast had been in his mind since the success of *Peter Ibbetson* in 1931, when he had written to Mary of his interest in Lady Gregory's play.

The delightful tale tells of an astrologer in ages past, "when there were kings and dragons in Ireland," who on the birthday of the headstrong princess foretells that unless she marries within the year, a dragon will come to consume her. The new chef (the king is obsessed with eating) is actually a disguised young king from a distant land who knows of the danger and has come to battle the dragon, should the beast appear. Then, the astrologer, because of a computational error, apologetically announces that the dragon is to appear that very day.

When the beast is seen in the distance, the young chef goes forth to master it and replaces the dragon's heart with that of a squirrel. The royal family watches from a distance, and the princess collapses. The young chef-hero sends the dragon away to find nuts to satisfy his new squirrel personality, then revives the princess, and a happily-ever-after ending ensues.

In shaping the libretto, Taylor followed the story line fastidiously. In so doing, he produced what is probably the best libretto of all four of his operas. Here was the world of fantasy, a domain that Taylor adored, with characters who showed human emotions in often humorous ways. One wonders why, especially because of the innate sense of wit that he possessed, it took him so long to come to a comic setting as a possibility for an opera.

Using music both new and from the never-produced *Moll Flanders,* Taylor created a lengthy one-act chamber opera, purposely composed to be singable by well-trained young vocalists. Only a few years earlier, in 1954, Aaron Copland had composed his only major attempt at opera, *The Tender Land,* for a similar purpose. Perhaps at an ASCAP meeting, Copland and Taylor had discussed this distinct need, especially because of the increasing number of universities with opera programs. One of these was New York University. Quite naturally, since he was an alumnus, Taylor offered the NYU music department his opera's premiere, an offer readily accepted.

For the January 1958 production, three professional singers took the principal roles in the twelve-person cast, with NYU students assuming the rest. The most important part given to a nonprofessional singer was that of the queen, a role taken by a student, Rita Falbel. Years later she recalled Taylor's presence at rehearsals, continually challenging the student singers to rise to their highest potential: "It was his insistence and support that gave me great confidence."[22]

And with that confidence she succeeded admirably, as the *Herald Tribune*'s music critic, Francis Perkins, noted in his review of the premiere. Perkins wrote that Falbel's role of the queen "was notable for poise and assurance, as well as for commendable singing." To provide such an operatic experience to a student was exactly what Taylor had hoped to achieve. Perkins also lauded the libretto, and "melodies [that] are well turned and appealing."[23] The *Times* critic said that Taylor "has written with high professional skill and consideration for young voices and student musical resources and stagecraft."[24]

Also seated in NYU's three-hundred-seat Hall of Fame Playhouse that night were Oscar Hammerstein and his wife. The next day Hammerstein wrote to his old friend to express his enjoyment: "Dorothy and I thought the score was charming, particularly the third act aria sung by the Princess. . . . I should [think] that the opera should do very well on the university circuit, and in fact anywhere it is played."[25] Hammerstein's assessment unfortunately did not come to pass, for *The Dragon* received no further productions during the twentieth century. An operatic gem awaits rediscovery.

The completion of *The Dragon* effectively ended Taylor's composing career. He did compose some songs later, based on Millay's poems, for the stage piece *A Lovely Light*. In this work, Dorothy Stickney attempted in a one-woman presentation to portray through Millay's poetry her heartaches and triumphs. Stickney liked Deems's songs very much, but in a preview of the show she learned that "every time we stopped for a song the bottom dropped right out of the play, and it had to be picked up off the floor and started over again."[26] Sadly, none of the songs were used for the production.

Ayn Rand Gives an Attentive Ear

Social and intellectual sustenance began to diminish for Taylor, for he had never been one to polish friendships to a persisting luster. Because of his daughter, Ayn Rand brought a special camaraderie to his later years. As a publicity assistant at Knopf, Joan read an advance copy of Rand's *Atlas Shrugged* and found the book fascinating. She wrote a letter of appreciation to the author, who responded by inviting her to lunch. The two women established a friendship, partly because of Joan's deep interest in Rand's highly personal "Objectivism." For Joan, Rand blended literary aptitude and economic philosophy into an attractive package. Her "me first" view became a capitalist commandment for many others as well.

When Joan introduced Rand to her father, the novelist was charmed by him. No one could accuse Rand of being young and beautiful, the usual prerequisites for a Taylor girlfriend, but she offered energy, brains, and a love of music. She also appeared at the right time, because by the late 1950s none of Taylor's music remained in symphonic or operatic repertoire, which made him feel left out of the new world of musical culture. He probably made it clear to her that as a composer he was a loner; romantic and impressionistic music had been supplanted in the national music scene by the modernists. He must have told her how much it had hurt when, at a dinner, he had heard his fellow critic and composer Virgil Thomson brag about defeating "romantic composers by outliving them!"[27]

Sitting and listening to recordings of his works with Rand showed him that someone important still cared about his music. He played commercially released versions of the *Through the Looking Glass* suite and *Portrait of a Lady,* as well as off-the-air recordings he had acquired of his other compositions. Of these, Rand particularly loved the "Introduction and Fandango" from *Ramuntcho,* in a performance by Leopold Stokowski and the NBC Symphony.

Taylor chatted with Rand about fantasy and the difficulties of composing. Impressed by the music she heard, she asked him to consider writing an opera based on her short science-fiction novel *Anthem.* The plot looked to a distant future when "I" is lost from the language and only "We" is used. The hero is the one who rediscovers "I." Rand suggested a Schoenberg-type modernist music for the "non-I" portion, and then a change to romantic melodies of a Rachmaninoff-type when "I" is rediscovered. But Taylor declined. If he had not chosen to compose in modernist style during his more productive years, he would hardly do so now.[28] He also had to admit that the creative juices simply flowed no longer. Now, at age seventy-three, he could only hope that in his remaining years, he would hear some of his music played again. As it turned out, his aspiration was to come true in unusual ways.

20. The Final Years

A Farewell in Chicago

By 1959 there was no denying that Taylor's memory and general health were worsening. The physicians told Joan that there was not only arteriosclerosis, but also the psychosis associated with it: in other words, a form of dementia. Joan wanted to be closer to her father, yet she didn't want to oversee his every move. So she suggested that she become his part-time secretary, stopping in as needed after her regular job. He agreed, as long as she allowed him to pay her an appropriate wage.

Joan now brought an additional source of happiness to Deems, for the previous year she had married David Dawson, a talented writer and jack-of-all-trades in whom her father immediately found a friend, stimulating conversationalist, and good cook. Often on Sunday evenings David would prepare dinner, even inviting Mary Kennedy to join them. After dinner eight-year-old Michael would illustrate the progress he had made in his violin studies, and then everyone would settle in the living room to watch *Maverick* on television.

In addition to these homely pleasures, Thanksgiving and Christmas holidays now were truly special because for the first time the entire Taylor family could get together. Bill Davis had retired from the Air Force and settled with his wife, Virginia, and their four children—Charles, Carolynn, Michael, and Melanie—in New Canaan, Connecticut. As a result, with Deems and the Dawsons in Manhattan, Katy and her family just north in Scarsdale, and the

Davises in nearby Connecticut, each family took turns hosting festive holiday dinners, and very often Mary would join them. Taylor must have felt he now belonged to a complete family.

Because of Deems's diminishing income, George Bye contacted many magazines to see if they had interest in an article from Deems Taylor. When the unlikely door of *Sports Illustrated* opened, Taylor stepped through to write "Sports for Art's Sake." *Damn Yankees,* the musical about baseball, was a current success on Broadway, and this gave him the idea to consider identifying operas that featured a sport. In the article he gave *sport* a broad definition and found fifteen operas with a sporting event in their plots, including card games, duels, bullfighting (in *Carmen*), archery (Rossini's *William Tell*), hunting (in German operas especially), and the Basque sport of pelote in his own *Ramuntcho.*[1]

If the $1,500 for the *Sports Illustrated* story was an unexpected bonus, even more so was an invitation from the Chicago Symphony to be the host and commentator for *Great Music from Chicago,* a major series of television concerts for the Midwest. One can imagine the thrill Taylor experienced in once again providing his musical insights to an audience, this time for a twenty-six-week Sunday evening series. He accepted even though it would demand weekly trips to Chicago. The Chicago Symphony had held a special place in his heart ever since Frederick Stock had been the host thirty years earlier, when Taylor had visited Chicago in his Midwest tour of orchestras.

The Chicago Symphony, a pioneer in regional television presentations, expected their finest season yet, since the concerts would be telecast in color. An advertising blitz was made for the promised classical music from conductors such as Fritz Reiner (then the symphony's permanent conductor), Sir Thomas Beecham, and Sir John Barbirolli. Taylor's personal appearances received equal publicity because of his "national reputation, authenticity, and the ability to communicate with every viewer."[2]

Joan accompanied her father on the first trip, especially concerned about his difficulty in walking. On arrival they met with the officials in charge, and Joan took them aside to tactfully point out that her father, at age seventy-three, was prone to lapses in memory. Taylor himself emphasized his age in an interview with a *Chicago Tribune* reporter, when he told of being old enough to have seen the real Annie Oakley at the Chicago Columbian Exhibition of 1893. He added, "She left me cold."[3]

The first program, like most of the rest, originated not from a concert hall but from the grand ballroom of the Sheraton Hotel, where the large, flat space allowed for more fluid camera movement. What the viewers saw was an aged Taylor with a hoarse voice, who spoke briefly before each number.

The *Chicago Sun-Times*'s review of the concert next morning was headlined, "Symphony 'Great' in New TV Series."[4]

But a few weeks later, complaints surfaced that the combination of Taylor's comments and the commercials made the program too talky, with not enough music. The format changed to a brief introduction and a few words at sign-off, with Taylor's program notes handed out to the audience before the concert. As far as the program itself, in the words of one critic, it was "the year's most important TV project on the local scene."[5]

In a letter to Lucille, Taylor explained that his television experience was a mixed blessing: "They pay well, of course—$1,000 a week—but I never see that. By the time the station has extracted the withholding tax, and my traveling expenses, and my agent's commission I'm lucky to net about four hundred. I admit that is still money, at that. But the strain isn't worth it."[6] He complained that it took him two or three days to prepare the program notes, and he indicated an awareness that he could no longer rely a great deal on his memory: "I've got to be completely accurate in everything I say, otherwise the wolves will be at my heels. And that means burying my nose in books—biographies, dictionaries, encyclopedias." After seven months of weekly flights and persisting health difficulties, Taylor left the program and closed another door on his life—that of a music commentator.

Peter Ibbetson Revived

Taylor's life was becoming strenuous, but after the Chicago series he received a major psychological boost when he learned of plans for a revival of *Peter Ibbetson*. The opera had not been staged since the Metropolitan production, but an off-the-air recording had been made of the Saturday afternoon broadcast of March 17, 1934. It was the discovery of this recording that created interest in a revival. Locked into the fifty aluminum discs of the recorded broadcast were the voices of Lawrence Tibbett, Lucrezia Bori, Edward Johnson, and Gladys Swarthout. The voices could be released only by way of a record player with cactus needles, but the problem was solved, as Taylor explained in a letter to Lucille:

> Since there ain't no more cactus needles . . . Joan's new husband (and what a nice guy!) said "I bet I can put those platters on tape." Which he did, making his own cactus needles out of strips from a bamboo back-scratcher. We now have a fine tape recording of a complete performance. It's not perfect, but it's surprisingly good for an old timer. We played it for Lucrezia Bori and she almost

jumped out of her skin. Then Gladys Swarthout, who was also a member of the original cast, got interested. Frank Chapman [Swarthout's husband] has now interested a guy who puts on a season of opera every summer. The whole thing may blow up, of course—those things generally do—but just the same—well, who knows?[7]

In spite of Taylor's wariness, the New York Empire Music Festival did present *Peter Ibbetson* as its first summer offering of the 1960 season. For the previous five years these productions had been held in a large tent near Bear Mountain, just south of West Point. The festival went first class for *Ibbetson*. Licia Albanese, then a star soprano at the Metropolitan, accepted the key role of Mary, Duchess of Towers, and was coached by her longtime friend Lucrezia Bori, who had originated the role. (Unfortunately, Bori died two months before the performances.) Another link to the original production delighted Taylor: the music director would be Wilfrid Pelletier, who had conducted most of the Metropolitan Opera performances. The orchestra would be members of the former NBC Symphony, renamed the Symphony of the Air after Toscanini left in 1954.

Though *Peter Ibbetson* was to open the festival in the second week of July, nature decreed otherwise. "We have been having what they call 'a spot of trouble' here," Taylor wrote a friend. "The tent in which Ibbetson was to be given has been blown down. . . . However, it has just been decided that a re-assembled cast, with some replacements, will be able to give two performances."[8] The delay did not diminish the interest of friends and an inquisitive press, who wanted to hear the opera that still held the Metropolitan record for the number of performances of an American work.

Reviewers rushed off after the first performance to write their evaluations. Most labeled the opera pleasant but old-fashioned. In the opinion of Jay Harrison of the *Herald Tribune,* "not a note of it—not even the sometimes pithy clashes of tonality—does much to suggest the opera's time of origin. It is a Romantic piece."[9] The *Newsweek* critic, recalling Taylor's curtain speech at the premiere of *Peter Ibbetson,* compared him to that evening of 1931: "To all those who watched the composer bowing and nodding, it was obvious that Deems Taylor was a completely happy person once again."[10]

Indeed, Taylor was pleased by the production, but even more so by what had happened earlier. He and Joan had gone to all the rehearsals, and during the breaks, many of the orchestra members had sought him out to compliment him on the knowledge of their instruments that he had shown in the orchestration. In the years ahead, he would mention this compliment over and over to Joan.

The performance was recorded and later played over a New York radio station. If anything dulled Taylor's excitement for the *Peter Ibbetson* revival, it was a letter received the previous April informing him that his apartment building, his home of twenty years at 2 East Sixtieth Street, was slated for destruction, and he would have to vacate by the end of summer. His seventh-floor apartment, praised by his grandson as "elegant with a killer view of Central Park," had provided the longest residence of his life. It was the center of his universe. Sadly, at age seventy-four Deems Taylor spent the summer looking for an apartment. With Joan's help he found one only a few blocks across town, in the Century Apartments at 25 Central Park West. He moved there in September.

Taylor had never enjoyed playing host for parties in the old apartment. He was comfortable in simply inviting friends over to visit, chat, and listen to music, or stay over after a particularly heavy night on the town. The latter usage had suited the novelist John O'Hara, who for many years had been one of Taylor's chatting and drinking buddies. Their friendship was another example of the interlinked lives of people in the arts during the 1920s, generated by the social world of those days. Early in his reportorial career O'Hara had been secretary to Heywood Broun, undoubtedly through whom he had met Taylor. As early as 1929, O'Hara wrote to a friend in admiration of Taylor's multiple talents: "I hate to think that the world will have to wait for his obituary to learn what a versatile, able guy is Taylor."[11]

Like Taylor, O'Hara loved the social life and believed in free speech, which in his case meant highly descriptive sexual episodes in his novels. That proclivity may have been the reason that O'Hara was continually passed over for election into the conservative National Institute of Arts and Letters, a phenomenon to which he referred as "My Annual Snub."[12] Taylor pushed hard for O'Hara's election, as he had for Jerome Kern's, and when it finally happened in 1957, the author wrote to thank him for "going to bat for me all these years."[13]

As a small token of his gratitude, he invited Taylor to a preview of *Ten North Frederick,* the movie based on his novel of the same name, a book that had been banned as obscene in both Albany and Detroit. "I am inviting a few friends to eat an early meal and go see the picture. Since you qualify as few friends, will you meet us at '21' at seven o'clock? . . . I am paying for the dinner myself, which means it will not be a large one in the populous sense, although you can eat and drink within reason. No seconds on the filet mignon is what I mean. . . . Wear your Legion of Decency ribbon."[14]

When O'Hara learned about the change in apartments, with tongue in cheek (since he had now left his drinking days behind) he let his friend know he was not pleased:

> I got home from Europe yesterday and what do I find? I find you have moved from 2 East 60th to Central Park West. What kind of management is that? Now where can I go when I stumble out of the Copa [Copacabana nightclub] at 4 A.M.? I resigned from the Metropolitan Club years ago because I thought I could always use your flat, and now you do this to me. If you think I am going all the way across the Park you have another think coming. And don't try to placate me by pretending you moved to be closer to the Lincoln Center. I never go there, and you know it. You just did it to be mean, you prick, you. Ever, J. O'Hara.[15]

Two years later O'Hara did lift one glass to honor his old friend, when NYU presented Taylor with the Gallatin Medal.

Throughout his lifetime Taylor had found special friends in the literary world, such as Broun, O'Hara, FPA, and Millay. His closest friends in the music world were the composers of popular songs: George Gershwin, Jerome Kern, and Richard Rodgers. That he had no real friends among the classical composers is not that surprising. Friendship is two-sided, and Taylor, in his glory years of composing, exuded self-sufficiency and independence. Perhaps jealousy also arose in other composers, who saw Taylor rise so quickly into prominence through his operas and radio appearances. More likely, most concert-music composers simply traveled paths that did not intersect with Taylor's.

What Virgil Thomson said about Emerson Whithorne, a composer and a contemporary of Taylor's, could just as easily have been said about Taylor: "[He] was not a bad composer. He was simply not a chum of ours—he wasn't a modernist composer. He wasn't of any group involving Harvard or Boulanger or Copland or any of that."[16] In addition, Taylor lived a vital heterosexual social life, quite different from many of the New York modernist crowd, who were homosexual.

Summers at the National Music Camp

Early in 1959 Taylor received a letter that established a late but ultimately firm friendship with Don Gillis, another composer and wit. Gillis, like Taylor, had had to make his living in other ways. "Although it has been some time since we met," Gillis wrote, "I hope you will remember me as the former producer for the NBC Symphony and Sigmund Romberg shows." Taylor did indeed remember the Missouri-born Gillis, who had achieved special musical fame because of one particular orchestral work, his *Symphony 5½, A Sym-*

phony for Fun, premiered by Toscanini with the NBC Symphony. Gillis explained in his letter that he was now the director of development for a new American opera workshop at the National Music Camp at Interlochen, Michigan. He asked Taylor to be one of their guests "whose significant achievement in operatic writing, performance, and conducting will give the students additional inspiration."[17] Flattered by the invitation, Taylor accepted. He began four consecutive summers of visits that gave the aging composer the joy of hearing performances of his orchestral works by some of the nation's most gifted young musicians.

During his lifelong concern for developing American musicians, Taylor had recognized the importance of the Interlochen camp. On November 29, 1940, the New York Philharmonic had broadcast its Sunday performance from the University of Michigan before a crowd of nearly six thousand. Taylor, making his intermission remarks from the New York studios, had taken the opportunity to praise the National Music Camp and its president, Dr. Joseph Maddy, then also a professor at the university. He told of Maddy's dream of a summer music camp for students, and of how it had become a reality in 1927. "The Interlochen camp, and others, have done invaluable work in training our own native orchestral musicians," Taylor said. "Twenty years ago, 70% of the players in our major symphony orchestras were foreign born. To-

Taylor at the National Music Camp, Interlochen, Michigan.
(Courtesy of Yale University Music Library)

day that proportion has been exactly reversed." After the program, a grateful Maddy had written to Taylor, extending an invitation to visit the camp; Gillis reactivated the invitation twenty years later.

Each summer from 1959 to 1962, Taylor spent at least a week at the four-hundred-acre camp between the two lakes that gave Interlochen its name. For Taylor, a man slipping from public view after decades of fame, Interlochen proved a haven of peace, filled with appreciative young musicians. He began an enduring friendship with Gillis, a man with as wild a wit as his own. During Taylor's visits, Gillis and Maddy provided opportunities for him to meet with students, discuss music, and answer questions about composing. Among the students was Jeff Davis, a teenager to whom Gillis was like a father. Years later, as one of the country's finest carillonists, Davis, with insight and fondness, thought back on the impact Taylor had made on his life:

> He was one of the few truly brilliant persons I have met, and he spoke of music with passion and humor. Interlochen students were not allowed to either drink or go into faculty houses, yet many evenings Don [Gillis] would take me over to Deems's lodgings where we would talk of music. Deems always offered me a drink. These were times of clarification for me. Deems had strongly held opinions on practically every subject imaginable. . . . I think it was over those summers that I came truly to understand that differences of professional opinion stand everyone in good stead. . . . Deems taught me that composing is a way of life, a habit of living. . . . Opposing nearly every composer with whom I have spoken, he advised against working at a keyboard. "You'll end up writing what you can play," he told me. I took that advice to heart, struggling for years to let my aural imagination roam unrestricted by what hands can do. I am truly thankful for that advice. As Deems said to me, "Why do they expect composers to be performers? They don't expect playwrights to be actors."[18]

In his first summer at Interlochen, Taylor shared billing with another guest composer, the television personality Hugh Downs, whose ten-year-old daughter was attending the camp that summer. When he had been a youngster himself, Downs had found music his first love, and had composed pieces by age thirteen. "Some years ago," he wrote later, "I spoke on a radio program with Deems Taylor, who called himself America's most unprolific composer. I told him that as a composer I had him beat, insofar as I was even more unprolific than he."[19]

Taylor was hardly unprolific, having written a half-dozen orchestral works. And during each of his four summers at the camp, an orchestra played at least one of these. In both 1959 and 1962, Joseph Maddy insisted on conducting the *Looking Glass* suite, a special favorite of his. Otherwise he turned the conducting over to A. Clyde Roller, longtime instructor at the Eastman School of Music, whom Maddy had brought to Interlochen in 1951. Roller's experience was broad: he had conducted a symphony orchestra of GIs in France, assembled near Paris after the city had been liberated in World War II; regional orchestras in Texas; and the Boston Pops Esplanade Orchestra.

In his younger years, Roller had listened faithfully to Taylor's Philharmonic intermission commentaries. Meeting him in person proved to be a great thrill for Roller, a poignant moment that he shared with the student orchestra when he introduced Taylor to them: "This is the man whom I have admired so long from his New York Philharmonic broadcasts. It is a great honor to be on the same stage with him." After the introduction, Roller turned to Taylor and saw an aging man with tears in his eyes.[20] An emotional bond joined them from that moment, and they chatted as if old friends.

On one occasion Roller asked Taylor if he had ever conducted an orchestra. The composer indicated he had, and then recounted the time when the Chicago Symphony had invited him to conduct *Circus Day*. He had arrived for the concert only to learn, happily, that the symphony's permanent conductor, Frederick Stock, had rehearsed the orchestra completely. Taylor proceeded to conduct a perfunctory run-through and received the musicians' polite applause. Feeling that he should say something in appreciation, he advised the musicians bluntly: "Gentlemen if anything goes wrong at tonight's performance—for God's sake don't look at me!"[21]

In 1960 Roller conducted the first Interlochen performance of *Marco Takes a Walk,* with the University of Michigan Symphony Orchestra. The next year, again with the same orchestra, Roller brought Taylor's *Three Centuries Suite* to life for the first time in the United States. It proves to be the composer's most melodic work. A courtly, regal pavane serves as an overture, with a melody that equals in beauty that of the "Dedication" of the *Looking Glass* suite. After the pavane, a saraband's deliberate, slow step moves smoothly to a rigadoon, a type of French quickstep. A jig follows, which transforms smoothly into a sweeping waltz melody of the final section, "Bartholomew Fair." A double-time version of the waltz gives the suite a perky Broadway-type final flourish.[22]

On the day of the *Three Centuries Suite* performance, Taylor visited his nine-year-old grandson, Michael Cook, who was spending the first of three summers at Interlochen as a violin student. All of his fees were paid through a quid pro quo arrangement between Maddy and Taylor. Cook remembers the first day his grandfather came to see him at the camp:

> I was swimming across the lake, a feat we all tried to achieve, being monitored by a counselor in a rowboat. I made it, and when I came out of the lake, Deems was on the shore waiting for me. I remember standing awkwardly with him—I guess we were both shy with each other. . . . In any event, I went that night to a concert with him, and sat with him and Don Gillis; both of them had pieces being played. They played a piece he wrote called *Three Centuries Suite,* which is really nice, with some stirring romantic melodies.[23]

At the end of that performance, the Kresge Hall audience applauded long and vigorously. Taylor sat in the front row with a camp hostess, and, following a preconcert arrangement, rose to walk up the stairs to the stage. He was clearly having some difficulty, and a concerned conductor reached down to give him a hand. Taylor slowly mounted the four steps and stood with Roller facing the audience as the applause continued. After acknowledging the appreciation, a smiling Taylor returned cautiously to his seat, then turned to his hostess and asked a quite unexpected question: "Have you ever had to climb stairs with your underwear down around your knees?"[24]

Taylor's grandson remembers another postconcert incident: "Afterwards, people came by to get autographs, and this young flute player (a girl), rushed up to him and said 'Oh Mr. Taylor, thank you so much for writing it!'"[25] The girl was Nancy Howe from Cedar Falls, Iowa, already a special person from Taylor's point of view, for they had met the previous year at Interlochen in a most surprising way, as she recalled years later:

> I first met Deems Taylor the summer of 1959 when I was fourteen years old. It was my first year in the High School division, and I was playing first chair flute, much to my amazement. One of the programs included Deems Taylor's *Through the Looking Glass.* Dr. Maddy told the orchestra that he had phoned Mr. Taylor about the performance and was told, 'Impossible! I don't care how talented they are. No high school orchestra could possibly play that work well!' Dr. Maddy . . . promptly invited Mr. Taylor to be a guest of Interlochen for that week so that he could hear for himself! Mr. Taylor gamely wore the camp uniform, name badge and all, along with his beret.

Nancy Howe's musical abilities impressed Taylor deeply. He chose a special day to present her with a gift. Every Friday morning "challenges" were held as a way for orchestral members to move up in their sections. They accomplished this by challenging those ahead of them to be judged in comparison performances of the same solo work. "When we finished the dreadful challenges," Howe remembered, "I went out to discover my mother was there and she gave me a container of those wonderful black cherries grown in the area. Then I saw Mr. Taylor who handed me this odd bundle of something wrapped in newspaper. When I opened the bundle there was a very old, four-keyed wooden flute! I didn't know what to say, except thank you, and didn't have anything to give him, so I handed him my container of black cherries."[26] The flute that her admirer gave her, made of cocoa wood with ivory rings on each of its three joints, was about 150 years old. The gift established a friendship that persisted in correspondence for many years.

After Taylor's second Interlochen visit in 1960, Gillis wrote to tell him, "I vote you the highlight of my summer program by large odds. It is sunny out but . . . I'd rather sit here and pound this typewriter at you in a vain attempt to recreate the most pleasant mood that surrounded my being able to talk with you while you were here." In 1961 Gillis's deep admiration for Taylor resulted in a unique gift to the composer on his seventy-fifth birthday: a brochure entitled "A Salute to Deems Taylor," listing all his published compositions. Gillis sent it to music schools, symphony orchestras, and everyone on the Interlochen mailing list, urging the programming of the composer's works during the coming year in his honor.[27] A deeply touched Taylor called it one of the nicest things anyone had ever done for him.

But in 1962, when Taylor arrived at Interlochen for what turned out to be his last visit, Gillis was not there to greet him. Disagreements with Joseph Maddy, an aging benevolent autocrat, had led to Gillis's resignation. Writing about his departure to a friend, the conductor Richard Korn, Gillis called the National Music Camp a great institution that had suffered "because of our growing schism and the inevitable separation. Have you ever grown schisms? They are rather difficult to raise in cold climates, but he [Maddy] manages it somehow."[28] Gillis and his wife moved to New York City the following year and became regular visitors to Taylor's Central Park West apartment, where the two men matched wits. "Deems Taylor was one of the wittiest people I have ever known," remembers Gillis's wife, "and Don was not far behind him. There were times when it almost seemed like a contest. I was never sure which one won."[29]

Still, Taylor's downhill mental slide became all too evident to visitors such as the Gillises. His had been a long life of heavy smoking and too much alcohol. Joan, who saw her father every day in her secretarial role, continually wondered how long he would be able to live by himself. Visits from

Opening night of Mary Kennedy's children's play *Ching Ling and the Magic Peach,* 1961. From left: Taylor, David, Joan, Michael, Mary. *(Courtesy of Joan Kennedy Taylor)*

friends perked him up at times, but such occasions became less frequent as his condition worsened. One regular visitor was Mary Kennedy, who would often come by on Sundays to read the *Times.*

But, faithful as Mary remained, her former husband could now take only so much of her at any one time. "To Mary everything is a federal case," Taylor once told his grandson, and when she particularly annoyed him, he called her his "clinging oak." One Sunday morning when Joan and her son stopped by, Mary sat comfortably reading the paper while Taylor remained in his bedroom. "Joan looked in on him," Michael Cook recalled, "and he asked her: 'Is Mary still here?' When Joan responded that she was, her father said: 'Do me a favor. Go into the living room, and when you see her, act surprised, and say: "Oh! Are you still here?"'"[30]

The independent spirit that Taylor had long nurtured was slowly crumbling. Whether he realized it or not, his memory was functioning in erratic spurts. In addition, his financial security had begun to sag considerably; his income in 1962 came to only $8,000, half of which went to pay the rent. He had no health insurance, and medical bills took a good bit of money. As her father's savings accounts crept lower and lower, Joan saw the need to sell the one major asset that remained, the Monet *Nymphéas* painting that ASCAP had given him twenty years earlier. Billy Rose agreed to act as the agent for sale, with no commission. The painting sold for $65,000, money that became the backbone of Taylor's financial future.[31]

NYU Bestows the Gallatin Medal

Nothing lifted Taylor's spirits in 1962 more than the letter he received from James M. Hester, the president of New York University. "It gives me great personal pleasure," wrote Hester, "to inform you of your selection as the recipient of the N.Y.U. Gallatin Medal for 1962. I sincerely hope you will consent to accept this award. . . . Each year, since 1956, the Gallatin Medal has been awarded to an alumnus of N.Y.U. who has made a contribution of lasting significance to society."[32] The president then provided a list of the previous recipients, including Dr. Jonas Salk, developer of the polio vaccine, and Dr. Ralph Bunche, U.S. representative to the United Nations.

One can imagine the smile of appreciation that must have come across Taylor's now-furrowed face upon reading this letter. Other honors had come throughout his active years, including the honorary degrees. But until now, the one honor he had particularly cherished had been the New York Society for the City of New York's 1939 choice of him as "the native son who has by his devotion and zeal done most to add to the prestige of our city."[33]

The Gallatin award dinner at the Hotel Pierre on November 7, 1962, was a bittersweet event. Among the 450 attendees were many of Taylor's friends who probably realized that this would be a final public acknowledgment of what Deems Taylor had meant not only to the university, but also to New York City and to the nation. His family was there, of course: Joan and her husband, David Dawson; his grandson, Michael Cook; his sister, Katy Stranathan, and her husband; his nephew, Bill Davis, and his wife, and the clinging oak, Mary Kennedy. Friends included John O'Hara, Ayn Rand (who insisted on being seated next to O'Hara, whom she had never met), and Howard Barlow, the conductor who had been such an important part of Taylor's musical life. As Taylor looked out from the dais, he must have reflected on friends who could not be present because they had died: Robert Benchley, Lawrence Tibbett, Joseph Urban, Edna St. Vincent Millay, and FPA.

Seated along with Taylor were the requisite NYU dignitaries as well as ASCAP's president, Stanley Adams, Richard Rodgers, and William Schuman, the composer and head of Lincoln Center. At the conclusion of dinner, Schuman officially introduced the guest of honor and called attention to his category of talents ("at least those that can be repeated at a dinner"): "composer, speaker, popularizer, writer, author, critic, translator, editor, and

Taylor and the novelist John O'Hara admiring the 1962 Gallatin Award, presented to Taylor by NYU. *(Courtesy of Yale University Music Library)*

judge of Miss America." In a beautiful sentence he summed up why Deems Taylor had been chosen: "He is," Schuman said, "a man for all reasons." As the audience applauded, the honoree rose with some difficulty and, beaming with joy, approached the microphone. When the applause ceased, the audience heard a man whose voice was a pale shadow of the one they had heard in former times:

> Thank you, Dr. Schuman. This award is doubly important to me, for it comes from the university that has in so many ways helped to shape my life, and it has been presented by a fellow musician. When I looked over the list of past winners of the Gallatin Award, as I read the names of those distinguished people, I couldn't help wondering how a musician could make a contribution to society comparable to that made—for example—by a statesman or an eminent jurist. I

think that it is one of the triumphs of human civilization that this is considered to be so—that people have time not only for what keeps them physically alive, but for what they enjoy. It was at New York University that I first learned that. When I said that it has helped to shape my life, I meant that it was my college days that made me realize how many fields were open to me. I entered N.Y.U. determined to be an architect. But while there, I had the time to write music, and hear people play music that I had written—and I graduated from N.Y.U. determined to be a composer. Alma Mater is not just someone to be obeyed and admired. She says: "Here is the sum total of human knowledge. Now what do you want? And are you willing to work for it?" In the many, many years since then, N.Y.U. has kept on encouraging me. It was at this university that my first comic opera was performed—in 1906. It was this university that performed my most recent opera—in 1958. And as for tonight, well, in the course of a lifetime, I have experienced certain rare moments, I think we all do, moments when we say to ourselves, "This I shall remember all my life." For me, this is one of those moments. Thank you.[34]

A Downhill Slide

Joyful as the evening was for Taylor and his family and friends, grim reality struck the following morning when Joan went to her father's apartment and discovered a befuddled awardee; he had slept all night in sartorial disarray, unable to get out of his tuxedo. Joan decided then and there that her father could no longer live alone. Not only were his mental faculties impaired, but also there were significant physical problems. His friend Lyn Murray confirmed this on December 20, 1962, several weeks after the Gallatin dinner: "Took Deems Taylor to lunch at Pierre's," Murray wrote in his journal on that day. "He is barely able to walk now. Sad."[35]

Joan and David decided that Deems must come to live with them. First they considered renting a larger apartment, but financially that was impossible, so they chose another plan: the rearrangement of their six-room Eighty-fifth Street apartment. When Joan told her mother of the proposed solution, Mary opposed the idea because to her the Dawsons' West Side apartment was déclassé. After her former husband's years on Fifth Avenue and then Central Park West, how could she allow him to move into an Eighty-fifth Street apartment? Mary had closed her eyes to the extent of his physical deterioration, but Joan opened them using his post-Gallatin confusion as ammunition.

That very day Mary did a complete turnaround and spoke to Deems, stating emphatically that she believed it best that he move in with Joan, David, and his grandson. Mary's approval was all Taylor needed to hear, for she was still a guide. He agreed to the plan with one proviso: he insisted on helping financially. In addition to the fifty dollars a week that he paid Joan for her secretarial work, he would now pay two hundred for room and board.

Taylor left the Century Apartments and moved in with the Dawsons early in 1963. Joan incorporated many of his favorite pieces of furniture into both his new bedroom and their joint living area to assure his comfort. After he had settled in, she kept her mother informed about his physical and mental condition: "He's been reading and watching TV, but nothing else—no answering letters, or sorting papers—just reading, TV and getting dressed, with an occasional talk with a guest."[36] In spite of his difficulties, Joan and David were determined to take him to any concerts that had programmed a Taylor composition. Twice they flew to Miami during 1963: in July Taylor heard the Miami Pops, conducted by his old friend Howard Barlow, perform the *Looking Glass* suite, and in December another old friend, Fabien Sevitzky, conducted a performance of a symphonic poem from orchestral portions of *Peter Ibbetson*. At least someone was remembering him as a composer.

The King's Henchman Returns to Say Good-bye

Taylor's first year with the Dawsons went well enough, though he was becoming increasingly feeble, but in the summer of 1964 the unexpected visit of two nuns energized him. Sister Helen Jean Sullivan and Sister Mary Brigid from Mercyhurst College in Erie, Pennsylvania, came to seek his permission to produce *The King's Henchman* the following spring for the Fine and Lively Arts Festival in the Erie area. The small Catholic college had a strong music department headed by Sister Helen, a graduate of the New England Conservatory. But the main interest in the opera came from Sister Mary, who headed Mercyhurst's drama department and admired Millay's poetry. The request aroused Taylor's enthusiasm for an unexpected reason, as the nuns found out. He told them that the opera had been dedicated to his daughter and her mother, but that his daughter had never seen a production of it. This would give Joan that opportunity, so he gave his blessing to the nuns and told them that he would attend, if his health permitted.

The nuns returned to Mercyhurst in high spirits, though they realized that *The King's Henchman* would be the most difficult production they had ever attempted at the college. Nevertheless, for Sister Helen it became "one of my fondest memories of my years at Mercyhurst."[37] Preparation for the early May performances involved dozens of students, including drama club members who transformed some two hundred yards of material into seventy-five costumes.[38] In addition, five knitters prepared the cloth that, when sprayed with a copper-colored solution, gained a chain-mail armor effect. Sister Mary Brigid oversaw the staging, while Sister Helen conducted rehearsals. Some of the student singers had to balance family and song, as did Boyd Dolan, who sang the role of Aethelwold, the king's henchman. Dolan was already the father of two children, and every night his pregnant wife played the score on the piano for him to learn his difficult role. Hers was no easier—their baby was born two days before opening night![39]

Taylor's memory and speech had deteriorated noticeably by the time of the production, yet Joan and David insisted he attend. They believed the trip would lift his spirits. When their plane landed at Erie's airport the day of the first performance, an enthusiastic contingent of Mercyhurst students and a mayor's representative met them with a banner proclaiming "Deems Taylor Day in Erie." A newspaper reporter and several nuns accompanied Taylor and his family to their motel, where he repeatedly mentioned the joy he had in knowing that his daughter would finally see her opera.[40] After the nuns had left, the reporter overheard him asking his daughter, "Now that the girls are gone, can I have a cigarette?"[41] On doctor's orders he had ended more than forty years of smoking, so in place of cigarettes Joan gave her father butter-rum Life Savers. The fastidious Taylor's new habit was to put the very last part of the candy into an ashtray as if stubbing out a cigarette.

Being used to professional presentations, Taylor must have wondered what he would be seeing and hearing as he approached the Weber Memorial Theatre for the first Mercyhurst performance of *The King's Henchman*. Not unexpectedly, as a reviewer would describe, what he saw in the first minutes was "a group of rather frightened young performers trying too hard to tell the tenth century story with Taylor's 20th century music." However, the young singers quickly gained confidence and, with the two-piano accompaniment, ultimately provided a performance that was "colorful and very satisfactory."

Taylor took his bows and joined the excited crowd of students, nuns, and Mercyhurst friends backstage. Though memory lapses now were all too common, he rallied to give a short speech telling the singers and stage personnel that "he was truly astonished at the remarkable and lovely performance and felt that great credit was due [them] for the beauty of both the staging and the singing."[42] Nothing could have been sweeter to him than having seen and heard his first opera "child" while surrounded by the joy of spirited young singers, the hospitable Mercyhurst nuns, his daughter, Joan, and her husband.

On returning to New York, another pleasant surprise awaited: the

ASCAP board had voted him $10,000 a year for life, a token of thankfulness for his thirty years of loyalty, labor, and love. Very likely they had learned of his financial difficulties and decided to help out.

Only months after the notification of this yearly gift, Joan had to write one of the most painful letters she ever would: she informed ASCAP president Stanley Adams of her father's resignation from the ASCAP board. Though the reason was not in the letter, everyone concerned understood that his mental and physical state no longer permitted involvement. Adams quickly responded: "The Board reluctantly accepted the resignation but instructed me to stress the inadequacy of words in expressing the appreciation and gratitude of everyone connected with the Society towards the one and only Deems Taylor."[43]

The following spring, Joan informed close friends of her father's downward spiral. Among those to whom she wrote was the English character actor Reginald Gardiner:

> [He] has been having a very hard time this spring. . . . [H]e had a rather bad fall in which he cut his head, and a mild thrombosis attack. He has also been failing even more mentally and although we have an electric eye up in his room now, so that even if I am in another part of the house, I will know when he gets up and tries to walk around, the doctors have decided that he should go into a nursing home. . . . As a matter of fact, his doctor thinks that a new environment and the need to be charming to the nurses may actually result in an improvement in his condition.[44]

But a nursing home was not needed, for soon after writing this letter, Joan found her father collapsed on the floor of his bedroom. He was rushed to the Medical Arts Center Hospital on Fifty-seventh Street, where he survived in a semicoma for six weeks. There he would take food only from his daughter or from Mary Kennedy, the woman whose approbation he continually had sought from the day they had met.

On July 4, 1966, the *New York Times* opened an honored place on its front page to announce that Deems Taylor, a New Yorker who had shared his multiple talents with the world, had died the night before. Upon Joan fell the sad necessities of making the funeral arrangements.[45] Because it was the Fourth of July, she informed special friends by telegram that the services would be held two days later at the Frank Campbell funeral home. She cabled Lucille in Paris. Word spread and telegrams arrived, some from friends such as Yolande Betbeze Fox and Giuliana Taberna Fields, who had shared the joys of his companionship. Others came from famed musicians such as Jascha Heifetz and Duke Ellington, the latter extolling Taylor as "a great man whose many credits were not as many as he deserved."[46] Especially touching words came from William Grant Still, words from the heart of a man who knew of the many battles that Taylor had fought for him and other American composers: "We are sorry that your father's time here has come to an end for we wish he could have stayed longer. However his monumental contribution to our culture will always live in our minds and hearts. We regard his passing as a tremendous personal loss."[47] Years later, Still's daughter Judith recalled a touching scene: "My father wept when Deems died."[48]

As the mourners arrived at the mortuary chapel, the organ played Taylor's songs written for Mary Kennedy's book *A Surprise to the Children.* They saw their friend lying in an oak coffin, which Joan had chosen because it "looked rather Jacobean . . . the kind of coffin he would have made."[49] He was dressed in white tie and tails, with the button of the American Academy of Arts and Letters in his lapel. Among the sixteen pallbearers were Marc Connelly, Richard Rodgers, John O'Hara, and Stanley Adams. Taylor's family filled the front pews: Joan, David, Michael, Mary ("his widow," as she thereafter insisted on being called), his nephew Bill Davis, and the Davis family. Katy and her family had left on vacation just prior to his death. Because of this, and her Christian Science beliefs opposing funeral services, she chose not to return.

At the beginning of the service, William Hess sang the "Ave Maria" from *Ramuntcho.* To deliver a eulogy Joan chose Don Gillis, for no friend had been closer to her father in the final years. An emotional Gillis arose and told of his admiration for the multi-gifted man: "He was a gentle man . . . a man to whom achievement was but a natural thing and to whom, when honors came (as they did in abundance), they were to be tolerated, not worn in ostentation."[50] Gillis shared portions of a letter from Ross Hastings, a composer and writer Taylor had not known but who represented the thousands whose lives he had changed.[51]

The Hastings letter had arrived while Taylor remained in a semicoma, too late for him to appreciate the gratitude in it: "You were a real inspiration to me and to the gang with whom I passed the 1930s," wrote Hastings, pointing out reasons such as "the wonderful Philharmonic intermission talks" and *Fantasia.* From Taylor's appearance on *Kraft Music Hall,* he recalled an example of his wit in explaining the importance of the saxophone: "John Philip Sousa was one of the first bandmasters to employ the saxophone. This later led to the World War." After the laughter had subsided, Gillis continued with Hasting's tribute: "These things taught us much, not just music, but wit, the beauty of clear thinking, and above all, that one need not necessarily be a kook to be a music lover. Every guy I knew, whether he planned to be a musician or not, wanted to grow up to be like you. . . . None of us ever made it, of course, but we certainly were a lot better off for having tried. My dear friend, please accept my humble and belated thanks."[52]

With the memorial service over, family and friends drove north some thirty miles from midtown Manhattan to the Kensico cemetery in Valhalla, New York. There they gathered in a small chapel, to be with their friend one last time. Simply and sorrowfully, the silence of the world of the dead was broken by the sounds of music and a familiar voice from a 1942 radio broadcast: it was the final scene of *The King's Henchman,* the death of Aethelwold, and above the music Deems Taylor was heard describing the action. Nothing could have been more appropriate—the music of his greatest triumph in a recording made of a radio broadcast that included his own voice, played on this day in Valhalla, a name made famous by Taylor's "Monster," Richard Wagner. The three major talents of this extraordinary man—composer, radio personality, and writer—joined in a final tribute.

And what of an epitaph? Years earlier, the composer himself had considered his end and words to summarize his feelings about it. His choice was uncomplicated and to the point: "Here lies Deems Taylor—under protest!"[53]

Epilogue

After a sleep of forty years, Deems Taylor's operatic spirit awoke in the spring of 1999, not in New York, as might be expected, but in Seattle. But it was a New Yorker—maestro Gerard Schwarz, champion of early-twentieth-century composers' music—who breathed life into Taylor's music. He chose to highlight the inaugural year of the Seattle Symphony's new home, Benaroya Hall, by conducting two performances of a concert version of *Peter Ibbetson*.

The hall's beautiful main auditorium, with 2,500 rust-red seats and reddish-brown wood-paneled walls, was filled both evenings. In the audience were Joan, his grandson, Michael, his nephew Robert Stranathan, and his grandnephew Michael Davis. Absent, though probably there in spirit, were Deems's gatekeeper, Mary, who had died in 1987, and David Dawson, who had died in 1979. Lucille, still living in Paris and pursuing her career as an artist, was unable to attend.

The Seattle Symphony, the symphony chorus, and three top-notch American soloists—Lauren Flanagan, Anthony Dean Griffey, and Richard Zeller—gave impassioned, first-class performances. From the waltz melodies of the opening scene to the somber orchestral threads underlining Peter Ibbetson's death sentence, the presentation greatly pleased nationally known critic Byron Belt, who called it "a rich restoration of a truly wonderful opera."[1] In its own way, the performance supported the contention of the American music historian Nicholas E. Tawa: "Taylor deserves recognition as a major composer who knew how to write music."[2]

Although today's average music lover may not know Deems Taylor's compositions, Taylor himself is remembered fondly by those who grew up during the golden years of radio. Writers on the subject of music also know the name well, for many have garnered one of the annual ASCAP–Deems Taylor awards, established by the society a year after Taylor's death to honor "the gifted composer-critic-commentator."[3]

Of Character and Circumstances

The Canadian historian Donald Creighton (1902–79) defined history as "the record of an encounter between character and circumstances."[4] How well this applies to the life of Deems Taylor. He had the character to succeed in all the areas of his multiple talents, and circumstances allowed them to fit the cultural needs of the early twentieth century. When music critics were major forces on the New York scene, he became a successful one by incorporating into his reviews a broad band of wit, musical knowledge, and experience as a composer. When the Metropolitan continued its search for a successful opera by a native-born composer, he filled the vacuum by writing not one but two and thereby provided, as Carolyn Guzski has noted, "a significant foundation upon which future efforts could rest."[5] When radio became a presence throughout the country, Deems Taylor became one of its best-known voices, particularly as the spokesman for "good music," which in his mind meant much more than just classical music. And when ASCAP desperately needed a president to smooth troubled waters, the diplomatic Taylor was there to lead his beloved organization.

His clarity of thought, nonjudgmental nature, and humor made him a welcome guest among the leaders of the arts in New York City, the cultural capital of the United States. Socially, his charm and puckish nature drew women to him. But what prevented Taylor's growth, as we have explored, was his preoccupation with youth, as well as with what appeared to be a search for the perfect woman.

One is reluctant to call that quest an obsession, but nothing sheds more light upon these preoccupations than the subject matters of many of his musical compositions. In *The Siren Song,* the beauty of enchantresses lures men to their deaths. *Through the Looking Glass* takes us into the world of eternally young Alice. *Portrait of a Lady* is a musical picture of an idealized woman. *Jurgen* is a fantasy journey to find eternal youth and a woman of beauty with whom to share life. *Circus Day* tells of a child's special day at a one-ring circus. In *Peter Ibbetson,* a dream-journey seeks lost youth and happiness. *The Dragon* shows us a disguised young prince who saves a beautiful young princess, and the music of *Three Centuries Suite* was inspired by the literary Everywoman Moll Flanders.

How Taylor came to such preoccupations must be left to psychologists, but it does seem that Taylor, like Peter Pan, did not want to grow up, either as a person or as a composer.

Some Reflections on Deems Taylor's Music

If all of Taylor's orchestral works were played in sequence, they would occupy one's attention for just over two hours. From *Siren Song* in 1913 to his final work in 1960, *Three Centuries Suite,* Taylor's orchestral music remained consistently within the romantic and impressionistic world. He never developed a style that would make a listener say, "Ah, this must be by Deems Taylor." What his works do disclose is an effective approach to orchestration, modeled greatly on Tchaikovsky's economy of instruments, which Taylor himself identified as "Not what can I put in, but what I can do without."[6] For Taylor, pianissimos far outweigh fortissimos, and subtlety is the order of the composer's day.

The conductor A. Clyde Roller has brought a variety of Taylor's orchestral works to life. His comments about the music have the ring of both admiration and experience:

> There is a certain naiveness about Taylor's manner of composing that makes him uniquely what he is. There is no pretentiousness about his composition and . . . whether it be *Through the Looking Glass* suite, *Circus Day,* or *Marco Takes a Walk,* the musical pictures come through with much clarity. . . . I never get the feeling that he tries to overpower you with a compositional egotism just to prove what a brilliant student of music he is. Rather, he uses the most basic methods in structure and color to achieve his unique results. He uses the orchestra (large or small) to convey the pictures that he would have you enjoy and not over-orchestrate just for the sake of showing off.[7]

Through the Looking Glass is his masterpiece. Most critics were amazed that someone who was self-taught in orchestration could provide such unusual instrumental color so early in a career. In his monograph *Deems Taylor,* the music historian and composer John Tasker Howard speaks of the suite as "impressions clearly delineated, and painted with a sparkle and brilliance that prove irresistible and dazzling."[8] Nicholas Tawa, in *Mainstream Music of Early Twentieth Century America,* simply states: "This outstanding work deserves life."[9] Taylor himself listed the suite as his "most important and characteristic work."[10]

Other significant Taylor compositions for orchestra can be counted on the fingers of one hand. Of these, *Marco Takes a Walk* follows close behind *Looking Glass* in quality and importance in Taylor's output of musical fantasy. This work never received a commercial recording. If it had, it probably would have become a standard for children's concerts, because its musical depiction of a child's imagination at work—transforming a simple horse and wagon into colorful animals pulling exotic carriages—has charm and verve. Roller conducted the work many times with regional orchestras, often with a narrator describing the transformations with the words that inspired the composition, Dr. Seuss's *And to Think That I Saw It on Mulberry Street*. The result he found highly effective.

Circus Day also never received a separate commercial recording, though it exists as part of the release of the September 1940 ASCAP concert in San Francisco (see appendix 2). Here too is a charming work that would benefit any children's concert. Howard Taubman wrote of the "moments of delightful humor in it; the grunting of the lion, the waltzing elephants, the precariously situated tight-rope walker. But the piece is too long."[11] William Rose Benet was "fascinated by what one might call the onomatopoetic effects" of the composition.[12] Performing a judicious selection of portions of the suite could provide a special experience for children.

Portrait of a Lady and *Jurgen* (later transformed into a slightly different version, *Fantasy on Two Themes*) both have elements of fantasy. *Portrait of a Lady*, with a piano representing the lady, has the lightness of the aforementioned works; its character is that of the atmosphere of New York City in the 1920s. *Jurgen,* on the other hand, has a musical depth that demands attention because, quite unlike other Taylor works, it is musically murky on first hearing. Both John Tasker Howard and Christopher Mehrens expound critically on the themes of *Jurgen,* but Mehrens is more critical. He sees the music as "safely conventional . . . [with] little in terms of originality." In addition, he points to the "dense harmonic language and mundane thematic material."[13]

Yet throughout repeated playings of both the Michael Keith recording (produced via a music synthesizer) and an off-the-air recording of *Fantasy on Two Themes,* there remains a haunting quality in the work. With an inspired conductor, *Jurgen* or *Fantasy on Two Themes* should prove to be a moving musical experience for an audience. On quite another level, *Three Centuries Suite,* with some of Taylor's most effective melodies, has immediate audience appeal.

As to why the operas have disappeared in spite of their original success, there is a simple answer: fame in the arts is often ephemeral, for what is popular in one generation may be cast aside by the next. Taylor's music and librettos looked back rather than forward, and as a result, his music lost out to the modernist compositions that infused the musical domain from the 1930s onward. Now that tastes have turned back to tonality and lyricism, Taylor's music is due for reconsideration.

About *The King's Henchman* Nicholas Tawa suggests, "It is no small thing to write a fine theater piece replete with music that catches the public's fancy." Tawa's findings on *Peter Ibbetson* are that "the music is excellent throughout, though none of it boasts great individuality."[14] The ever-critical Paul Rosenfeld, five years after the premiere of *Peter Ibbetson,* admitted that the opera was "the Metropolitan's outstanding American success" and that Taylor was "the equal of the Mascagnis, the Wolf-Ferraris, and other European makers of effective operas."[15]

As for Taylor's third opera, *Ramuntcho,* Tawa notes that it "met with the usual enthusiasm from the audience, and the usual denunciation from the reviewers for its lack of originality. No one questioned the craftsmanship or the musicalness of the score, nor the aptness for the stage. It, like his previous two operas . . . was undeservedly relegated to the dustbin. All three stage works merit better treatment."[16] The one-act *Dragon* met a similar fate, but as it is Taylor's best libretto, when rediscovered it should prove a valuable addition to opera ensembles of young singers. In that regard, so should *Ramuntcho.*

Thoughts in Conclusion

It is clear that after completing *Ramuntcho* in 1937, Deems Taylor, the man who considered himself first and foremost a composer, cut back severely on his activities as a composer. He had become subsumed into radio, a financial siren song that he could not resist. But there is another aspect to consider: Taylor had achieved success too early, initially by winning a national competition in his first attempt at orchestral writing, then by presenting two successful cantatas. Afterward, both *Through the Looking Glass* and *The King's Henchman* were highly lauded achievements. Such success gave Taylor a severe case of independence. Unlike Aaron Copland, who ultimately would far exceed him in fame as a composer, Taylor never took the time to be challenged by others in his musical development. So far as is known, after his months of study with Oscar Coon, he never sought to learn from another teacher or even to solicit advice about how to develop his compositional skills.

He also painted himself into a corner where musical inspirations came from literature, as was the case with *Jurgen* and *Peter Ibbetson*. Why he never wrote a symphony is understandable, because for this genre form must precede content, something contrary to his impressionistic style of composing.

Often a person's writings are camouflaged autobiography, and Taylor, in his verbal depiction of the White Knight in *Looking Glass,* may well have been describing himself. The knight was "mild, chivalrous, ridiculous, and rather touching . . . a gentle soul, with good intentions."[17] If we add to that the word *multitalented,* we have Deems Taylor. Yet, a multitude of talents is not necessarily an advantage, as he wrote regarding his good friend Joseph Urban, the scenic designer and architect: "Because he stood for more than a single phase of his art, he could not be trade-marked; and a man who cannot be trade-marked is at a disadvantage in an era of specialization."[18] As successful as Taylor was in so many areas, he did not hone any of his talents to the level of persisting fame.

In the final analysis, Deems Taylor's skills entertained millions and influenced thousands of musicians. There is no way to quantify his impact as his era's articulate spokesman for American music and musicians, but clearly it was highly significant. Consider the millions of listeners who tuned into the New York Philharmonic Sunday broadcasts and heard him speak imaginatively about highbrow music and the human nature of its composers, people like himself, who had to try out their wings and fly. In his day, no one came near him as a representative of the world of classical music.

Later in television, Leonard Bernstein, through his exceptional gifts as composer, conductor, and speaker (not to mention his physical appeal), attracted millions of Americans, especially the young, to knowledge of the forms of classical music. Now there is no one who has taken on the mantle of teacher. At a time when classrooms are linked to the Internet, those who still believe that we need to keep an appreciation for music's past have the vehicle, but not the voice.

Today there remain many tangible legacies of Deems Taylor: his music, his writings, and his appearance in *Fantasia*. His music deserves to be heard and enjoyed, his books warrant being read and reread, and his presence in the Disney masterpiece among the cartoon characters ought to be cherished forever. In a manner of speaking, *Fantasia* is the ideal environment in which he should be remembered.

Appendix 1: Chronological List of Compositions

Following are the compositions of Deems Taylor, both published and unpublished. The composer prepared a list in September 1941, and I updated it for this book. For Taylor's song arrangements, see John Tasker Howard's monograph *Deems Taylor*. Both the 1927 and 1940 editions include a complete list.

The Deems Taylor Papers at the Irving S. Gilmore Music Library of Yale University are a major source of his original manuscripts and copies of published music. Some original manuscripts are also in the Library of Congress.

At the time of writing this book, some of Taylor's orchestral works with full orchestra parts were available from:

[BM] Belwin Mills Rental Catalog
c/o European American Music Distributors
15800 NW 48th Avenue, Miami, FL 33014
Phone: (305) 521-1604. E-mail address: eamdc@eamdc.com

Some orchestral works are on deposit at:

[FLE] Edwin A. Fleisher Collection of Orchestral Music
The Free Library of Philadelphia
1901 Vine St., Rm. 125, Philadelphia, PA 19103
Phone: (215) 686-5313

The far right column identifies the location of the orchestral parts as BM and/or FLE.

Name of Composition		Composed	Publisher	Available
——	Songs for NYU show			
	The Isle of Skidoo	1906	Unpublished	
——	Songs for NYU show *The Oracle*	1907	Unpublished	
——	Seven songs from NYU show			
	Cap'n Kidd and Co.	1908	George Lunt	
——	Vocal selections from *The Echo*	1909	Wm. Maxwell	
Op. 1	*Two Indian Love-Lyrics:*			
	"The Dawn Breeze,"			
	"Alone I Wait"	1910–11	Unpublished	
Op. 2	*The Siren Song* (symphonic poem			
	for orchestra)	1912	Unpublished	BM
Op. 3	"Witch Woman" (song for voice			
	and piano)	1912	Oliver Ditson	
Op. 4	*Two Songs* (voice and piano):			
	"The Rose," "The Lake"	1913	Unpublished	
Op. 5	*Two Studies in Rhythm* (piano):			
	"Prelude," "Poem"	1913	J. Fischer	
Op. 6	*Plantation Love Song*			
	(voice and piano)	1913	J. Fischer	
Op. 7	*The Chambered Nautilus*			
	(cantata for mixed chorus)	1914	Oliver Ditson	
Op. 8	*The Highwayman*			
	(cantata for women's chorus)	1914	Oliver Ditson	
——	Songs for *A Breath of Scandal*			
	(Dutch Treat Club)	1916	Dutch Treat Club	
Op. 9	*The City of Joy* (song cycle			
	for voice and piano)	1916	Oliver Ditson	
Op. 10	"Time Enough" (voice and			
	piano)	1915	Oliver Ditson	
Op. 11	*Three Part-Songs* (voice and piano):			
	"May Eve,"	1915	J. Fischer (1918)	
	"Tricolor"	1917	J. Fischer (1918)	
	"Valse Ariette"	1918	J. Fischer	
——	Folksong arrangements for			
	Schumann Club	1917–20	J. Fischer	
Op. 12	*Through the Looking Glass*			
	(suite—chamber orch.):	1917–19	Unpublished	BM
	"Dedication," "Jabberwocky,"			

Name of Composition	Composed	Publisher	Available
"Looking-Glass Insects," "White Knight"			
Through the Looking Glass (suite—full orchestra): "Dedication," "Garden of Live Flowers," "Jabberwocky," "Looking-Glass Insects," "White Knight" "Dedication" (arr. for organ by Charles Courboin)	1922 1924	J. Fischer (1923) J. Fischer	BM, FLE
Op. 13 *Three Songs* (voice and piano): "The Rivals," "A Song for Lovers," "The Messenger"	1919	J. Fischer	
Op. 14 *The Portrait of a Lady* (rhapsody for strings, wind, and piano)	1919, 1924	J. Fischer (1932)	BM, FLE
Op. 15 *Traditional Airs* (voice and piano)	1918–20	J. Fischer	
——— Songs for *What Next?* (musical revue)	1920	Unpublished	
——— Songs for *Heigh-Ho* (musical revue)	1920	Unpublished	
——— Incidental music for *Liliom* (drama)	1921	Unpublished	
——— Incidental music for *Will Shakespeare* (drama)	1922	Unpublished	
——— "I Have a Rendezvous with Death" (voice and piano), for stage production *Humoresque*	1923	Unpublished	
——— Incidental music for *Rita Coventry* (drama)	1923	Unpublished	
——— Incidental music for *The Adding Machine* (drama)	1923	Unpublished	
——— "Captain Stratton's Fancy" (voice and piano)	1923	J. Fischer	
——— Incidental music for *Casanova* (see Op. 22)	1923	Unpublished	
Op. 16 Incidental music from *Beggar on Horseback:* *A Kiss in Xanadu* (piano)	1924	J. Fischer	
——— Motion picture score for *Janice Meredith*	1924	Robbins-Engel, Inc.	

Name of Composition		Composed	Publisher	Available
Op. 17	*Jurgen* (symphonic poem for orchestra)	1925	J. Fischer	
	Revised and renamed *Fantasy on Two Themes*	1942	J. Fischer	BM
Op. 18	*Circus Day: Eight Pictures from Memory*			
	Orchestrated by Ferde Grofé for jazz orchestra	1925	Unpublished	
	Orchestrated by composer for full symphony	1933	J. Fischer (1934)	BM, FLE
Op. 19	*The King's Henchman* (lyric drama in three acts)	1926		
	Piano-vocal score		J. Fischer (1927)	BM
Op. 20	*Peter Ibbetson* (lyric drama in three acts)	1929–30		
	Piano-vocal score		J. Fischer (1931)	BM
	"Dream Finale," "Inn Music," "Waltzes"			BM
———	"Page's Air" for Millay's *Princess Marries the Page*	1932	J. Fischer Unpublished	
———	Four songs for *A Surprise to the Children*	1933	Doubleday, Doran	
———	Incidental music for *Lucrece*	1932	Unpublished	
Op. 21	*Lucrece Suite* for string quartet	1933	J. Fischer	
———	*The Smugglers* (piano solo)	1936	Carl Fischer	
Op. 22	Ballet music from *Casanova*	1937	J. Fischer	BM
———	"Tandis qu'amour dormait"	1938	Unpublished	
———	"Choric Song" from *The Lotus Eaters*	1939	Unpublished	
Op. 23	*Ramuntcho* (lyric drama in three acts)	1937–40		BM
	Piano-vocal score		J. Fischer (1941)	
	"Introduction and Ballet"	1940	J. Fischer	BM, FLE
———	Music for *Cavalcade of America* program:	1940	Unpublished	
	"Battle Hymn of the Republic," with A. Woollcott			
———	*Processional* for National Inst. of Arts & Letters	1941	Unpublished	
———	Music for Norman Corwin radio drama, *Job*	1941	Unpublished	

Name of Composition		Composed	Publisher	Available
Op. 24	*A Fanfare for Russia*	1942	Unpublished	
	An arrangement in *Ten Fanfares by Ten Composers for Brass and Percussion*	1944	Boosey & Hawkes	FLE
Op. 25	*Marco Takes a Walk: Variations for Orchestra*	1942	Unpublished	BM
——	*A Christmas Overture*	1943	Unpublished	
——	"Variation" for *Variations on a Theme of Goossens*	1945	Unpublished	
——	*Elegy for Orchestra*	1945	Unpublished	BM
——	*Moll Flanders* (lyric comedy in two acts)	1947	Unpublished	
——	*Restoration Suite*. Renamed *Three Centuries Suite*	1950	Unpublished	BM
——	Songs to poems of Edna St. Vincent Millay	1950–?	Unpublished	
——	*The Dragon* (chamber opera)	1956	Unpublished	

Appendix 2: Commercial Recordings of Compositions

The following is a list of the commercial recordings made of Taylor's compositions. Some of his works exist also in off-the-air recordings, as well as in private recordings of concerts (e.g., Interlochen) or operas (such as the Mercyhurst College production of *The King's Henchman*). Most of the noncommercial recordings can be found in either of two important collections: the Yale University Historical Sound Recordings and the Rodgers and Hammerstein Archives of Recorded Sound of the New York Public Library, Lincoln Center Performing Arts division. The Rodgers and Hammerstein Archives are available to the general public (and noted "R & H Archives" below).

When known, the year of recording is stated. As of this writing, except for some of the compact discs (CDs), most of the commercial recordings are no longer available. Some may appear occasionally on Internet auction sites such as eBay.

Orchestral Works

Through the Looking Glass, op. 12
>Howard Barlow and the Columbia Symphony Orchestra. Columbia Records, no. 350, 78 rpm; recorded 1938.
>Howard Hanson and the Eastman-Rochester Philharmonic. Mercury Classics, no. MG40008, 33$\frac{1}{3}$ rpm, American Music Festival Series, vol. 9; recorded 1953.

Joseph Maddy and the Interlochen Youth Orchestra. "Van Cliburn Conducts," RCA Victor Red Seal, no. LM-2807, 33⅓ rpm, recorded 1964.
Gerard Schwarz and the Seattle Symphony. Delos CD, no. DE 3099; recorded 1990. Also part of a three-CD set entitled "All American Favorites," Delos CD, no. DE 3180.

Portrait of a Lady, Rhapsody for Strings, Winds, and Piano, op. 14
Walter Hendl and the Vienna Symphony Orchestra. Desto Records, D-417, 33⅓ rpm; American Composers Series. Reissued on American Recording Society no. ARS 23, 33⅓ rpm. (R & H Archives)

Circus Day, op. 18
Edwin McArthur and the San Francisco Symphony. "Carousel of American Music," box of four CDs, Music & Arts, no. B00004ST84; recorded live at the ASCAP concert of 24 September 1940, Golden Gate International Exposition.

Orchestral suite from *Peter Ibbetson,* op. 20
Howard Barlow and the Columbia Symphony Orchestra. Columbia Records, 78 rpm, no. CX-204; recorded 1941[?]. (R & H archives)

Ballet music from *Casanova,* op. 22
Richard Korn and the Philharmonia Orchestra of Hamburg. "A Panorama of American Orchestra Music," Allegro-Elite Records, 33⅓ rpm, no. LRX 1823. (R & H Archives)

Fanfare for Russia, op. 24
Jorge Mester and the London Philharmonic Orchestra. "Twenty Fanfares for the Common Man," Koch International CD, no. 3-7012-2 H1.

Vocal Selections

"A Song for Lovers," op. 13, no. 2
Kirsten Flagstad, with Edwin MacArthur, piano. "Schubert, Brahms, Strauss Songs," RCA Victor Records, 33⅓ rpm, no. LM-1870; recorded 1955. (R & H Archives)

"Captain Stratton's Fancy"
Randolph Symonette, with Leslie Harnley, piano. Colosseum Records, 33⅓ rpm, no. CLPS 1008. (R & H Archives)

The King's Henchman. Selections
Act I: "O Caesar, Great Wert Thou!"
Act III: "Nay, Maccus, Lay Him Down"
Lawrence Tibbett, Giulio Setti with Metropolitan Opera Orchestra and Chorus. Victor Records, 78 rpm, no. 8103; recorded 5 April 1928; reissued on New World Records, "Toward an American Opera, 1911–1954," 33⅓ rpm, no. NW 241.

Act III: "God Willing, We Leave This House Tonight."
Alfred Wallenstein and Orchestra, Vivian Della Chiesa and Jan Peerce. "Souvenirs from American Operas," International Record Collectors' Club CD, no. 818. "Souvenirs" also includes the Tibbett recording of "O Caesar, Great Wert Thou," and an extended finale of the opera, "Eadgar, Eadgar!," sung by Lawrence Tibbett on a radio broadcast of 20 November 1934.

Peter Ibbetson. Complete opera
Unique Opera Records, no. UORC 143. This is the off-the-air recording of the Metropolitan Opera performance of Saturday, 17 March 1934, conducted by Wilfrid Pelletier, with Lawrence Tibbett, Edward Johnson, Lucrezia Bori, and Gladys Swarthout (R & H Archives).

The complete *Peter Ibbetson* was performed and recorded in Seattle on 29 April and 1 May 1999 by Gerard Schwarz, the Seattle Symphony, soloists, and chorus. In fall 1999 it was broadcast over Seattle radio station KING-FM. The recording has not yet been released commercially.

Act I: "I would never dedicate my days."
Licia Albanese and Symphony of the Air, conducted by Wilfrid Pelletier from a radio broadcast of the *Peter Ibbetson* performance of the Empire State Music Festival in July 1960. "Souvenirs from American Operas," International Record Collectors' Club CD, no. 818.

Deems Taylor as Commentator

Benjamin Britten, *The Young Person's Guide to the Orchestra*
Antal Dorati and the Minneapolis Symphony Orchestra. Deems Taylor, narrator. Mercury Records, $33\frac{1}{3}$ rpm, no. MG 50055. Later released on Mercury Storyteller Records, $33\frac{1}{3}$ rpm, no. SLP 116.

Peter Ilyich Tchaikovsky, *1812 Festival Overture* (original scoring)
Antal Dorati and the Minneapolis Symphony Orchestra. Deems Taylor, commentator. Mercury Records, $33\frac{1}{3}$ rpm, no. SR 90054. Also released on Mercury CD 434 360-2. Recorded 1958.

Appendix 3: "Haec Olim Meminisse Iuvabit," by Deems Taylor

"Haec Olim Meminisse Iuvabit" is a line from Virgil's *Aeneid*, meaning "Perhaps one day it will be useful to remember even these things." Franklin P. Adams (FPA) judged it to be the best submission for his "Conning Tower" column during 1919. This witty history of Taylor's years as a student at New York University was first published in the *New York Tribune* on 21 August 1919.

I

Oh, back in the fall of nineteen-two, when I was a Freshman green,
I planned to be one of the cultured few, with a high and beetling bean.
   So I took on Latin, and German IV,
   French, History V (to the Civil War),
   Trig, Algebra I—a ghastly bore—
   —and Freshman chemistree;
Here, then, are the facts I still retain from nineteen-two and -three:
We[1] won the bloody Monday fight, and made the Sophs retire:[2]
Dear Lehigh licked the football team, by a score that was something dire;[3]
   Bill[4] came on from Chicago U.
   With some barroom stories—and good ones, too;[5]
I got on the Glee Club, and made Psi U, and sang in the chapel choir.

II

As a sophomore, I am proud to state, I was taking the hurdles clear;
I dreamed of copping the old Phi Bete by the end of my Junior year.
 I soaked up Logic, and Physics III,
 French Lit. (I was there with the loud oui, oui*),*
 Psychology, Shakespeare, Verse—not free—
 —and a couple of courses more.
Here's what I recall as I look back on nineteen-three and -four:
Weary chairmaned the Junior prom (his girl was Harriet White);[6]
I played third quarter on the football scrub, while Loup played center and right;
 Joe Bauderman ran a record mile,
 The baseball team was perfectly vile,[7]
I made the track team after a while, and fussed[8] *each Saturday night.*

III

By Junior year I had laid away all hopes of a Phi Bete key,
But I toyed with the thought of a proud M.A., and a possible Ph.D.,
 So I grabbed off Plato, and Kant, and such,
 Church History, Banking (the worldly touch!),
 The German Bards—whom we termed the "Dutch"—
 —such French as I might contrive;
And the following info still adheres from nineteen-four and -five:
Tom Reilley's[9] *team smeared R. P. I. to the tune of a large amount:*[10]
I made the gym and track teams both;[11] *they ducked young Blum*[12] *in the fount;*
 The Glee Club trip was a Lakewood treat,
 The baseball team got badly beat,[13]
And I got third on the Wesleyan meet[14]*—but third place didn't count.*

IV

As a Senior now, I was bald and gray with the studious life I'd led,
But proud of the knowledge stowed away in my small but well-formed head.
 I killed International (so-called) Law,
 Took Spanish and Chaucer (the latter's raw),
 Wound up with a thesis on Bernard Shaw
 —how much of that stuff still sticks?
Well, here is the dope I recollect from nineteen-five and -six:
Bill and I wrote the Senior show (his book was a mere detail),

> *And Loup played "Elsie, the Cannibal Queen," and looked like a half-dressed*
>   *whale;*
>   *The Senior ball was a dream divine,*[15]
>   *The Senior banquet was mostly wine,*
> *And F. P. A. ran a piece of mine*[16] *in the* New York Evening Mail.

1. That is, the class of 1906.
2. Weary [Reinald Werrenrath] won't like this, but it's true.
3. 46–0, if you must know.
4. William Le Baron.
5. And a wonderful song, "Kansas."
6. And maybe he wasn't stuck on her!
7. As usual.
8. Some girl, too. She married shortly after that.
9. Major T. T. Reilley, D.S.C.
10. 53–0, no less.
11. I was pretty good, too, but badly handled. I know I could have done the low hurdles in 26 if Mike McCann had only understood me. Stimmie Draper (Arthur S. Draper of the *New York Herald Tribune*) did the pole-vault that year. He was rotten.
12. I'm not sure of the name. He was going to sue the university, but didn't.
13. See Note 7.
14. The track up there is so narrow that only three of us could run.
15. I took Adele Martin, a queen. She married Bill Wildman almost immediately afterward.
16. It wasn't very good.

Notes

Abbreviations

DTP: The Deems Taylor Papers, Irving S. Gilmore Music Library, Yale University
MKP: The Mary Kennedy Papers, Beinecke Library, Yale University
JKT: Joan Kennedy Taylor personal collection
MWD: Michael W. Davis personal collection

Chapter 1. The Early Years of (Joseph) Deems Taylor, 1885–1906

1. Joseph S. Taylor to Reuben B. Moyer, 31 December 1885, DTP.
2. The author is indebted to Michael W. Davis, Taylor's grandnephew, for sharing the information he has assembled on both the Schimmel and Taylor families. Much information came from the journals kept by Taylor's father, Joseph Schimmel Taylor. Information on pp. 169–70 of journal "No. 79" proved especially valuable. The article "Joseph S. Taylor Pays Tribute to Reuben B. Moyer," *Quakertown News* (Pa.), 20 August 1920, pasted on p. 70 of the "1920 Vacation Diary," was the source of the quote.
3. The quotation is from the entry "Joseph S. Taylor" in "Class of 1878: A Biographical History 1878–1888," published in 1888 by the Pennsylvania State Normal School, Millersville, Pa. (now Millersville State University). MWD.
4. John B. Weaver, "Charles F. Deems: The Ministry as Profession in Nineteenth-Century America," *Methodist History* 21 (1983): 156–68. The relationship of Deems and Commodore Vanderbilt is described in Joseph S. Taylor, ed., *A Romance of Providence: Being a History of the Church of the Strangers* (New York: Wilbur B. Ketcham, 1887).
5. Arthur T. Vanderbilt II, *Fortune's Children: The Fall of the House of Vanderbilt* (New York: William Morrow, 1989), 46. According to the author, Reverend Deems was also the man who convinced the commodore to give one million dollars to the Central University of Nashville, then renamed Vanderbilt University.

6. Taylor, *A Romance of Providence,* 22–33.

7. W. S. Gilbert, *Plays and Poems of W. S. Gilbert,* preface by Deems Taylor (New York: Random House, 1932), xiii–xiv. The book was reprinted in 1998 by Black Dog and Leventhal Publishers.

8. Madeline Goss, *Modern Music-Makers* (New York: E. P. Dutton, 1952), 103.

9. Deems Taylor, *The Well-Tempered Listener* (New York: Simon and Schuster, 1940), 316.

10. Joan Kennedy Taylor shared the information that *Sentimental Tommy* had been one of her father's favorite books, along with the story of the hoped-for goat.

11. John Allwood, *The Great Exhibitions* (London: Studio Vista, 1977), 81–94. An Internet site with photos and history of the Columbian exhibition is Bruce R. Schulman, "Interactive Guide to the World's Columbian Exhibition," users.vnet.net/schulman/Columbian/columbian.html (10 April 2003) (the address is case sensitive).

12. Rudi Blesh and Harriet Janis, *They All Played Ragtime,* 4th ed. (New York: Oak Publications, 1971), 41.

13. "Deems Taylor Was Versatile Boy," unknown Philadelphia newspaper, 14 March 1931, DTP.

14. Tacy-Knight Robinson to Joseph S. Taylor, 24 April 1931. Letter in Joseph S. Taylor journal "79," 92, MWD.

15. Author unidentified, "Biography of Deems Taylor," one spiral-bound notebook, 1–2, DTP. This thirty-six-page, handwritten biography ends in the early 1940s. Several statements strongly suggest it was written in 1942. The information in the biography is consistent with material in Taylor letters.

16. Deems Taylor, "Ethical at the Turn of the Century," *Ethical Culture Schools,* n.d.: 35.

17. Ibid., 36–39.

18. Ibid., 40.

19. Deems Taylor, "Herbert Talk," DTP.

20. Deems Taylor, *Of Men and Music* (New York: Simon and Schuster, 1938), 294.

21. Deems Taylor to James F. Berry, 8 March 1927, DTP.

22. "The University College," chap. 10 in *New York University, 1832–1932,* ed. Theodore Francis Jones (New York: New York University Press, 1933).

23. Louis A. Banks, "The Hall of Fame," in *The Land of Contrasts: 1880–1901,* ed. Neil Harris (New York: G. Braziller, 1970). Originally published in Louis A. Banks, *The Story of the Hall of Fame* (New York: n.p., 1902).

24. Deems Taylor, "Words and Music," *New York American,* 5 June 1931.

25. Author unidentified, "Biography of Deems Taylor," 6.

26. Taylor, *The Well-Tempered Listener,* 319–21.

27. Taylor, "Herbert Talk," DTP.

28. Deems Taylor, *Some Enchanted Evenings: The Story of Rodgers and Hammerstein* (New York: Harper and Brothers, 1953), 10; Meryle Secrest, *Somewhere for Me: A Biography of Richard Rodgers* (New York: Alfred A. Knopf, 2001), 38–41. Rodgers's first varsity show collaboration was with Columbia alumnus Lorenz Hart. The team of Rodgers and Hart created the great Broadway musicals *Pal Joey* and *The Boys from Syracuse.*

29. Deems Taylor, "My Dream Girls of the Theatre," *Stage,* October 1935, 48.

30. Thomas Vinceguerra, "Sing a Song of Morningside," *Columbia College Today,* fall 1994 (www.columbia.edu/cu/varsity/html/article6.html) (26 December 2002).

31. Author unidentified, "Biography of Deems Taylor," 5.

32. Deems Taylor, "Haec Olim Meminisse Iuvabit," in *The Week End Companion,* compiled by Franklin P. Adams, Deems Taylor, Helen Rowland, Percival Wilde (1925; reprint, Cleveland: World Publishing Co., 1941). The entire poem is in Appendix 3.

Chapter 2. The Emergence of Taylor as Composer and Writer, 1906–1916

1. By 1906 Theodore Roosevelt had published more than a dozen books.
2. Newman Levy, *My Double Life: Adventures in Law and Letters* (Garden City, N.Y.: Doubleday, 1958), 35.
3. Ibid.
4. Newman Levy, "Versatility Personified," *New Yorker,* 6 June 1925, 9.
5. Taylor, "Herbert Talk," 15, DTP.
6. Taylor, *The Well-Tempered Listener,* 71.
7. *Cap'n Kidd and Co.* Selections, vocal score, DTP.
8. Levy, *My Double Life,* 36.
9. "Press Notices Last Year," *1909 Varsity Show "The Echo,"* pamphlet, DTP.
10. Goss, *Modern Music-Makers,* 104.
11. Taylor, *Of Men and Music,* 9–11.
12. Author unidentified, "Biography of Deems Taylor," 9.
13. Ibid.; Gerald Bordman, *Jerome Kern, His Life and Music* (New York: Oxford University Press, 1980), 61.
14. "Lots of Charm to 'The Echo' at Globe," *New York Times,* 18 August 1910.
15. Deems Taylor to Charles Dillingham, 25 August 1910, Charles Bancroft Dillingham papers, 1903–31, New York Public Library.
16. Taylor's 1909 appointment book has the following entry for Sunday, 21 November 1909: "Meet Jane Anderson; Plainfield 2:14." Throughout December, almost every day shows an entry for Jane.
17. Jeffrey Meyers, *Joseph Conrad: A Biography* (New York: Charles Scribner's Sons, 1991), 295–96. The most extensive information on Jane Anderson currently in one source is Meyers's book, chap. 16, "Jane Anderson, 1916–1917"; appendix 1, "The Later Life of Jane Anderson, 1918–1947"; appendix 2, "The Quest for Jane Anderson."
18. Rebecca West to Ian Watt, quoted in John Halverson and Ian Watt, "Notes on Jane Anderson: 1955–1990," *Conradiana,* spring 1991, 74.
19. Jane Anderson to Theodore Dreiser, 24 March 1910, Theodore Dreiser Papers, University of Pennsylvania.
20. Marriage certificate, 27 September 1910, Joseph Deems Taylor and Jane Foss Anderson, DTP.
21. Time sheets for "The Echo" company, Dillingham Papers.
22. Charles B. Dillingham to Taylor, 1 September 1911, Dillingham Papers.
23. Taylor to Charles B. Dillingham, 24 October 1911, Dillingham Papers.
24. Author unidentified, "Biography of Deems Taylor," 11.
25. Newman Levy, unpublished manuscript, "Biography of Franklin Pierce Adams," 1, Newman Levy papers, New York University.
26. Author unidentified, "Biography of Deems Taylor," 11–12.
27. P. L. Thomson to Taylor, 18 February 1943, DTP.
28. Deems Taylor, "To Tommy," DTP.

29. Deems Taylor, "Between All of Us," *New York Press,* 12 December 1912.

30. Deems Taylor, "My Second Prize Start," DTP.

31. National Federation of Music Clubs to Taylor, telegram, 14 March 1913, DTP.

32. Deems Taylor, "Talk for Lecture Tour, 1958," DTP.

33. Deems Taylor, National Music Camp, 1959, audiotape, Yale University Historical Sound Recordings.

34. Author unidentified, "Biography of Deems Taylor," 14.

35. A.W.K., *Musical America,* 16 May 1914.

36. Author unidentified, "Biography of Deems Taylor," 15.

37. The Yale University Historical Sound Recordings provided a cassette copy of an off-the-air recording of the cantata, conducted by Alfred Wallenstein on 13 July 1940, over radio station WOR in New York. So far as is known, it is the only existing recording of the work.

38. The Kramer quote (*Musical America,* 29 August 1914) and the Liebling quote (*Musical Courier,* 26 August 1914) were found in the pamphlet "Deems Taylor" (Boston: Oliver Ditson Company, n.d.), DTP.

39. Author unidentified, "Biography of Deems Taylor," 15. The story was confirmed by Taylor's daughter, Joan Kennedy Taylor.

40. "The Schola Cantorum," *New York Times,* 8 March 1916.

41. Kurt Schindler to Taylor, 8 March 1916, DTP.

42. John Tasker Howard, *Deems Taylor.* Studies of Contemporary American Composers (New York: J. Fischer and Bro., 1940), 13.

43. Franklin P. Adams, *The Diary of Our Own Samuel Pepys,* vol. 1, *1911–1925* (New York: Simon and Schuster, 1935), 84.

44. Ibid., 73.

45. Levy, *My Double Life,* 54.

46. "The Conning Tower," *New York Tribune,* 4 August 1915.

47. Levy, *My Double Life,* 55.

48. I have been unable to discover a listing of all the "coveted time-piece" winners. Levy, in his unpublished biography of Adams, mentions the following in addition to himself and Taylor: Julian Street, author; James Montgomery Flagg, artist; George S. Bryan, historian/biographer; J. M. Kerrigan, Irish actor for the Abbey Players; and Edna St. Vincent Millay (under the pseudonym Nancy Boyd). Millay wrote to thank Adams for the honor (Edna St. Vincent Millay, *Letters of Edna St. Vincent Millay,* ed. Allan Ross Macdougall [New York: Harper & Brothers, 1952], 207) and asked that he consider, instead of a watch, substituting "a silver candelabrum" for her bedroom.

49. "The Conning Tower," *New York Tribune,* 11 July 1922.

50. Meyers, *Joseph Conrad,* 297.

Chapter 3. The War Years, 1916–1919

1. John H. Hobbs interview, Federal Bureau of Investigation, Jane Anderson Files, Baltimore, Md., File No. 61-584. This file provides the account of Hobbs's involvement with Jane. Joseph Poprzeczny kindly supplied a copy of the entire F.B.I. file on Anderson.

2. Jane Anderson to Taylor, in Halverson and Watt, "Notes on Jane Anderson: 1955–1990," 61–64.

3. Jessie Conrad, *Joseph Conrad and His Circle,* 2d ed. (Port Washington, N.Y.: Kennikat Press, 1964), 204.

4. Joseph Conrad quoted in Meyers, *Joseph Conrad,* 303.

5. Joseph S. Taylor, "1916 Journal," 14 August 1916, MWD.

6. Meyers, *Joseph Conrad,* 300–307.

7. Billy Altman, *Laughter's Gentle Soul: The Life of Robert Benchley* (New York: W. W. Norton, 1997), 80–82.

8. Sally Ashley, *F.P.A.: The Life and Times of Franklin Pierce Adams* (New York: Beaufort Books, 1986), 96–97.

9. "The Conning Tower," *New York Tribune,* 5 April 1916. This is a logical assumption based on the entry: "Old Deems Taylor visited the Tower office for three or four hours, Eastern time, yesterday afternoon."

10. Will Irwin, "History of the Dutch Treat Club," in *Thirty-Eighth Anniversary of the Dutch Treat Club* (New York: privately printed, 1943).

11. *Leslie's Weekly* first published Flagg's illustration as the cover of the 6 July 1916 issue, with Uncle Sam pointing his finger at the viewer and asking "What Are *You* Doing for Preparedness?"

12. Robert Benchley, "Journal," 28 February 1916, Robert Benchley Papers, Boston University.

13. Benchley, "Journal," 8 May 1916, Benchley Papers.

14. "1775 Mennonite statement to the Pennsylvania Assembly," quoted in "Mennonites," *New Encyclopedia Britannica,* 15th ed. (Chicago: Encyclopedia Britannica, 1994).

15. Author unidentified, "Biography of Deems Taylor," 20.

16. Taylor to Joseph and Katherine Taylor, 23 August 1916, DTP.

17. Joseph S. Taylor, "1916 Nova Scotia Journal," 27 August 1916, 76, MWD.

18. Taylor to Robert Benchley, 14 November 1916, Benchley Papers.

19. Taylor to Robert Benchley, 8 December 1916, Benchley Papers.

20. Deems Taylor, "The Conning Tower," *New York Tribune,* 8 January 1917.

21. "Papers—Paris trip—1916," DTP.

22. M. B. Biskupski, "Spy, Patriot or Internationalist? The Early Career of Jozef Retinger, Polish Patriarch of European Union," *Polish Review* 43, no. 1 (1998): 51.

23. Borys Conrad, *My Father: Joseph Conrad* (New York: Coward-McCann, 1970), 122–25.

24. George Seldes, *Witness to a Century* (New York: Ballantine Books, 1987), 56.

25. Paul Scott Mowrer to Taylor, n.d., DTP.

26. Author unidentified, "Biography of Deems Taylor," 22.

27. Kurt Schindler, *Sixty Russian Folk-Songs* (New York: G. Schirmer, 1918), iii.

28. Joan Kennedy Taylor, e-mail to author, 2 November 2000.

29. Taylor's appointment books for 1919 and 1920 show numerous entries for "Jane" in the spring of both years. There can be little doubt that this is Jane Anderson, for Deems entered an appointment with a person by the first name only for his closest friends.

30. John Carver Edwards, *Berlin Calling* (New York: Praeger, 1991), 47.

31. Gilbert, *Plays and Poems of W. S. Gilbert,* xviii.

32. Taylor to William Arms Fisher, 26 November [1918], DTP.

33. Taylor to Gladys Tipton, 1961, DTP.

34. Deems Taylor, "Krehbiel Obituary," *New York World,* 21 March 1923.

35. H. E. Krehbiel, "New Works Heard at Concert of the Chamber Music Society," *New York Tribune,* 19 February 1919.

36. "Fine Chamber Concert Music," n.p., Taylor scrapbook, DTP.

37. *Rocky Mountain News,* 22 June 1919, sec. 2, 12.

38. "Empress Theater Advertisement," *Denver Post,* 23 July 1919.

39. *Denver Post,* 30 July 1919, 19.
40. Joan Givner, *Katherine Anne Porter: A Life* (New York: Simon and Schuster, 1982), 120.
41. Ibid., 123.
42. Katherine Anne Porter, "Settings for Little Theater," *Rocky Mountain News,* 6 July 1919.
43. At the time, the New York production of the very popular musical *Maytime* was playing in Denver. The ticket prices: $2.00 and $1.50 for orchestra seats; $1.00 and $0.50 in the balcony.
44. Katherine Anne Porter, "It's Easy to Be Mad Nowadays," *Rocky Mountain News,* 13 July 1919.
45. Joseph S. Taylor, "1919 Journal," MWD.
45. Author unidentified, "Biography of Deems Taylor," 23–24.
47. F.E.W., "Amusements," *Denver Post,* 8 August 1919.
48. Katherine Anne Porter, "Old Melodies Please at Nursery Benefit," *Rocky Mountain News,* 8 August 1919.
49. Katherine Anne Porter to Donald Stalling, 28 March 1956, Katherine Anne Porter Papers, University of Maryland.

Chapter 4. The Theater Beckons Again, 1920–1921

1. Mercedes de Acosta, *Here Lies the Heart* (New York: Reynal, 1960), 95.
2. Ibid., 97.
3. "What Next!" sketches, DTP.
4. "Amateurs Act 'What Next!'" *New York Times,* 27 January 1920.
5. Eugene Lockhart to Taylor, 31 January 1920, DTP.
6. Marc Connelly, *Voices Offstage: A Book of Memoirs* (Chicago: Holt, Rinehart and Winston, 1968), 56.
7. Taylor's appointment books for 1920 and 1921 evidence the numerous times that the Kaufmans fed the two men.
8. Charles G. Shaw, *The Low-Down* (New York: Henry Holt, 1928), 21.
9. Taylor to Kennedy, 24 December 1920, MKP.
10. From her mother's family came strong Catholic roots: an uncle who was vicar general of Georgia, and an aunt who was Mother Superior of the Sisters of Mercy.
11. Divorce decree, Rhode Island, 10 January 1920, DTP. All that is known of the marriage comes from the final decree, 9 July 1920, of the State of Rhode Island and Providence Plantations Superior Court: "Mary Hawley vs. James Blaine Hawley . . . dissolved upon the ground of wilful desertion. And it is further ordered, adjudged and decreed that the petitioner be allowed to resume her maiden name of Mary Kennedy."
12. Katherine Taylor to Taylor, 16 July 1939, DTP.
13. Taylor to Kennedy, n.d. [1920], MKP.
14. Kennedy to Taylor, 26 November 1920, MKP.
15. Taylor to Kennedy, 3 November 1920, MKP.
16. Author unidentified, "Biography of Deems Taylor," 25.
17. Taylor to Kennedy, 24 November 1920, MKP.
18. Author unidentified, "Biography of Deems Taylor," 26.
19. Taylor to Kennedy, 4 December 1920, MKP.
20. Taylor to Kennedy, 18 December 1920, MKP.
21. Deems Taylor, "Commemorative Tribute to John Alden Carpenter," 28 May 1952, Archives of the National Institute of Arts and Letters, New York City.

22. Taylor to Kennedy, 18 December 1920, MKP.

23. James R. Gaines, *Wit's End: Days and Nights of the Algonquin Round Table* (New York: Harcourt Brace Jovanovich, 1977), 22–29.

24. Peggy Wood, *How Young You Look: Memoirs of a Middle-Sized Actress* (New York: Farrar and Rinehart, [1941]), 130. Peggy Wood insisted that this oft-quoted remark originated with her father.

25. Quotes of the Algonquin wits are taken from Robert E. Drennan, ed., *The Algonquin Wits* (Secaucus, N.J.: Citadel Press, 1968).

26. Taylor to Kennedy, 26 January 1921, MKP.

27. *Nonsenseorship*, G. P. P., ed. (New York: G. P. Putnam's Sons, 1922), iii.

28. Christopher Mehrens, "The Critical and Musical Work of Deems Taylor in Light of Contemporary Cultural Patterns" (Ph.D. diss., University of North Carolina, 1998), 154.

29. Taylor to Kennedy, 27 December 1920, MKP.

30. The exchange of letters can be found in *Between Friends: Letters of James Branch Cabell and Others,* ed. Padraic Colum and Margaret Freeman Cabell (New York: Harcourt, Brace and World, 1962), 210–11.

31. Taylor to James Branch Cabell, 5 January 1921, James Branch Cabell Papers, University of Virginia.

32. Taylor to Cabell, 10 March 1921, Cabell Papers.

33. Taylor to Kennedy, 7 January 1921, MKP.

34. Taylor to Kennedy, 9 January 1921, MKP.

35. Taylor to Kennedy, 28 January 1921, MKP.

Chapter 5. Taylor Becomes the Music Critic of the *New York World,* 1921–1922

1. Mark N. Grant, *Maestros of the Pen* (Boston: Northeastern University Press, 1998), 106. Chap. 4, "Gilded Age Gadfly," covers Huneker's work as a writer of music criticism.

2. Arnold T. Schwab, *James Gibbons Huneker: Critic of the Seven Arts* (Stanford, Calif.: Stanford University Press, 1963), 65.

3. James Boylan, "Introduction," in *The World and the 20's, The Golden Years of New York's Legendary Newspaper* (New York: Dial Press, 1973), 3.

4. "Story for a Child," recollections of Mary Kennedy, 1 November 1932, MKP.

5. Taylor to Herbert Bayard Swope, 19 February 1921, DTP. H. L. (Henry Louis) Mencken—as reporter, magazine editor, and author of the highly regarded study of American speech idioms *The American Language*—had great impact in the literary world during the first half of the twentieth century. As Grant points out in *Maestros of the Pen* (134), Mencken also was "America's most outspoken but unappreciated, unsung, and unheralded music critic." He did not, however, as did other famed music critics, hold such a singular role for a newspaper. Most of his criticisms came in magazine essays.

6. Taylor to Kennedy, 25 February 1921, MKP.

7. Taylor to Kennedy, 27 February 1921, MKP.

8. Alexander Woollcott, "The Play," *New York Times,* 22 March 1921.

9. *Time,* 30 June 1924, 16.

10. Taylor to Kennedy, 3 June 1921, MKP.

11. Heywood Hale Broun, *Whose Little Boy Are You?* (New York: St. Martin's/Marek, 1983), 47–55. Broun provides a valued and unique insight into "Mac." For young Broun, Mac

was one of two men who often visited the home of his parents and became his boyhood heroes. The other was the actor/singer Paul Robeson.

12. *Paterson Press,* 1 May 1913.

13. Ibid.

14. "M'namara Makes First Night Hit," *Paterson Morning Call,* 9 October 1914.

15. "Caruso Takes First Pupil," *New York Times,* 7 December 1915.

16. Broun, *Whose Little Boy Are You?* 49.

17. She and her close friend Mary Curtis Bok believed in being sponsors of up-and-coming composers, including Samuel Barber and Gian Carlo Menotti.

18. Deems Taylor, 1920 appointment book, DTP.

19. Edith Evans Braun journal, New York Public Library for the Performing Arts.

20. Joseph S. Taylor's "1921 Journal," 13 July 1921, MWD.

21. Lucille Watson-Little Térouanne, letter to author, 19 February 1997. Lucille married Deems Taylor in 1945.

22. Herbert Bayard Swope to Taylor, 19 September 1921, JKT.

23. Grant, *Maestros of the Pen,* 58–62.

24. Copy of *Musical Progress* in collection of Western Connecticut State University library.

25. Henry F. Gilbert, "Composer Gilbert on America's Music," *New York Times,* 27 March 1918.

26. Carol J. Oja, *Making Music Modern: New York in the 1920s* (New York: Oxford University Press, 2000). The development of modern music organizations and the role played by affluent women therein are well documented in chap. 12, "Women Patrons and Activists."

27. "A Farewell Symphony," *New York World,* 16 April 1922.

28. Alfred Pessolano, letter to author, 7 April 1997.

29. Taylor, *The Well-Tempered Listener,* 300.

30. Deems Taylor, "Own Verse," DTP.

31. Joseph S. Taylor to Deems Taylor, 23 April 1922, DTP.

32. Deems Taylor, "Finis Coronat Opera," *New York World,* 23 April 1922.

33. Deems Taylor, *New York World,* 28 May 1922.

34. Adams, *The Diary,* vol. 1, 315.

35. Quoted in Brian Gallagher, *Anything Goes: The Jazz Age Adventures of Neysa McMein and Her Extravagant Circle of Friends* (New York: Times Books, 1987), 75.

36. Ibid., 69–87.

37. Deems Taylor's New York Philharmonic intermission script, 24 December 1939, DTP.

38. Broun, *Whose Little Boy Are You?* 10.

39. Newspaper Guild of New York, *Heywood Broun as He Seemed to Us* (New York: Random House, 1940), 20.

40. Harold E. Stearns, ed., *Civilization in the United States: An Inquiry by Thirty Americans* (New York: Harcourt, Brace, 1922), iii.

41. Van Wyck Brooks, *Days of the Phoenix: The 1920s I Remember* (New York: E. P. Dutton, 1957), 167.

42. Frederick Manning, "The Younger Generation," *Yale Review,* October 1922, 14.

43. Kerin R. Sarason and Ruth L. Strickland, *American Writers in Paris, 1920–1939,* vol. 4 of *Dictionary of Literary Biography* (Detroit: Gale Research, 1980), 358.

44. Stearns, *Civilization,* 199.

45. Ibid., 214.

46. Barbara L. Tischler, *An American Music: The Search for an American Musical Identity* (New York: Oxford University Press, 1986), 182.

47. Stearns, *Civilization,* 205.
48. Ibid.
49. Walter Damrosch, *My Musical Life* (New York: Scribner, 1926), 323.
50. A lengthy assessment of Taylor's chapter "Music" in the Stearns book is found in Mehrens, "Critical and Musical Work of Deems Taylor," 54–87.
51. Edna Ferber, *A Peculiar Treasure* (New York: Literary Guild of America, 1939), 272.
52. Donald Ogden Stewart, *By a Stroke of Luck* (New York: Paddington Press, 1975), 109.
53. Ferber, *A Peculiar Treasure,* 273.
54. Taylor, *Of Men and Music,* 53.
55. Ibid., 57.

Chapter 6. The *World* Years, 1922–1923

1. Paul Rosenfeld, "Musical Chronicle," *The Dial,* January 1922, quoted in Oja, *Making Music Modern,* 50.
2. Cornelia Otis Skinner, "Those Starring Days," *New Yorker,* n.d., MKP.
3. Elmer Rice, *Minority Report: An Autobiography* (New York: Simon and Schuster, 1963), 195.
4. Richard Aldrich, "The Philharmonic Society," *New York Times,* 12 January 1923.
5. Richard Aldrich, "The New York Symphony," *New York Times,* 12 March 1923.
6. A copy of this review and several others of the 11 August 1925 Promenade concert are found pasted into Taylor's father's "1925 Journal," 322, MWD.
7. A map entitled "In and Around Great Neck, Pictured from the Description of a Weekend Guest," drawn by John Held, appeared in the *New Yorker* in 1927 and identified the location of the Great Neck homes.
8. Howard Dietz, *Dancing in the Dark* (New York: Quadrangle Books, 1974), 234.
9. Beatrice Kaufman and Joseph Hennessy, *The Letters of Alexander Woollcott* (New York: Viking Press, 1944), 76. The phrase is referred to in Woollcott's letter to Edna Ferber, 21 July 1922.
10. Ring Lardner Jr., *The Lardners: My Family Remembered* (New York: Harper and Row, 1976), 171.
11. Herbert Bayard Swope Jr., telephone conversation with author, 15 September 1996.
12. Mary Kennedy journal, 1 November 1932, MKP.
13. Deems Taylor, "A City Fellow Goes Rustic," *American Magazine,* July 1934, 53.
14. Ibid.
15. Joseph S. Taylor, "1923 Journal," entry of 30 September 1923: "Katherine and I went to Deems' farm. He met us at Stamford in his depot wagon, the gift of Mrs. Freuauff [*sic*]." MWD.
16. John Corbin, "Old Glamer," *New York Times,* 27 September 1923.
17. Donald Ogden Stewart to Kennedy, 12 September 1923, MKP.
18. Kennedy to Taylor, 10 September 1923, MKP.

Chapter 7. The *World* Years, 1923–1924

1. Ralph Pulitzer to Taylor, 16 October 1923, DTP.
2. Alexander Woollcott, *Enchanted Aisles* (New York: G. P. Putnam's Sons, 1924), 3–9.
3. F. D. Perkins, "De Pachmann Gives Recital and Omits Diverting Features," *New York Tribune,* 17 November 1923.

4. Deems Taylor, "Talk for Lecture Tour, 1958," DTP.

5. Deems Taylor, "Mischa Levitzki," *New York Times,* 5 December 1923.

6. Andre Kostelanetz, *Echoes: Memoirs of Andre Kostelanetz* (New York: Harcourt Brace Jovanovich, 1981), 211.

7. Deems Taylor, "George Gershwin," *New York American,* 7 October 1931.

8. Background information on Eva Gauthier was found at www.association-gauthier.org/anglais/famous/evaa.html (10 April 2003).

9. Isaac Goldberg, *George Gershwin: A Study in American Music* (New York: Simon and Schuster, 1931), 130.

10. Paul Whiteman and Mary Margaret McBride, "An Experiment," in *Gershwin in His Time,* ed. Gregory R. Suriano (New York: Gramercy Books, 1998), 16. Originally published in Paul Whiteman and Mary Margaret McBride, *Jazz* (New York: J. H. Sears, 1926).

11. Oja, *Making Music Modern,* 323.

12. Paul Rosenfeld, *An Hour with American Music* (Philadelphia: J. B. Lippincott, 1929), 15.

13. Connelly, *Voices Offstage,* 118.

14. John Corbin, "Jagged Expressionism," *New York Times,* 13 February 1924.

15. John Corbin, "Among the New Plays," *New York Times,* 17 February 1924, sec. 7, 1.

16. Years later George Kaufman and Moss Hart wrote the smash hit *The Man Who Came to Dinner* based on personalities they knew from the Algonquin Circle, particularly Alexander Woollcott and Harpo Marx.

17. George S. Kaufman and Marc Connelly, *Beggar on Horseback,* in *Three Plays about Business in America,* ed. Joseph Mersand (New York: Washington Square Press, 1964).

18. Ken Bloom, *American Song: The Complete Musical Theatre Companion, 1877–1995,* 2d ed. (New York: Schirmer Books, 1996), 20.

19. Olin Downes, "Carroll Put to Music," *New York Times,* 26 March 1924.

20. Sergei Rachmaninoff to Taylor, date unspecified, JKT. Rachmaninoff referred to the Stokowski concert of 25 March 1924: in his letter, written the day after the concert, Rachmaninoff said he was leaving for Europe "tomorrow," which would have been 27 March. The *New York Times* reported that the pianist did leave on the *Duilio* for Italy on 27 March.

21. James Pegolotti, "Howard Barlow and the Rise and Fall of Classical Music on Commercial Radio," *Connecticut Review* 17 (spring 1995): 1–15.

22. Howard Barlow to Taylor, 17 April 1924, Howard Barlow Papers, Western Connecticut State University.

23. Howard Barlow, "The Reminiscences of Howard Barlow," interview by Frank Ernest Hill, 1951, transcript, Columbia University Oral History Research Office, New York. A copy of the interview is also in the Howard Barlow Papers, Western Connecticut State University.

24. Taylor to Kennedy, 22 April 1924, MKP.

25. Richard Koszarski, *An Evening's Entertainment: The Age of the Silent Feature Picture, 1915–1928* (New York: Charles Scribner's Sons, 1990), 286. Mary Kennedy had a featured role in *Yolanda,* and when she asked LeBaron in 1954 about a print of it, he responded: "Darling, there ain't no such thing as stills of *Yolanda,* nor even a print of the picture. They had a fire years ago and all the old Cosmopolitan stuff was destroyed. *Yolanda* was lovely wasn't it?" William LeBaron to Kennedy, 1 October 1954, MKP.

26. The information about Hearst's Cosmopolitan studio operations was distilled primarily from articles about William LeBaron supplied by the Margaret Herrick Library, Beverly

Hills, Calif., and Louis Pizzitola's *Hearst over Hollywood: Power, Passion and Propaganda in the Movies* (New York: Columbia University Press, 2002).

27. "The Spirit of '76," *New York Times*, 6 August 1924.
28. "Editorial," *Musical Courier*, 11 September 1924, 71.
29. *Time*, 30 June 1924, 16.
30. *Music Illustrated Monthly Review* 1, midsummer 1924.

Chapter 8. The *World* Years, 1924–1925

1. Stark Young, "A Fresh Family Comedy," *New York Times*, 6 January 1925.
2. Burns Mantle, ed., *The Best Plays of 1924–1925* (New York: Dodd, Mead, 1925), 223–65.
3. Olin Downes, "Music," *New York Times*, 4 February 1925.
4. Millay to editor of *New York World*, 4 February 1925, in Allan Ross Macdougall, ed., *Letters of Edna St. Vincent Millay* (New York: Harper and Brothers, 1952), 191–92.
5. Deems Taylor, "Talk for Lecture Tour, 1958," DTP.
6. Aaron Copland and Vivian Perlis, *Copland: 1900 through 1942* (New York: St. Martin's/Marek, 1984), 104.
7. "Order Gershwin Music," *New York Times*, 22 April 1925.
8. George Martin, *The Damrosch Dynasty: America's First Family of Music* (Boston: Houghton Mifflin, 1983), 290.
9. Taylor to James Branch Cabell, 7 June 1925, DTP.
10. Joseph S. Taylor, "1926 Journal," 13 November 1926, MWD.
11. Taylor to Kennedy, n.d. [probably 23 July 1925], MKP. The resignation is noted in a letter sent to Miss Mary Kennedy, c/o Guaranty Trust Co., 50 Pall Mall, London.
12. John Tasker Howard, *Contemporary American Composers* (New York: J. Fischer and Bro., 1928), 10–11.
13. Grant, *Maestros of the Pen*, 182–83.
14. Barbara Meuser, "The Criticism of New Music in New York: 1919–1929" (Ph.D. diss., City University of New York, 1975), 14.
15. Taylor to Kennedy, 28 May 1925, MKP.
16. Joseph S. Taylor, "1925 Journal," 5 July 1925, MWD.
17. Kennedy to Taylor, letters of 7 July 1925, 9 July 1925, and 11 July 1925, MKP.
18. Kennedy to Taylor, 13 July 1925, MKP.
19. Kennedy to Taylor, "Tuesday," n.d. [probably 14 July 1925], MKP.
20. Kennedy to Taylor, "Saturday afternoon," n.d. [probably 18 July 1925], MKP.
21. Taylor to Kennedy, 11 July 1925, MKP.
22. Altman, *Laughter's Gentle Soul*, 164.
23. Babette Rosmond, *Robert Benchley: His Life and Good Times* (New York: Paragon House, 1989), 12.
24. Marion Meade, *Dorothy Parker: What Fresh Hell Is This?* (New York: Villard Books, 1988), 148–56. Meade implies that the Parker-Taylor affair began before the summer visits.
25. Robert Benchley to Gertrude Benchley, Benchley Papers.
26. Taylor to Kennedy, 7 August 1925, MKP.
27. Taylor to Kennedy, 27 December 1920, MKP.
28. Taylor to Kennedy, 13 August 1925, MKP.
29. Taylor to Kennedy, 6 August 1925, MKP.

30. Taylor to Kennedy, 13 August 1925, MKP.
31. Joan Kennedy Taylor, e-mail to author, 2 November 2000.
32. Braun journal.
33. Deems Taylor to James Branch Cabell, n.d., DTP.
34. Though a commercial recording of *Jurgen* does not exist, Michael Keith generously pro-
    vided a copy of one he had made utilizing the score from the Library of Congress and an
    electronic synthesizer. Also an off-the-air recording of *Fantasy on Two Themes* exists,
    dated May 1943, by Frank Black and the NBC Symphony (Yale University Historical
    Sound Recordings). *Fantasy* is *Jurgen* revised by Taylor in 1942.
35. W. J. Henderson, *New York Sun,* 20 November 1925.
36. Olin Downes, "Premiere of Deems Taylor's Jurgen," *New York Times,* 20 November
    1925.
37. Taylor, *The Well-Tempered Listener,* 239–40.
38. *Musical Courier,* 19 December 1925.
39. "Paul Whiteman Gives 'Vivid' Grand Opera," *New York Times,* 30 December 1925.
40. Olin Downes, "Paul Whiteman's Novelties," *New York Times,* 2 January 1926.
41. Joan Kennedy Taylor, e-mail to author, 8 January 2001.

Chapter 9. *The King's Henchman,* 1925–1927

1. Theresa M. Collins, *Otto Kahn: Art, Money, and Modern Time* (Chapel Hill: University of
   North Carolina Press, 2002), 81.
2. Giulio Gatti-Casazza, *Memories of the Opera* (New York: Charles Scribner's Sons, 1941;
   reprint, New York: Vienna House, 1973), 236.
3. Henry Finck, *My Adventures in the Golden Age of Music* (New York: Funk and Wagnalls,
   1926), 371.
4. Gatti-Casazza, *Memories,* 238.
5. Carolyn Guzski, "American Opera at the Metropolitan, 1910–1935: A Contextual History and Critical Survey of Selected Works" (Ph.D. diss., City University of New York,
   2001), 2. The most comprehensive assessment of the American operas produced during
   Gatti-Casazza's managership is contained in this excellent dissertation. Guzski lists the
   works performed prior to Taylor's *King's Henchman* in 1927, with name, composer, premiere date, and number of performances: *The Pipe of Desire* (one-act), Frederick Converse, 18 March 1910, 3 perfs.; *Mona,* Horatio Parker, 14 March 1912, 4 perfs.; *Cyrano,*
   Walter Damrosch, 27 February 1913, 6 perfs.; *Madeleine* (one-act), Victor Herbert,
   24 January 1914, 6 perfs.; *The Canterbury Pilgrims,* Reginald De Koven, 8 March 1917,
   7 perfs.; *Shanewis,* Charles Wakefield Cadman, 23 March 1918, 8 perfs. (two seasons);
   The Legend (one-act), Joseph Breil, 12 March 1919, 3 perfs.; *The Temple Dancer* (one-act),
   John Adam Hugo, 12 March 1919, 3 perfs.; *Cleopatra's Night,* Henry Kimball Hadley, 31
   January 1920, 9 perfs. (two seasons).
6. Gatti-Casazza, *Memories,* 242.
7. Newman Levy, "Versatility Personified," *New Yorker,* 6 June 1925.
8. Nancy Milford, *Savage Beauty: The Life of Edna St. Vincent Millay* (New York: Random
   House, 2001), 271.
9. Deems Taylor, "Edna St. Vincent Millay, 1882–1950," in *Commemorative Tributes of the
   American Academy of Arts and Letters, 1942–1951* (New York: American Academy of Arts
   and Letters, 1951), 104.
10. William Shirer, *20th Century Journey* (New York: Simon and Schuster, 1976), 47.

11. Richard Lamparski, "High Tea with Dorothy Parker," radio interview, 1966.

12. Milford, *Savage Beauty;* Daniel Mark Epstein, *What Lips My Lips Have Kissed: The Loves and Love Poems of Edna St. Vincent Millay* (New York: Henry Holt, 2001). Two memoirs bring special light to her life, since they were written by close friends of the poet: Vincent Sheean, *The Indigo Bunting* (New York: Shocken Books, 1973), and Edmund Wilson, *The Shores of Light* (New York: Farrar, Straus and Young, 1952), 744–93.

13. Taylor, *Commemorative Tributes,* 106.

14. Taylor to Kennedy, 30 July 1925, MKP.

15. Goss, *Modern Music-Makers,* 108.

16. Milford, *Savage Beauty,* 271.

17. Eugen Boissevain to Arthur Ficke, 4 November 1925. Arthur Ficke Papers, Beinecke Library, Yale University. In this letter Eugen refers to "two acts" that Millay had completed before she gave up.

18. Elaine Bremer Apczynski, "The Making of *The King's Henchman:* An American Opera" (master's thesis, State University of New York at Buffalo, 1991), 61–62. Apczynski relates that in Millay's Steepletop library she found a well-thumbed *Anglo-Saxon Reader,* but she also believes that Millay found the story of Eadgar and Aethelwold in a book completed in 1125 by William of Malmesbury, *Chronicle of the Kings of England.*

19. John Joseph Patton, "Edna St. Vincent Millay as a Verse Dramatist" (Ph.D. diss., University of Pennsylvania, 1962), 131–71.

20. In addition to the libretto, Millay published *The King's Henchman: A Play in Three Acts* (New York: Harper and Brothers, 1927), a slightly expanded version; the venture brought her $10,000.

21. "Deems Taylor Goes to Curtis Institute," *Hartford Courant,* 13 December 1925. The archives of the Curtis Institute provided information to confirm that the course ran from December 1925 to May 1926.

22. Braun journal.

23. Taylor, *Commemorative Tributes,* 107.

24. Eugen Boissevain to Taylor, 5 January 1926, Millay Collection, Library of Congress.

25. Taylor to Millay, January 1926, copy of letter provided by John Patton.

26. Boissevain to Taylor, n.d., MKP.

27. Taylor to Millay, February 1926, transcription of letter provided by John Patton.

28. Millay to Taylor, February 1926, MKP.

29. Millay to Taylor, 28 March 1926, MKP.

30. Millay to Taylor, telegram, 14 April 1926, MKP.

31. Taylor to Kennedy, 7 May 1926, MKP.

32. Kennedy to Taylor, 9 May 1926, MKP.

33. Taylor to Kennedy, 11 May 1926, MKP.

34. Taylor to Kennedy, 12 May 1926, MKP.

35. Kennedy to Taylor, 13 May 1926, MKP.

36. Kennedy to Taylor, 17 May 1926, MKP.

37. Kennedy to Taylor, 20 May 1926, MKP.

38. Braun journal.

39. Taylor's own typed and handwritten assessment of the composing time for *The King's Henchman* is as follows: Act I: Feb. 8–April 10 (62 days); Act II: April 15–May 31 (47 days); Act III: June 5–July 14; Aug. 26–Sept. 3 (49 days). Total days: 158.

40. Joseph S. Taylor, "Journal," 26 September 1926, MWD.

41. Olin Downes, "A Twelfth 'American Opera,'" *New York Times,* 17 October 1926.

42. Deems Taylor, "The Scenic Art of Joseph Urban," *Architecture,* May 1934, 276. This issue focused on the work of Joseph Urban.

43. James MacKenzie, letter to author, 11 January 2001.

44. Hertzel Weinstat and Bert Wechsler, *Dear Rogue: A Biography of the American Baritone Lawrence Tibbett* (Portland, Oreg.: Amadeus Press, 1996), 69. In the 6 January 1926 letter from Eugen to Deems, Millay's husband indicated her feeling on the choice: "Tibbett is too darn tall to play Eadgar, if the truth were known, Eadgar being known for his small stature, but as the truth is not known, perhaps it does not matter."

45. Taylor to Kennedy, 21 November 1926, MKP.

46. Joseph S. Taylor, "Journal," 20 November 1926.

47. Taylor to Kennedy, 26 November 1926, MKP.

48. Taylor to Kennedy, 16 December 1926, MKP.

49. Marjorie Kummer Young to Mary Kennedy, n.d., JKT.

50. Millay and Boissevain to Arthur Ficke and Gladys Brown, 31 December 1926, Arthur Ficke Papers, Beinecke Library, Yale University.

51. Alexander Woollcott to Mary Kennedy, n.d., JKT.

52. Joseph S. Taylor to Kennedy, 23 December 1926, JKT.

53. Deems Taylor, "A City Fellow Goes Rustic," typescript, 10, DTP. A greatly revised version with the same title was published in *The American Magazine,* July 1934, 52–53, 92–94. The typescript is more informative about dates than the published article.

54. Shaw, *Low-Down,* 24.

55. Apczynski, "The Making of *The King's Henchman,*" 53. The letter from Taylor to Millay of 30 January 1927 is quoted here.

56. Lawrence Tibbett, *The Glory Road* (privately printed, 1933), 66–67.

57. "Native Opera Sung to Society Folk," *New York Times,* 16 February 1927.

58. Deems Taylor, *Musical Digest,* 4 January 1927.

59. Gladys Brown to Arthur Ficke, 18 February 1927, Ficke Papers. This letter details the Mixter-Millay contretemps. It is also described in Milford, *Savage Beauty,* 289.

60. "Laurels for Two," *New York Times,* 18 February 1927.

61. Brown to Ficke, 18 February 1927, Ficke Papers.

62. Richard Stokes, *New York Evening World,* 18 February 1927.

63. These congratulatory messages, along with many others, are found in the scrapbook "Articles and Correspondence Regarding The King's Henchman," DTP.

64. Edwin P. Hoyt, *Alexander Woollcott: The Man Who Came to Dinner* (New York: Abelard-Schuman, 1968), 208.

65. Herbert Peyser, "Cross-Examining 'The King's Henchman,'" *Singing,* March 1927, 15.

66. Charles Henry Meltzer, "The King's Henchman," *Outlook,* 2 March 1927, 269.

67. Rosenfeld, *An Hour with American Music,* 113–14.

68. Ibid., 44.

69. Taylor made a choral arrangement of this folksong among the dozens that he provided for J. Fischer and Bro. from 1917 to 1920.

70. Apczynski, "The Making of *The King's Henchman,*" 87.

71. Ibid., 96.

72. Wilson, *Shores of Light,* 198.

73. Giulio Gatti-Casazza to Kahn, 20 April 1927, Kahn Papers, Manuscripts Division, Department of Rare Books and Special Collections, Princeton University Library.

74. Gerald Fitzgerald, ed., *Annals of the Metropolitan Opera: The Complete Chronicle of Performances and Artists,* 2 vols. (New York: Metropolitan Opera Guild; Boston: G. K. Hall,

1989). Fourteen performances were at the Manhattan venue, one in Brooklyn (1928), and two in Philadelphia (1927, 1929).

75. *Musical America,* 9 July 1927, 8.
76. E.E.P., "'King's Henchman' Wins Washington at First Rendition," *Washington Post,* 5 November 1927.
77. "St. Paul Pleased with 'Henchman,'" *Musical America,* 28 January 1928, 17.
78. "5 Noted Americans Get Honors at N.Y.U.," *New York Times,* 9 June 1927.

Chapter 10. The Road to *Peter Ibbetson,* 1927–1931

1. Joseph S. Taylor, "1927 Journal," 3 April 1927, MWD.
2. Joan Kennedy Taylor, e-mail to author, 8 January 2001.
3. Taylor to Kennedy, 1 April 1927, MKP.
4. "5 Noted Americans Get Honors at N.Y.U."
5. "Deems Taylor Finds Ideal Collaborator," *New York Times,* 1 October 1927.
6. Deems Taylor, "A Declaration of Intentions," *Musical America,* 27 August 1927, 1.
7. Randolph Carter and Robert Cole, *Joseph Urban: Architecture, Theater, Opera, Film* (New York: Abbeville Press, 1992), 223–25. An excellent summary of the story of the Metropolitan house that was never built is found on pages 221–31, along with many drawings.
8. Otto Kahn, speech, October 1925. Attached to 14 April 1932 letter from Kahn to Taylor, Kahn Papers.
9. Otto Kahn to R. Fulton Cutting, 26 December 1925. In Carter and Cole, *Joseph Urban,* 223.
10. "Opera Box Holders Agree on New Home," *Musical America,* 23 April 1927, 4. Also see John Briggs, *Requiem for a Yellow Brick Brewery* (Boston: Little, Brown, 1969), 321–24.
11. Carter and Cole, *Joseph Urban,* 223.
12. Taylor to Kennedy, 5 October 1927, MKP.
13. Guzski, "American Opera," 348. Guszki identifies an Associated Press release of 18 February 1927, immediately following the *King's Henchman* premiere, that indicates the next Taylor opera would open the new opera house.
14. Deems Taylor, *Musical America,* 8 October 1927, 1.
15. "New Opera Plans Reveal Rift in Project," *Musical America,* 15 October 1927, 1.
16. Ibid., 13.
17. "Urban Opera Plan Rouses Chorus of Praise," *Musical America,* 22 October 1927, 1.
18. "Opera Directors Look for Another Site," *Musical America,* 25 February 1928, 1.
19. A good summary of the entire episode of Kahn's attempt to build a new Metropolitan Opera house can be found in Irving Kolodin, *The Metropolitan Opera, 1883–1935* (New York: Oxford University Press, 1936), 363–78.
20. George H. Douglas, *The Early Days of Radio Broadcasting* (Jefferson, N.C.: McFarland, 1987), 1–21.
21. According to the broadcasting historian Elizabeth McLeod, when NBC formed in 1926, it assimilated two "networks" of local New York stations. The feeder stations were New York stations WJZ and WEAF, and these became the anchors for the two NBC networks, Red and Blue. AT&T historian William Banning indicates the names were taken from the "colored pencil lines used to trace the network circuits on the AT&T long-lines maps." Elizabeth McLeod, "Red and Blue Networks," in "AM Broadcasting History, Various Articles, Part 1," www.members.aol.com/jeff560/jeff.html (26 December 2002).

22. Millay to Arthur Ficke, 19 September 1927, Ficke Papers.
23. Martin, *The Damrosch Dynasty,* 368–69.
24. Deems Taylor, "Radio Develops into Great Art Factor," *Musical America,* 17 December 1927, 27.
25. Ibid., 1.
26. "Carrying the Best Music Afield," *Musical America,* 4 February 1928, 21. I recall vividly hearing my first live concert by a major artist. The singer was Bidú Sayão, then at the Metropolitan Opera, and the event in spring 1951 was sponsored by the Community Concert organization of Eureka, California.
27. Joseph S. Taylor, "1926 Journal," 20 November 1926, MWD.
28. "Deems Taylor Gets a Juilliard Grant," *New York Times,* 3 February 1928.
29. Joan Taylor to Deems Taylor and Mary Kennedy, telegram, 19 April 1928, JKT.
30. Edward Jablonski, *Gershwin* (1987; reprint, Boston: Northeastern University Press, 1990), 170.
31. Taylor to Kennedy, 11 May 1928, MKP.
32. Jeffrey Meyers, *Scott Fitzgerald: A Biography* (New York: HarperCollins, 1994), 141.
33. Taylor to F. Scott Fitzgerald, 21 July 1925, Fitzgerald File, Princeton University.
34. Fitzgerald to Taylor in Matthew J. Bruccoli, ed., *A Life in Letters: F. Scott Fitzgerald* (New York: Scribners, 1994), 126.
35. Taylor to Kennedy, 26 May 1928, MKP.
36. "To the Readers of Musical America," *Musical America,* August 1929, 16.
37. Heywood Broun, *Collected Edition of Heywood Broun,* Heywood Hale Broun, compiler (New York: Harcourt, Brace, 1943), 224.
38. Taylor to Millay, [?] June 1928, MKP.
39. Millay to Taylor, 26 June 1928, MKP.
40. Several drafts of *Gandle Follows His Nose* are found in Box 42, MKP.
41. "Shelves New Opera after 2 Years' Work," *New York Times,* 18 February 1929.
42. Olin Downes, "Mr. Taylor's Opera," *New York Times,* 10 March 1929.
43. Richard Kelly, "George Du Maurier," in *Late Victorian and Edwardian British Novelists,* first series, ed. George M. Johnson (Detroit: Gale Research Co., 1995), 76–79.
44. "Taylor's New Opera on 'Peter Ibbetson,'" *New York Times,* 22 November 1929.
45. "Mr. Taylor's New Opera," *New York Times,* 25 November 1929.
46. Alexander Woollcott to Julie Woollcott Taber, 14 February 1918, *The Letters of Alexander Woollcott,* ed. Beatrice Kaufman and Joseph Hennessey (New York: Viking Press, 1944), 54.
47. Deems Taylor, introduction to George Du Maurier, *Peter Ibbetson* (New York: Modern Library, 1932). The novel had begun as a *Harper's Monthly* serial in 1891, followed by the book version the next year. Du Maurier's second novel, *Trilby* (1894), had even greater success on both sides of the Atlantic and introduced the name Svengali into everyday language.
48. *English Society: Sketched by George Du Maurier* (New York: Harper and Brothers, 1897), unnumbered plate.
49. Constance Collier to Taylor, 4 May [1930], DTP.
50. Taylor to Edward Ziegler, June [1930], Metropolitan Opera Archives.
51. "Metropolitan Opera Stars in Six Puccini Broadcasts," *New York Times,* 10 November 1929.
52. "Alda as Butterfly on the Air Tonight," *New York Times,* 16 November 1929.
53. John Vansant, letter to author, 15 May 1997.

54. Taylor's own typed and handwritten assessment of the composing time for *Peter Ibbetson,* DTP.

55. Taylor indicated his debt to Damrosch in an answer to a question about influential individuals in his life. Questionnaire from Storm Bull, professor of music, University of Colorado, 13 May 1961, JKT.

56. Olin Downes, "An American Composer's New Opera," *New York Times,* 1 February 1931.

57. Deems Taylor, *Peter Ibbetson: Lyric Drama in Three Acts* (New York: J. Fischer and Bro., 1930), 826–27.

58. Lehman Engel, *This Bright Day: An Autobiography* (New York: Macmillan, 1974), 45.

59. *New York Times,* 8 February 1931, 1, 26.

60. Ruby Mercer, *Tenor of His Time* (Toronto: Clarke Irwin, 1976), 147.

61. Grenville Vernon, "Peter Ibbetson," *Commonweal,* 25 February 1931, 470.

62. Benjamin Grosbayne, "Deems Taylor's New Opera," *Metropolitan Opera House Program,* 7 February 1931, 23. Author's personal collection.

63. Ibid.

64. Adams, *The Diary,* 1014.

65. Lawrence Gilman, "Deems Taylor's New Opera Heard by Notable Audience," *New York Herald Tribune,* 8 February 1931.

66. Walter Damrosch, "Concerning Taylor's 'Peter Ibbetson,'" *New York Herald Tribune,* 15 February 1931.

67. Taylor to Lawrence Gilman, 30 June 1932, Lawrence Gilman Papers, Georgetown University.

68. Oscar Thompson, quoted in "Taylor's New Opera, 'Peter Ibbetson,'" *Literary Digest,* 28 February 1931, 17.

69. Paul Rosenfeld, "Taylor, Carpenter and Loeffler," *New Republic,* 18 March 1931, 128.

70. Rosenfeld, *An Hour with American Music,* 128.

71. Taylor to Kennedy, 6 August 1931, MKP.

72. "'Peter Ibbetson' Is Acclaimed with Enthusiasm at Ravinia," *Chicago Journal of Commerce,* 4 August 1931. Quoted in Guszki, "American Opera," 385.

73. Fitzgerald, *Annals of the Metropolitan Opera.* Of the twenty-two performances, sixteen were at the Manhattan venue; one each in Boston (1935), Brooklyn (1931), Cleveland (1931), and Washington, D.C. (1931); two in Philadelphia (1931, 1932).

74. The role of Mimsey was the first acting experience for June Lockhart, whose career moved from motion pictures into television, with lengthy runs in the series *Lassie, Lost in Space,* and *General Hospital.*

75. Mercer, *The Tenor of His Time,* 174.

76. Ibid., 147.

77. Ibid., 148.

Chapter 11. Rough Times after *Peter Ibbetson,* 1931–1934

1. "Thirteenth Try," *Time,* 16 February 1931, 24.

2. Deems Taylor, "Ein Heldenleben," *New York World,* 19 November 1922.

3. Ben M. Hall, *The Best Remaining Seats: The Story of the Golden Age of the Movie Palace* (New York: Bramhall House, 1961), 175. When Rothafel became manager of Radio City Music Hall, he took along the Roxyettes, doubled their number, and initiated the Rockettes.

4. One of the four Roxy conductors, Charles Previn, moved to California. There he became head of Universal Studios' music department and paved the way for his nephew, André Previn, to escape with his family from Germany and join him in Hollywood.

5. Paul Jackson, *Saturday Afternoons at the Old Met: The Metropolitan Opera Broadcasts, 1931–1950* (Portland, Oreg.: Amadeus Press, 1992), 8. For a concise history of opera and radio, see Thomas A. DeLong, *The Mighty Music Box* (Los Angeles: Amber Crest Books, 1980), 89–103.

6. Taylor, script from first Metropolitan Opera NBC broadcast, 25 December 1931, DTP.

7. Ibid.

8. "What Happened on the First Met Broadcast?" Tape *LT-10 2840, New York Public Library, Rodgers and Hammerstein Archives of Recorded Sound.

9. Taylor, script from fourth Metropolitan Opera NBC Broadcast, 9 January 1932, DTP.

10. Taylor to Kennedy, 31 March 1932, MKP.

11. Otto Kahn to Taylor, 11 April 1932, Kahn Papers.

12. Taylor to Otto Kahn, 12 April 1932, Kahn Papers.

13. Guzski, "American Opera," 447.

14. Ibid., 391.

15. Pitts Sanborn, *New York World-Telegram,* quoted in *Metropolitan Opera Annals* (New York: H. W. Wilson Co., 1947), 626.

16. Edward Johnson and the Metropolitan board did not turn their backs completely on American opera during the next ten years. In the spring of 1937 the Metropolitan produced the American premiere of Richard Hageman's *Caponsacchi* for two performances and the world premiere of Walter Damrosch's *The Man without a Country.* For the next decade, any American operas performed were one act in length. Gian Carlo Menotti's amusing opera *Amelia Goes to the Ball* premiered in 1937 in Philadelphia, and it entered the Metropolitan repertoire for two seasons (1938–39). The success of *Amelia* led to the world premiere of Menotti's *Island God* in the spring of 1942. It survived one season. In 1947 *The Warrior,* with music by Bernard Rogers and libretto by Norman Corwin, earned one season of performances. This version of the story of Samson and Delilah was presented with *Hänsel und Gretel,* creating one of the strangest pairings in Metropolitan Opera history.

17. Taylor to Kennedy, 6 August 1931, MKP.

18. Taylor to Kennedy, 25 May 1932, MKP.

19. Joseph Taylor, "1932 Journal," MWD.

20. Katherine Taylor Davis to Kennedy, 22 May 1934, MKP.

21. Joseph S. Taylor to Deems Taylor, 23 April 1922, DTP.

22. Shaw, *Low-Down,* 18.

23. Author unidentified, "Biography of Deems Taylor," 8.

24. Gilbert, *Plays and Poems,* xviii.

25. From the poem "The Bustle in the House," by Emily Dickinson.

26. Taylor to Kennedy, 29 June 1932, MKP.

27. According to Joan Kennedy Taylor, her mother indicated that Deems's decision to take the Kraft Music Hall position played a significant part in her decision to file for divorce.

28. Taylor to Kennedy, [?] January 1934, MKP.

29. Phillip I. Earl, "This Was Nevada," *Las Vegas Review-Journal,* 15 February 1998, www.reviewjournal.com/lvrj_home/1998/Feb-15-Sun-1998/lifestyles/6921009.html (26 December 2002).

30. Curtis Bok to Kennedy, 27 March 1934, MKP.

31. Kennedy journal, 11 March 1934, MKP.
32. Joan Kennedy Taylor, e-mail to author, 20 April 2002.
33. Katherine Taylor Davis to Kennedy, 22 May 1934, MKP.
34. Joan Kennedy Taylor, interview with author, Stockbridge, Mass., 17 June 1996.
35. Taylor to Kennedy, 2 May 1934, MKP.
36. John Updike, ed., *A Century of Arts and Letters* (New York: Columbia University Press, 1998), 1.
37. Deems Taylor, speech at Juniata College, 17 April 1931, DTP.
38. "New Opera: Deems Taylor Is Busied with a Rip Van Winkle from China," *Newsweek,* 18 August 1934, 25.

Chapter 12. Hollywood, Colette d'Arville, and *Ramuntcho,* 1934–1936

1. "Paramount," *Fortune,* March 1937, 202.
2. Richard Barrios, *A Song in the Dark: The Birth of the Musical Film* (New York: Oxford University Press, 1995), 4.
3. Ibid., 137.
4. Taylor to Kennedy, 2 September 1934, MKP.
5. Taylor, 1934 appointment book, DTP.
6. Barrios, *A Song in the Dark,* 410.
7. John Hammell to Joseph I. Breen, 7 September 1934, Margaret Herrick Library, Academy of Motion Picture Arts and Sciences, Beverly Hills, Calif.
8. Joseph I. Breen to John Hammell, 8 September 1934, Herrick Library.
9. Joseph I. Breen to Will H. Hays, 14 September 1934, Herrick Library.
10. "Pétain Welcomed to City by Mayor: Charmed by 'Marseillaise,'" *New York Times,* 27 October 1931.
11. "D'Arville Recital," *New York Times,* 23 January 1934.
12. Taylor to Kennedy, n.d., MKP. The letter spoke of the success of the Chase and Sanborn Opera Program, a radio show that began in December 1934 and lasted four months. Thus the letter was probably written early in 1935.
13. Giovanni Martinelli to Taylor, 5 April 1928, DTP.
14. James A. Drake, *Rosa Ponselle: A Centenary Biography* (Portland, Oreg.: Amadeus Press, 1997), 195.
15. John Dunning, *On the Air: The Encyclopedia of Old-Time Radio* (New York: Oxford University Press, 1998).
16. Taylor to George Bye, 15 December 1934, James Oliver Brown Papers, Columbia University.
17. "Opera: 'Rigoletto' Is Put to Work Booming Coffee Sales," *Newsweek,* 8 December 1934, 33.
18. Taylor to Kennedy, n.d. [1934 or 1935], MKP.
19. Author unidentified, "Biography of Deems Taylor," 14.
20. Taylor to Kennedy, n.d. [1934 or 1935], MKP.
21. Taylor, script of *Fleischmann Yeast Hour,* 1 August 1935, DTP. The Italian word for water closet is *gabinetto.*
22. Guzski, "American Opera," 453.
23. In 1908 Gabriel Pierné composed incidental music for a play based on Loti's book, and in 1921 the French composer Stefano Donaudy fashioned a lyric drama that played in Milan once and then disappeared. Pelote, or pelota, is a game similar to jai alai.

24. Walter Damrosch to Taylor, 15 November 1937, JKT.
25. George Gershwin to DuBose Heyward, quoted in Jablonski, *Gershwin,* 278. Taylor mentions being summoned by Gershwin in the script he wrote for a Gershwin memorial concert, *Everybody's Music,* 10 July 1938, DTP.
26. Taylor to Kennedy, 6 April 1936, MKP.
27. Taylor to Kennedy, 12 June 1936, MKP.
28. A review of the will of Colette d'Arville shows that her birth name was Marie Marthe Cescosse, and that there was a bequest "to my son, Gaston Etienne Cescosse." It is assumed the child was born out of wedlock (Manhattan Borough Probate Records, File #80/1945; Liber 1782; page 475). Joan Kennedy Taylor states that she does not believe her father ever knew about the son, but it is possible that he did find out.
29. Taylor to Kennedy, 23 July 1936, MKP.
30. Deems Taylor, *Music to My Ears* (New York: Simon and Schuster, 1949), 7.
31. Ibid., 8.

Chapter 13. The Philharmonic Intermissions Begin, 1936–1938

1. Leon Crist Hood, "The Programming of Classical Music Broadcasts over the Major Radio Networks" (Ed.D. diss., New York University, 1955), 38–39.
2. Dunning, *On the Air,* 179.
3. Ibid., 257.
4. Sally Bedell Smith, *In All His Glory: The Life of William S. Paley* (New York: Simon and Schuster, 1990), 135.
5. Arthur Judson to Marshall Field, 1 October 1936, New York Philharmonic Archives.
6. Douglas Coulter to Arthur Judson, 23 October 1936, New York Philharmonic Archives.
7. Arthur Judson to Douglas Coulter, 23 October 1936, New York Philharmonic Archives.
8. Joseph Horowitz, *Understanding Toscanini* (New York: Alfred A. Knopf, 1987; reprint, Minneapolis: University of Minnesota Press, 1988), 142.
9. Deems Taylor, "The Philharmonic," *New York World,* 31 January 1925.
10. "Prussian Disciplinarian Will Rule the N.Y. Philharmonic," *Newsweek,* 7 March 1936.
11. "Transition," *Newsweek,* 21 March 1936.
12. Horowitz, *Understanding Toscanini,* 443.
13. "Writing about Music," *World in Books,* 14 May 1959, WEVD-FM, New York. Tape of broadcast in author's personal collection.
14. Throughout this chapter, the inclusion of a Philharmonic broadcast date indicates that I have seen the original script in the Taylor Papers at Yale Music Library.
15. Alton Cook, *New York World-Telegram,* 30 November 1936.
16. Horowitz, *Understanding Toscanini,* 443–45. Though this was the control side of Judson, he nonetheless did offer sound advice to Barbirolli; for example, he suggested that "the William Walton Symphony has been played several times in America and has been totally unsuccessful. Whether you want to play a work of this nature on your first visit to New York and so early in your season, is an open question" (p. 95).
17. Taylor, *Of Men and Music,* 95, 106. The scripts for the 1937 broadcasts by Taylor on modern music are not among the Deems Taylor Papers, nor are they available from the New York Philharmonic Archives. It is assumed that the chapter entitled "The Tolerant Ear I," which is concerned with modern music, is essentially from those broadcasts.

18. Arnold Schoenberg to Taylor, 24 April 1939, Schoenberg Papers, Library of Congress.

19. Dika Newlin, *Schoenberg Remembered: Diaries and Recollections (1938–76)* (New York: Pendragon Press, 1980), 148.

20. Arnold Schoenberg to Taylor, 21 January 1940, Schoenberg Archives, Vienna, Austria. Therese Muxeneder, director of the Schoenberg Archives, stated that the letter may never have been sent.

21. Arnold Schoenberg to Taylor, 12 February 1941, Library of Congress.

22. Taylor, *Music to My Ears,* 260.

23. Newlin, *Schoenberg Remembered,* 308.

24. Arnold Schoenberg to Taylor, draft of telegram, 10 March 1941, Library of Congress.

25. Don Herold, "Deems Taylor," *Judge,* June 1937, 22, quoted in Anthony Slide, *Selected Radio and Television Criticism* (Metuchen, N.J.: Scarecrow Press, 1987), 88.

26. Aaron Copland, "America's Young Men of Promise," *Modern Music,* March/April 1926, 13–20. Copland humbly did not include himself in that list, although most other composers of the time would have put him at the head of any such list.

27. Taylor, script of NBC Orchestral Awards broadcast, 1 May 1932, DTP.

28. Ibid. Other winners were: second prize of $2,500 to Max Wald for *The Dancer Dead;* third prize of $1,250 to Carl Eppert for *Traffic;* fourth prize of $750 to Florence Grandland Galajikian for *Symphonic Intermezzo;* and fifth prize of $500 to Nicolai Berezowsky for *Sinfonietta.*

29. Gerard Schwarz, interview with author, 13 January 2002. Schwarz stated that David Diamond informed him of the Whiteman scholarship and Taylor's role in the award.

30. Taylor, quoted in Albert D. Hughes, "Radio Proves Valuable Agent for Promotion of Good Music," *Christian Science Monitor,* 9 November 1937.

31. Copland and Perlis, *Copland: 1900 through 1942,* 255.

32. The composers for the 1938 commissions were Robert Russell Bennett, Nathaniel Dett, Vittorio Giannini, Jerome Moross, Quincy Porter, and Leo Sowerby. Time has proved these to be on a secondary level when compared with the composers of the first year's commissions.

33. Edward Jablonski, letter to author, 6 April 1999.

34. Taylor to George Bye, 15 December 1934, James Oliver Brown Papers, Columbia University.

35. Taylor, *Of Men and Music,* 59.

36. George Stevens, "Friend of Music," *Saturday Review,* 27 November 1937, 12.

37. Deems Taylor, "A Critic of Music," *Dial,* September 1920, 313–19.

38. Paul Rosenfeld, "Some Sprightly Musical Variations by Deems Taylor," *New York Times Book Review,* 26 December 1937, 3.

39. Fraser Macdonald, letter to author, 5 October 1998.

40. Fraser Macdonald to Taylor, 7 November 1937, copy provided by Fraser Macdonald.

41. The letter to Taylor changed Macdonald's life completely. It became the basis for "Guest Speaker," a chapter in Taylor's second successful book of musical essays, *The Well-Tempered Listener.* A friend of Macdonald's read the book, got in touch with him, and brought him from the Canadian wheat fields to Toronto and the Canadian Broadcasting System, where he worked in the music department for thirty-five years doing "the work that I should have been doing all along, instead of trying to teach school!" Letter to author, 5 October 1998.

42. "Record of New Operas Submitted to the Met: 1919–1950," 157, Metropolitan Opera Archives. Taylor played the score for them on 18 November 1937.

43. Harold E. Stearns, ed., *America Now: An Inquiry into Civilization in the United States* (New York: Charles Scribner's Sons, 1938), 70–71.
44. "'The Nutmeg'—a Great Idea, 10 Publishers, One Reporter, and No Editor," *Newsweek,* 23 May 1938, 23.
45. John Erskine, "Editorial," *Connecticut Nutmeg,* 26 May 1938.
46. "The Nutmeg," *Newsweek,* 23 May 1938, 23.
47. Joan Kennedy Taylor, interview, 19 March 1996. A local paint store supplied the team with caps bearing the initials B. P. S., for "best paint sold." Bye developed the name Bye's Prehistoric Sluggers to take advantage of the initials.
48. Joan Kennedy Taylor provided a drawing of the apartment's layout as well as her recollections of many visits there.
49. "Colette d'Arville's Recital," *New York Times,* 9 January 1938.

Chapter 14. The *Fantasia* Years, 1938–1940

1. Walt Disney to Taylor, 4 August 1938, Walt Disney Archives, Burbank, Calif.
2. John Culhane, *Walt Disney's Fantasia* (New York: Henry N. Abrams, 1983). Chap. 1, "The Making of Fantasia," provides a full description of the movie's evolution.
3. Taylor to Kennedy, 5 September 1938, MKP.
4. David R. Smith, "The Sorcerer's Apprentice: Birthplace of Fantasia," *Millimeter,* February 1976, 18.
5. Culhane, *Walt Disney's Fantasia,* 13.
6. "BBC Radio interview with Stokowski by John Bowen, 1959," quoted in Oliver Daniels, *Stokowski: A Counterpoint of View* (New York: Dodd, Mead, 1982), 379–80.
7. Ibid., 380.
8. Culhane, *Walt Disney's Fantasia,* 18.
9. Deems Taylor, "The Philadelphia Orchestra," *New York World,* 17 October 1923.
10. "*Fantasia.* Dance of the Hours—Ponchielli. Notes taken from story meetings," 19 September 1938, DTP. Some of Taylor's own copies of the Disney story meetings on *Fantasia* are in the Taylor Papers.
11. "*Fantasia.* Night on the Bare Mountain—Moussorgsky. Notes taken from story meetings," 16 September 1938, DTP. The composition is more commonly known as *Night on Bald Mountain.*
12. Culhane, *Walt Disney's Fantasia,* 182.
13. "Story meeting," 13 September 1938, DTP.
14. Deems Taylor, "Music," *New York World,* 1 February 1924.
15. "Story meeting," 30 September 1938, Walt Disney Archives.
16. Taylor to Kennedy, 4 October 1938, MKP.
17. "Story meeting," 30 September 1938, DTP.
18. Kevin Starr, *The Dream Endures: California Enters the 1940s* (New York: Oxford University Press, 1997), 282. Starr, whose books on the history of California delve into every side of the state's personality, writes that "Hollywood adored the British for a variety of reasons, including their ability to speak the English language with grace and clarity—and to act."
19. Ginger Rogers, *Ginger: My Story* (New York: HarperCollins, 1991), 85.
20. Arturo Toscanini, *The Letters of Arturo Toscanini,* ed. Harvey Sachs (New York: Alfred A. Knopf, 2002), 351–52.

21. John Davis, *The Guggenheims* (New York: William Morrow, 1978), 203. Guggenheim always emphasized the need to be generous. His penchant for art and his generosity may well explain why after d'Arville's death, an auction of her art properties in March 1945 brought nearly $36,000, a significant amount at that time. "Art Sale Brings $35,676," *New York Times,* 4 March 1945.

22. "Deems Taylor, 53, Talks, Writes, Paints, and Composes—But He Still Can't Add," *Newsweek,* 26 December 1938.

23. "Ten Million Listeners," *Fortune,* February 1939, 13.

24. Deems Taylor honorary degree citation, Dartmouth College, 18 June 1939, Rauner Library Archives, Dartmouth College.

25. "Rochester Honor to Mrs. Lindbergh," *New York Times,* 20 June 1939.

26. Taylor to Stuart Buchanan, 22 February 1939, DTP.

27. Bob Jones, quoted in Robin Allan, *Walt Disney and Europe* (Bloomington: Indiana University Press, 1999), 145.

28. Taylor's 1939 appointment book details each day's meetings while he was in Hollywood.

29. Michael Mok, "Miss Gish Looks Back," *New York Post,* 14 November 1939, MKP.

30. Broun, *Collected Edition of Heywood Broun,* 229–31.

31. *New Yorker,* 20 April 1940, 23.

32. Taylor, script of first program of *Musical Americana,* 25 January 1940, DTP.

33. Taylor, script of *Musical Americana,* 1 February 1940, DTP.

34. "All-American Program: Deems Taylor and a Symphony to Wave Musical Flag," *Newsweek,* 29 January 1940, 44.

35. Students were selected from Chicago Conservatory, Cincinnati Conservatory, Cleveland Institute of Music, Curtis, DePaul University, Drake University, Eastman, Ellison-White Conservatory (Portland, Oreg.), Iowa State College, Juilliard, Kansas City Conservatory of Music, New England Conservatory, Northwestern University, Oberlin Conservatory, University of Michigan, University of Minnesota School of Music, and University of Southern California.

36. Nathan Stutch, telephone conversation with author, 6 April 2000.

37. Harry Herforth, telephone conversation with author, 29 March 2000.

38. Sidney Mear, telephone conversation with author, 29 March 2000.

39. Elis Ronbeck, telephone conversion with author, 9 April 2000.

40. David Falvay, telephone conversation with author, 7 April 2000.

41. Walt Disney to Taylor, 27 July 1940, MKP.

42. Scott MacQueen, "Audio Commentary," *Walt Disney's Fantasia,* DVD release, 2000.

43. F. Scott Fitzgerald to Zelda Fitzgerald, 5 October 1940, *The Letters of F. Scott Fitzgerald,* ed. Andrew Turnbull (New York: Charles Scribner, 1963), 126.

44. Katherine Taylor to Deems Taylor, 2 October 1940, DTP.

45. Bosley Crowther, "The Screen in Review," *New York Times,* 14 November 1940.

46. Dorothy Thompson, "Minority Report," *New York Herald Tribune,* 25 November 1940.

47. Otis Ferguson, "Both Fantasy and Fancy," *New Republic,* 25 November 1940, 724.

48. Katherine Taylor, journal, "A Line a Day," DTP.

49. *Fantasia* became a moneymaker only after several rereleases, especially that of 1969, when many viewers augmented its Technicolor brilliance with drug enhancement. With the video release in the early 1990s, *Fantasia* zoomed around the world; Taylor, however, was entirely cut out of overseas editions. With the English-language DVD version recre-

ating the "road-show" original, all of Taylor's commentaries were restored, with one significant difference: unable to find the Taylor voice tracks but having the original scripts, Disney engineers recorded another person's voice.

50. Walt Disney to Taylor, 14 September 1940, MKP. The introductions requested and prepared were for Stravinsky's *Firebird,* Debussy's *La Mer,* John Alden Carpenter's *Adventures in a Perambulator,* Richard Strauss's *Don Quixote,* and Mussorgsky's *Pictures at an Exhibition.*

Chapter 15. Radio Daze, 1940–1942

1. The information on the interactions of Taylor and his girlfriends comes from his appointment books in the Taylor Papers.
2. Leila Hadley Luce, telephone conversation with author, 26 October 1998.
3. Norman Corwin, telephone conversation with author, 11 March 1995.
4. Howard Taubman, "The Well-Tempered Musical Essays of Deems Taylor," *New York Times,* Book Reviews, 11 February 1940, 2.
5. R. D. Welch, "From a Fireside Commentator," *Yale Review,* spring 1940, 645.
6. I reviewed Taylor's personal checks, which are part of the Deems Taylor Papers.
7. *America Preferred* script, 6 September 1941, DTP.
8. A year later, when the Treasury Department found some difficulties with his tax returns, Deems wrote a letter to his accountant: "Not that it is entirely relevant, but I can't help having a faintly wry feeling at the vigilance of the Treasury Department's janissaries, in view of the fact that during the past twelve months I have written and delivered forty Savings Bond broadcasts for the U.S. Treasury Department. These services were rendered free of charge, of course. At my regular fee, they would have cost a commercial sponsor exactly $30,000." Letter to Appel, 1 February 1943, JKT.
9. Deems Taylor income tax return, 1942. DTP.
10. Clifton Fadiman, letter to author, 8 May 1997.
11. Dunning, *On the Air,* 343.
12. Ibid., 345.
13. *America Preferred* script, 6 December 1941, DTP.
14. Samuel Barber to Taylor, 3 October 1941, DTP.
15. Taylor to Joan Kennedy Taylor, 27 January 1942, JKT.
16. "Grand Operetta," *Time,* 23 February 1942, 58.
17. Linton Martin, "'Ramuntcho' Is Given World Premiere," *Philadelphia Inquirer,* 11 February 1942.
18. Taylor to Joan Kennedy Taylor, 17 February 1942, JKT.
19. Dorothy Sarnoff (no relation to NBC's David Sarnoff) later justified the praise with a two-year run on Broadway in *Rosalinda,* an English-language version of Johann Strauss's *Die Fledermaus;* she also originated the role of Lady Thiang, the king's principal wife, in Rodgers and Hammerstein's *King and I.*
20. Henry Pleasants, "Opera 'Ramuntcho' Has Its World Premiere Here," *Evening Bulletin-Philadelphia,* 11 February 1942.
21. Howard Taubman, "Premiere Is Given of Taylor Opera," *New York Times,* 11 February 1942.
22. Eddy, "Phila. Bow for Taylor Opera," *Variety,* 11 February 1942, 33.
23. Linton Martin, "The Operatic Composer Who Is Also Librettist," *Philadelphia Inquirer,* 15 February 1942.

24. Taylor, *The Well-Tempered Listener,* 57.

25. Erika Mann, "Erika Mann Protests," *New York Times,* 15 February 1942. It had been Erika who warned her novelist father, the winner of the 1929 Nobel Prize in literature, not to return from a 1933 vacation because Hitler had condemned his works. Thomas Mann's inevitable journey then began: first to Switzerland, then to Princeton, and finally to Los Angeles.

26. Katherine Anne Porter, "Question of Royalties," *New York Times,* 8 March 1942.

27. Alfred Frankenstein, "How to Make Friends by Radio," *Modern Music,* 21 (1943–44), 6.

Chapter 16. ASCAP Fades In and Intermissions Fade Out, 1942–1945 (Part 1)

1. *New Grove Dictionary of Music and Musicians,* 2d ed., s.v. "copyright." The first society was the Société des auteurs, compositeurs et éditeurs de musique (SACEM).

2. Deems Taylor, "Fame Pays No Bills," *ASCAP,* 31 July 1940.

3. John Tasker Howard, *Our Contemporary Composers* (New York: Crowell, 1941), 335.

4. Mark Murphy, "Play for Pay," *Hearst's International Combined with Cosmopolitan,* June 1951, 138.

5. John Ryan, *The Production of Culture in the Music Industry* (Lanham, Md.: University Press of America, 1985), 20.

6. "5,000,000 Songs," *Fortune,* January 1933, 29.

7. Taylor, "Fame Pays No Bills."

8. W. C. Handy, *Father of the Blues: An Autobiography* (New York: Collier Books, 1970), 301. In chap. 21, Handy provides a detailed account of the entire day's events.

9. *Carousel of American Music: The Fabled 24 September 1940 San Francisco Concerts,* Music and Arts CD-971, 4 compact discs.

10. Richard Frohlich, telephone conversation with author, 13 February 1998. Mr. Frohlich was in charge of public relations for ASCAP from 1939 to 1979.

11. John Tasker Howard, "Stephen Collins Foster," in *A Treasury of Stephen Foster* (New York: Random House, 1946), 13.

12. Jonathan Yardley, *Ring: A Biography of Ring Lardner* (New York: Random House, 1977), 259.

13. "Buck Out as ASCAP Prez," *Variety,* 29 April 1942, 41.

14. "Passing of Buck," *Time,* 4 May 1942, 40.

15. Taylor's financial records indicate that for 1942 his gross income (rounded off) was $63,000; payment to Mary Kennedy, $21,500; his net income (after taxes), $22,500.

16. Richard Frohlich, telephone conversation with author, 13 February 1998.

17. Deems Taylor, "My Friend Billy," *New York Post,* 23 September 1952.

18. Ben Bodec, "ASCAP's 'Just Chums' Dinner," *Variety,* 4 November 1942, 41.

19. Taylor to Joan Kennedy Taylor, 1 November 1942, JKT.

20. Ben Bodec, "'New' and Better ASCAP Highlighted Quiet Music Yr.," *Variety,* 6 January 1943.

21. Francis Chase Jr., *Sound and Fury* (New York: Harper, 1942), 265.

22. "Music Biz Plenty Forte in U.S.," *Variety,* 13 December 1944, 1.

23. *Articles of Association of the American Society of Composers, Authors, and Publishers* (New York: ASCAP, 1981), 31.

24. Agatha Fassett, *The Naked Face of Genius: Béla Bartók's American Years* (Boston: Houghton Mifflin, 1958), 271.

25. "The MacDowell Colony," *Musical America,* 7 April 1928, 10.

26. Mrs. Edward MacDowell to Lewis M. Isaacs Jr., 17 January 1952, Library of Congress, MacDowell Collection.

27. Olin Downes to Taylor, 15 October 1946, Olin Downes Papers, University of Georgia.

28. Memo to Miss Sylvia Rosenberg from ASCAP accounting department, 12 July 1962, JKT.

29. "Problems Facing Television Tough, Says Deems Taylor," *New Bedford* [*Mass.*] *Sunday Standard-Times,* 11 August 1946. I am grateful to Eulalie Regan of the *Vineyard Gazette* (Edgartown, Mass.) for providing a copy of this article.

30. Caleb Milne to Taylor, n.d., in Caleb Milne, *"I Dream of the Day . . .": Letters from Caleb Milne, Africa, 1942–1943* (New York: Longmans, Green, 1945), 63–64.

31. Ibid., 63.

32. David Mason Greene, *Greene's Biographical Encyclopedia of Composers* (Garden City, N.Y.: Doubleday, 1985), 1041.

33. *Prudential Family Hour* script, 27 June 1943, DTP.

34. Taylor to Joan Kennedy Taylor, 27 October 1943, JKT.

35. Jack Gould, "One Thing and Another," *New York Times,* 28 November 1943.

36. Taylor to Joan Kennedy Taylor, "21st" [January 1944], JKT.

37. Transcription by author from Yale Collection of Historical Sound Recordings cassette, radio station WOR broadcast, 11 November 1945.

38. Dunning, *On the Air,* 349.

39. Recording of *It Pays to Be Ignorant,* 6 October 1944, Yale University Music Library.

40. *Duffy's Tavern* radio script, 25 January 1944, DTP.

Chapter 17. Taylor as Author, Father, and Composer, 1942–1945 (Part 2)

1. George Bye to Taylor, 6 September 1940, James Oliver Brown Collection, Columbia University.

2. Deems Taylor, *A Pictorial History of the Movies* (New York: Simon and Schuster, 1943). Marcelene Peterson and Bryant Hale are given credit for assisting Taylor.

3. Martin Scorsese, "Modern Library Goes to the Movies: Series Introduction by Martin Scorsese," July 1999, www.randomhouse.com/modernlibrary/seriesmoviesdet1.html (8 April 2003).

4. *A Personal Journey with Martin Scorsese through American Movies,* prod. Florence Dauman, British Film Institute, [1998], 3 videocassettes. The quote is a transcription from Scorsese's introductory remarks.

5. Richard Lamparski, telephone interview with author, 7 March 2001.

6. Joan Kennedy Taylor, conversation with author, 17 September 2001.

7. Taylor to Joan Kennedy Taylor, "21st" [January 1944], JKT.

8. Taylor to Joan Kennedy Taylor, 17 February 1942, JKT.

9. David L. Strauss to Taylor, 14 July 1940, DTP.

10. Taylor to Kennedy, 18 December 1920, MKP.

11. "Muses Honored by Art Institute," *New York Times,* 19 January 1941. Edna St. Vincent Millay, who read her "Invocation to the Muses" at the 18 January ceremony, also wrote "Chorale," words for *Processional.*

12. Helen A. F. Penniman, "Barlow, Taylor Win Plaudits at Symphony," *Baltimore News-Post,* 28 April 1941.

13. The fanfares were found listed on the Cincinnati Symphony's Internet site, www. cincinnatisymphony.org/aboutus/fanfare.htm (10 April 2003).

14. Deems Taylor, quoted in *Great Orchestral Music: A Treasury of Program Notes,* ed. Julian Seaman, rev. ed. (New York: Collier Books, 1962), 357.

15. New York Philharmonic intermission script, 15 November 1942, DTP.

16. Noel Straus, "Casadesus Plays at Concert Here," *New York Times,* 15 November 1942.

17. Olin Downes, "Barbirolli Offers Villa Lobos Suite," *New York Times,* 12 February 1943.

18. Taylor to Joan Kennedy Taylor, 8 March 1943, JKT.

19. Walt Disney to Taylor, 2 July 1943, DTP.

20. Roger Plummer, telephone interview with author, 7 August 1993.

21. Olin Downes, "Berezowsky Music Is Well Received," *New York Times,* 24 December 1943.

22. Taylor to Joan Kennedy Taylor, 4 February 1944, JKT.

23. Taylor to Joan Kennedy Taylor, "Abe's Natal Day" [12 February 1944], JKT.

24. Isabel Morse Jones, "Kabalevsky Work Highlights Music Event," *Los Angeles Times,* 5 January 1945.

25. "Lady Haw-Haw," *Time,* 19 January 1942, 30.

26. Deems Taylor interview, Federal Bureau of Investigation, Jane Anderson Files, Baltimore, File No. 61-791 A.S.

27. John Carver Edwards, *Berlin Calling: American Broadcasters in Service to the Third Reich* (New York: Praeger, 1991), 49.

28. "American Woman Freed of Espionage in Spain," *New York Times,* 11 October 1936.

29. "Blacklist Is Laid to U.S. Radicals," *New York Times,* 28 February 1938.

30. Edwards, *Berlin Calling,* 41–56. Edwards details the entire story of Anderson's road from her marriage to the Spanish nobleman to her disappearance after the war.

31. Ibid., 55.

32. Ralph Blumenthal, *Stork Club: America's Most Famous Nightspot and the Lost World of Café Society* (Boston: Little, Brown, 2000), 13.

33. Broun, *Whose Little Boy Are You?* 49.

34. "Edward McNamara, Actor, Dies: Ex-Policeman Sang Way to Stage," *New York Times,* 10 November 1944.

35. "Colette d'Arville, Soprano, 42, Is Dead," *New York Times,* 17 December 1944.

Chapter 18. More Beginnings and Endings, 1945–1951

1. Henry S. Cohn and David Bollier, *The Great Hartford Circus Fire* (New Haven, Conn.: Yale University Press, 1991), 8–14.

2. *Ringling Bros. and Barnum & Bailey Circus Magazine,* 1945 ed., 52. Author's personal collection.

3. Emily Coleman, telephone interview with author, 5 August 1998. Ms. Coleman interviewed Taylor as one of her first assignments for *Newsweek.* Their conversation was published 26 December 1938, but did not mention his hobbies.

4. Térouanne, letter to author, 28 November 1996.

5. Térouanne, letter to author, 11 November 1996.

6. Robert D. Stranathan, letter to author, 18 April 1999.

7. "14,000 at Opening of the Circus Here," *New York Times,* 5 April 1945.

8. "Show Clicks," *Billboard,* 14 April 1945.

9. Taylor to Kennedy, 17 April 1945, JKT.

10. Joan Kennedy Taylor, e-mail to author, 1 September 1998.

11. Barbara Boston, "Deems Taylor in Big Top Elopement," *New York Daily News,* 18 April 1945.

12. Térouanne, letter to author, 21 January 2000. In a later letter (10 April 2001), she wrote the following: "When Deems and I married, I was 23 years old, *not 20.*"

13. Eugen Boissevain to Taylor, n.d., New York Public Library, Music Letters Collection.

14. George T. Bye to Taylor, 20 April 1945, New York Public Library, Music Letters Collection.

15. Leila Hadley Luce, conversation with author, 26 October 1998. Giuliana Taberna married Michael Field in Caracas, Venezuela, on 13 July 1949.

16. Verna Arvey, "Deems Taylor Talks of Cabbages and Kings," *Opera and Concert,* June 1947, 40.

17. The following identifies Deems Taylor's shared income from 1934 to 1944. "Summary of Payments made to Mary Kennedy, 1934–1944," DTP.

Gross Income		Payment to Mary	Taylor's After-Tax Net
1934	34,495	17,648	12,595
1935	31,132	18,043	7,918
1936	26,832	12,099	11,334
1937	38,843	15,701	16,311
1938	56,589	25,317	21,256
1939	30,679	13,753	14,823
1940	56,030	24,365	17,414
1941	32,149	12,663	9,912
1942	63,135	21,440	22,484
1943	54,061	20,875	18,784
1944	46,560	19,722	13,910

Taylor paid the taxes on both his and Mary's shares.

18. Térouanne, letter to author, 11 November 1996.

19. Térouanne, letter to author, 19 February 1997.

20. Térouanne, letter to author, 25 March 2000.

21. Script of *The RCA Show: The Battle of Music,* 2 December 1945, Jane Weld personal collection. Jane Weld, a daughter of Raymond Paige, graciously provided the background information on "The Battle of Music."

22. Jack Gould, "Radio Notebook," *New York Times,* 9 December 1945.

23. Taylor, *The Well-Tempered Listener,* 206.

24. Robert Ringling to Taylor, 21 December 1945, Circus World Museum Archives, Baraboo, Wisc.

25. Pat Percell, "Majestic in Garden Bow," *Billboard,* 6 April 1946, quoted in Joseph T. Bradbury, "The Season of 1946," *White Tops,* November–December 1982. Provided by Circus World Museum Archives.

26. "Mrs. Joseph S. Taylor," *New York Times,* 26 March 1946.

27. Katherine Johnson Taylor to Deems Taylor, 10 September 1942, DTP.

28. Katherine Johnson Taylor to Deems Taylor, 5 March 1942, DTP.

29. Katherine Johnson Taylor to Deems Taylor, 13 November 1938, DTP.

30. Katherine Johnson Taylor to Deems Taylor, 5 March 1942, DTP.

31. Katherine Johnson Taylor to Deems Taylor, 22 August 1940, DTP.

32. Térouanne, letters to author, 11 November 1996, 16 May 1997.

33. Theresa Helburn to Taylor, 23 May 1947, DTP.
34. William Hess, interview by Oliver Daniels, 15 July 1978, Rare Books and Manuscript Library, University of Pennsylvania.
35. "ASCAP Reelects Entire Slate; Votes Prexy Deems Taylor $25,000 a Year," *Variety,* 1 May 1946, 49.
36. "ASCAP Board Holds First of Series of Meetings on Television Problems," *Variety,* 3 December 1947, 89.
37. "See Fred Ahlert Succeeding Taylor as ASCAP Prez: Decision This Month," *Variety,* 14 April 1948, 37.
38. Ibid.
39. U.S. Department of Justice, Federal Bureau of Investigation, "Deems (Joseph) Taylor Summary," 8 June 1953. Two pages, released to author 21 January 1998. FOPIA Request No. 425436.
40. Joan Kennedy Taylor, conversation with author, 23 July 1995.
41. Joan Kennedy Taylor, conversation with author, 18 February 2001.
42. Shirlee P. Newman, *Marian Anderson: Lady from Philadelphia* (Philadelphia: Westminster Press, 1965), 105–6.
43. U.S. Department of Justice, Federal Bureau of Investigation, Deems Taylor file.
44. Stewart, *By a Stroke of Luck,* 228.
45. Taylor to Emil Hilb, 23 December 1948, New York Public Library.
46. Louis D. Frohlich to Taylor, 5 May 1948, DTP.
47. "Deems Taylor May Be Next ASCAP Prez," *Variety.* This was a clipped article with no date, DTP.
48. John Crosby, "Radio in Review," *Philadelphia Bulletin,* 4 August 1949.
49. Taylor, *Music to My Ears,* 5–6.
50. Ibid., 23.
51. Deems Taylor, *Moments Mousical* (Chicago: Ziff-Davis, 1949), [10].
52. Ibid., [36].
53. Gladys Swarthout to Taylor, 15 November 1949, DTP.
54. Térouanne, letter to author, 27 October 2000.
55. Ibid.
56. Boissevain to Taylor, n.d., JKT.
57. "Eugen Boissevain, Retired Importer," *New York Times,* 31 August 1949.
58. Deems Taylor, "Edna St. Vincent Millay," 108.
59. Milford, *Savage Beauty,* 508. The book is the first to detail Millay's addiction to drugs.
60. Térouanne, letter to author, 25 March 1997.
61. Térouanne, letter to author, 21 January 2000.
62. Taylor to "Mrs. Still" (Verna Arvey), 13 March 1951, William Grant Still Collection, University of Arkansas Library.
63. Joan Kennedy Taylor, conversations with author.
64. Térouanne, letter to author, 16 May 1997.
65. Ibid.
66. Shaw, *Low-Down,* 21.

Chapter 19. A Life with Friends, the 1950s

1. Kennedy to Taylor, 3 December 1920, MKP.
2. Kathy Kemp, "More Than 'A Flesh Show,'" *Kansas City Star,* 16 September 1995.

3. Yolande Betbeze Fox, telephone conversation with author, 27 January 1997. Betbeze married Matthew Fox in 1954.

4. George Trow and Irving Lieberman, "Billy, the Cultured Rose," *New York Post,* 21 September 1952.

5. Deems Taylor, "My Friend Billy," *New York Post,* 23 September 1952.

6. Betbeze Fox, telephone conversations with author, 27 January 1997, 9 April 1997, and 16 March 2001.

7. Eleanor Holm, telephone conversation with author, 20 September 1997.

8. Deems Taylor, *The One-Track Mind: Love Poems of Seventeenth and Eighteenth Century France* (New York: Library Publishers, 1953), xi.

9. Ibid., 32–33.

10. In 1932 Taylor provided a sixty-page preface to the *Plays & Poems of W. S. Gilbert.* In addition, he edited *A Treasury of Gilbert & Sullivan: The Words and the Music of One Hundred and Two Songs from Eleven Operettas* (New York: Simon and Schuster, 1941).

11. "Musical Play Team Called Immortal," *New York Times,* 23 October 1950.

12. Updike, *Century of Arts and Letters,* 1.

13. Ibid., 48.

14. Deems Taylor to Julian Street, 7 January 1944, Julian Street Papers, Princeton University.

15. Deems Taylor to David Ewen, n.d., DTP.

16. Linda Rodgers Emory, telephone conversation with author, 18 November 2000.

17. Ibid.

18. Betbeze Fox, telephone conversation with author, 27 January 1997.

19. Matthew Fox, after marrying Betbeze in 1954, purchased the entire film library of RKO Radio Pictures for release to television, the first major library to find its way onto television. All other studios ultimately followed. Fox made millions and died in 1964, leaving Yolande with one child. She never married again.

20. For the 1954 Miss America pageant, Deems shared the judges' stand with another lovely woman, Grace Kelly. The future princess of Monaco found Deems to possess the same charming, gentlemanly ways that so many other women had found beguiling. Though they never became an item in the social scene, according to Joan Kennedy Taylor they exchanged many letters.

21. Lyn Murray, *Musician: A Hollywood Journal* (Secaucus, N.J.: Lyle Stuart, 1987), 161.

22. Rita Falbel, telephone conversation with author, 21 March 2001.

23. Francis Perkins, "The Dragon—Premiere of Deems Taylor's Opera," *New York Herald Tribune,* 7 January 1958.

24. E. D., "N.Y.U. Singers Give Deems Taylor Work," *New York Times,* 7 February 1958.

25. Oscar Hammerstein II to Taylor, 7 February 1958, JKT.

26. Dorothy Stickney, *Openings and Closings* (Garden City, N.Y.: Doubleday, 1979), 138.

27. Joan Kennedy Taylor, conversation with author, 6 August 1998.

28. Ibid. Joan Kennedy Taylor provided all the information regarding her father's relationship with Ayn Rand.

Chapter 20. The Final Years

1. Deems Taylor, "Sport for Art's Sake," *Sports Illustrated,* 14 December 1959, 72. Card games included poker in *Girl of the Golden West;* throughout *A Hand of Bridge,* by Gian Carlo Menotti and Samuel Barber; the Germont-Baron game in *La Traviata.* Duels were

found in *Don Giovanni* and *Eugene Onegin.* Taylor forgot to include William Schuman's 1953 one-act opera about baseball, *The Mighty Casey,* based on the poem "Casey at the Bat" by Ernest L. Thayer.

2. Advertising copy for "Great Music from Chicago," Rosenthal Archives, Chicago Symphony Orchestra.

3. "Great Music from Chicago," *Chicago Tribune,* 17 October 1959, Rosenthal Archives.

4. Robert C. March, "Symphony 'Great' in New TV Series," *Chicago Sun-Times,* 19 October 1959, Rosenthal Archives.

5. Paul Molloy, "'Great Music' Local TV's Finest Hour," *Chicago Sun-Times,* 16 December 1959. Copy provided by Rosenthal Archives.

6. Taylor to Lucille Térouanne, 29 [January 1960], Lucille Térouanne personal collection.

7. Ibid.

8. Taylor to Don Gillis, 13 July 1960, Interlochen Center for the Arts Papers, University of Michigan.

9. Jay S. Harrison, "'Peter Ibbetson' Revived at Empire State Festival," *New York Herald Tribune,* 25 July 1960.

10. "Sentimental Moment," *Newsweek,* 1 August 1960, 54.

11. John O'Hara to Katherine Angell, October 1929, in *Selected Letters of John O'Hara,* ed. Matthew J. Bruccoli (New York: Random House, 1978), 42.

12. John O'Hara to Taylor, 23 January 1957, in *Selected Letters of John O'Hara,* 261.

13. Ibid.

14. O'Hara to Taylor, 19 April 1958, John O'Hara Papers, Pennsylvania State University Library.

15. O'Hara to Taylor, 2 November 1960, John O'Hara Papers.

16. Oja, *Making Music Modern,* 176. This quote is from an Oja interview with Virgil Thomson in which she asked his opinion of the composer Emerson Whithorne.

17. Don Gillis to Taylor, 11 March 1959, Interlochen Papers, University of Michigan.

18. Jeff Davis, e-mail to author, 25 August 2001.

19. John Bell Young, "For the Love of Composing: An Interview with Hugh Downs," *Clavier,* July–August 1998.

20. A. Clyde Roller, telephone conversation with author, 19 March 2000.

21. Taylor, *The Well-Tempered Listener,* 133–34.

22. Copies of a recording of the *Three Centuries Suite* performed at the National Music Camp, Interlochen, Michigan, were provided both by the Yale Collection of Historical Sound Recordings and by Barbara Gillis.

23. Michael Cook, e-mail to author, 11 March 1997.

24. A. Clyde Roller, telephone conversation with author, 29 March 2000.

25. Cook, e-mail.

26. Nancy Howe Webster, e-mail to author, 22 April 2000.

27. Taylor to Barbara Gillis, 6 March 1961, DTP.

28. Don Gillis to Richard Korn, 23 January 1962, Richard Korn Papers, Princeton University.

29. Barbara Gillis, e-mail to author, 13 August 2000.

30. Cook, e-mail.

31. The value of the Monet *Nymphéas* painted in 1905 was $7,000 in 1944 and $65,000 in 1962. A 1906 Monet *Nymphéas,* similar in size, sold for $22,000,000 in 2000.

32. James M. Hester to Taylor, 13 February 1962, DTP.

33. "Taylor Wins 'Native Son' Honor," *New York Times,* 14 April 1939.

34. Albert Gallatin Award Dinner, 7 November 1962, "Address by Pres./Presentation by Dr. Wm. Schuman/Speech by Deems Taylor," Yale University Historical Sound Recordings.

35. Murray, *Musician: A Hollywood Journal,* 245. The date was 20 December 1962.

36. Joan Kennedy Taylor to Mary Kennedy, 3 April 1963, MKP.

37. Sister M. Helen Jean Sullivan, telephone conversation with author, 24 April 2000.

38. Georgina Cantoni, "'The King's Henchman' Cast Rehearses: Backstage Crew Prepares for Operetta," *The Merciad,* 8 April 1965. Provided by Sister M. Lawrence Franklin Archival Center, Mercyhurst College.

39. Boyd Dolan, e-mail to author, 21 July 2000.

40. Sullivan, telephone conversation with author, 24 April 2000.

41. Dave Stout, "Deems Taylor 79 but He Thinks Young," *Erie Daily Times,* 8 May 1965.

42. B.D., "'Henchman' Excellent," *Erie Daily Times,* 8 May 1965.

43. Stanley Adams to Joan Kennedy Taylor, 19 November 1965, DTP.

44. Joan Kennedy Taylor to Reginald Gardner, 16 May 1966, DTP.

45. Joan Kennedy Taylor to Lucille Térouanne, 7 July 1966, DTP. This letter describes in detail the funeral arrangements and the funeral itself.

46. Duke Ellington to Stanley Adams, [n.d.] July 1966, DTP.

47. William Grant Still to Joan Kennedy Taylor, telegram, [n.d.] July 1966, DTP.

48. Judith Anne Still to author, 18 August 1997.

49. Joan Kennedy Taylor to Lucille Térouanne.

50. Don Gillis, eulogy for Deems Taylor, DTP.

51. Ross Hastings (1915–91) grew up in Los Angeles learning music from his father, the organist for the Los Angeles Philharmonic Orchestra. His life consisted of work as a choral conductor and freelance arranger, then as an editor for several publishing firms. He composed music throughout his mature years. The Hastings Papers are at the University of Wisconsin, Eau Claire.

52. Don Gillis to Joan Kennedy Taylor and David Dawson, 7 July 1966, DTP. Gillis provided a copy of the eulogy with his letter.

53. Bennett Cerf, *Try and Stop Me* (New York: Simon and Schuster, 1945), 180.

Epilogue

1. Byron Belt, "American Composers Get Their Due," Newhouse News Service, n.d. I am grateful to Roger Dettmer for providing a copy of this article.

2. Nicholas E. Tawa, *Mainstream Music of Early Twentieth Century America* (Westport, Conn.: Greenwood Press, 1992), 91.

3. *ASCAP Today,* winter 1968, back cover.

4. *Simpson's Contemporary Quotations,* comp. James B. Simpson (Boston: Houghton Mifflin, 1988), 224.

5. Guzski, "American Opera," 390.

6. Taylor to Storm Bull, 13 May 1961, JKT. Bull, professor of music at the University of Colorado, questioned Taylor about his musical life.

7. A. Clyde Roller, e-mail to author, 10 April 2002.

8. Howard, *Deems Taylor,* 28. The same pagination will be found in the 1940 revision.

9. Tawa, *Mainstream Music,* 88.

10. Taylor to Storm Bull, 13 May 1961, JKT. To answer Bull's question ("Which of your works do you consider the most important and characteristic?") Taylor put *Looking Glass* at the top, then listed, in descending order, *The King's Henchman, Jurgen, Ramuntcho,* and *Marco Takes a Walk.*

11. H.T., "Native Program Given at Stadium," *New York Times,* 5 July 1934.

12. W.R.B., "Cursing and Discoursing," *Saturday Review of Literature,* 23 January 1926, 514.

13. Howard, *Deems Taylor,* 30–32; Mehrens, "Critical and Musical Work of Deems Taylor," 173.

14. Tawa, *Mainstream Music,* 90.

15. Paul Rosenfeld, *Discoveries of a Music Critic* (New York: Harcourt, Brace, 1936), 282.

16. Tawa, *Mainstream Music,* 90–91.

17. Deems Taylor, "Program Notes for *Through the Looking Glass,*" in Charles O'Connell, *The Victor Book of Overtures, Tone Poems and Other Orchestral Works* (New York: Simon and Schuster, 1950), 511.

18. Deems Taylor, "The Scenic Art of Joseph Urban," *Architecture,* May 1934, 288.

Selected Bibliography

Acosta, Mercedes de. *Here Lies the Heart*. New York: Reynal, 1960.

Adams, Franklin P. *The Diary of Our Own Samuel Pepys*. 2 vols. New York: Simon and Schuster, 1935.

Adams, Franklin P., Deems Taylor, Helen Rowland, Percival Wilde, compilers. *The Week End Companion*. 1925. Reprint, Cleveland: World Publishing Co., 1941.

Altman, Billy. *Laughter's Gentle Soul: The Life of Robert Benchley*. New York: W. W. Norton, 1997.

Apczynski, Elaine Bremer. "The Making of *The King's Henchman:* An American Opera." Master's thesis, State University of New York at Buffalo, 1991.

Ashley, Sally. *F.P.A.: The Life and Times of Franklin Pierce Adams*. New York: Beaufort Books, 1986.

Author unidentified. "Biography of Deems Taylor." Handwritten in spiral notebook, 36 pages, [1942].

Ballenger, Stephen Ray. "The Music Criticisms of Deems Taylor." Master's thesis, University of Florida, 1991.

Barrios, Richard. *A Song in the Dark: The Birth of the Musical Film*. New York: Oxford University Press, 1995.

Bergreen, Laurence. *Look Now, Pay Later: The Rise of Network Broadcasting*. Garden City, N.Y.: Doubleday, 1980.

Boylan, James. *The World and the 20's, The Golden Years of New York's Legendary Newspaper*. New York: Dial Press, 1973.

Briggs, John. *Requiem for a Yellow Brick Brewery.* Boston: Little, Brown, 1969.

Broun, Heywood Hale. *Whose Little Boy Are You?* New York: St. Martin's/ Marek, 1983.

Cabell, James Branch. *Between Friends: Letters of James Branch Cabell and Others.* Edited by Padraic Colum and Margaret Freeman Cabell. New York: Harcourt, Brace and World, 1962.

Collins, Theresa M. *Otto Kahn: Art, Money, and Modern Time.* Chapel Hill: University of North Carolina Press, 2002.

Connelly, Marc. *Voices Offstage: A Book of Memoirs.* Chicago: Holt, Rinehart and Winston, 1968.

Culhane, John. *Walt Disney's Fantasia.* New York: Henry N. Abrams, 1983.

Daniels, Oliver. *Stokowski: A Counterpoint of View.* New York: Dodd, Mead, 1982.

DeLong, Thomas A. *The Mighty Music Box.* Los Angeles: Amber Crest Books, 1980.

Drennan, Robert E. *The Algonquin Wits.* Secaucus, N.J.: Citadel Press, 1968.

Dunning, John. *On the Air: The Encyclopedia of Old-Time Radio.* New York: Oxford University Press, 1998.

Edwards, John Carver. *Berlin Calling.* New York: Praeger, 1991.

Epstein, Daniel Mark. *What Lips My Lips Have Kissed: The Loves and Love Poems of Edna St. Vincent Millay.* New York: Henry Holt, 2001.

Fitzgerald, Gerald, ed. *Annals of the Metropolitan Opera: The Complete Chronicle of Performances and Artists.* 2 vols. New York: Metropolitan Opera Guild; Boston: G. K. Hall, 1989.

Gaines, James R. *Wit's End: Days and Nights of the Algonquin Round Table.* New York: Harcourt Brace Jovanovich, 1977.

Gatti-Casazza, Giulio. *Memories of the Opera.* New York: Charles Scribner's Sons, 1941; reprint, New York: Vienna House, 1973.

Gilbert W. S. *Plays and Poems of W. S. Gilbert.* Preface by Deems Taylor. New York: Random House, 1932; reprint, New York: Black Dog and Leventhal Publishers, 1998.

Givner, Joan. *Katherine Anne Porter: A Life.* New York: Simon and Schuster, 1982.

Goss, Madeline. *Modern Music-Makers.* New York: E. P. Dutton, 1952.

Grant, Mark N. *Maestros of the Pen.* Boston: Northeastern University Press, 1998.

Guzski, Carolyn. "American Opera at the Metropolitan, 1910–1935: A Contextual History and Critical Survey of Selected Works." Ph.D. diss., City University of New York, 2001.

Horowitz, Joseph. *Understanding Toscanini.* New York: Alfred A. Knopf, 1987; reprint, Minneapolis: University of Minnesota Press, 1988.

Howard, John Tasker. *Deems Taylor.* Studies of Contemporary American Composers. New York: J. Fischer and Bro., 1927, 1940.

Jablonski, Edward. *Gershwin.* 1987; reprint, Boston: Northeastern University Press, 1990.

Kennedy, Mary. *A Surprise to the Children.* Garden City, N.Y.: Doubleday, Doran, 1933.

Levy, Newman. *My Double Life: Adventures in Law and Letters.* Garden City, N.Y.: Doubleday, 1958.

Martin, George. *The Damrosch Dynasty: America's First Family of Music.* Boston: Houghton Mifflin, 1983.

Meade, Marion. *Dorothy Parker: What Fresh Hell Is This?* New York: Villard Books, 1988.

Mehrens, Christopher E. "The Critical and Musical Work of Deems Taylor in Light of Contemporary Cultural Patterns." Ph.D. diss., University of North Carolina, 1998.

Meyers, Jeffrey. *Joseph Conrad, A Biography.* New York: Charles Scribner's Sons, 1991.

Milford, Nancy. *Savage Beauty: The Life of Edna St. Vincent Millay.* New York: Random House, 2001.

Millay, Edna St. Vincent. *Letters of Edna St. Vincent Millay.* Edited by Allan Ross Macdougall. New York: Harper and Brothers, 1952.

O'Hara, John. *Selected Letters of John O'Hara.* Edited by Matthew J. Bruccoli. New York: Random House, 1978.

Oja, Carol J. *Making Music Modern: New York in the 1920s.* New York: Oxford University Press, 2000.

Rosenfeld, Paul. *An Hour with American Music.* Philadelphia: J. B. Lippincott, 1929.

Ryan, John. *The Production of Culture in the Music Industry.* Lanham, Md.: University Press of America, 1985.

Shanet, Howard. *Philharmonic: A History of New York's Orchestra.* Garden City, N.Y.: Doubleday, 1975.

Shaw, Charles. *The Low-Down.* New York: Henry Holt, 1928.

Stearns, Harold E., ed., *Civilization in the United States: An Inquiry by Thirty Americans.* New York: Harcourt, Brace, 1922.

———. *America Now: An Inquiry into Civilization in the United States.* New York: Charles Scribner's Sons, 1938.

Tawa, Nicholas E. *Serenading the Reluctant Eagle: American Musical Life, 1925–1945.* New York: Schirmer Books, 1984.

———. *Mainstream Music of Early Twentieth Century America: The Composers, Their Times, and Their Works.* Westport, Conn.: Greenwood Press, 1992.

———. *American Composers and Their Public.* Metuchen, N.J.: Scarecrow Press, 1995.

Taylor, Deems. *Of Men and Music.* New York: Simon and Schuster, 1938.

———. *The Well-Tempered Listener.* New York: Simon and Schuster, 1940.

———. *A Pictorial History of the Movies.* New York: Simon and Schuster, 1943.

———. *Moments Mousical.* Chicago: Ziff-Davis, 1949.

———. *Music to My Ears.* New York: Simon and Schuster, 1949.

———. *The One-Track Mind: Love Poems of Seventeenth and Eighteenth Century France.* New York: Library Publishers, 1953.

———. *Some Enchanted Evenings: The Story of Rodgers and Hammerstein.* New York: Harper and Brothers, 1953.

Taylor, Joseph S., ed., *A Romance of Providence: Being a History of the Church of the Strangers in the City of New York.* New York: Wilbur B. Ketcham, 1887.

Index